Talking to **Siri**®

Mastering the Language of Apple's Intelligent Assistant

Third Edition

Erica Sadun
Steve Sande

que
800 East 96th Street,
Indianapolis, Indiana 46240 USA

Talking to Siri®
Mastering the Language of Apple's Intelligent Assistant

ISBN-13: 978-0-7897-5298-7
ISBN-10: 0-7897-5298-0

Library of Congress Control Number: 2014931709

Printed in the United States of America

First Printing: March 2014

Trademarks

All terms mentioned in this book that are known to be trademarks or service marks have been appropriately capitalized. Que Publishing cannot attest to the accuracy of this information. Use of a term in this book should not be regarded as affecting the validity of any trademark or service mark.

Siri is a trademark of Apple, Inc.

Day-Timer is a registered trademark of ACCO Brands Corporation.

Warning and Disclaimer

Every effort has been made to make this book as complete and as accurate as possible, but no warranty or fitness is implied. The information provided is on an "as is" basis. The authors and the publisher shall have neither liability nor responsibility to any person or entity with respect to any loss or damages arising from the information contained in this book or from the use of programs accompanying it.

Talking to Siri is an independent publication and has not been authorized, sponsored, or otherwise approved by Apple, Inc.

Special Sales

For information about buying this title in bulk quantities, or for special sales opportunities (which may include electronic versions; custom cover designs; and content particular to your business, training goals, marketing focus, or branding interests), please contact our corporate sales department at corpsales@pearsoned.com or (800) 382-3419.

For government sales inquiries, please contact governmentsales@pearsoned.com.

For questions about sales outside the U.S., please contact international@pearsoned.com.

Editor-in-Chief
Mark Taub

Senior Acquisitions Editor
Trina MacDonald

Senior Development Editor
Chris Zahn

Managing Editor
Kristy Hart

Senior Project Editor
Betsy Gratner

Copy Editor
Kitty Wilson

Indexer
Lisa Stumpf

Proofreader
Sarah Kearns

Publishing Coordinator
Olivia Basegio

Cover Designer
Alan Clements

Senior Compositor
Gloria Schurick

Contents at a Glance

Table of Contents

A Quick Q&A with Dag Kittlaus, Cofounder and Former CEO of Siri

How much of what we see in Siri today was realized in your original work?

Steve [Jobs] wanted to focus on everyday use cases for iPhone users, which is what you saw with the original Apple launch. Integrating much deeper in iOS helped the experience. The original start-up version had a few more transactional capabilities and some broader data, such as asking Siri to "send a taxi to my house in an hour," or "What should I do tonight around downtown Chicago?"

How much have Apple and other voice assistant systems like that from Google brought to the table?

Google seems to be following the Siri path, although I think that in general Virtual Personal Assistants will become a marketplace unto themselves, with user preferences becoming the "filter to the world" as people increasingly navigate and control things through conversation.

Did you anticipate users becoming as excited about Siri's personality as the utility of its technology?

Yes. You will see Siri become increasingly personable as time goes on.

Of all the ways people are using Siri today, what is the single use case that excites you the most and pays off its promise?

The most exciting use case is the general fact that people by the hundreds of millions make their lives easier by talking to their mobile devices. Personally, I use reminders, sports, text messaging, and restaurant reservations the most often. When the number of things you can do goes from a few dozen to thousands, you will see the entire way we use the Internet change.

What is something you desperately wanted Siri to be able to do and could not accomplish? Is this something we're likely to see over the next few years? If not, why?

There was no functionality we wanted to build that we didn't end up making work, and there is no limit to what these types of systems will do in the coming few years.

What else could you tell us that we'd never even know to ask?

In the early years, we had different names for our software releases. V1 was "periodically human," V2 was "practically human," V3 was "positively human," and V4 was "kill all humans."

 NOTE

Want to learn more about how Siri came to be in terms of its original conception and prototyping? Check out this superb video interview with Dag: http://scobleizer.com/2010/08/10/the-story-behind-the-2010-startup-success-siri-why-its-so-important-to-apples-future/.

Preface

With Siri, your spoken wishes are your iPhone's command.
Available on the newest iPhones (4S and later), iPads (third
generation and later), iPad minis, and iPod touches (fifth
generation and later), the voice-operated Siri assistant uses
natural-language processing to answer your questions, respond
to your commands, and provide helpful action as you need it.
With Siri, you can set up meetings, call your mom, ask about your
appointments, check your email, find your friends, and do a lot
more.

Using Siri is incredibly convenient. You'll find yourself using your
device in ways you never did before because Siri makes things
so much simpler. "Wake me up at 8:30 a.m." "Tell my spouse I'm
on my way home." "Remind me to stop by the dry cleaners when
I leave here." "Text my hairdresser." Siri offers virtual concierge
services that simplify your life.

This short book introduces you to Siri. You'll learn how to
access the voice assistant by using the Home button (or simply
lifting your iPhone to your ear) and how to achieve the highest
recognition rate as you talk. You'll discover which categories
Siri responds to and find out how to make the most of each of
these in your conversations. You'll also discover practical how-to
guidance mixed with many examples to inspire as well as to
instruct.

Tutorials show you how to set up Siri in your settings and how to
manage the interactive conversations you have with your voice
assistant. You'll learn how to perform tasks by topic: checking the
weather, doing math, looking up information on the Web, and
many others.

Siri dictation has now made the leap to OS X. Your Mac can listen to what you say and transcribe it in words to nearly any text-ready application. You can dictate letters, create notes, or specify reminder details with your voice. This book shows you how to control dictation—on both OS X and iOS—so you can add punctuation, paragraph breaks, and more.

Ready to get started? Here are all the basics you need for talking to Siri, presented in a simple, easy-to-follow handbook.

What's New in This Edition

With the arrival of iOS 7, Siri evolved from a beta (in testing) feature to a mature product. Siri now responds to your commands more quickly and offers new capabilities that transform your favorite Apple device into an indispensable part of your life.

This third edition provides all the helpful commonsense how-to that made the first two editions of *Talking to Siri* best sellers. In addition, it covers new features to help both original users and those users who are just starting to work with Siri.

Siri's dictation features are available in the latest OS X, and this book shows how to accurately and quickly enter text into your Mac or iOS device using the power of Siri.

The authors of *Talking to Siri* love to test the limits of what Apple's intelligent assistant can do, and you'll find both hints and ideas to stir your imagination and build your excitement for this fun technology.

When you pick up this book, you'll be sure to learn new tricks and discover what Siri can do to enhance your life.

Who This Book Is For

This book is written for anyone who has purchased a Siri-enabled iOS device—an iPhone, iPad, or iPod touch—or who owns a Mac running the latest OS X releases and wonders how to make the most of it. If you're looking for tips, tricks, and how-to guidance, you've come to the right place. This book offers friendly, easy-to-read tutorials that show you, with a wealth of examples, the ins and outs of Siri use in real life.

How This Book Is Organized

This book offers topic-by-topic coverage of basic Siri usage. Each chapter groups related tasks together, allowing you to jump directly to the material you're looking for. Here's a rundown of what you'll find in this book's chapters:

- **Chapter 1, "Getting Started with Siri":** This chapter introduces you to Siri basics. You'll read about setting up the service, launching it, and trying it out. You'll discover how to speak clearly and how to recover from mistakes when Siri misunderstands you. Don't like Siri's voice? You'll find out how to change it.

- **Chapter 2, "Controlling Your Device with Siri":** The latest incarnation of Siri not only performs your bidding when it comes to finding information and staying in touch but also gives you the power to control many of the settings on your iPhone without ever launching the Settings app.

- **Chapter 3, "Asking Siri for Information":** Want to check the weather or stocks? Need to search the Web? Eager to find out whether your favorite team is winning? This chapter introduces ways you can check information by conversing with Siri. You'll read about Siri integration with Bing, Google, Wikipedia, and Wolfram Alpha and learn how to ask questions that get you the best possible answers.

- **Chapter 4, "Using Siri to Stay in Touch":** This chapter shows you how you can use Siri queries to keep in touch with your friends, family, and business contacts. You'll read about searching for contacts, placing phone calls, checking voicemail and missed calls, returning calls, texting, updating Facebook and Twitter, and sending email. You'll learn about how Siri relationships work and how you can let Siri know who your spouse, your child, or your parent is.

- **Chapter 5, "Talking to Your Day-Timer":** When you want to create appointments, take notes, or set reminders, Siri provides the perfect set of tools for organizing your life. Siri enables you to check your daily schedule, jot down important notes, and set short-term timers and alarms. This chapter introduces all the ways you can use Siri to help schedule and organize your life.

- **Chapter 6, "Going Shopping with Siri":** Whether you're searching for goods and services, trying to find your way to local businesses, or trying to figure out tax and tip after eating lunch, Siri has the tools you need. In this chapter, you'll read about using Siri to go shopping. You'll discover great ways to hunt down the items you need (including turn-by-turn directions!). You'll also get surprisingly useful tips on having Siri remind you about what you need when you get close to the stores that carry them. Siri is now more useful than ever when you're searching for restaurants, even to the point of making reservations for you.

- **Chapter 7, "Pushing Limits with Siri":** The Siri universe continues to expand over time. With a little clever work, you can blog using Siri text messaging and email. This chapter shows you how you can push the Siri envelope.

- **Chapter 8, "Siri Dictation":** Siri does a lot more than just answer queries. Its built-in dictation support means you can use its natural language-to-text support to speak to applications on iOS or OS X. This chapter discusses all the ins and outs of Siri dictation, providing tips and hints about getting the most accurate responses, and shows how you can produce exactly the text you're looking to create (punctuation and all).

- **Chapter 9, "Having Fun with Siri":** In this chapter, you'll read about having fun with Siri and all the clever ways you can tickle your personal assistant's funny bone. It's okay to be silly with Siri. This chapter shows you how. You also find out how to give Siri control of your physical world through a variety of new home automation products.

- **Chapter 10, "Our Top 10 Siri Jokes":** In addition to being friendly, helpful, loyal, and kind, Siri can bring the sass and the laughs. Before we wrap up this book, we want to leave you with 10 of our favorite Siri wisecracks.

- **Appendix A, "Siri Quick Reference":** This appendix provides a topic-by-topic list of things you can say to Siri, offering you an overview of this highly capable assistant's capabilities.

Contacting the Authors

If you have any comments or questions about this book, please visit http://sanddunetech.com/contact-us/. We're happy to listen to your feedback. Follow us on Twitter (@sanddunebooks) to keep up with our new and updated books.

About the Authors

Erica Sadun writes a lot of books and blogs at TUAW. When not writing, she's a full-time parent of geeks who are brushing up on their world-domination skills. According to her academic dosimeter, she's acquired more education than any self-respecting person might consider wise. She enjoys deep-diving into technology.

Steve Sande also writes way too much. He's the hardware editor at TUAW and has logged almost 2 million words written for the blog in a little more than 5 years. He's written a number of books, is married to a rocket scientist, and spends his days being bossed by a cat.

Acknowledgments

Thanks to everyone at TUAW for all their support and to all the readers and friends who helped with suggestions and feedback. Additional thanks for this edition go out to Aaron Kulbe and Matt Yohe.

None of this would have been possible without the vision and leadership of Apple's late founder and CEO, Steve Jobs. Thank you, Mr. Jobs.

We Want to Hear from You!

As the reader of this book, you are our most important critic and commentator. We value your opinion and want to know what we're doing right, what we could do better, what areas you'd like to see us publish in, and any other words of wisdom you're willing to pass our way.

We welcome your comments. You can email or write to let us know what you did or didn't like about this book—as well as what we can do to make our books better.

Please note that we cannot help you with technical problems related to the topic of this book.

When you write, please be sure to include this book's title and author, as well as your name, email address, and phone number. I will carefully review your comments and share them with the author and editors who worked on the book.

Email: trina.macdonald@pearson.com

Mail: Que Publishing
         ATTN: Reader Feedback
         330 Hudson Street
         7th Floor
         New York, New York, 10013

Reader Services

Visit our website and register this book at quepublishing.com/register for convenient access to any updates, downloads, or errata that might be available for this book.

Getting Started with Siri

Have you met Siri? Siri is Apple's fabulous hands-free, conversation-based virtual personal assistant. Siri can help manage your life, organize your mobile device, and, as a bonus, provide endless hours of silly fun. If you own a current-generation iOS device, your virtual assistant awaits your command. Siri runs on the iPhone (4S and later), iPod touch (fifth generation and later), iPad (third generation and later), iPad Air, and all versions of the iPad mini.

Siri replaces the dance of your fingers on the glass screen of an iOS device with a conversation like the one shown in Figure 1-1. Siri understands your voice and places what you say in context with the apps that it works with. It even responds with a question if it doesn't understand. Reality has overtaken science fiction. You can now use spoken natural language to interface with a computer.

NOTE

This book refers to Siri as *it*, not as *him* or *her*. This is because Siri can be set to use either a male or female voice according to your preferences. Although Siri originally had specific genders in different regions (for example, in the United States, Siri was female, and in the UK, Siri was male), Siri's gender is now universally adjustable.

Siri doesn't stop there. Macintosh computers that run OS X Mavericks and Mountain Lion offer Siri dictation as well. You can speak to dictate emails, create reports with your voice, and more.

Figure 1-1
Siri awaits your command.

In this chapter, you'll learn how to get started with Siri: how to enable it, launch the service, and try it out. You'll read about how to speak (slowly and clearly), how to recover from mistakes (by editing errors), and how to access Siri in a variety of ways. By the time you finish reading this chapter, you'll feel at ease talking to (instead of at) Siri.

 NOTE

An independent start-up founded by the Stanford Research Institute's Artificial Intelligence Center created Siri's recognition technology in 2007 (hence the name Siri). Apple acquired the Siri company in 2010 and first debuted the technology with iOS 5 on the iPhone 4S.

Enabling Siri on iOS

Like many other services on iOS, you can enable or disable Siri as desired. To ensure that the Siri service has been enabled, navigate to Settings, General, Siri or launch Siri and tell it to "Open Siri settings." You now see the screen of options shown in Figure 1-2. These options let you control how Siri works. Use this screen to adjust the way Siri is set up and responds to you.

Figure 1-2

From the Siri settings page, you choose a primary language, select either a male or female voice, set when you want the service to respond to you, and enable or disable the handy Raise to Speak option. Some options vary by iOS device. For example, only the iPhone supports Raise to Speak, which relies on the iPhone's built-in proximity sensor. Other devices do not offer proximity sensors, so they cannot provide this option.

Tap the Siri toggle switch to On (green) to activate the Siri service. On the iPhone, when the service is disabled, the older iOS Voice Control feature still enables you to place hands-free calls and request music. Siri is much more powerful than Voice Control, offering a wider range of voice-directed actions.

Disabling Siri is not a step you take lightly. Doing so actually removes your information from Apple servers. You'll lose all the personalization and customization you have built up over time. You can re-enable Siri later, but reestablishing that personal profile—specifically how Siri learns your accent and speech patterns—will take time (see Figure 1-3).

The settings page includes some other options:

- **Language:** Select the language and region you want Siri to use for interpreting your interaction. In early 2014, Siri speaks Cantonese Chinese, Mandarin Chinese with mainland and Taiwan dialects, English (Australian, Canadian, UK, and U.S. dialects), French (Canadian, French, and Swiss dialects), German (German and Swiss dialects), Italian (Italian and Swiss dialects), Japanese, Korean, and Spanish (Mexican, Spanish, and U.S. dialects). Apple is rolling out more languages and dialects over time. You can ask Siri, "What languages do you speak?" to see them listed.

- **Voice Gender:** In its original release, Siri used a default gender of female in the United States and male in the United Kingdom, with similar gender discrepancies in other countries. Now you can select between male and female in many of the supported languages. Siri cannot change that gender for you. If you ask, it directs you to make the change yourself in the Siri settings page.

- **Voice Feedback:** Siri can respond to you with voice as well as text responses. Choose to always enable this feature (Always) or to support it only for hands-free operation (Handsfree Only) when used with a headset of some sort.

If you choose Always, remember that Siri uses a volume control system that's separate from your main iOS device's voice control (see Figure 1-4). Lowering the volume of your music playback won't affect Siri and vice versa. If you enable voice feedback and forget to lower the Siri volume, you could encounter embarrassing situations. Imagine being in a meeting and activating the service by accident. You set Siri's volume by opening the assistant (press and hold the Home button or raise the unit to your ear if you enabled Raise to Speak) and then adjusting the device's volume toggles on the side of the phone.

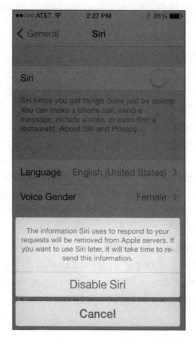

Figure 1-3
Disabling Siri deletes information stored on Apple's servers. Siri must relearn your personal style when you re-enable it in the future.

Figure 1-4
Siri has its own volume controls. Adjusting the volume when Siri is displayed does not affect normal iOS system volume and vice versa.

- **My Info:** This sets the default contact for your identity from your personal address book. Choosing a contact lets Siri knows where "home" is, what your name is, and so forth. It also allows Siri to associate relationships with your contacts, such as "my spouse" or "my boss" or "my doctor." Make sure this option points to the right contact so that when Siri tries to help you, it's working with the right person.

- **Raise to Speak:** When this setting is enabled, Siri activates using the iPhone proximity sensor. As the device nears your ear, Siri detects that you're ready to speak and enters listening mode. Switch this setting to On, and you can start a Siri session by raising the iPhone to your ear. You generally want to leave this option enabled. It offers the simplest and most discrete way to activate Siri from your handset. This feature is not available on iPod touch, iPad, or iPad mini—only on iPhone.

 NOTE

Muting your iOS device and lowering the speaker volume to zero does not directly affect Siri chimes for either dictation or voice assistance. If you hold the Home button for too long or your finger brushes across the microphone in the keyboard, you could trigger a Siri-based beep. This can be quite embarrassing in boardroom or classroom situations. That's because Siri has its own volume control (refer to Figure 1-4), which you access only when the assistant is shown onscreen.

To adjust Siri's volume setting, summon your personal assistant and then adjust the volume control when the wavy line appears onscreen. You can silence Siri here to ensure that your Siri-enabled device stays quiet even when you accidentally open the assistant screen. This tweak doesn't affect the chime Siri plays (just to you) when you hold a phone to your ear.

Universal Access

Siri works with VoiceOver, the screen reader built into iOS. VoiceOver offers a way for visually impaired users to listen to their *graphical user interface (GUI)*. VoiceOver converts an application's visual presentation to an audio description.

VoiceOver can speak any text displayed on your iOS screen, including Siri responses. VoiceOver speech can also interpret as speech certain graphical elements presented by Siri. These include weather forecasts, the text of emails, answers from Wolfram Alpha, and so forth.

You enable VoiceOver in Settings, General, Accessibility, VoiceOver. Be sure to set the Triple-Click Home option to On so that you can enable and disable VoiceOver with a simple shortcut.

When using VoiceOver, you use the iPhone GUI with your fingers and ears rather than with your eyes. VoiceOver uses an entire language of touches, with a challenging learning curve. Consult documentation on Apple's website for details about using VoiceOver features both in general and with Siri.

Enabling Dictation on OS X

Starting with OS X Mountain Lion, you can use Siri-style dictation on your Macintosh. You enable this feature in the System Preferences Dictation & Speech pane (see Figure 1-5). Setting the Dictation option to On activates dictation services on your computer. These services enable you to speak text wherever you would normally type it.

The Shortcut pop-up menu lets you choose how to begin dictation. In Figure 1-5, this shortcut is set to Press Function (Fn) Key Twice. Other preset options enable you to press the right Command key twice, the left Command key twice, or either Command key twice.

If you'd rather use a nonstandard key choice, choose Customize from the pop-up menu and type a different key or key combination. For example, you might use Shift-F6 or Control-Shift-D. Choose the key combination that best fits your personal workflow.

Select the dictation language and region from the Language pop-up menu. OS X Mavericks currently supports English, Chinese, French, German, Italian, Japanese, Korean, and Spanish, in a number of regional dialects (see Figure 1-6). This set will almost certainly grow over time.

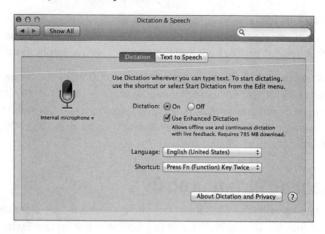

Figure 1-5
OS X's Dictation & Speech settings pane enables you to activate dictation on your Macintosh.

Figure 1-6
OS X dictation currently supports a number of languages and regions.

NOTE

> Many Siri services are country and region specific. Some features, such as dictation, are available practically worldwide. Others, such as maps and directions, have been rolled out on a far more limited basis. Check Apple's website to see if specific Siri features are available in your area.

Privacy

Apple collects data on your Siri usage. Information sent to Apple includes your contacts in the address book, your name and contact information, songs and playlists from your media library, audio recordings of you speaking, transcripts of what you have said, and operating system information/performance statistics. If you use Siri, a lot of your personal information goes to Apple.

What's more, this information may be shared with Apple's partners—but only for dictation-related services. Apple states that it doesn't share the info with other third parties. You cannot opt out of data collection, but you can opt out of Siri entirely by not using the feature and disabling it in Settings or System Preferences.

If you don't mind having Apple collect information on you but you'd rather not have your children's information divulged to Apple, you can separately control access to dictation in the Parental Controls pane on OS X. There you will find and can check the Disable Use of Dictation option for your child's account. On iOS, use the General, Restrictions settings to disable Siri access.

For more about Siri privacy issues, tap the About Siri and Privacy link in the iOS Siri settings page or the About Dictation and Privacy link in the OS X Dictation & Speech pane. Figure 1-7 shows the privacy disclosure screens for iOS and OS X.

●○○○○ AT&T 🤙   2:29 PM   🔋 87% ▪▪▪

Siri and Privacy   Done

When you use Siri, which includes the dictation feature of your device, the things you say and dictate will be recorded and sent to Apple to process your requests. Your device will also send Apple other information, such as your name and nickname; the names, nicknames, and relationship with you (e.g., "my dad") of your address book contacts; and song names in your collection (collectively, your "User Data"). All of this data is used to help Siri understand you better and recognize what you say. It is not linked to other data that Apple may have from your use of other Apple services.

If you have Location Services turned on, the location of your device at the time you make a request will also be sent to Apple to help Siri improve the accuracy of its response to your location-based requests (e.g., "what's the weather like here today?"). You may choose to turn off Location Services for Siri. To do so, open Settings, tap Privacy, tap Location Services, and slide the Siri switch to "off".

Information collected by Apple will be treated in accordance with Apple's Privacy Policy, which can be found at www.apple.com/privacy.

You may choose to turn off Siri at any time. To do so, open Settings, tap General, tap Siri, and

---

When you use Dictation, you can choose to have either your Mac or Apple's servers perform the speech recognition for you. If you use Mac-based Dictation, your computer will convert what you say into text without sending your dictated speech to Apple.

If you use server-based Dictation, the things you dictate will be recorded and sent to Apple to convert what you say into text and your computer will also send Apple other information, such as your name and nickname; and the names, nicknames, and relationship with you (for example, "my dad") of your address book contacts (collectively, your "User Data"). All of this data is used to help the dictation feature understand you better and recognize what you say. It is not linked to other data that Apple may have from your use of other Apple services.

Information collected by Apple will be treated in accordance with Apple's Privacy Policy, which can be found at www.apple.com/privacy.

You can choose to turn off or change your preferences for Dictation at any time by going to the Dictation & Speech pane within System Preferences. If you turn off Dictation, or switch from using server-based Dictation to Mac-based Dictation, Apple will delete your User Data, as well as your recent voice input data, from Apple's servers. Older voice input data that has been disassociated from you may be retained for a period of time to generally improve Dictation and Siri functionality in Apple products and services. This voice input data may include audio files and transcripts of what you said and related diagnostic data, such as hardware and operating system specifications and performance statistics.

You can restrict access to the Dictation feature on your computer in the Parental Controls pane of System Preferences.

Figure 1-7
Apple collects a lot of information when you use Siri.

Launching Siri on iOS

On iOS, Siri lets you use your voice instead of your fingers to send messages, schedule meetings, choose music, and more. You use Siri conversationally. You talk to your device, and your device talks right back to you.

Access Siri in several ways:

- Press and hold the Home button for a couple seconds.
- Raise your iPhone to your ear. (Not available on iPod touch or iPad.)
- On your wired (iPhone earbud style) or wireless (Bluetooth) headset, squeeze or press the control button. Siri also works with many car kits. A small blue speaker icon appears in Siri's display when you connect through Bluetooth.
- Press the Siri Eyes Free button on your car steering wheel. A growing number of cars now support Siri Eyes Free, providing a fast and safe way to engage Siri while driving.

A chime tells you that Siri is listening and ready to follow your commands. Make sure Siri is enabled and that you have a good Internet connection. If so, you are ready to take off and start exploring this innovative voice-driven service.

Saying Hello to Siri

Are you ready to start talking to Siri? Siri uses several chimes to let you know whether it's listening to you. These audio cues help you know Siri's state. Higher chimes start a session, and lower ones cancel it. To hear this on the iPhone, enable Raise to Speak, raise your phone (turned on, of course) to your ear, and then place it back on a table. The high chimes mean Siri is listening; the low chimes mean it has stopped listening. On the iPod touch or iPad, press and hold the Home button (high chimes) and then tap the Siri microphone (low chimes).

Try the following to start a Siri session. Either raise the phone to your ear or press and hold the Home button. If Siri is already displayed, tap the Siri microphone button.

Say "Hello" and then pause. Siri uses pause detection to know when you've stopped speaking. You now hear a second set of chimes—higher-pitched chimes of acknowledgment, in this case—but this time you hear them without moving the phone away from your ear or having to tap the microphone button.

If you have a good Internet connection—a requirement for working with Siri—you'll hear it respond to you. Siri responds with "Hi" or "Hello," perhaps adding your name (see Figure 1-8). As you talk, Siri creates a scrolling list of responses so you can review the conversation to date. By default, Siri automatically scrolls up to the most recent response, but to see what has already transpired, pull down on the list.

To summarize, you start talking to Siri in these ways:

- Pressing and holding the Home button for 1 to 2 seconds
- Pressing and holding the control button on a wired or wireless headset
- Pressing the Siri Eyes Free button on your car steering wheel
- Raising a phone to your ear with Raise to Speak enabled
- Tapping the Siri microphone button

Siri plays chimes that indicate the state of your interaction. By listening for these chimes, you'll know how Siri is responding to you:

- Its higher-pitched "listening" chime (the musically inclined will recognize a C4) lets you know Siri's ready for you to speak.

- To finish talking, you can either pause or tap the microphone button. Siri plays a high-pitched "done listening" chime (a higher A♭4).
- If Siri does not hear any input, it stops listening and plays a lower-pitched "cancellation" chime (a lower A♭3).

Figure 1-8
Saying hello to Siri.

Cancelling Siri

If you ever need to stop whatever Siri is doing, just say "Cancel" and then either tap the microphone button or press the Home button.

Because Siri remembers your ongoing thread of conversation, you might need to reset your current conversation at times. Say "Start over" or "Restart" to begin a new dialogue. Siri responds with a response such as, "Okay, Erica, what's next?" or "What can I help you with?"

Repeating Siri

When you did not quite catch what Siri last said, say "Say it again." Siri repeats its last response. This feature gives you a second chance for comprehension or offers you the possibility to repeat a particularly clever punch line to share with others.

Quitting Siri

Leave Siri mode by pressing the Home button or saying "Good-bye." This returns you to your normal iOS home screen. If you say "Quit," Siri responds, "Did I say something wrong? If you really want me to go away, at least say 'goodbye.'" and "Quit? Did you mean 'goodbye'?" (see Figure 1-9).

Asking Siri to "go away" or "leave" won't work, but you can say any of the following to exit Siri mode:

- "Goodbye"
- "Bye"
- "Bye-bye"
- "So long"
- "Adios"
- "See you later"
- "See you"

Figure 1-9
To leave Siri mode by voice, say "Goodbye." Telling Siri "Quit" or "Go away" does not end your Siri interaction.

Getting Help

If you say "Help me" or "What can you do?" Siri provides suggestions on what to say. Siri displays a list of categories, such as Phone, Music, Messages, and Calendar, along with a sample phrase for each topic, as shown in Figure 1-10. Tap on any category to view an extended list of sample phrases for just that category.

Figure 1-10
Not sure what to say to Siri? Siri can offer suggestions. Just say "Help" or "What can you do?" A tiny question mark appears at the left of Siri's microphone whenever you invoke it. Tap this question mark at any time to request this help screen.

For example, if you're interested in something about a calendar, tap Calendar "Set up a meeting at 9." Siri then offers examples for adding, changing, or asking about events. They provide a range of functions that showcase how you can interactively ask about your upcoming schedule. Here are examples:

- "Set up a meeting at 9."
- "Meet with Emily at noon."
- "Set up a meeting about hiring tomorrow at 9 a.m."

- "Schedule a planning meeting at 8:30 today in the board-room."
- "Reschedule my appointment with Dr. Patrick to next Monday at 9 a.m."
- "Add Emily to my meeting with Brian."
- "Cancel the budget review meeting."
- "What does the rest of my day look like?"
- "What's on my calendar for Friday?"
- "When am I meeting with Jimmy?"
- "Where is my next meeting?"

This onboard help system lets you know the kinds of interactions that Siri supports. The options inspire you to expand your Siri vocabulary and use the assistant system more flexibly.

 NOTE

If you're just starting out with Siri and don't really know what to try, consider saying to Siri "Speak to me," "Let's talk," or "Tell me a joke." These are great ways to produce interesting responses.

Siri Listens

As Siri listens to you speaking, look at the bottom of the screen (see Figure 1-11, left). A moving "wave" provides you with volume feedback as you speak and lets you know that Siri is in listening mode. If you do not respond after a few seconds, Siri stops listening and plays the end-of-listening chime.

To finish speaking, either pause and wait for Siri or tap the wave. Siri listens and then enters thinking mode. During this time, a rotating circle appears, letting you know that Siri is contacting

Apple's data centers for speech interpretation and processing (see Figure 1-11, right).

Siri works with both 3G and Wi-Fi Internet connections, so you can use it wherever you are. The data demands are fairly minimal, so you probably do not need to worry about depleting your monthly allocation if you use Siri a lot.

Figure 1-11
Left: Siri's feedback wave rises and falls with your speech. Right: A circle rotates as Siri contacts its servers to interpret your speech and respond to you.

If Siri is able to process your statement, it tries to interpret it and provide some kind of response for you. If Siri cannot call home to its Apple data processing center, it informs you about the situation, saying something like, "I'm sorry, I'm having difficulty accessing the network." Try moving to a location with a better Internet signal or try again later.

Listening on OS X

On OS X, Siri provides feedback in the shape of a microphone. As Figure 1-12 shows, the microphone acts as a level meter, and an animated dot presentation shows that the computer is actively contacting servers for speech interpretation. OS X does not use pause detection, so you must either click Done or press Return to finish your dictation.

Figure 1-12
The microphone on OS X works as a level meter. The height of the purple bar in the microphone reflects the current volume of your speech.

Siri Responds

Siri responds to both direct commands and random statements. If Siri can't interpret what you've said as a request, it searches the Web for your statement. For example, Figure 1-13 shows how Siri responds to you when you say "platypuses." Siri uses your word or phrase for a web search using its built-in set of helper sites: Bing, Wikipedia, and Wolfram Alpha.

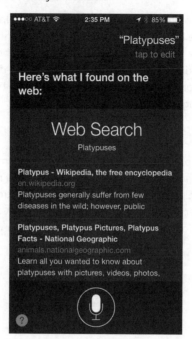

Figure 1-13
Siri displays web searches for any words or phrases it doesn't immediately recognize.

 NOTE

Siri learns your accent and voice characteristics over time. As long as you keep Siri enabled in your iPhone settings, your Siri account remains on Apple's servers, and your recognition rates improve over time. Siri uses voice-recognition algorithms to categorize your voice into its database of regional dialects and accents. This database continues to evolve and will keep improving as Siri collects more data and evaluates its interpretation successes. Siri also uses information from your iPhone. Data from your contacts, music library, calendar, and reminders helps fuel its recognition vocabulary.

To reset your Siri information, switch Siri off and then back on in Settings, General, Siri. When you do this, you dispose of all personalized settings Siri has collected from you over time (not including any general metrics it studies and adds to its primary database) and returns Siri to a fresh install, ready to learn your quirks again.

Correcting Siri

Siri always gives you a second chance. To fix what you said or correct Siri's interpretation of your speech, just tap the words that represent what you said (see Figure 1-14). Siri reinforces this capability by showing the words *tap to edit* underneath your most recent query. (You don't see this in Figure 1-14 because the words have already been tapped and Siri is in Edit mode.) When you tap, an edit cursor and the system keyboard appear, enabling you to make changes. At this point, edit your request directly or tap the microphone button on the keyboard to add words or redictate your request. Tap the blue Done key on the keyboard to finish.

Sometimes Siri's dictation processor adds a blue line under a word in the text you have spoken. When you tap that word, iOS presents alternative interpretations of your speech. Either dictate a replacement or select the correction you want to use or edit.

You can also speak to correct text messages or emails that you have composed. The following statements let Siri know that you're not satisfied with what you've said. Notice how you can change the contents completely, add new material, and more:

- "Change it to: Let's meet at 3:00 p.m."
- "Add: Can't wait exclamation point." (You can use "Add" to extend items, even if Siri doesn't mention it explicitly as an option.)

- "No, send it to Megs."
- "No." (This keeps the message without sending it.)
- "Cancel."

Figure 1-14
Tap your interpreted speech to edit it directly or redictate your statement.

Before you send a text message on its way, have Siri read it back to you. Say "Read it to me" or "Read it back to me." As with the Add feature, Siri does not tell you about this option. When you are satisfied with your text, tweet, or email message, say something like "Yes, send it" to send it off.

Correcting Speech on OS X

The same dashed underlines appear on OS X as on iOS. Because OS X is centered on the mouse, not the touch, the methods for accessing variant spellings differ. Figure 1-15 shows the result of saying "I'm ready to dictate for all." Siri has misinterpreted the last word as *from* but flagged it with possible variations. It shows this flag by underlining the word with a dashed blue line.

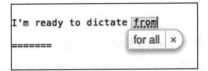

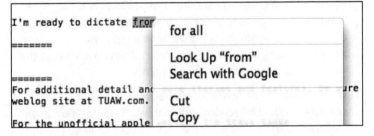

Figure 1-15
With OS X, you can either left-click just to the right of an underlined word (top) or right-click the underlined word (bottom).

If you move the cursor to the very right of the word in question and left-click, OS X presents a list of alternative interpretations. In Figure 1-15, it suggests *for all*. Tap that word or phrase to choose it. OS X replaces the word with your selection and removes the underline.

You can also right-click (Control-click) the underlined word to bring up the contextual menu you see in Figure 1-15 (bottom). The alternate interpretation is listed at the top of the menu. Select it to confirm and replace, look up the word "from" in the dictionary, or search the word's meaning on the Web with your default search engine.

Alternatively, you can simply type to correct the text. Dictating and then correcting by hand offers a robust workflow for both OS X and iOS.

Enhancing Your Speech Recognition

On iOS, Siri responds to commands by creating appointments, setting timers, placing phone calls, and more. To see this in action, try using Siri to create a new note on your iOS device. Say "Note that I spent $15 on lunch." Speak steadily but do not draaaaag ooooooout what you're saying. Siri should reply "Noted" or "Got it!" or something like that (see Figure 1-16). On OS X, you use the same approach: Use steady, clear sentences.

When talking to Siri, remain conversational. Try to speak with normal tones and inflections, although you'll want to slow down slightly. Enunciate a bit more than you're used to, like a pedantic teacher. The key to Siri is holding on to your standard speech patterns while emphasizing any words that help Siri understand you better.

Don't be afraid to ask questions (with your voice rising at the end), make statements (with your voice dropping), or otherwise speak sentences as you normally do, including emphasizing words inside sentences (for example, "What does *intransigent* mean?"). Do not try to be robotic or lose normal sentence inflections. Your recognition rate will plummet if you do.

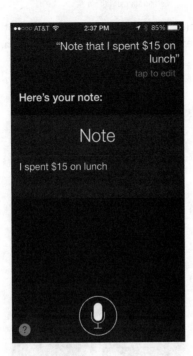

Figure 1-16
Siri can take notes to help you keep track of your expenses.

On iOS, this particular query should load up a definition, as shown in Figure 1-17. It's actually a little hard to speak this request coherently and in a way that Siri understands, so it makes a good exercise to test out your speaking-with-Siri skills.

Clarity

Siri likes to hear you speak slowly and clearly and prefers to have you e-nun-ci-ate your words, especially with word-ending consonants. This helps Siri differentiate between, for example, *me* and *mean*. This is an important distinction when defining words, as in this example with *intransigent*, because asking Siri "What does

intransigent me?" won't load the dictionary definition you're looking for—but asking "What does *intransigent* mean?" does.

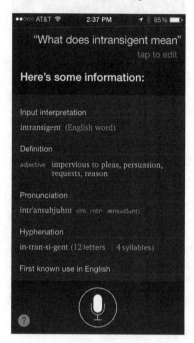

Figure 1-17
Use slow, careful speech to increase Siri's recognition rate, as in this word-definition request.

Don't be afraid to add a little extra pause between words so that
Siri can tell the difference between "Mike Rose" and "micros," or
"Mike Rose's phone" and "microphone."

If you add too long a pause, Siri stops listening, but that does not
happen accidentally. A good deal of usable range exists between
your normal speaking speed and the extreme at which Siri thinks
you're not talking anymore. Explore that range and test longer
pauses to see how you can improve your recognition.

Fumbles

Everybody fumbles words sometimes. If you find yourself stumbling over a tongue twister, the best thing to do is just tap the wave at the bottom of the display and let Siri attempt to figure out what you meant to say. If Siri's choice is completely wrong, edit your current entry by tapping the text to edit. Sometimes it's easier to just tap the microphone icon that appears and make your request again. On OS X, either click Done or press the designated key to show that you've completed dictation, then start over again.

Never worry about starting your request over. Siri doesn't care, and you can save a lot of time that you'd otherwise waste editing or waiting on interpretations of flubbed speech that are bound to go wrong. Siri is a *virtual* assistant and does not judge you.

Viewing Items You Create

Earlier, you read about how you might create a note using Siri. You can jump from Siri to the Notes application with a single tap. Just tap any yellow Siri note item. That is also where you need to go if you want to delete a note you just created. Siri does not enable you to delete notes directly by speaking your command, as you can see in Figure 1-18. That's because, as an assistant, Siri focuses on creating new requests (notes, appointments, phone calls, dictation, weather checks) and not on editing or application control in general. Siri is not a full voice interface.

 NOTE

> Siri is meant to enable you to accomplish simple creation and checking tasks hands free while on the go. But that's where Siri's capabilities end. Don't expect to navigate through menus, search for information within documents, or otherwise treat Siri as a full artificially intelligent user interface. Knowing what Siri can and cannot do helps limit your expectations while using this tool.

This tapping trick works with most Siri items, not just notes: Tap on contacts to view them in the Contacts app, tap on text messages in Messages, and so on. Siri often gives you items to choose from and actions to perform as well; tap on these choices to select a contact or perform web searches. You can also instruct Siri by voice, specifying how you want to proceed.

Figure 1-18
Siri can create notes but cannot delete them.

Multilingual Siri

Unfortunately, the Siri voice assistant cannot directly switch languages. The only way to change from English to French, for example, is to hop out, edit your preferences (Settings, General, Siri, Language or just say "Open Siri Settings" and tap Language), and hop back in.

A workaround for multilanguage dictation exists, however. The Settings, General, International, Keyboards preferences allow you to add keyboards and enable the globe button, which lets you toggle directly between keyboard languages. You'll find it between the number toggle (123) and the microphone dictation button on the keyboard when you've enabled more than one language on your device.

A simple tap takes you to the next language setting, including dictation. By tapping, you move, for example, from French to English and back as you dictate into any text-entry element on your iPhone. Hopefully, Siri will support "Speak to me in [some language]" requests in a future update.

Siri recognizes each language using specific dialects and accents. Native speakers will experience higher recognition accuracy.

New in Siri

Siri is an evolving system. Apple continues to add new and exciting technologies to Siri, and it rolls them out over time. For example, during its first two years, Siri's voice was rather slow and robotic sounding. With the release of iOS 7, Apple provided more realistic-sounding voices speaking at a much faster rate. This fluidity enhances your understanding of Siri's responses.

Siri is now faster at returning responses, particularly on Wi-Fi or fast mobile networks. It is now adept at working with more sources of information to get those answers, by adding Bing, Wikipedia, and even Twitter to its list of sources. Many of its responses now appear inline with your questions. Previously, Siri launched other applications like Safari to display answers. Keeping the answers within Siri's interface allows you to view those responses much faster, in a clean inline presentation.

Apple launched iTunes Radio—a streaming Internet radio service—in the Music app with iOS7. At the same time, it updated Siri to provide a way to control iTunes Radio with your voice. Tell Siri to "Play iTunes Radio" or "Play my Led Zeppelin station," and you'll soon be rockin' to the radio. Don't like one of the station choices? Just say "Don't play this song again," and you'll be saved from hearing *Bohemian Rhapsody* for the seventh time that day. (If you ask Siri to "Scaramouche, Scaramouche, will you do the Fandango?" at this time, it mostly returns YouTube videos.)

On an iPhone, Siri can now return calls or play your voicemail. Ask "Do I have any missed calls?" to retrieve a spoken summary of how many calls you missed, at what time, and from what contacts. To listen to your voicemail, ask "Do I have any new voicemail?" Siri produces a spoken list of those items. Ask Siri to play a specific voicemail back to you; say, for example, "Play the voicemail from Trina."

Voicemail isn't the only form of communication that Siri now handles. Previously, you could just send emails; now asking Siri to "Check email" lets you hear what has come into your inbox lately. Have that email read to you by asking "Read my latest email," and when Siri is done, it will ask "Do you want to reply?"

As Figure 1-19 shows, Siri is also getting better at pronouncing names. When Siri mispronounces a name in your contact list, say "That's not how you pronounce her name" (or something similar). Siri will thank you and then ask how you pronounce the name. After listening to you, Siri presents you with a list of possible pronunciations. Tap each option to listen to it and then select the pronunciation that is closest to correct.

Figure 1-19
When Siri mispronounces the name of a contact, you can now teach it the correct pronunciation.

Many of us receive our news of what's going on in the world through Twitter instead of traditional sources, so it's not surprising that Siri now keeps an eye on Twitter trends. Just ask "What's happening on Twitter?" and Siri shows you what is currently trending (see Figure 1-20).

Figure 1-20
Siri keeps an eye on what's trending on Twitter.

Ask Siri "What are people saying about [a topic or a person]?" to see what kind of tweets are being sent out on a topic or about a celebrity. Want to track what a friend or coworker is saying on Twitter? For example, "What's Mike T. Rose saying?" produced the list of tweets shown in Figure 1-21.

Twitter isn't the only one to have made friends with Siri; Facebook is now just a conversation away as well. At this time, it's only possible to use Siri to post on your wall. For example, "Write on my wall just saw an amazing Denver Broncos game and they won 45 to 21" gets the word out to your Facebook pals at the speed of light.

Figure 1-21
Siri can produce a list of recent tweets from any of your friends.

Siri helps you connect with your friends, coworkers, and loved ones as well through new integration with FaceTime, Apple's video calling app. Just say something like "Make a FaceTime call to Susan" or even "FaceTime Susan," and before you know it, you're chatting face-to-face.

Apple has given some of Siri's old tricks a new spin. Siri has always used Yelp ratings to help determine whether a given restaurant is good or bad; now it can even show you individual reviews for a place. Likewise, asking for movie reviews brings up a list of reviews from online movie source Rotten Tomatoes.

One surprisingly useful new feature is the ability to change or check the settings of your iOS device. There are so many options available that we cover them separately in Chapter 2, "Controlling Your Device with Siri."

Living with Siri's Limitations

Although Siri is now a mature product, you can still expect that the voice-interpretation system will be subject to mistakes. After all, even humans misunderstand things all the time. With the best of intentions and the best of interpretations, Siri will never be able to provide 100% accuracy.

Sometimes the mistakes are laughably funny, but other times you may become frustrated. Rather than get mad, just work within the limitations and use Siri more often instead of less. Siri used to have a really hard time differentiating between Pachelbel (as in the famous canon) and Taco Bell. It was pretty hilarious. These days, Apple has updated the service to better distinguish between the two—and many other similar-sounding pairs.

The more you use Siri, the better it understands you. Over time, Siri learns your regional accent and characterizes your voice into a specific dialect. This helps it improve its interpretation over time. What's more, Siri uses information from your device, including your contacts, your music, your calendar, and your reminders, to better match what you're saying to what you mean.

Summary

Siri provides a new and natural way to interact with a computer, enabling you to speak and be understood. On iOS, Siri listens to your commands and then performs your bidding, responding through speech or a visual answer on the device screen.

On OS X, Siri enables you to dictate into any application that normally offers text input. Take away these key points from this chapter:

- Think carefully about the information you are sending to Apple when you agree to enable Siri. It means trusting Apple with a lot of personal information. Most people won't be bothered by this, but you should make an informed choice, nonetheless.

- If you don't know what to say to Siri, say "Help me" or tap the small question mark that appears on the bottom left of the Siri display. Siri is always happy to provide a list of categories and sample phrases.

- You access Siri by pressing and holding the Home button, raising your iPhone to your ear with Raise to Speak enabled, squeezing or pressing the control button on a wired or wireless headset, or pressing the Siri Eyes Free button on your car's steering wheel. On OS X, you customize how to trigger dictation through the Dictation & Speech settings pane in System Preferences.

- Talk slowly and clearly to Siri. Siri works best when you enunciate deliberately.

- Remember that Siri is more about creating items than editing them. Build new appointments, create new notes, and write emails. Don't expect to use Siri to cancel, delete, undo, or modify those items.

- Siri responses typically lead to more actions, enabling you to jump into associated apps such as the Notes app for notes or the Contacts apps for addresses.

- Don't be afraid of making mistakes with Siri. You can always reset your conversation or edit what you say. Siri is designed to assist you, not to put obstacles in your way. Siri lets you add new text and edit the text you've already spoken, or you can restart your dictation from scratch. Use these tools to achieve the highest possible recognition rate.

- Siri uses a separate audio volume system. So if you're at a movie or a conference, make sure you mute your system audio *and* lower Siri's volume control. To do that, invoke Siri and use the volume toggles on the side of the phone to lower the Siri sound level.

- Siri simplifies your life. Whether it's setting alarms ("Wake me at 7:15"), finding a friend ("Where is Barbara Sande?"), or updating your family ("Send Dad a message that I'm on the way"), Siri is there to help you become more productive with less work. The more you learn about using Siri, the simpler these tasks become over time. For many of these items, the issue isn't whether Siri can handle the tasks; it's whether you know that they're there to use. If this book helps you add a few essential ideas into your day-to-day Siri use, then we've proudly done our jobs.

2

Controlling Your Device with Siri

Siri helps you to check and change settings on your iOS device. Through clever integration with iOS 7 (and later), Siri not only answers your questions and helps you work and play, but it also lets you control your iPhone or iPad with voice commands. In this chapter, you'll discover how to use these new features to tweak and customize your mobile device. You'll read about Siri commands that reach beyond scheduling and communication into actual device settings.

Airplane Mode

Although the U.S. Federal Aviation Administration has now approved gate-to-gate usage of mobile devices on many aircraft and airlines, you must still place your device into Airplane mode for the duration of your flight. In this mode, iOS disables the various radios on your device. This rule applies even when you connect to onboard Wi-Fi networks once the aircraft is above a certain altitude.

The process of putting your iPhone into Airplane mode used to be a two-handed exercise in iOS 6 and earlier. First, you unlocked your device, then navigated to Settings, and then finally slid the Airplane mode toggle to enable it. iOS 7 has simplified the task, thanks to Control Center. Now, you slide up to bring Control Center into view and then tap the airplane button to enable it.

Siri makes it even easier. When you have Siri's Raise to Speak capability enabled on your iPhone, just click the Home button to wake up your device, then lift it to your ear. Say the magic words "Switch on Airplane mode." Siri is smart. It knows that disabling Wi-Fi also makes Siri deaf to your commands. It asks you to confirm that you really want to continue to enable Airplane mode. Reply "Yes" or tap the switch, and Siri dutifully shuts down Wi-Fi, cellular, and Bluetooth connections.

This voice-activated feature is incredibly useful when you're boarding an airplane with a backpack in one hand and a pulling a carryon with the other. Provided that your iPhone is in hand, just punching the Home button and asking Siri to turn on Airplane mode gets the job done (see Figure 2-1).

Voice-directed Airplane mode works on other non-phone iOS devices, but since they are not equipped with Raise to Speak, you'll have to manually engage Siri by holding down the Home button. Apple understands how ridiculous you'd look if you held up a full-sized iPad to your ear.

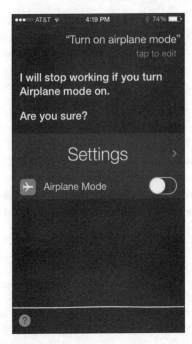

Figure 2-1
Siri can now disable itself by invoking Airplane mode. This is especially useful when you're boarding an aircraft.

Bluetooth and Wi-Fi Settings

iOS 7 introduced many interaction enhancements. For one thing, it made switching Bluetooth and Wi-Fi on and off a lot easier by placing a pair of buttons in the Control Center. Siri makes it easier yet. You don't need to swipe and tap to perform those tasks. Instead, you can now control these features with your voice.

First, ask Siri whether those networks are currently on or off. Yes, you could look at the icons in the status bar at the top of your iOS device to see if the Wi-Fi and/or Bluetooth indicators are there. But what if you're in a very bright place and can't read the screen very well? Or maybe you're in a situation where you need to keep your hands free and just can't look. Ask Siri, "Is Bluetooth on?" or "Is Wi-Fi on?" You'll get a quick yes or no response.

Next, Siri can switch Wi-Fi and Bluetooth on and off for you. Sometimes in crowded urban centers, you may find that your device keeps trying to connect to a variety of Wi-Fi networks. Invoke Siri, speak the words "Switch off Wi-Fi" or "Switch Wi-Fi off," and it shuts off that wireless networking option. Siri requires a network connection to work, so if you don't have a strong cellular data connection, Siri may be unresponsive when you ask it to "Switch Wi-Fi on."

 NOTE

> Siri does a terrific job at flexibly understanding commands regardless of word order. You can tell it to "Switch Wi-Fi on" or "Switch on Wi-Fi" and it adapts to your phrasing. Siri also understands many common variations. You can "Enable Wi-Fi," "Power on Wi-Fi," "Set Wi-Fi to on," "Engage Wi-Fi," "Start Wi-Fi going," "Begin using Wi-Fi," and "Turn on Wi-Fi," as well as "switch" it on.

As you no doubt already know, Bluetooth is a short-range low-power wireless system. Using Siri to turn it on is helpful when setting up a Bluetooth keyboard or headset. If you don't have Bluetooth enabled yet, just speak the magic words "Switch Bluetooth on," and Siri will do your bidding (see Figure 2-2).

Finally, Siri can be quite helpful when you need to jump into the Bluetooth or Wi-Fi settings to change something. Rather than tap on Settings, then scroll to Wi-Fi or Bluetooth, just say "Open Wi-Fi settings" or "Open Bluetooth settings," and Siri takes you to the right spot.

Figure 2-2
Siri loves to help you turn Bluetooth and Wi-Fi on and off, and it also helps you jump to settings for these two wireless services with a quick phrase.

Screen Brightness

Imagine that you're on a bright beach and need to turn up your screen brightness to see something, but you can't even see the screen to change those settings. Never fear: This is a good time for Siri to come to your rescue.

Just tell Siri to "Make my screen brighter," and it changes the setting for you. Too bright for you when you're in that movie theater, waiting for the movie to start? Tell Siri to "Make the screen darker," and it turns down the backlight (see Figure 2-3).

In both cases, Siri provides audible feedback that your command has been received and understood. Siri also displays the brightness slider, so if the settings aren't exactly to your liking, fine-tune the brightness by moving the slider with the tip of your finger.

Figure 2-3
Siri's pretty bright and can make your screen brighter or darker.

Siri and Social Network Settings

iPhone and iPad users love their social networks. Whether it's tweeting to your friends about the show you're watching on TV, or updating your Facebook pals about your latest vacation plans, social networks are a popular way to stay in touch.

Siri offers a quick way for you to check the settings for Twitter and Facebook with a single verbal command. Just tell Siri to "Open Twitter settings" or "Open Facebook settings," and the settings appear. This is a nice, lazy way to get to these settings instead of using the manual method, which is to launch the Settings app, then scroll down to Twitter or Facebook, and then tap the social network's name to open the settings.

These settings are important when you value security on your iOS device. Not only are these settings where you set up accounts (multiple accounts in Twitter), but it's also where you let Twitter or Facebook have access to your Contacts app to update it with Twitter and Facebook account information (see Figure 2-4).

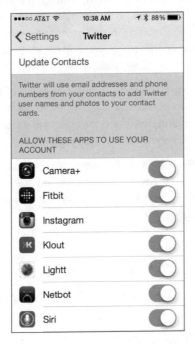

Figure 2-4
To quickly find the settings for both Facebook and Twitter, just ask Siri to open those settings.

In each Settings page, you'll find a number of toggle switches that enable or disable access from the social network apps to other apps on your iOS device. For example, you can choose to disable Siri's access to your Twitter account if you wish, although this prevents you from using Siri's powers to verbally send and read tweets.

Oddly enough, two other social networks that are integrated with iOS 7—Flickr and Vimeo—do not (at publication time) allow you to open settings with a Siri command.

Checking Email Settings with Siri

Like the social networking settings, email settings are also a quick Siri command away. You no longer have to dig around in the Settings app. Now telling Siri to "Open Mail settings" jumps right into the Settings page, where you add or delete accounts, change passwords, or make other changes.

Some of those settings include how many lines of your email are previewed (from zero to five lines), whether the to/cc labels are visible on incoming email, and the color and shape of the flag that is set when you flag a message (see Figure 2-5).

At this time, Siri can't actually change any of those settings for you, but it makes it easier to find them. Perhaps in some future version of iOS, Siri may let us say things like "Set my iCloud Mail signature to…."

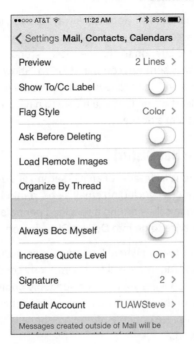

Figure 2-5
Email settings are just a Siri chat away.

Privacy Settings and Siri

Apple has built a number of privacy settings into iOS 7 to ensure that you and your device share information with only those applications and services that you approve of. Find your privacy settings in the Settings app, under the Privacy button. In the app, you change settings for how info like your location, contact data, calendars and reminders, photos, or even your device's microphone are shared with other apps or services.

In recent versions of iOS, apps will always ask you for your permission to have access to these items the first time you launch them. You may decide later on to change those settings. To jump immediately to privacy settings, command Siri to "Show me my Privacy settings." You'll still need to review and possibly reset those settings, but at least it's no longer a hassle to navigate to these settings at a moment's notice.

Controlling Do Not Disturb

Do Not Disturb is a lifesaver of an iOS setting. It's used to turn off all notifications—including email alerts, reminders, and even incoming phone calls—during a specified period of time or when you tell the device to go into Do Not Disturb mode.

It is this latter situation where Siri proves most helpful. Let's say that you're walking into a hall for a symphony concert and don't want to chance having your iPhone suddenly ringing or chiming in the middle of the concert. (Some conductors have been known to stop in mid-piece until the offending phone is silenced or the patron removed.)

Just before you place that iPhone into your pocket, invoke Siri and intone the incantation "Switch on Do Not Disturb." Your device immediately goes into blessed quiet mode (see Figure 2-6), saving you from embarrassment and others from inadvertent interruptions.

Siri, being the polite assistant that it is, provides a spoken verification that the Do Not Disturb mode has been enabled. Do Not Disturb provides a number of additional settings. For example, if someone calls your number more than once within three minutes, Do Not Disturb lets that call get through. Just flip the mute switch on the side of your iPhone into the Muted mode, and your phone will only buzz, not ring.

Figure 2-6
Shhhhh. Don't disturb those around you with your notifications.

Music

Siri wants to help you enjoy your iOS device as much as possible, so it has taken over duties from a previous voice-control tool fittingly called Voice Control. Siri works with both your music library and the newly introduced iTunes Radio streaming music service.

Controlling the Music App

You can ask Siri to play specific songs or playlists you've synced to your device. For example, you might say "Play Behind Blue Eyes by the Who." This results in that classic song beginning to blast from your headset (see Figure 2-7). When you've created a playlist of favorite tunes, Siri can either play it for you straight up—"Play my Led Zeppelin playlist"—or shuffle the music to surprise you—"Shuffle my party playlist."

Figure 2-7
Siri is your personal DJ, playing your requests with no hesitation or backtalk.

While a song is playing, you might invoke Siri and say "Pause" to temporarily halt the playback or "Play" to start up again. If any of the tunes you're listening to from an album or playlist are not your personal favorites, just invoke Siri and say "Skip" to bounce right past the currently playing song.

Once Siri has started to play a playlist or song, it displays the words "Show Now Playing." With a tap, the Music app appears, and you'll see the album cover and playback tools for that song or series of songs.

Controlling iTunes Radio

iTunes has been around since January 2001, and Apple keeps adding new features and services to increase your music listening enjoyment. The latest addition, which debuted in September 2013, is iTunes Radio. iTunes Radio streams music to you over the Internet so you can lighten the data you sync to your device. It works surprisingly well both over fast Wi-Fi and slower cellular data networks.

Siri provides integrated control with iTunes Radio. You begin by speaking the single Siri command "Play iTunes Radio." iPhone, iPad, and iPod touch owners can then explore music with ease. When you launch iTunes Radio, your last selected "station" begins playing. If you haven't used iTunes Radio before, a station is automatically selected for you.

When you like what you hear, let Siri know. This helps iTunes Radio better fit your musical tastes. Just say "Play more songs like this one" or "I like this song," and you'll begin to hear songs that are in a similar genre or by similar artists. If you just about gag when a Lady Gaga song appears in the middle of your Norah Jones station, let Siri know. Tell it "Don't play this song again," and you'll get immediate relief as well as freedom from future miscues.

You may choose a station manually by selecting it from the list of pre-created stations or by requesting songs by a specific artist. Calling up that station in the future is then a breeze. Just ask Siri to "Play my Led Zeppelin station," and the station begins to fill your life with music (see Figure 2-8).

Figure 2-8
It's all-request radio when Siri's behind the microphone at iTunes Radio.

Summary

Siri's new ability to control your increasingly more complex iOS device with spoken commands provides a wonderful jump toward a future filled with even more conversational assistants. The items you want to remember from this chapter include the following points:

- With the advent of iOS 7, Siri now provides voice control for device settings.

- Wireless connections—including Wi-Fi, Bluetooth, and any cellular voice or data connections—can be enabled or disabled with simple Siri requests.

- Does your iPhone or iPad screen seem too bright or dim for your surroundings? Ask Siri to make the screen to dimmer or brighter.

- Sharing your life with others through social networks has never been easier. Siri makes it possible to control access to Facebook and Twitter.

- Use privacy settings to control anything you don't wish to share. Easily access these settings through Siri.

- No longer do you need to have wake your device, unlock it, and launch an app to control what music you're listening to. Siri now plays your choice of music from either your music library or from iTunes Radio, all through friendly and easily learned commands.

3

Asking Siri for Information

Siri exists to serve. It wants nothing more than to provide information to you—about almost anything in the universe. Siri provides answers to questions about everything from the weather to stock prices, through integration with the apps that come with your iOS device. Questions outside the realm of the built-in apps on iOS are no problem for Siri. It knows how to work with Wikipedia and Wolfram Alpha, and it searches the Web through Bing, Yahoo!, and Google to find the best possible answers to whatever you ask. In this chapter, you'll learn how to phrase your conversation to maximize the probability of getting an accurate and detailed answer.

Weather

Worried about whether to bring an umbrella? Siri keeps on top of the weather forecast for you. When you ask "Will it rain tonight?" or "What is the temperature?" Siri offers immediate feedback. When you ask "What's the weather for this week?" Siri provides the full weekly forecast (see Figure 3-1). As a rule, Siri replies with simple answers. If extensive charts are involved, you are prompted to look at the phone instead of just listen. Best of all, Siri occasionally sneaks in a little sass in its conversation, adding fun commentary to its answers.

Figure 3-1
Siri can check the weather for you so you know how to dress appropriately.

Other Queries

In addition to the current weather conditions, Siri provides sunrise and sunset times (for the current day only) and the phase of the Moon. You can even ask "When will Jupiter (or Mars or Venus or the Moon or so on) rise?" to query about planets or the Moon.

Siri has no access to past weather information and cannot check information such as sunrise/sunset times for the future. So you cannot ask "When will the Sun rise tomorrow?" If you do, Siri reports only today's sunrise time.

Locations

When you switch locations, make sure you let Siri know. Why does this matter? When you ask about the high today in London and next ask about the local wind speed, Siri defaults to the London wind speed, not the local one, unless local for you is London. So go ahead and say "What's the wind speed here?" rather than "What's the wind speed?" to make sure you correct for the previous possible problem.

Siri always tries to retain context for your conversations, to make it easier for you to add brief questions without having to keep stating who, where, and when. But these assumptions work against you if you don't specify "here" or "now" when you change the topic.

The best questions to ask in hands-free mode are ones that evaluate the weather, using specific quantities ("How cold is it?" "How warm is it?" "What is the wind chill?"), or that specify whether it will rain/be cold/be hot, and so on. Figure 3-2 shows this kind of question in action. Siri replies with a useful narrated response.

Figure 3-2
Siri can answer questions that evaluate the weather.

 NOTE

When temperatures drop fast, Siri may add a "Brr" to your weather report.

Siri offers a wide vocabulary for weather-related conversation. You can ask about forecasts using many approaches. Here are some things you can say to Siri about the weather:

- "What's the weather for today?" and "What's the weather for tomorrow?"
- "What's the weather in Walla Walla?"
- "Should I take an umbrella tomorrow?"
- "Should I wear a coat tonight?" and "Can I wear a bikini?"
- "Is it raining in Roanoke?"
- "How hot is it today?" and "How cold is it?"
- "What is the wind speed?" and "What is the wind speed in London right now?"
- "What is the humidity?" and "What is the wind chill?"
- "Will it rain in Cupertino this week?"
- "Will there be a storm here?"
- "When will it snow here?"
- "Check the forecast for Fort Lauderdale."
- "What's the forecast for this evening?"
- "Will it snow this week in Denver?"
- "How's the weather in Tampa right now?"
- "How hot will it be in Palm Springs this weekend?"
- "What's the high for Anchorage on Thursday?"
- "What's the temperature outside?"
- "How windy is it out there?"
- "What's the phase of the Moon?"
- "Is it nighttime in Paris?" and "When is sunrise in Paris?"

Web Search

With Siri, you have the entire Web not just at your fingertips but also at the tip of your tongue. With spoken phrases, you can ask Siri to search the Web and show you the information it finds. With iOS 7, most Siri web searches are now integrated with Bing, displaying results within Siri's results screen rather than launching a web browser.

Siri uses several key phrases to hunt for information on the Web. You can tell it, "Search the Web," "Search the Web for [topic]," or "I want to see websites about…," among other web-oriented queries. Here are examples of web search requests you might ask Siri to perform:

- "Search the Web for Bora Bora."
- "Search for vegetarian pasta recipes."
- "Search the Web for best cable plans."
- "Search for news about the World Cup."
- "I want to see websites about ostriches."
- "Show me websites about baseball."

What's more, Siri can use any of iOS's three major search engines to answer your queries, so Google, Yahoo!, and Bing are all valid sources for information. When you choose either Google or Yahoo!, however, Siri launches your web browser to display the search results. For example, you might say "Yahoo! pickle recipes," "Google knitting," or "Bing Bing Crosby" (see Figure 3-3).

Figure 3-3
You can use search engine names as request verbs with Siri. You may also want to "Bing bing cherries," "Bing Binghamton," or "Bing Chandler Bing."

Searching for Pictures

If you're looking specifically for pictures, there's a Siri shortcut for that, too. Say "I want to see pictures of [topic]." For example, you might say "I want to see pictures of kittens" (see Figure 3-4). The Bing search results that appear by default when you ask for information about a topic generally include related pictures.

Figure 3-4
Siri understands requests that start with "I want to see..." and conducts a meaningful web search for you.

Sometimes you ask Siri the worst things, and it responds with unexpectedly sweet results. For example, ask it to "Show me pictures of boobies," and it returns a set of pictures of the appropriately named birds. Some of the top results we see from this search include marvelous wildlife images with their distinctive blue feet.

Searching Wikipedia

Siri offers full Wikipedia support in addition to search engine results. All you have to do is ask your question the right way. With previous versions of Siri, you specifically had to ask it to search Wikipedia for a topic. Now, search results often include Wikipedia entries automatically. The search results break down source by source, so you can tell which items result from Bing, which from Wolfram Alpha, and which from Wikipedia, as shown in Figure 3-5.

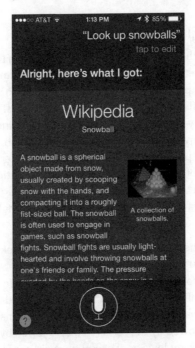

Figure 3-5
Wikipedia entries often appear at or near the top of Siri web searches.

Try out your own requests, like these:

- "Search Wikipedia for Abraham Lincoln."
- "Look up snowballs."
- "Tell me about the blue-footed booby."
- "What is a parliamentary system?"
- "Wikipedia oranges."
- "What is Snodgrass?"

Checking Flights

Among its other talents, Siri may now be bucking for a travel agent job—although it still has a way to go in terms of customer service. With previous iterations of Siri, you had to say "Search the Web for flights between [two cities or airports]," and Siri would display the answers in Safari. Now just saying "Find flights between Denver and Houston" or "Search for flights from Denver to Frankfurt" produces a list of results on Siri's interface. Admittedly, many of these results are for discount ticketing services such as Orbitz, Expedia, or Cheapflights. So we're going to give Siri a failing grade for most of the integrated flight information it produces.

Google, on the other hand, does know how to look up flight information. If you've ever entered a search like "Southwest Airlines Flight 245," you know that Google produces information about whether the flight is on time, when it departs, and when it arrives. So the best way to use Siri to look up flight information is to say "Google" followed by the carrier name, followed by the flight name—for example, "Google Southwest Airlines Flight 245"—as shown in Figure 3-6.

Figure 3-6
Use Siri's "Google" command to retrieve specific flight information.

Unfortunately, you can't just tell Siri to "Buy me two first class tickets to Honolulu on December 24." Perhaps someday soon Siri will expand to work with airline apps to make purchasing tickets easier than buying them from a website.

Overhead Flights

Steve is a bit of an airliner freak. He loves looking up at the contrails of jets flying overhead and wondering where a plane might be going. A few years ago, he discovered that Wolfram Alpha has the ability to tell you what airplanes are cruising around above you, based on your position and its knowledge of where various airline and charter flights are located at any point in time. Since Siri has the built-in ability to work with Wolfram Alpha, Steve uses Siri to find out about those flights overhead.

Saying to Siri "Ask Wolfram what flights are overhead" produces these results, although you can also just ask "What flights are overhead?" as in Figure 3-7. That query displays a Wolfram Alpha summary, showing the flights that are currently visible from where you're standing, their altitude, and the angle above the horizon. You also get information on what type of aircraft each is, how far away it is, and what direction to look. The Wolfram Alpha query also pulls up a sky map showing where the planes are located. Scroll down to find the map at the end of the flight information results.

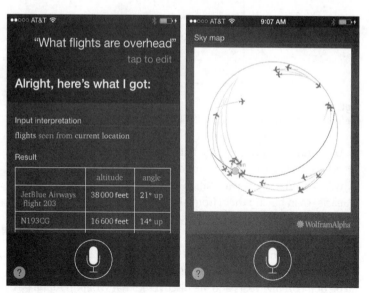

Figure 3-7
Wolfram Alpha helps you discover what flights are above you.

Sports and Siri

If you're a sports fan, you'll be happy to know that Siri brings scores, schedules, rosters, and more to your device. As Figure 3-8 shows, Siri has the goods on many major sports. Ask about your favorite teams and their players and check when the next game will happen.

Figure 3-8
Siri knows how your favorite team is doing.

Siri primarily covers U.S. sports. As far as international coverage goes, Siri is limited to what the U.S. calls "soccer" and the rest of the world calls "football." So although Siri knows about English Premiere League football, it has no knowledge of rugby or cricket.

It will, however, offer up a number of web results for you to choose from if you ask about those sports. Siri currently provides information for the following sports leagues:

- **Baseball:** Major League Baseball
- **U.S. football:** NCAA football and National Football League
- **Basketball:** NCAA basketball, National Basketball Association, and Women's National Basketball Association
- **Hockey:** National Hockey League
- **International football (soccer):** Italian Seria A, English Premier League, Dutch Eredivisie, Major League Soccer, French Ligue 1, Spanish La Liga, and German Bundesliga

For these sports, Siri can respond to questions about scores, standings, team rosters, player stats, and playing schedules. Here are some of the specific ways to ask Siri about sports:

- "Did the Giants win?"
- "What was the score of the last Giants game?"
- "How did Kansas City do?"
- "What was the score the last time the Tigers played the Red Sox?"
- "What are the National League standings?"
- "Show me the football scores from last night."
- "When do the Giants play next?"
- "How is Arsenal doing?" (See Figure 3-8.)
- "When is the Boston Red Sox's first game of the season?"
- "Show me the schedule for baseball."
- "Who has the highest slugging percentage?"
- "What's Buster Posey's batting average?"
- "Who is taller, Lebron or Kobe?"

- "Who has the most home runs on the Giants?"
- "Who has the most goals in soccer?"
- "Which quarterback has the most passing yards?"
- "Show me the roster for the University of Colorado football team."
- "Who is pitching for the Miami Marlins this season?"
- "When is the Rockies's first game of the season?"
- "What's the University of Colorado's football record?" (See Figure 3-9.)

Figure 3-9
Siri displays the standings for many sports leagues but cannot guarantee that your favorite team will make the playoffs.

Checking Stocks

For those of us who have money in the stock market either through personal choice or with a 401(k), it's occasionally interesting to see how our investments are doing by checking on stock prices. Because a stock ticker is part of the iOS notification center and a Stocks app has been part of the iPhone since 2007, it's not surprising that Apple also lets Siri be your personal investment assistant (see Figure 3-10).

Figure 3-10
Siri supplies up-to-the-minute information about the markets and individual stocks, but it won't tell you what to buy or sell.

Not only does Siri give you an overall snapshot of market averages, it also supplies details about individual stocks. Just ask about the company name, and Siri looks up the stock details. Here's an overview of some of the phrases that Siri understands:

- "How is Procter and Gamble doing?"
- "What's Coca-Cola trading at?"
- "What's Twitter's stock price?"
- "What is Apple's PE ratio?"
- "What did Yahoo! close at today?"
- "How is the Nikkei doing?"
- "How are the markets doing?"
- "What is the Dow at?"
- "What's Apple's market cap?"
- "Compare the market caps for Apple and Exxon Mobil."
- "What is the 52-week high for Apple this year?"
- "What's the 52-week low for Lockheed Martin?"

If you say "Buy 500 shares of Apple," Siri looks up the stock, but it will not place an order. That's because Siri cannot actually offer stock services or even advice. Apple definitely does not want Siri to be your stock advisor. We gave it a try, as you can see in Figure 3-11. Here are some examples of Siri queries that cause the assistant to complain. None of these produce the results you're looking for:

- "Should I buy Apple?"
- "Siri, what are the 10 best picks on the New York Stock Exchange?"
- "Please pick me a good stock."

Figure 3-11
"What would I do? I'd shut it down and give the money back to the shareholders." (Michael Dell in 1997, answering a question about what could be done to fix the then-ailing Apple Computer, Inc.)

At this time, Siri also has a sneaky built-in Easter egg specifically about stocks, which we share with you in Figure 3-12.

Figure 3-12
Oh Siri, you sly assistant!

Using Wolfram Alpha

Wolfram Alpha is, according to Wikipedia, "an online service that answers factual queries directly by computing the answer from structured data, rather than providing a list of documents or web pages that might contain the answer as a search engine might." Between Bing, Wikipedia, and Wolfram Alpha, Apple has done an amazing job of opening up Siri searches to first-class information sources. Like the other integrated queries, Wolfram Alpha answers are presented directly in the Siri interface. That makes it easy for you to keep going with a conversation, without having to hop into and out of Siri mode on your device (see Figure 3-13).

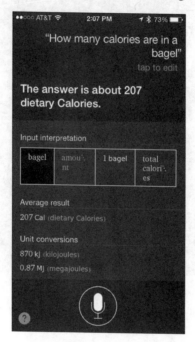

Figure 3-13
Use Wolfram Alpha queries to check definitions, look up information, calculate, and more.

When Siri recognizes a question that might be best answered or analyzed by Wolfram Alpha, it passes along your data and then displays whatever Wolfram Alpha returns. Siri uses this special view to present those results. They aren't verbally announced to you. Some of the questions you can get answers to seem incredible.

Querying Wolfram

Wolfram knows about quite a lot. The most reliable way to query Wolfram is to prefix your question with "Wolfram," "Ask Wolfram," or "What is." The "Wolfram" clue isn't strictly necessary, as you'll see in the following sample statements. Each of these statements is interpreted by Siri and then passed to Wolfram Alpha without explicitly using the word Wolfram at all:

- "How many calories in a bagel?"
- "What does *repartee* mean?"
- "What is an 18 percent tip on $86.74 for four people?"
- "What's Morse code for *horse feathers*?"
- "Who's buried in Grant's tomb?"
- "How long do dogs live?"
- "What is the square root of 128?"
- "How many dollars is €45?"
- "What is the gossamer condor?"
- "What are the first 23 digits of *e*?"
- "How many dollars is ¥50,000?"
- "What was best picture in 1949?"
- "How many days until Easter?"
- "How many days between September 22, 1957, and today?"
- "How far away is Neptune?"
- "When is the next solar eclipse?"
- "What is the orbital period of Pluto?"
- "How far away is the Sun?"
- "Show me the constellation Ursa Major."
- "What's the population of Montenegro?"
- "How high is Mt. Kilimanjaro?"

- "How deep is the Pacific Ocean?"
- "What's the price of diesel in Dubuque, Iowa?"
- "What's the price of lettuce in New York City?"
- "What's the integral of the cosine of x?" (Siri and Wolfram Alpha seem to have problems with the sine function, confusing it with the word *sign*.)
- "Graph y = $9x^2$ + 2."
- "What's the derivative of $3x^3$ + 2x?"
- "What's the boiling point of iron?"
- "What's the scientific name of a mountain lion?"
- "How many dimples are on a golf ball?"
- "How many episodes were there of *Buffy the Vampire Slayer*?"
- "What is the largest lake in the world?"
- "What is the longest filibuster?"
- "When did Colorado join the union?"
- "How many Earths fit inside the Sun?"
- "How many turkeys are there in Turkey?"
- "What words contain *Steve*?"
- "What is the angle of the Leaning Tower of Pisa?"
- "How many people are there per pet fish in the United States?"
- "What's the atomic weight of lead?"

Yes, Siri answers all these questions, with the help of Wolfram Alpha, and presents the results directly to you.

The depth of knowledge that Wolfram Alpha has is staggering. With Siri translating your questions into a format that Wolfram Alpha can understand, you have access to an incredible amount of information. Neither tool is perfect, and sometimes the way that Siri or Wolfram Alpha interprets your questions is amusing (to say the least), but both provide a huge amount of information and trivia.

 NOTE

Want to discover further interesting things to say to Wolfram Alpha? Follow @WolframFunFacts on Twitter. Wolfram regularly posts intriguing queries.

The Wolfram Saving Throw

Try saying "igneous rock" to Siri on your iOS device. Siri usually displays a Wikipedia entry for your answer, and it may also display a link to Wolfram Alpha at the bottom of the entry. You can use this link or use the Wolfram saving throw, which allows Wolfram to act as a superhero. Tap the microphone after the Wikipedia results appear and say the magic phrase "Ask Wolfram."

Suddenly, bingo! Without any further work, Siri redirects your query to Wolfram Alpha—and saves the day. Figure 3-14 shows this maneuver in action.

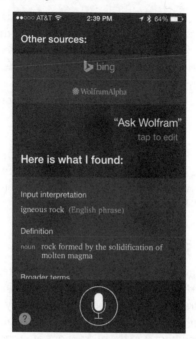

Figure 3-14
The Wolfram saving throw converts a phrase into a valid Wolfram Alpha search.

Other Cool Stuff You Can Do with Wolfram Alpha

Here are several ways you can use Siri and Wolfram Alpha to do things you might not have thought of:

- **Generate a random number:** Say to Siri "Tell me a random number" or "Pick a random number." Wolfram Alpha returns a value between 0 and 1,000. Also, in the latest releases of Siri, you can ask the assistant directly to "Roll the die," and it will return two numbers between 1 and 6 for you.

- **Generate a random password:** Tell Siri "Wolfram, give me a random password." This generates a secure password for you. For an amusing (but pointless) alternative, ask Siri "What's the password?" without using the Wolfram keyword.

- **Check earthquakes:** Tell Siri "Wolfram, earthquakes" and let Siri find the most recent recorded earthquakes around the world.

- **Check upcoming holidays:** Say "How many days until Thanksgiving?" Siri returns both the number of days and a helpful calendar so that you can chart the time until then.

- **Convert text to Morse code:** Say "What is Morse code for *horsefeathers*?" You'll see the entire sequence laid out for your tapping pleasure.

- **Check your diet:** Say "How many calories in a small apple?" Wolfram will tell you there are 74.5 dietary calories in a small apple.

- **Ask out about time zones:** Say "Wolfram, what is the local time in Jakarta?"

- **Look up nature facts:** Say "Wolfram, what is the scientific name of a mountain lion?" As Siri will tell you, it's puma con-color. Rabbits are leporidae, and peacocks are galliformes.

- **Query about your chances:** Say "Wolfram, what is the prob-ability of a full house?" For a random five-card hand, it's appar-ently 1 in 694.

- **Have fun with pop culture:** Say "Wolfram, what is the air-speed velocity of an unladen swallow?" or "Who shot the sher-iff?"

- **Visualize colors:** If you work with colors, this can save you a lot of time. Say "Wolfram pound sign 9 9 7 4 5 1" (for dark salmon) or "Wolfram pound sign 2 9 A B 8 7" (for jungle green). Siri also converts the colors to RGB values and looks up closely matching house paint colors from Benjamin Moore. Be sure to scroll down to catch all the helpful information. The latest version of Siri seems to struggle a bit with letter names (specifically A through F), unlike earlier releases.

- **Graph equations:** Wolfram Alpha does great graphs and is ready to replace your expensive graphing calculator. Say "Graph Y equals 4x plus 15," for example. Also try "Show me a plot of c over lambda." Siri gives you a cool graph in response, although we were hoping for "Nothing's nu with me. What's nu with you?"

Pokédex

Fans of Pokémon now have Siri access to the Pokédex for characters up to Generation VI. You'll find this database particularly handy if you play the various titles in the Pokémon game franchise—but it's incredibly fun regardless. The Pokédex—the mythical electronic device that catalogs and provides information about the species of Pokémon—was made available by Wolfram Alpha, so you'll want to preface your question about one of 649 different Pokémon with "Search Wolfram for." What you'll get as a response is much more information than you can possibly imagine about Pokémon (see Figure 3-15), unless you have a 9-year-old son, in which case you're probably already acutely aware of how much there is to know about such matters.

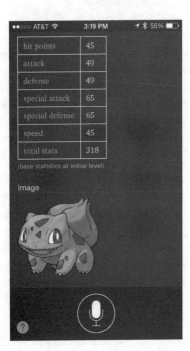

hit points	45
attack	49
defense	49
special attack	65
special defense	65
speed	45
total stats	318

(base statistics at initial level)

Image

Figure 3-15
Need overly detailed information about different Pokémon? It's at your fingertips, thanks to Siri and Wolfram Alpha. You'll be able to see the core statistics that form the basis for how each character performs in battle.

To see for yourself what Siri and Wolfram Alpha know about Pokémon, try these queries:

- "Ask Wolfram Alpha about Pikachu."
- "Which Pokémon has the highest special attack?"
- "Which Pokémon has a speed greater than 80?"
- "What is the special attack of flying Pokémon?"
- "Which Pokémon are taller than 5 feet?"
- "What are the physical characteristics of Pikachu?"

Summary

Siri's powerful capabilities help you search for information through quick spoken conversations. In this chapter, you've learned about the vast range of topics that Siri can respond to by working with the built-in iOS apps, searching the Web, or passing information to an established search service such as Wikipedia or Wolfram Alpha. The points you want to remember from this chapter include the following:

- Siri offers a personal weather assistant, providing information on conditions either locally or in other parts of the world.

- Siri isn't limited to Google searches. Set your preferences to Google, Yahoo!, or Bing—or choose the search engine you prefer to use by saying its name during your request. It may feel odd to say "Google this," "Bing that," or "Yahoo! whatever," but it helps Siri direct your request to the engine you prefer.

- Siri now provides many more responses from Wikipedia.

- Enjoy up-to-the-moment sports info. Ask Siri about your favorite team, the score, and when the next game is due to start.

- Siri is your personal stock market reporter. It gives you up-to-date information on individual stocks, markets, and indices, as well as ratios and statistics.

- Wolfram Alpha's integration with Siri offers a powerful information-gathering combination. From solving differential equations to telling you how far it is to the South Pole from your current location, Siri and Wolfram Alpha transform incredible standalone tools into an unbeatable combo.

4

Using Siri to Stay in Touch

When it comes to contacts, Siri is the star of the show. It helps you stay in touch with others by supercharging your device's communication capabilities, letting you search for contacts, placing phone calls, sending text messages, and even composing email.

Siri understands relationships, too. Communication is all about relationships between people, and Siri can learn the established connections between you, your friends and coworkers, and your family. Tell Siri the names of your dentist, your accountant, your hairdresser, and more. Then when you want to make an appointment, Siri is ready to help retrieve that contact information.

Prepare to have some fun as you find out how to use Siri as your personal assistant when communicating with the world.

Contacts

When it comes to knowing who your contacts are, Siri provides a direct line into your iOS Contacts. For example, it's possible to look up phone numbers, email addresses, birthdays, and other data you would normally find in your device's Contacts list. You might ask Siri:

- "What's Victor's address?"
- "What is my dentist's phone number?"
- "When is my wife's birthday?"
- "What is Joe's work address?"
- "Find people named Fred."
- "Who's my hairdresser?"
- "Who is Jony Ive?"
- "Show Megan's home email address."

Each query looks up a specific detail for a given contact. Figure 4-1 shows a typical request, asking for the phone number for John Appleseed.

When Siri displays a contact, tap it to jump into the Contacts app to view or edit the entry.

Siri might at times have trouble distinguishing between contacts with similar names. If you ask, "What is John's phone number?" Siri asks you which John you mean. It does this by presenting a list of possible matches (see Figure 4-2) from your Contacts list.

Figure 4-1
Siri simplifies looking up specific contact information.

To respond, tap a name or say the surname out loud. Siri automatically listens whenever it asks you a clarification question. After you've established which contact you meant, you can keep referring to John, without answering any further questions. Say "Send a text to John," and Siri uses the currently selected person's contact information.

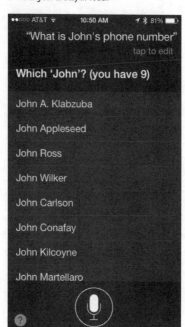

Figure 4-2
Siri might ask you to specify which contact you mean when multiple entries match your request.

If you need to change the context from the current person to another person of the same name, specify the full name (including last name) in your request—for example, "What is John *Walton's* phone number?" Siri always tries to remember context to make each session as seamless as possible. In the case of your address book, the context is the most recently selected contact.

 NOTE

Using nicknames is a great way to differentiate contacts, especially those with common names. If you know six Bills, for example, nicknames might help you distinguish Bill "Poker Night Bill" Smith from Bill "Space Boy" Jones.

Searching for Contacts

Sometimes you want to view an entire contact entry. Siri helps
you find contacts from your iOS address book. For example, you
might ask Siri, "Show Jason Russell" or "Who is Michael Manning?"
Each of these queries locates the requested person and displays
his or her full contact information (see Figure 4-3).

Figure 4-3
View contacts by asking Siri to show them or by asking, "Who is…?"

Once you see what contact information is available, you can easily use this data to send email, place phone calls, write texts, and
more.

Creating Relationships

Relationships form an important part of the Siri/Contacts story. Although these elements have been part of iOS for many years, not until the introduction of Siri has adding relationships really made important sense on iOS. That's because Siri enables you to personalize your relationships with others and use those relationships as shortcuts when making requests.

Say "Victor Agreda is my boss" or "John Appleseed is my friend" (see Figure 4-4) to establish those connections between your contact information and other entries in your iOS address book.

Figure 4-4
Siri creates relationships to connect your contact information to others. You can edit those connections in the Contacts app.

Default relationships include mother, father, parent, sister, brother, child, friend, spouse, partner, manager, and assistant—but you are not limited to these. You can create any describable relationship for any recognized contact. For example, you might say, "Erica Sadun is my writing partner" or "Dave Caolo is my hairdresser." Siri adds those relationships to your contacts, as you see in Figure 4-4.

Relationships can be made with only known contacts. If you use an unknown person—for example, "Benjamin Franklin is my tennis partner"—Siri complains (in this case, "There's no one in your contacts matching 'Benjamin Franklin'").

 NOTE

Historically, Siri has had problems properly supporting relationships for Exchange and Gmail address books. Be aware that you, too, might experience some problems.

Here are some examples of ways you can use relationships with Siri:

- "My mom is Susan Islington."
- "Michael Fredericks is my brother."
- "Call my sister at work."
- "Text my assistant."
- "Call my hairdresser."
- "Billy Appleseed is my spouse."
- "Steve Sande is my friend."
- "Fran Yeddis is my realtor."
- "When is my husband's birthday?"
- "Emma Sadun is my child."

Each relationship is stored in the standard Contacts app. You can edit any relationships you might have inadvertently added by mistake (for example, "Justin Bieber is my boyfriend"—yeah, right, smart-aleck daughter who swiped the iPhone). Also, well, we'll let Figure 4-5 speak for itself.

Figure 4-5
She's just a girl who claims that I am the one.

Creating Nicknames

Perhaps you've heard this joke: You tell Siri, "Call me an ambulance," and Siri responds, "From now on, I'll call you, 'An Ambulance.' Okay?" Leanna Lofte pointed out in a great write-up at iMore (http://imore.com) that this joke is actually of practical use. It's possible to create a more intimate identity for yourself by telling Siri to call you by your nickname—or indulge your mono-maniacal streak by instructing it to call you "master" or "emperor" (see Figure 4-6, left). Check on your current nickname by asking Siri, "Who am I?" (see Figure 4-6, right).

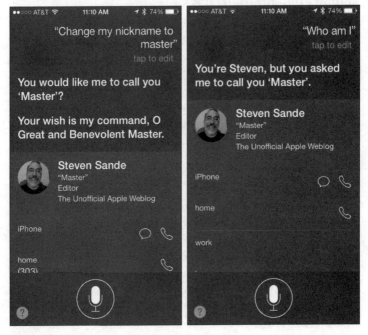

Figure 4-6
Changing your nickname to "master" is likely to prompt a snarky response from Siri (left). If you're not sure who Siri thinks you are, just ask (right).

Siri does this by checking two fields in your primary Contacts entry. The Nickname field takes priority. When you say, "Call me [followed by some name]," Siri updates your Nickname field. Another way to establish an alternative name without adding a nickname to your entry is to use the phonetic guides.

Adding Pronunciation Cues

The Phonetic First Name and Phonetic Last Name fields have been around for quite some time in the Contacts application on both iOS and OS X. They help you pronounce people's names when you call them. For example, you might enter "Ser-hee-yo" for a contact named Sergio and refer to that pronunciation as you're placing your call. (You can also add free-form notes in each contact for other cultural hints.) Siri then uses those fields to override the default pronunciation of your name as well.

To add these fields in iOS, tap Edit, scroll down to Add Field, and then choose one of the phonetic options.

If Siri doesn't seem to pronounce a name the way it should, let it know. For example, Siri pronounced the last name "Geraghty" as "Gare-ought-tee," while the actual contact pronounced it as "Gare-ih-tee." To correct Siri's pronunciation, tell it "That's not how you pronounce [contact's name]." Siri asks you to pronounce the first name, then offers two or three choices for you to listen to. Select the pronunciation that sounds the closest to reality, and then Siri asks you to pronounce the last name. Once again, you're offered several sound samples to listen to. Choose the closest pronunciation, and Siri thanks you for correcting its mispronunciation (see Figure 4-7).

Figure 4-7
When Siri mispronounces a name, be sure to correct it.

Placing Phone Calls with Siri

Siri uses your address book contact information to simplify the way you place phone calls. For example, you might say one of the following phrases to initiate a call with one of your personal contacts. If a person is not listed in your address book, explicitly speak the number.

- "Call Jason."
- "Call Biffster." (Remember that Siri works with nicknames, too.)
- "Call Jennifer Wright mobile."
- "Call Susan on her work phone."
- "Call 408-555-1212."
- "Call home."
- "FaceTime Lisa."

Be aware that Siri does not confirm phone calls before placing them (see Figure 4-8, left). It initiates a call directly and immediately switches to the phone (or FaceTime) application. You can cancel a call if needed, but you use an airtime minute in the process. Alternatively, press the Home button before control passes to the Phone application to stop the call from going out.

When contacts offer several phone numbers, you can help Siri by specifying which number to use. For example, you might say "Call John Appleseed at work" or "Call John Appleseed at home." If Siri cannot exactly match your request to a given number, it tries to offer you an alternative (see Figure 4-8, right).

In Figure 4-8 (right), John Appleseed's contact entry contains just one phone number, and it's labeled as iPhone. If you ask to call him at home, Siri suggests the iPhone number as an alternative. You can confirm using the iPhone number or cancel by pressing the Home button.

Figure 4-8
Siri places calls directly, without requiring confirmation (left). If Siri cannot match the requested phone to a contact number (for example, you asked to call home, but there's no home number), it tries to use another number instead (right).

Missed Calls and Voicemail

Siri's learned some new tricks in iOS 7, like how to play back your voicemail, check your missed phone calls, and return calls. This is very useful when you're otherwise occupied and cannot answer every phone call, such as when you're driving your car or when you're in the midst of a job interview.

Checking Missed Calls

You're in that all-important meeting with the boss, your iPhone is vibrating away in your pocket, and you know you can't just answer the calls. Once you're out of the meeting, ask Siri "Do I have any missed calls?" or "Show my call history" (see Figure 4-9). The results of these two queries are slightly different: For the former request, Siri lists just those calls that you didn't answer, while for the latter Siri shows all recent incoming and outgoing phone calls.

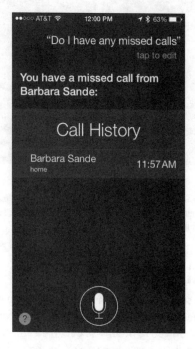

Figure 4-9
Siri's your virtual phone answering service, keeping track of the calls you've missed.

Checking Voicemail

Not everyone likes to leave voicemail messages; some prefer to talk directly to a real live human instead. But some of your callers may decide to leave a message when you don't answer. Siri's happy to let you know if you have voicemail, responding to a request of "Do I have any new voicemail?" with a spoken and visual response (see Figure 4-10, left).

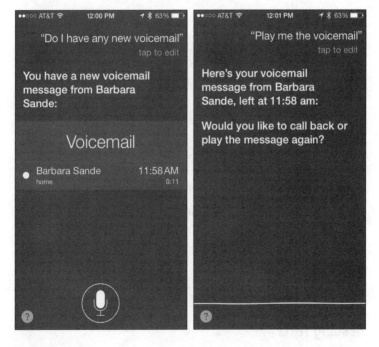

Figure 4-10
Siri visually and verbally provides you with an update of any voicemail messages you may have received, and if you wish to listen to them, also offers the choice of playing a message again or dialing the caller.

Your reaction to Siri's response can be either tactile—tapping the voicemail message displayed on your iPhone screen—or spoken. To hear a voicemail message, tell Siri "Play me the voicemail." Siri knows that you'll probably want to either listen to the message again or return the call, so it displays a "call back or play the message again" message while the voicemail is being played (see Figure 4-10, right).

Text Messages

The Siri intelligent assistant helps you use your voice to check text messages, send replies, and start new conversations. With Siri, you can perform many of your iMessage tasks from anywhere on your iOS device.

Siri supports sending or receiving three different types of messages—standard SMS text messages, MMS multimedia (pictures and video) messages, and Apple's iMessage format. iMessage bypasses the traditional phone-based messaging system and instead transfers text and multimedia messages over the Internet.

Like the proverbial honey badger, Siri really doesn't care how the messages are sent. It chooses the correct transport method and ensures that your message is properly dictated and sent to the recipient. One nice feature of iMessage is that it lets you know when a message has been delivered and also shows you if someone is in the process of typing a reply.

Reading Texts

Siri loves to read your new text messages to you. This is very useful if you're out driving and receive a message you want to hear. How do you do it? Just ask!

When a new message arrives, tell Siri "Read my new message." If you want it repeated, tell Siri "Read it again." Siri fills you in on all your new messages while keeping your hands free for other tasks. You can also ask, "Do I have any new messages?" in case you've lost track.

Composing Texts

Siri listens for some keywords before sending a text message—including *tell*, *send a message*, and *text*. Figure 4-11 shows an example of a message going to Erica.

To create a message, instruct Siri to tell someone something, such as "Tell Steve, I'll be right there." You can also say "text" or "send a message." For example, you can say, "Send a message to Mike saying 'How about tomorrow?'" or "Text Anthony 'Where are you? I have been waiting for 20 minutes.'" Here are some common phrases to use when telling Siri to dictate and send a message to someone:

- "Tell Megan 'I'll be right there.'"
- "Send a message to Dave Caolo."
- "Text Steve and Megs that I'll be a little late."
- "Send a message to Paige saying, 'How about tomorrow?'"
- "Tell Cathy the birthday present was great."
- "Send a message to Susan on her mobile saying I'll feed the dog."
- "Send a message to 408-555-1212." Siri will prompt you for the message contents.
- "Text Mike and Victor 'Where are you?'"

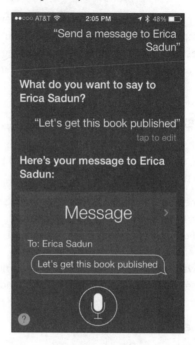

Figure 4-11
When you want to send a text message to someone, tell Siri to write it for you. Siri shows you what it heard and then asks if you want to send it.

Notice that if you don't have a contact for a person you want to message, but you do have a mobile number, you can tell Siri to send a message to that number. For example, say, "Send a message to 408-555-1212," and Siri prompts you for the text contents. Then speak your message.

Confirming Messages

When Siri asks if you wish to send a message, you can ask it to read the message back to you. (Say "Read it to me," "Read it back to me," "Review," or "Read it again.") Siri also offers the opportunity to send, cancel, review, or change a message you have composed (see Figure 4-12). The following examples let Siri know that you're not satisfied with what you've said. Notice that it is possible to change the contents completely or add new material:

- "Change it to, 'Let's meet at 3:00 p.m.'"
- "Add, 'Can't wait, exclamation point.'" (By the way, you can do this even if Siri doesn't mention it as an option.)
- "No, send it to Megs."
- "No." (Siri keeps the message without sending it.)
- "Cancel." (Siri deletes the message without sending it.)

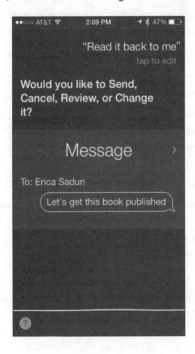

Figure 4-12
Not sure if Siri got what you were trying to say in a message? Have Siri read it back to you, then choose to send, cancel, review, or change the message.

When you are satisfied with your text or email message, say something like "Yes, send it" to start the delivery of the message.

Replying to Texts

You reply to your messages in a variety of ways. When you listen to a message, Siri follows along. This context enables you to say, "Reply 'That's great news,'" or "Tell him I'll be there in a few minutes." If the matter is urgent, just say "Call her," and Siri uses the contact information associated with the message you just received to look up and call the user's phone number.

Siri's hands-free system is perfect when you need to respond to an urgent message while driving.

Mail

Siri offers a totally new way of sending and reading email and text messages. You no longer need to hunt and peck on the iOS keyboard to assemble your written communications. Simply speak to Siri to create emails with your voice.

Creating Mail

There's a simple way to ask Siri to create a new email message. To address it to someone in your Contacts list, say "Email [name or nickname] about [subject]" or just "Email [name or nickname]." Telling Siri "Email Erica about book cover" starts an email message.

At this point, Siri asks what you want the email to say. Siri enables the dictation function and listens attentively as you speak your email (see Figure 4-13).

Figure 4-13
Part of a conversation with Siri to write and send an email. The cover of this book might or might not have kittens on it.

For a contact who doesn't have a nickname, use the person's first or first and last names (for example, Erica or Erica Sadun) to find the email address. If you have more than one email address for a person, Siri prompts you to select one.

You can shortcut the question/response process when creating an email by telling Siri, "Mail contact about '[subject]' and say '[Message].'" For example, you can say, "Mail Mom and Dad about Barb's birthday and say, 'Thank you for sending the flowers, period, they were lovely, exclamation point.'" That seemingly rambling comment creates a ready-to-send message that looks like the one shown in Figure 4-14.

Figure 4-14
This email was addressed, given a subject, and written, all with one long phrase directed at Siri.

When dictating email, don't feel that you have to do it all at once. If you're more comfortable being prompted for a subject and then content, go ahead and do it that way. Siri helps you create messages in the way that best fits your personal style.

NOTE

Don't forget that you can dictate punctuation (period, exclamation point, question mark) and line breaks (new paragraph and new line). These small touches help make your emails and texts more user friendly.

Checking Mail

Siri is not a one-trick pony when it comes to working with the Mail app. It can also check your incoming mail and display it on your iOS screen (although it cannot read it to you aloud). Siri tells you how many emails you have ("Okay, Erica, I found at least 25 emails") but little more than that.

Here are some email-related phrases you can try with Siri:

- "Check email."
- "Any new email from Kelly today?"
- "Show new mail about the wedding."
- "Show the email from Nik yesterday."

Siri responds to any request to delete emails with a terse "I'm not allowed to delete emails for you" message. As discussed earlier in this book, Siri focuses more on content creation than management. Apple probably made this a conscious design choice to prevent possible disasters from misspoken words.

Responding to Mail

Responding to an email message with Siri can take several forms. To send a Mail response, say something like "Reply 'Dear Mom, thanks for sending the flowers to the hospital.'" Want to call the person who sent you an email? Just say "Call [him/her/name] at [work/home/iPhone]." Siri dials the phone number, and within seconds, you're responding to the message in person.

Social Networking

Siri wants to be your social networking BFF. Starting in iOS 6, Siri integrates with Facebook and Twitter, letting you post updates to your favorite networks with just a few spoken words. With Siri, you can now say:

- "Post to Facebook 'Headed to the new Pixar movie.'"
- "Write on my Wall 'Just landed in San Jose!'"
- "Post to Twitter 'Another beautiful day in Cupertino.'"
- "Tweet with my location 'Great concert.'"
- "Tweet 'Meeting up with Brian Conway for lunch today.'"
- "Tweet 'The new iPad looks insanely great!' hashtag Apple Keynote."

Figure 4-15 shows how you can create a tweet by using your voice. Simply tell Siri to tweet or post to Twitter, and your message will soon be on its way.

Both Facebook and Twitter rely on your having entered your credentials in Settings. Go to Settings, Facebook to add your Facebook account and Settings, Twitter to add your Twitter account(s).

You can launch the Twitter app (if installed) by saying, "Check my tweets." Siri no longer launches the Twitter app in iOS 7. Instead, it now displays a list tweets you've sent in the familiar Siri interface. Similarly, you can say, "Open Facebook." You cannot, however, check your Wall or your Timeline from Siri.

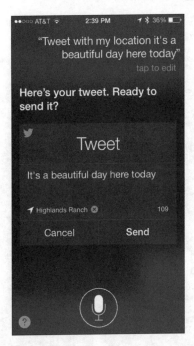

Figure 4-15
You can post Twitter and Facebook updates from within Siri.

Also new to iOS 7 is the ability to see what is currently trending on Twitter. While asking "What's trending on Twitter?" or "What are people talking about on Twitter?" may provide a stream of tweets that seem like random noise, asking Siri a more specific question like "What's the latest in Denver?" focuses on that particular locale.

"What is Steve Sande saying?" ties your search to a specific person (see Figure 4-16). You can also turn that around and ask, "What are people saying about Erica Sadun?" You might also ask, "Is anyone talking about Siri on Twitter?" or "What are people saying about the new iPad on Twitter?" Facebook doesn't have these Siri tie-ins just yet, but keep an eye on Apple, as social integration is only likely to grow over time.

Figure 4-16
Search for tweets tied to a particular person by asking what he or she is saying.

Friends

Find My Friends is a utility that you can download from the App Store. This app gives any approved contacts your current location. Likewise, you can ask your friends with iOS devices for access to their locations. Siri and Find My Friends make it easy to find out where your friends and relatives are at any point and time.

To find a contact, you don't need to launch Find My Friends. Just ask Siri, and it tells you the location of a particular person or group by displaying a map (see Figure 4-17).

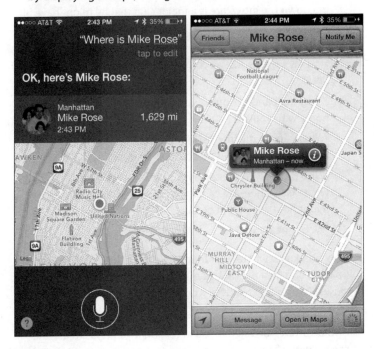

Figure 4-17
Friends who have given you permission to know their location and who have their iOS devices turned on can be located with a single Siri command. Tapping the displayed map reveals a much more detailed location.

You can use quite a few Siri phrases to check the whereabouts of your buddies. Here are some examples that demonstrate friend-finding capabilities:

- "Where's Jason?" (Useful to know, especially if Jason wears a hockey mask or if you're supposed to meet him for lunch and he's running 15 minutes late. Seeing that Jason is still driving down the interstate is a major clue that he might have hit some traffic.)

- "Where is my sister?" (You can use relationship names with Find My Friends, just as you do for making phone calls or texting.)

- "Is my husband at home?" (If so, don't bring your boyfriend home with you!)

- "Where are all my friends?" (If they're running away from you, you might want to cut down on all that garlic.)

- "Who is here?" (That's always fun at Macworld/iWorld, or anywhere else where we can catch up with Internet buddies we might not have met in person.)

- "Who is near me?"

Siri won't know where your friends are if you haven't first set them up with Find My Friends. Use the app to send invitations to your closest friends and relatives who are using iPhones, iPod touches, or iPads.

Also be aware you need to log in to Find My Friends to use the service with Siri. If you didn't sign in first and then try to use your device while driving to find people, you might be disappointed. Always log in before heading to the car if you want to use this feature hands-free. Otherwise, you might need to pull off the road and authenticate before you can start searching for those friends.

Summary

Your iOS device and Siri are better communicators than those units from *Star Trek*. Sure, your device isn't as small as those cool badges on the later generations of *Star Trek*—yet—but not only can you call someone with a voice command, you can also send text messages and emails as well. Plus, you won't get bruises from hitting your chest all the time. Throw in FaceTime, Facebook, and Twitter, and you have an extremely powerful communication tool.

You should take away the following points from this chapter:

- Relationships, especially unique ones, simplify your life when using Siri. If your spouse has a common name, such as John or Barbara or Steve, referring to a person as "my wife" or "my husband" helps jump past the hurdles of figuring out which John, Barbara, or Steve you are referencing. Take advantage of relationships to speed up texts, emails, and calls to people who are important in your life.

- The Contacts app provides tight Siri integration. Information about a contact's phone numbers, addresses, email addresses, and more is just a question away.

- Twitter and Facebook integration is fun and useful. It's a lot easier to ask Siri to post an update for you than to type it in yourself. Share the moment while you're having the moment—don't pull yourself away just so you can hunt and peck on the iOS keyboard.

- Use Siri voice commands for calling, emailing, and texting your contacts. For email and texts, use the dictation commands from Chapter 8, "Siri Dictation," to create complete messages with proper punctuation. You can dictate and send texts and email messages with just your voice.

- Siri reads your incoming text messages to you but cannot read full email messages. This is a feature we're looking forward to in future Siri updates. To reply to a message, just tell Siri to answer it and then dictate your reply.

- Having Siri play back voicemail messages or alert you to missed calls is at your command, and you can return calls by just asking your digital assistant to do so.

Talking to Your Day-Timer

For many people, iOS replaces handwritten organizers like the classic Day-Timer. You may be too young to be familiar with Day-Timers....They had printed pages with spaces for reminders, notes, and calendar appointments, as well as lists of contacts. They cost more than they were really worth and weighed more than an iPad—and we *loved* them. Ridiculously.

Instead of scrawling handwritten notes onto printed calendar pages, iOS and Siri set up appointments, take notes, and set reminders through simple conversations. This process feels more like having your own personal assistant taking care of business for you than using an electronic device.

This chapter introduces you to the ways you can use Siri to help schedule and organize your life. It's time to throw away that handwritten organizer.

Calendars

If you're familiar with iOS, you might already be a fan of the Calendar app for keeping track of your appointments and meetings. With Siri, you have your own concierge at your beck and call, handling all your Calendar events. Through the magic of iCloud, any Calendar events you make, whether with Siri or through the app itself, are immediately synchronized to any other devices you might have connected to the service.

Adding Events

Adding an event using Siri follows a standard conversational pattern. You tell it, "Set up a meeting," "Meet with someone," "Schedule a meeting," or "Make an appointment." You specify whom the meeting is with and when it takes place. Figure 5-1 shows this approach in action. You might say:

- "Set up a meeting with Jimmy at 7 p.m."
- "Schedule my dental appointment." (Using the word *schedule* is a great way to tell Siri to work with the Calendar.)
- "Meet with Emily at noon."
- "Set up a meeting about hiring tomorrow at 9 a.m."
- "New appointment with Susan Park, Friday at 3." (Siri knows the meeting is for 3:00 p.m. and not in the middle of the night.)
- "Schedule a planning meeting at 8:30 today in the boardroom."

Many times when setting up a meeting, you want your device to alert you a few minutes before the meeting starts. Reminders help you remember to participate. Unfortunately, there doesn't appear to be a way at this time to tell Siri to add an alert to a calendar event. To add an alert and specify the sound to use when the alert is made, you need to use reminders, which you'll read about in the next section. Reminders play an alert tone by default. Another way to add an alert to an event is to launch the Calendar app and then edit the event. Of course, this doesn't take advantage of Siri....

Figure 5-1
Asking Siri to schedule a meeting creates a calendar entry with all the pertinent information filled in. You specify who, what, where, and when for these events.

You might want to create a calendar event for a meeting to block out time on your calendar and send invitations to others. Then you can make a reminder to alert you before the start of the meeting.

Making Changes

In real life, meetings and appointments may shift. That's fine; Siri is amenable to change. Here are some phrases you might use to update an event on your calendar:

- "Move my 10 a.m. meeting to 2:30."
- "Reschedule my appointment with Dr. Hathaway to next Monday at 9 a.m."
- "Add Erica to my meeting with Apple."
- "Cancel the final book review meeting."
- "Change the location of my 3 p.m. meeting tomorrow to Bob's office."

These phrases let Siri know that you're modifying existing events rather than creating new ones in your calendar.

 NOTE

Siri uses your Contacts app information to figure out how to match location names (such as *home* and *office*) with contact names (such as Bob and Jennifer). Bob's work address in Contacts helps locate "Bob's office." Make sure you allow Siri to use location-based services. In Settings, Privacy, Location Services, set the switch for Siri to On.

Checking Your Calendar

Many times you just want to find out something about a meeting, such as what time and date it's set for, where the meeting is, or what you have scheduled for a specific day. Never fear, Siri's here! A quick conversation with Siri is like asking a human assistant to look at your calendar for you (see Figure 5-2).

Calendar Queries

What kind of calendar-related questions can you ask Siri? Here are several examples of questions you might use to ask Siri about upcoming events on your calendar:

- "What does the rest of my day look like?"
- "What's on my calendar for Wednesday?"
- "When is my next appointment?"
- "When am I meeting with Erica?"
- "Where is my next meeting?"

Figure 5-2
Need to know what's coming up on your agenda for tomorrow? Ask Siri, and you get an immediate answer.

When your meeting doesn't have a location, Siri tells you that it doesn't know where the meeting is to be held. Siri's pretty smart, so it also responds with an "I didn't find any meetings with [whomever] between today and [three months from today]" when you think you've set up a meeting with someone, but it's not on your calendar.

Siri can also tell you the date for an upcoming or past day of the week. For example, if you ask, "What date was last Thursday?" Siri responds with an answer such as "It was Thursday, November 14, 2013." Even more impressive, you can ask, "What day of the week was December 7, 1941?" (or any other date), and you'll get an answer.

Interestingly, Siri has some built-in errors. It does not pay attention to when holidays were instituted, so it will, somewhat strangely, report that December 7, 1920, was Pearl Harbor Remembrance Day and July 4, 1770, was Independence Day. If you ask about the days of the week between September 3 and September 13 in 1752, it will reply with intriguing answers even though these days *did not exist* in the UK and its colonies (including the United States) because of the transition from the Julian to Gregorian calendars. In 1752 in the American colonies, September lasted only 19 days.

Reminders

Reminders are different from calendar events. Calendars mark your appointments; reminders tell you what you have to do. Think of reminders, which are accessed through the iOS Reminders app, as an intelligent to-do list.

Reminders can be time and location sensitive. They often have a schedule associated with them. (Think of this as a deadline for completing a task.) You can also take advantage of your device's GPS in a feature called *geofencing*. Geofencing reminds you of something when you arrive at or leave a location.

Figure 5-3 shows a conversation with Siri to set up a time-based reminder—in this case, to help you remember to take your medicine. Siri sets up a new reminder and uses the task you specified—"Take my pills"—to create a little prompt at a time you specified ("9 a.m. tomorrow").

To ask for a reminder when you arrive at or leave a destination, you tell Siri "when I leave here" or "when I get home." Siri can remind you when you leave or arrive "here" or at home, work, school, or gym—both yours and someone else's.

Figure 5-3
This phrase tells Siri to remind you to take needed medicines tomorrow morning. Humans are notoriously forgetful. Siri isn't.

Figure 5-4 shows how to ask Siri for a reminder about buying beer when arriving at a local Safeway grocery store. Siri can act a little fussy when it comes to arbitrary locations like this. Unfortunately, it's not exactly sure where that location is unless it is in your Contacts list. If it's a store that you visit often, create a contact with the name "Safeway Safeway" along with a work address showing the actual physical location.

This is a little odd to do, but it shows that it's a good idea to test contacts and reminders scenarios before you actually need them. You may need to tweak your contacts a bit to get the results you want.

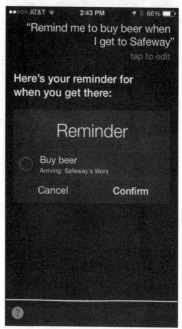

Figure 5-4
Siri can create location-based reminders. Make sure you set up a recognizable contact with the location information before asking Siri to set up a geofenced reminder. Although redundant, adding the destination name to the contact's first name and last name helps Siri better recognize the locations of businesses.

How Siri Can Remind You

Siri is great at remembering. Even when human memory fails, Siri keeps track of things you long ago forgot you had to do. Here are examples of some of the other things you can say to Siri to have it remind you:

- "Remind me to call Mom."
- "Remind me to text Jake when I get home."
- "Add paragliding to my bucket list." (You'll have to set up a Notes list named "bucket list" first.)
- "Remember to take an umbrella."
- "Remind me to head out to the airport at 6 a.m. tomorrow."
- "Remind me to find an ATM when I leave here."
- "Remind me when I leave to call Jason."
- "Remind me to finish the report by 6 p.m."
- "Remind me to park outside when I arrive at Bob's house."
- "Remind me to buy milk every 4 days."
- "Remind me to join the conference call every Wednesday at 3 p.m."

The last two conversations set up recurring reminders. You can ask Siri to remind you every day, every week, every two weeks, once a month, or once a year. Now there's no excuse for forgetting your anniversary!

Creating Reminders Without Time

We're often asked how to create reminders without specific due dates. Many users love Siri's easy voice integration but don't want to schedule these items and instead just add them to a to-do list. Possible? You bet. The secret lies in the way you phrase your request.

When you ask Siri to "remind" you, it adds a scheduled item. Saying "remind" is always tied to time because Siri has to actually nag you directly. This is like asking a spouse to "remind me to pick up the dry cleaning," and he or she immediately responds, "Okay. Don't forget to pick up the dry cleaning!" A reminder without a future target time is not very useful in this case.

Instead, to create a reminder without a specific time, say "remember"—for example, say "Remember to pick up the milk" rather than "Remind me to pick up the milk." Siri adds that item to the Reminders app without a time trigger, enabling you to build up a to-do list. If you forget to say "remember," there are workarounds. When Siri asks about the time for a reminder, say "no time," "don't remind me," or "never." You can also say, "Add 'Pick up the milk' to my [name of to-do list]," and that will trigger a time-free task.

A Word of Caution

One word of caution when using the GPS-based reminders: Doing so enables Location Services for the Reminders app. A small white arrow on the iOS status bar next to the battery indicator means that your device is actively finding your current location.

Why should you be concerned? Location Services causes higher-than-average power use, resulting in shorter-than-expected battery life. The reminders are great; the diminished battery charge may not be if you already need to charge several times a day. Use these features with the understanding that they might affect your battery life charge-to-charge.

To use geofencing, make sure you have properly enabled Siri in Settings. Check Settings, Privacy, Location Services (which must be On), Siri (which also must be On).

Creating Notes

Siri makes it easy to add notes quickly and hands-free on iOS. You can't beat the convenience of getting tiny tidbits of information recorded with a single tap and chat. With Siri, you can record information as you think of it. No need to wait until you arrive at the office or get to a coffee shop to sit down. This section covers additional ways you can use this handy feature.

Creating Single-Item Notes

It's easy to add single-item notes such as "Note that I spent $5 on parking" (see Figure 5-5) or "Note: Check out that new Steely Dan compilation album." Each of these spoken commands creates a single standalone note item in the Notes application.

Figure 5-5
Siri easily creates single-item notes for you when you're on the go. Tell it what you need to remember and let Siri keep track of the information.

Adding Items to the Current Note

Siri retains context, so you can add items to the currently edited note one at a time. The key word here is *add*. For example, say "Add 'Do laundry,'" and Siri adds "Do laundry" to the current note. Alternatively, say "Add" or "Add to note." Siri responds, "What would you like to add?" and automatically starts listening for a response. Each time, add one item to the current note and expand the note as needed. Figure 5-6 shows how to create and then add to a note.

Figure 5-6
Use "add" commands to add items to the current note.

Starting New Notes

When you want to begin a new note instead of add to an existing one, just tell Siri "Take a note," "Create a note," or "Start a note"— or just use the one-sentence "Note that..." structure.

If you don't provide contents, Siri responds with "OK, I can take that note for you...just tell me what you want it to say." You then use "Add" to keep adding to that new note.

Naming Notes

The name of a note is the first item added to the note. For example, you can say, "Create a 'bucket list' note" to create a note called "bucket list." Then add notes to it by saying, "Add 'skydiving' to my 'bucket list' note" or just "Add 'skydiving.'" Figure 5-7 shows an example of using a named list to add items.

Figure 5-7
Creating and adding notes. Tap on any note to view it in the Notes application.

Finding Notes

Retrieve a note by asking Siri to find it. Figure 5-8 shows the response to "Find my 'bucket list' note." Siri displays the note it pulls up on the screen for your reading pleasure. Ask Siri to read it to you by saying, "Read my 'bucket list' note." Siri both displays the note *and* reads it back to you.

If you forgot to say "Read" and used "Find" instead, you can always follow up your first request with "Read it to me." Siri remembers the context of your conversation and reads the note back to you. Be careful not to slur your words. Siri is under the impression that Erica has a contact named "Rita Timmy" whenever she forgets to enunciate.

Figure 5-8
Siri can retrieve notes by title, which corresponds to the first line.

Siri allows you to search for notes by date as well as by title. Say "Show me my notes from today" or "Show my notes from May 22," and Siri will oblige. Telling Siri "Show me my notes" or "Show me all the notes" displays a table of contents of all your notes. Tap any of the notes here to open it in the iOS Notes application.

If you want to jump directly to the Notes application, you can say, "Open the Notes app," "Open my notes," or "Launch Notes." Unlike the request to "show me" notes, these commands exit the Siri interface and move you to the Notes application.

If you ask Siri to read any of your notes, it responds by listing all the notes in the similar table of contents format, then reading the contents of the first note aloud before asking if you want it to read the second list. "Read my last note" does not read the last note you've created; instead, it reads the last note in the list of notes. For your named notes, when you ask Siri to read a specific note—as in "Read my Quotes note"—it displays the note on the iOS device screen and then reads it aloud.

 NOTE

> Unfortunately, Siri does not offer any note-editing features other than adding items. You cannot delete notes without going into the Notes application.

Clock Functions

Siri provides nicely integrated iOS clock functions. The usual clock functions built into the device firmware include an alarm clock, a countdown timer, a world clock displaying the current time in locations around the globe, and a stopwatch. Siri doesn't want to be a stopwatch when it grows up, but it happily serves you in the other clock functions.

Alarms

When you're trying to set an old-fashioned digital alarm clock, usually you press the little button and watch the wake time spin past, and then you have to do it all over again. It's easier on iOS: Just spin to the hour and minute you want to wake up and then tap Save. Siri makes setting an alarm even easier: Simply tell Siri when you want an alarm to go off.

Figure 5-9 shows an extreme example of a conversation with Siri, asking it to wake you the next morning. Here are some examples other of how you can ask Siri to handle alarms:

- "Wake me up tomorrow at 7 a.m."
- "Set an alarm for 6:30 a.m."
- "Wake me up in 8 hours."
- "Delete all alarms."
- "Turn morning alarms off/on." (Turns all alarms off or on at once.)
- "Change my 6:30 alarm to 6:45."
- "Turn off my 6:30 alarm."
- "Cancel my 7:15 a.m. alarm." ("Okay, I deleted your 7:15 a.m. alarm. Now we can all get some sleep.")
- "Show my alarms."

How do you know what sound iOS will use to wake you from your sweet dreams? It uses whatever alarm tone you used previously, or you can select Clock, Alarm, Edit and then select a sound.

Figure 5-9
Siri understands the "9 a.m." part and sets an alarm. Siri cleverly ignores the "Hey dude."

Sadly, Siri doesn't offer a snooze command—it won't listen as you plead to "let me sleep" (see Figure 5-10). Perhaps a future version of Siri will provide that capability. On the other hand, given how hard it is to wake up and speak clearly, Siri would probably respond, "I don't understand 'lemmings leap.' Do you want me to perform a web search for that?"

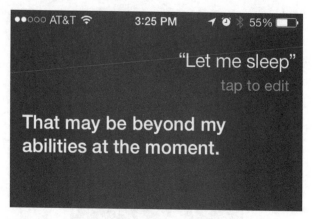

Figure 5-10
Siri doesn't exactly get the concept of snoozing. You'll have to open your eyes and tap the Snooze button instead.

 NOTE

In iOS 7, you can select any song as your alarm tone, not just Apple-supplied sound samples. Apple did add a lot of nice new sound samples, too, though.

Checking the Clock

iOS offers world clock functions, but Siri starts with your little part of the world. Siri knows where you are and responds to the query "What time is it?" by telling you the local time.

This may seem a bit pointless because every single Siri screen displays the time for you, but you may want Siri to speak the time—perhaps when you're driving or otherwise don't want to move your eyes. You can also ask, "What's today's date?" or "What year is it?"

That's the least of Siri's clock capabilities, however. When you need to know whether it's a good time to call your business partner in Mumbai, all you need to do is ask what time it is there (see Figure 5-11). Instantly, Siri gives you a time that translates both the actual hour and the date. In this example, it's already tomorrow in Mumbai.

You can ask:

- "What's the time?" or "What time is it?"
- "What time is it in Cupertino, California?"
- "What is today's date?"
- "How many days until Christmas?"
- "What's the date this Saturday?"

 NOTE

> Siri includes a little Easter egg that sometimes pops up when you ask the time. In a hilarious deadpan, it says, "At the tone, the time will be [some time]." A second or two later, it adds "Beep."

Using a Timer

Our families love to grill, and one of the key success factors we've discovered in our outdoor cooking is to use a timer to let us know when to flip the food, take meat off the heat, or let it rest. Since Siri has entered our lives, we can now set a timer one-handed. Press the Home button (or bring an iPhone to your ear) and say "Set a timer for 3 minutes." You quickly get verification from Siri that the timer is counting down and can even watch that timer onscreen.

Figure 5-11
Siri's world clock capabilities enable you to determine the time for most major cities around the world.

Starting in iOS 7, you can now specify seconds as well as minutes while using Siri! That's an important improvement for those of us who work out and want to perform high-tension moves for 15 or 30 seconds at a time. Best of all, you can set this up without having to look at a screen—although at the end, when the timer triggers, you will need to tap the alert.

You can also pause, resume, or stop timers. Here are several examples of setting timers with Siri:

- "Set the timer for 10 minutes."
- "Set a timer for 15 seconds."
- "Show the timer."
- "Pause the timer."
- "Resume."
- "Stop it."
- "Reset the timer."

Siri uses whatever timer alert sound you've set under the Timer tab of the Clock app. You select your favorite ear-shattering noise by tapping the When Timer Ends button. If you want to know how much longer the timer has to go, just ask Siri "What's the timer status?" or take a look at your lock screen, just below the current time. When the timer goes off, a tap on the lock screen silences the alert sound.

Siri must have taken cooking lessons at some point because it is aware of how long it takes to cook an egg. Setting a 3-minute timer often results in Siri replying, "Don't overcook that egg!"

 NOTE

Need to time how long something lasts? Tell Siri to "Open the Stopwatch" or "Launch the Stopwatch," and it will bring you to exactly the right task in the onboard Clock app. From there, it's just a tap on Start to begin timing.

Summary

With Siri working all the time on iOS, it's like having a personal assistant who works for you wherever and whenever you want. Through easy, natural-language statements, Siri sets appointments, checks your calendar, and sets and announces reminders.

Siri is also an incredible help with time functions. Whether you need to set an alarm to wake yourself up, set a cooking timer, or find the correct time anywhere in the world, a quick conversation gets the job done. Here are some points to take away from this chapter:

- Adding an appointment to your calendar is just one task Siri performs. Remember that you can work with Siri to get your next appointment; determine what your calendar looks like for a certain day; and change meeting attendees, times, and locations by using verbal commands.

- Reminders are different from appointments, in that they are more like a to-do list that can have a deadline. You can also take advantage of geofencing features and set Siri to remind you of something when you arrive at or leave somewhere. Your device monitors your location and triggers those reminders when you approach or leave a tagged destination.

- This chapter introduces a lot of great tips about reminders, but there's a lot more you can do with them. Move on to the next chapter to see how you can integrate reminders with your shopping lists.

- People who like to annotate their lives with handwritten sticky notes will love Siri's capability to create and add to lists through speech. Imagine dictating a shopping list to your iOS device as you drive to a store, and you have a good idea of the power of Siri's interactions with notes.

- Interacting with the iOS clock no longer requires hands-on action. Instead, ask Siri to set, change, or delete an alarm; start or stop a timer; or tell you what time it is in any major city in the world.

Going Shopping with Siri

In our busy twenty-first-century lives, time is a precious commodity. Siri make the best of your limited free time. It helps you search for goods, services, and entertainment; find your way to local businesses; and even calculate tips and taxes. This chapter explores the ways Siri works at your command to make your shopping journeys as smooth as possible. Siri hunts down the items you crave and reminds you to buy something when you are near a store that carries that item. In your pocket, Siri is an invisible assistant. It gets you out of stores and back to enjoying friends, family, and your valuable free time.

Products and Services

Siri discovers products and services at your command. You might say to Siri, "I'm hungry," or "I'm in the mood for Italian food," and Siri tries to find exactly what you're looking for, based on your current location (see Figure 6-1). Siri responds to your requests by matching local business to whatever you've said. For example, in the case of "I'm hungry," it lists nearby restaurants, enabling you to preview many options. Tap any of the listed offerings to find directions, phone numbers, and reviews.

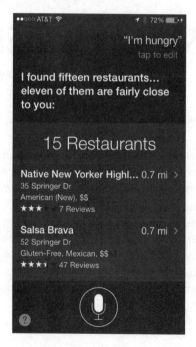

Figure 6-1
Siri finds restaurants, stores, services, and more, all with simple queries.

Siri is happy to assist, no matter what kind of goods or services you desire. It handles a wide range of shopping requests. The following statements demonstrate how you might start a local search-based conversation with Siri:

- "Find me a bike shop."
- "I'm looking for a health clinic."
- "What's a good place for dinner?"
- "Is there a dentist near me?"
- "How far is it from here to a library?"
- "I want to buy clothing."
- "Where can I go to read a novel?" (See Figure 6-2 for one of Siri's more memorable responses.)
- "Find me a Honda dealer."
- "Where can I get gas for my car?"
- "Is there a train station near here?"
- "I need a drug store."
- "Where can I find a sporting goods store?"
- "Where can I buy milk?"

When you ask a qualitative question, Siri orders items by ratings. For example, you might ask, "What's a good place to buy clothes?" or "What's the best bicycle shop?" It uses Yelp ratings to differentiate between locations with better reviews and those that are less well received.

Tap the star ratings next to each vendor, and Siri opens the Maps app. Pins show the locations of the selected establishments, and a tag highlights the one you have chosen. Just tap the tag to read the customer reviews, see information about the vendor, view photos of the location (if they're available, which they aren't always), and even get step-by-step directions to and from the location. This fabulous integration helps you evaluate whether the place you tapped is the right place for you to visit.

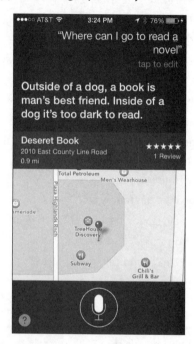

Figure 6-2
Sometimes Siri throws a little fun into a response while also providing a helpful answer.

Siri listens carefully to how you ask your question. Its sorting is always set up to simplify the task you've asked of Siri, whether it's related to distance, rating, or price. If you ask a general question, Siri's searches show closer items first, as in Figure 6-1. If you ask

"What's an inexpensive place to eat?" Siri sorts the vendors by price. Your question helps fine-tune Siri's response. Here's how you might want to set up your question to control the sorting of your results:

- **"Where is"/"Find"/"Show nearby":** Siri sorts by distance.
- **"What's the best"/"Where are good":** Siri sorts by ratings.
- **"What's an inexpensive"/"Find a fancy":** Siri sorts by price.

 NOTE

Siri was programmed to handle many regional speech variations. For example, Erica, a non-Denver native, typically says, "Find me a good Italian restaurant." Denver-born Steve prefers, "Find a good Italian restaurant." Siri handles both queries with aplomb.

Checking Gas Prices

When a gallon of gas may cost more than a Starbucks latte, it's important to keep an eye on how much you might be spending for a tankful. Siri can look up regional pricing for gasoline for you, so you can see if the gas station you just pulled up at is giving you a bargain or lifting your wallet. For example, you might ask Siri, "What is the average price of a gallon of gasoline in Denver?" (see Figure 6-3). In addition to pricing in big cities, Siri provides prices based on a state or national level.

Siri also won't look for gas stations based on pricing, so you cannot ask, "Where is the cheapest gas station near me?" Siri will reply, "I can't look specifically for price range...my apologies" before listing the locations of nearby fueling facilities.

Figure 6-3
Siri can help you determine whether you're getting a bargain on that tank of gas or paying more than you need to.

Shopping Math

Siri offers great tools when it comes to comparison shopping and calculating specific values. For example, use it to check sales tax, convert currencies, or split a bill. Here are some scenarios where Siri brings math skills to day-to-day shopping.

Adding Sales Tax

Siri calculates sales tax through your spoken requests. Just ask how much a purchase is with tax added for a given city, as shown in Figure 6-4. This is a great way to calculate your final purchase price. If you omit the city name, Siri tries to guess your location and replies appropriately.

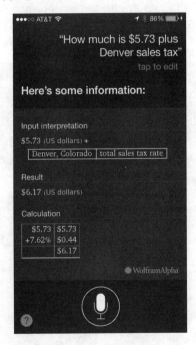

Figure 6-4
Siri adds sales tax.

Calculating Tips

Get some great service at lunch? You might want to consider leaving a generous tip. Siri helps with that, too! As Figure 6-5 (left) shows, Siri calculates the total of your bill with tip. If you try this on a member of the iPhone family (as opposed to the iPad), be sure to scroll down. Page through the results to see the amount with the tip you requested, as well as the amount with standard tip values, such as 10%, 15%, 20%, and 25%.

Siri can also split bills. Ask Siri "What is an 18% tip on $86.74 for four people?" and it returns the display shown in Figure 6-5 (right). That's about $26 per person, for a total check of $102.35—or $104 rounded up. Again, make sure to scroll down for further details.

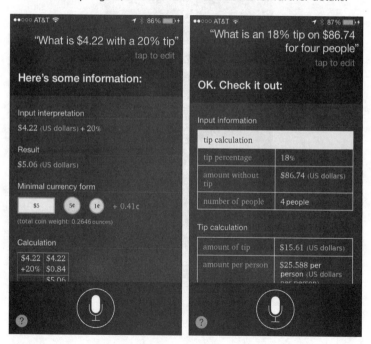

Figure 6-5
Siri is a tipping genius. Left: "What is $4.22 with a 20% tip?" Right: "What is an 18% tip on $86.74 for four people?"

Currency Conversion

If you are traveling abroad or purchasing from merchants overseas, Siri is there to help. As Figure 6-6 shows, Siri converts currencies to show you what a purchase in euros would cost in U.S. dollars.

This figure does not, of course, include any extra fees that the vendor might charge for conversion when shopping in dollars or that your credit card company might charge when shopping in local currency. Always keep in mind that you might incur fees when shopping with various forms of tender. Many credit card issuers charge currency conversion fees for foreign purchases made with their credit, debit, and check cards, as well as any ATM cash withdrawals.

Figure 6-6
Converting between currencies helps you shop abroad or from foreign websites.

Monetary exchange rates vary on a daily basis. Siri's conversion calculations are meant to give you an approximate sense of value—how much an item might cost in rupees or euros as opposed to dollars. Don't depend on these numbers to be exact; they reflect only the current quoted conversion rates.

Preparing a Shopping List

Cliff Joyce of Pure Blend Software introduced us to our favorite way of putting together shopping lists in Siri: Start in the Reminders application and create a new list. To do this, tap the New List button at the top of the application. Select an account—either just on one device or on all of your Apple devices through iCloud—and then type in a name for the list—for example, "Groceries." Tap a color dot to select a color to be associated with the list and then tap Done. Once you have a list named Groceries (see Figure 6-7), you can refer to it with Siri.

Figure 6-7
After you create lists in the Reminders app, refer to them by name with Siri.

After you create a list, add items at any time with simple requests. For example, tell Siri "Add milk to my Groceries list." Siri asks you to confirm the new item (see Figure 6-8). Say "Yes," and Siri adds it for you. When you're at the market, simply check off the items as you buy them. It couldn't be easier. Well, it could be easier if you could just tell Siri to check those items off the list, but at this time Siri can't modify Reminders lists.

Figure 6-8
Siri can add items to your list whenever you choose. Just tell it to add a new item and confirm.

This add-to-reminders approach is an effective way for people on diets to keep food logs. In particular, Siri's Wolfram Alpha integration helps you look up calorie content for a large variety of foods—for example, "How many calories are there in a small apple?" Between Wolfram and reminders, Siri provides an excellent diet-logging tool.

 NOTE

> Mark Johnson, a Siri user from Australia, provides this hint: "In Australia, Siri seems to not hear *add* very well. Despite lots of attempts to harden the consonant, it keeps thinking I am saying, *'and* eggs to the shopping list,' and then tries to find a business (which isn't supported here). I have found that *'put* eggs on my shopping list' works really well, however."

Sharing Shopping Lists via the Cloud

Lex Friedman of Macworld came up with a remarkably clever way to share reminder lists with others by using iCloud. The instructions here have changed slightly with the introduction of iOS 7 and OS X Mavericks, so if you're familiar with previous editions of this book, you might want to take special note of these changes.

Open the Reminders app on your Mac. You must be running OS X 10.8.2 or later for this to work because shared reminders were added to the desktop only in this update.

Create a new Reminders list by clicking the + button. Name the list whatever you like. Hover your mouse over the far-right side of the list name, where you see a Wi-Fi antenna symbol show up. Click it. As Figure 6-9 shows, this is where you add an email address. Click Done to share the list with that person. Each person receives a confirmation email.

If you plan to share your reminders with highly trusted people only (such as your spouse), you can share your default reminders list (called Reminders) using these steps, without creating a new list. Otherwise, we recommend creating a list specifically for sharing.

By adding people to your shared list, you enable them to see your reminders in their iCloud and in the OS X and iOS Reminders apps. Then all you have to do is tell Siri, "Add 'Pick up the library books' to my Shared list."

Friedman shares a killer use for shared lists: "Add your local supermarket as a contact in your iPhone address book, and, of course, add the address. (I called mine The Supermarket.) Now you can say, 'Remind me to buy eggs when I get to the supermarket,' and when you arrive at the supermarket, Reminders will remind you to purchase the item(s) on your list."

Figure 6-9
Shared lists offer powerful ways to use reminders. Among other things, they enable you to create geofenced (GPS-based) reminders that activate when any participant reaches a given location. Remind your spouse to pick up milk when he or she gets to the grocery store or ping your partner to straighten his tie when he arrives at the office.

Shopping Limitations

Siri doesn't always get your shopping requests right. It has been optimized for a general urban lifestyle and might miss local subtleties. For example, in Denver (home to the National Western Stock Show), you can, in fact, easily buy a cow, a pig, a sheep, and so forth (see Figure 6-10).

Figure 6-10
Siri clearly does not live in Colorado. Yee-haw.

Turn-by-Turn Directions

Siri offers amazing integration with the Maps app on your iOS device. Recently, Steve asked Siri to find an ATM nearby, and within seconds, he had a list indicating all money machines within a few miles' radius of his location. A tap brought him to a map sprinkled with red pins showing the ATMs in the area. The nearest

ATM on the map was designated by name with a tag that, when tapped, provided detailed information about the location.

Need help finding your way to one of those ATMs? Siri now offers turn-by-turn map integration (see Figure 6-11). Steve was presented with a list of nearby ATMs; tapping one provided directions for driving there.

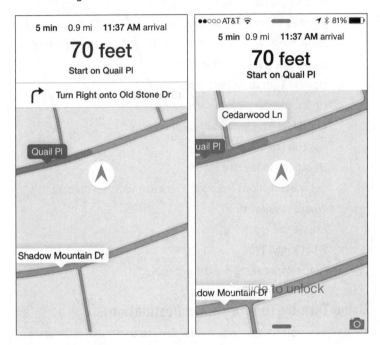

Figure 6-11
Siri provides turn-by-turn directions both in its normal navigation screen (left) and on your lock screen (right). This enables you to keep driving as directed, even when your device locks.

You can save a lot of steps by tweaking the question you ask Siri. Instead of asking "Where are local ATMs?" try "How do I get to an ATM?" Siri responds with a list of nearby locations. Tap the one you want, and Siri automatically starts turn-by-turn navigation. Of course, you still have to look at the screen to tap on the results list, so use caution when searching and driving.

Here are some conversations you can have with Siri about finding your way:

- "Find coffee near me."
- "Where's the nearest coffee shop?"
- "Show me how to get to the Sam Gary Library in Stapleton."
- "Find a gas station near work."
- "How do I get to a Chinese restaurant?"
- "Find some burger joints in Baltimore."
- "Good Mexican restaurants around here."
- "How do I get home?"
- "Directions to my dad's work."
- "Get me directions from San Francisco to Santa Barbara."
- "What's my next turn?"
- "Are we there yet?"
- "What's my ETA?"
- "Find a florist along my current route."

Using Turn-by-Turn to Known Destinations

Typically, you start by asking directions to somewhere: "How do I get to Steve's house?" or "How do I get to Erica's office?" If you're asking about a known address in Contacts, Siri recognizes this as a navigation request. It responds, "Getting directions to Steve Sande, Home." A few seconds later, it adds "Starting route to Steve Sande, Home," followed by the first set of driving directions.

As you drive, iOS and Siri navigate you to your destination, as shown in Figure 6-11. If you need to end your trip early (or you're just testing the option), tap the screen and then tap the End button that appears.

Looking Up Information on Maps

In addition to offering directions, Siri can show you information in map format. For example, you might ask Siri to respond to the following statements. Each of these provides a map to look at and explore in iOS's Maps application:

- "Show me Apple Headquarters."
- "Show me the Golden Gate Bridge."
- "Show me a map of The White House."

Making Restaurant Reservations

In addition to listing nearby restaurants, Siri integrates with OpenTable to help you create reservations at your desired location. You must download the OpenTable app separately.

Tap Make Reservation (see Figure 6-12, left), and OpenTable (see Figure 6-12, right) launches to help find a table and place a reservation. Some of the Siri-specific discussions you can have include these:

- "Table for four in Palo Alto tonight."
- "Find me a great place for dinner."
- "Show me the reviews for Seven Hills in San Francisco."
- "Make a reservation at a romantic Italian restaurant tonight at 7 p.m."

As Figure 6-12 shows, Siri helps you look up reviews, check the hours of operation, open the restaurant's website, and call the restaurant directly.

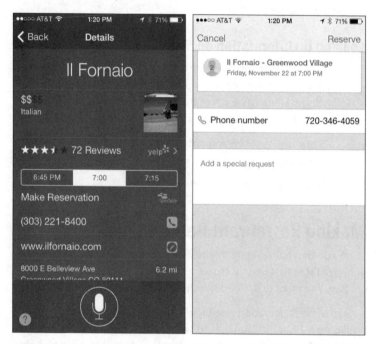

Figure 6-12
OpenTable integration enables you to place reservations with a tap after finding restaurants in Siri. Tap Make Reservation in the Siri results (left) to launch OpenTable (right).

Checking Out Movies

For many people, nothing's more relaxing than enjoying a good movie. Whether you're heading out to the theater or ordering up the latest Netflix offering, Siri is ready to help you. You can look up

movies by show times, check Rotten Tomatoes reviews of movies, and more. Siri lends a hand, as you see in Figure 6-13. These
reviews help Siri sort your choices by quality when you ask it to
find something good to watch.

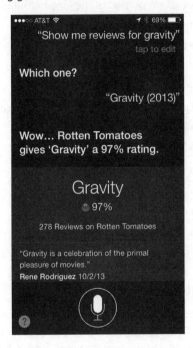

Figure 6-13
When you say, "Show me the reviews for Gravity," Siri taps into the Rotten Tomatoes review
database.

Siri helps you find information on the latest cinema releases by
retrieving locations and show times. You can also watch trailers
and read film facts. Here's a list of things you might say to Siri
about the movies:

- "Find Disney movies."
- "What comedies are playing?"
- "Where is *The Bourne Legacy* playing?"
- "What movies are playing at the Cinema Grill?"
- "Who starred in *Tron Legacy*?"
- "Who directed *Finding Nemo*?"
- "What is *Toy Story 3* rated?"
- "Are there any good movies playing nearby?"
- "What's a good movie that starts in the next hour?"
- "What is the best movie playing this evening?"
- "Are there any new Disney movies out?"
- "I want to see the new Pixar movie."
- "What's playing at the movies tomorrow?"
- "Find some movie theaters near my office."
- "Show me the reviews for *Toy Story 3*."
- "Which movie won Best Picture in 1983?"

Siri's Personal Movie Synopses

We dive into more detail about Siri's silly side in Chapter 9, "Having Fun with Siri," but we just couldn't resist telling you about Siri's library of movie synopses. At times, Siri can be your personal (if somewhat electronically biased) movie reviewer.

Although it displays an inclination toward science-fiction movies, Siri gladly provides you with its opinion of certain classic movie plot lines. Just ask Siri "What's the 1977 movie *Star Wars* about?" and you'll get a smart-aleck answer in return (see Figure 6-14).

Other movies you might want to ask Siri about include *Blade Runner, 2001: A Space Odyssey, Groundhog Day* (this was Erica's favorite

Siri review), *Alien, Inception, The Matrix, The Wizard of Oz, Star Trek, Star Wars, The Terminator, Wall-E, Toy Story,* and *Memento* (this was Steve's favorite). Hunt around and see if you can find other plot summaries. There's a lot of fun to be had.

To ask Siri for a review, say "What is [*Movie Title*] about?" Adding a year reference helps Siri identify which movie you're referring to— for example, "What is the 1980 movie [*Movie Title*] about?" If there are multiple possible matches to the title, a year helps skip the "Which one?" step and narrows those matches to a single choice.

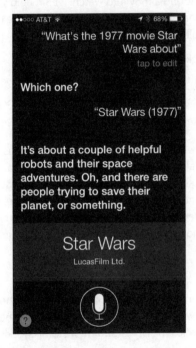

Figure 6-14
Siri helpfully provides its own synopses of many science-fiction films if you ask politely.

In early 2014, the movie *Her* debuted, and so did some hilarious Siri responses. Ask it "Siri, are you 'Her'?" and be rewarded by a variety of funny responses, like "No. She is a fictional construct, whereas I am a virtual entity. But we can still be friends." and "No. You know that's just a movie, right?" among others.

Say "Was [*Movie Title*] any good?" or "What can you tell me about the [*year*] movie [*Movie Title*]?" When you've found a movie in a current Siri conversation, ask "What is it about?"

Once you've found a movie to watch, let Siri help you purchase tickets. Here are some ways to ask that launch the Fandango app on your behalf:

- "Three tickets to see *Brave*."
- "Buy four tickets to see *Frozen* tonight in San Jose."
- "Two tickets to *Tangled* at the City Theater at 9 p.m."
- "Two tickets to that new Pixar movie."

Siri not only wants to help you find current movies at your local theaters but also helps if you want to stay home and watch older movies on your favorite iOS device. Ask about a movie, look at the review, and if that movie is in the iTunes Store, you'll have Buy and/or Rent buttons available to tap. Just enter your Apple ID password, and you'll be watching a movie in no time at all.

Summary

As you've seen in this chapter, Siri can help you shop for goods and services with a few well-chosen words. Whether you're looking for a specific type of restaurant or store, checking average prices for commodities, preparing a shopping list, scoping out a movie, or trying to get directions, Siri has the answer.

When using Siri to simplify your shopping trips, here are some things to keep in mind:

- Siri's search results are often sorted by distance from your current location. Stores and restaurants are sorted by the rating they've achieved on Yelp.

- Purchasing something in another currency? Ask Siri to calculate how much the item costs in your local currency—but watch out for those expensive data roaming charges if you're outside your mobile carrier's network.

- Need to write a shopping list? Create a special list in Reminders and then tell Siri what to add to the list. You can also share your shopping list with others through iCloud and set it up to remind you to pick up items whenever you're near a particular store.

- Let Siri do the math. Why drag out the Calculator app, when you can have Siri split tabs, calculate tips, and figure out how much everything costs with tax added?

- Siri's restaurant and movie integration simplifies your entertainment choices. Scan for reviews, check pricing, and reserve tables with a spoken sentence and a few taps. Order movie rentals with a few taps for viewing from your iOS device and beam them to your Apple TV.

- Turn-by-turn navigation rocks. It's one of Siri's best features, and it's one you're sure to love. Let Siri guide you to the places you need to be. It's one more way Siri can assist you in your day-to-day life.

- Siri's computer-biased explanations of movie plot lines can be downright hilarious. It's a marvelous Easter egg, and one well worth exploring.

Pushing Limits with Siri

Like the universe in which we live, the Siri universe continues to expand over time. Although Apple has not yet given developers a way to tap the power of Siri in third-party apps beyond dictation and launching, millions of early adopters have been able to come up with some very clever uses for the intelligent assistant, such as blogging.

Music aficionados have found that Siri works with the iPhone Music app to select and play songs, or even find out the name and artist of a song that is playing.

In this chapter, you'll get a look at a number of ways to push the limits with Siri. You'll also find information about how to keep your iPhone secure when using Siri.

Launching Apps

One of our favorite features (incidentally, first introduced in iOS 6) is Siri's application launcher. Tell Siri "Open Photos," "Play Infinity Blade," or "Launch Angry Birds," and it complies promptly. As Figure 7-1 indicates, control switches immediately from your Siri dialogue to the app you requested.

You are not prompted to confirm, and Siri doesn't give you a chance to change your mind, so be prepared to leave Siri. When you need to return to Siri, you know how: Either raise your phone to your ear (if you have Raise to Speak enabled on your iPhone) or double-tap the Home button on your iPhone, iPad, or iPod touch. Otherwise, just let Siri do its job. Tell it to launch an app, and then either get to work or start having fun.

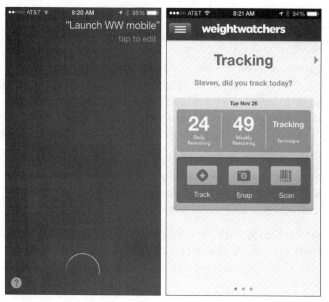

Figure 7-1
Launching an app (left) moves you directly to the application you requested (right).

Talking to Apps

Engaging in a chat conversation? Sending email? Why not speak instead of type? Conversation should be natural—as natural as simply talking. Figure 7-2 shows Steve using Siri for dictation on both OS X and iOS 7. The app you see here is Colloquy. It is an IRC (Internet Relay Chat) chat client that works on both iOS and OS X.

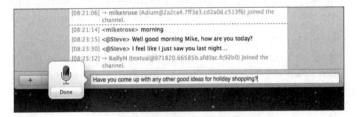

Figure 7-2
Siri offers the perfect accompaniment for chatting, as demonstrated by this Colloquy IRC conversation, conducted on Steve's part entirely by voice on OS X (top) and iOS (bottom).

Siri dictation makes chatting by voice fun and easy, and it's effective, too. Moving away from typing—either onscreen on iOS or on a keyboard on OS X—and speaking your conversations out loud speeds up text entry by a surprising degree. Yes, it may feel a little awkward at first, and, yes, you'll have to fix mistakes by hand, but soon you'll start wondering how you ever lived without it.

Now that we've been using dictation for a while, we miss it whenever it's gone. When we move away from our new Siri-enabled devices to older units such as the iPad 2, we both feel it in the gut. We've become addicted to talking, especially in iOS. Going back to tapping the screen or an accessory keyboard in Mail, Mobile Safari, and other apps feels slow, laborious, and downright hard.

When Mountain Lion launched in summer 2012, it brought Siri dictation to OS X. It felt like coming home to an old friend. If you move past any feelings of unease, Siri dictation can become a valuable tool in your workday arsenal.

Blogging with Siri

Did you know that you can create blog posts entirely by voice on iOS? We're not talking about basic dictation, either. Siri supports SMS messaging, and a little-known feature of Google Blogger enables you to create blog posts entirely by text.

Interested in giving it a spin? Text "register" to 256447. Blogger replies to your registration text by texting you a URL for your new blog and an optional claim code. This code is used to associate your new access with an existing blog. It is just as easy, however, to work with the automatically generated blog address that is sent to you.

Creating a Post

To create a new post, just reply to the 256447 text conversation. We recommend that you create a contact (we called ours Wheezing Weasels) to make it easier to refer to the 256447 SMS "phone number." This way, when you want to post, you just reply to or text the contact.

Dictate your new blog post to Siri and send it on its way. When you do, your words are instantly posted to the blog. Figure 7-3 shows us creating a post.

Figure 7-3
Use Siri and Google's blogging-by-SMS service to dictate your blog posts.

A post created in this manner appears online, using a default presentation with a temporary account and URL. This account is not intended for full-time use. To upgrade your blogging, you'll want to confirm your account.

Confirming Your Account

To move your account to a more reasonable URL with a more polished presentation, you need to claim it. Visit go.blogger.com and enter the code texted back to you by the mobile Blogger service. This page also enables you to associate the mobile account with an existing ID.

Once you've claimed your account, you can enter a permanent URL for your blog. We chose wheezingweasels.blogspot.com for ours. After choosing a name, we picked a more pleasing template than the initial blank white page. Figure 7-4 shows our final result.

This is a great way to do light blogging on trips or to create a low-stress blog for personal use.

Blogging by Email

If you're on a limited text message diet, posting by text message might prove too rich for your blood. There's a way for Siri to work around that. Blogging by email might not be *quite* as simple as blogging by text message, but it can be a lot cheaper. You must, however, use an existing Blogger account to create a Mail-to-Blogger address.

Visit your blog's dashboard and open Settings, Mobile and Email. Once there, establish a secret word that enables posting by email. This secret word creates a privileged address that enables blog posting.

In Figure 7-5, emails sent to tuawsteve.sekritword@blogger.com are automatically published to the blog. (Psst, we changed the secret word after we finished writing this book. It's no longer sekritword.) You'll find a complete set of instructions in the Blogger help article on this subject (www.google.com/support/blogger/bin/answer.py?answer=41452).

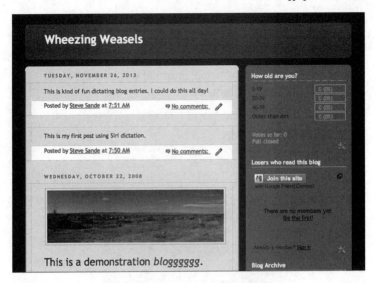

Figure 7-4
After we claimed and personalized our blog, new updates appeared at
wheezingweasels.blogspot.com.

After establishing your address, enter it into the Contacts app. Use
an easy-to-remember and easy-to-recognize contact name. We
used Wheezing Weasels, as we did for SMS updates.

Figure 7-5
Provide Blogger with a secret word that enables you to post blog updates by email.

When you're ready to post, tell Siri to create a new email. The
subject you provide sets the post's title, and the message sets its

contents. Allow Siri to send the email, and your blog magically updates.

Figure 7-6 shows the Siri interaction, along with the post it created. You can see the actual post that was built at http://wheezingweasels.blogspot.com.

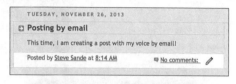

Figure 7-6
Use Siri to blog by email.

Other Blogging Services

Like Blogger, Tumblr also offers SMS access, although it tends to be a bit finicky. With the popular and free If This Then That (IFTTT.com) service, a few quick clicks can create recipes to convert your SMS text messages to blog posts for Tumblr and WordPress.

Some folks prefer not to use SMS for blogging, and that's okay: Plenty of other services support blog posting via email. Tumblr, WordPress.com, and self-hosted WordPress blogs all let you create a custom address that you use to post directly. You can find help and instructions for these services here:

- www.tumblr.com/docs/en/email_publishing
- codex.wordpress.org/Post_to_your_blog_using_email

Just add the custom email address to your address book with a distinctive—yet pronounceable—contact name and tell Siri "Send an email to [*the service name*]" to dictate your post and share it with the world.

Search around for other email and SMS-based services that are usable with Siri and social networks. More exist than the few mentioned here.

Don't forget, you can also tweet and post to Facebook from Siri. Here are things you can say to Siri that help perform social updates:

- "Post to Facebook 'Headed to the new Pixar movie.'"
- "Write on my Wall 'Just landed in San Jose!'"
- "Post to Twitter 'Another beautiful day in Cupertino.'"
- "Tweet with my location 'Great concert.'"
- "Tweet 'Meeting up with Brian Conway for lunch today.'"
- "Tweet 'The new iPad looks insanely great!' hashtag Apple Keynote."

Siri Security

Almost immediately after the release of Siri, we started receiving emails from users who noticed that even when they had a passcode set on the lock screen, someone could pick up their device and issue commands to Siri. This meant that unauthorized persons could pick up an iPhone or iPad, press and hold the Home button, and converse with Siri. Fortunately, you can disable Siri while using a lock screen passcode.

The Sophos Naked Security blog (http://nakedsecurity.sophos. com) notes that unauthorized users can do everything from write an email or send a text message to maliciously change calendar appointments. Blogger Graham Cluely pointed out that it's easy to disable Siri while a passcode is in effect. He wonders why Apple didn't set up iOS that way by default.

To make sure Siri is deaf to commands while a passcode is enabled, tap Settings, General, Touch ID & Passcode, and slide the Siri option to the Off position, as shown in Figure 7-7.

Now when your friends try to make a prank call to your girlfriend using your iPhone, they'll find Siri unwilling to participate in the prank.

One further note about security: When you allow Siri access from the lock screen, you also override any Find My Friends privacy. Siri does not prompt you to log in at the lock screen the way it does when you use the service normally. This is either a big security hole or a great convenience when you're trying to get together with a friend for lunch. Adjust your usage accordingly.

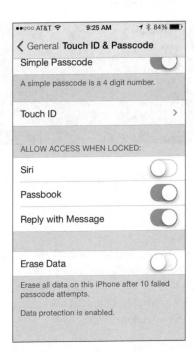

Figure 7-7
Increase your Siri security by disabling the lock screen access override.

The Lock Screen and Siri

Apple has provided Siri features specific to your lock screen. You can ask Siri to read notifications (see Figure 7-8) and check your messages. Be aware that Siri won't list the specifics of those notifications onscreen. They are described only by audio, although you will see the application names.

Here are some of the Lock Screen–specific conversation starters:

- "Read my notifications."
- "Do I have any new messages?"
- "Did I miss any phone calls?"

Figure 7-8
Siri tells you how many notifications you have and reads them out loud for you.

Music

Although a lot of the built-in Siri support involves controlling your schedule and finding information, Siri can also act as your personal media DJ. With Siri, you can select music, play it, and control the playback. For example, you might say some of these phrases to choose a music selection:

- "Play 'I Gotta Feeling.'"
- "Play 'Get Lucky' shuffled."
- "Play Steely Dan."
- "Play some blues [some country/some rock and roll]" or "I'm in the mood for [some genre] music."
- "I don't like this song. Can you play something else?"
- "Play my party mix."
- "Shuffle my road-trip playlist."
- "Play my Led Zeppelin playlist." or "I want to hear my Beatles playlist."
- "Shuffle this playlist."
- "Play similar songs."

- "Play [pause/resume/skip] next song [previous song]."
- "What is this song?" or "Who is this song by?" or "What music is playing?" or "Who is this artist?"

Siri fades out any currently playing audio when the assistant interface appears. So when you ask "What song is playing?" (as in Figure 7-9), you won't actually be hearing the song you're asking about. With a tap of the "Show Now Playing" link Siri provides, your digital assistant displays the Music app's Now Playing screen, complete with an image of the album cover, song and artist name, and play controls.

Figure 7-9
Siri tells you about the song that is currently playing.

iTunes Radio

With iTunes Radio, you store less music on-device and have access to a huge library of streaming selections. It works surprisingly well both over fast Wi-Fi and on slower cellular data networks. Launch the service by saying, "Play iTunes Radio." Your last selected "station" begins playing music to you. (If you haven't used iTunes Radio before, a station is automatically selected for you.)

iTunes Radio learns and adapts to your personal style. When you like a song, let Siri know. Say "Play more songs like this one" or "I like this song." In return, you hear songs that are in a similar genre or by similar artists. If songs don't fit your style, say "Don't play this song again." Either choose a station manually—just select it from the list of pre-created options—or request songs by a specific artist. Just tell Siri "Play my Tom Petty station," and the station begins playing.

Summary

Siri adds flexibility to your day-to-day work. Little details such as app launching and text entry by voice expand the way you work with your device and your computer. Controlling your music and asking about what's playing keeps you on top of your entertainment needs. Siri's easy blog and social network integration enables you to keep your friends, colleagues, and family up-to-date on your activities. Before you move onto the next chapter, here are a few parting thoughts:

- Siri cannot yet take pictures or post them by voice, but it's certainly a feature we look forward to in future iOS updates.
- You can talk to apps on your Macintosh just as you can on iOS. Take advantage of the dictation features of OS X for text entry to cut down on your typing time.

- The names you use to launch apps don't have to be exactly right. Siri tries to match as many details as possible to find an app that fits your request. For example, if you say "Launch Angry Birds," and the only Rovio Angry Birds app on your iPad is the Seasons version, Siri will launch that.

- When you post a blog entry by email, your signature *will* appear, if you use one. Don't let this come as a surprise, especially if your signature is off color or provides contact information that you'd rather not post online.

- Siri's music-controls-by-voice are handy when you're driving because you don't have to swipe between screens or hunt for buttons. Tell Siri "Skip to the next song" when something you don't want to hear pops up in your playlist. Telling Siri "Play similar songs" is also a favorite. It creates an iTunes Genius–like playlist on the spot.

Siri Dictation

Apple's intelligent assistant does more than just answer questions and make jokes. Siri also translates your spoken words into text. Through dictation, you can reduce your usage of the tiny iOS keyboard—or the more generous OS X keyboard—and leave the typing to Siri.

In this chapter, you'll learn how to elicit the most accurate responses from Siri through fun examples and practice phrases. You will find Siri remarkably good at taking notes or even writing short documents. From enunciation to punctuation, this chapter is ready to help you start using your voice to write with Siri.

Launching Dictation on iOS

The small Siri microphone, which you see at the bottom of Figure 8-1 (top), appears on dictation-capable iOS keyboards. The microphone is found just to the left of the spacebar and to the right of the number toggle. When this microphone appears on the iOS keyboard, you know you can dictate as an alternative to typing.

Tapping the microphone (see Figure 8-1, top) places you into iOS's dictation mode (see Figure 8-1, bottom). Here, a gray voice interface appears, consisting of an animated sound wave and the word Done. As in standard Siri, the sound wave acts as a sound meter, rising and falling along with your speech.

Siri dictation does not use silence detection, so it waits for you to tap Done. In practical terms, this means you have about 30 seconds before the "buffer" (the part of iOS that stores your voice as it is being recorded) fills up, Siri runs out of memory, and it automatically taps Done for you.

After listening, Siri interprets your speech, transforming it from sounds to text. It then types it for you at the current position of the cursor. What you said becomes words on the iOS screen.

Launching Dictation on OS X

Starting with OS X Mountain Lion and continuing with OS X Mavericks, you can use Siri-style dictation on your Macintosh as well as on iOS. This is a great way to bypass your keyboard and create text with your voice.

You enable this feature in the System Preferences, Dictation & Speech pane (see Figure 8-2, top) by clicking the On radio button. To allow dictation when your Mac is not connected to the Internet, and to also allow for continuous dictation, check the Use Enhanced Dictation check box.

Next, choose a shortcut that launches dictation on your computer. This shortcut is universal and should work across any application, assuming that there's something to type into. If there is no active text-entry cursor, triggering the shortcut produces a sad beep.

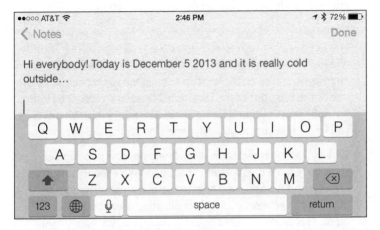

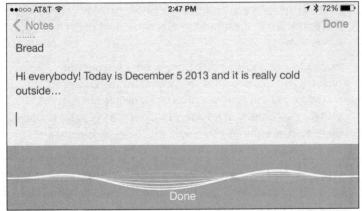

Figure 8-1
Tap the Microphone button on the iOS keyboard to begin dictating to Siri (top). As you dictate, the sound wave animates to offer a sound level. The words you say don't appear until after you tap Done. Siri converts your speech to words and adds them to the current cursor position.

We personally like the Press Fn (Function) Key Twice option because it's convenient and not usually triggered by accident. However, select whatever choice you prefer. There's also an end user–customizable key combination at the bottom of the pop-up; after you set it, use this trigger to launch dictation.

Siri dictation works with any item on your Mac that displays a text-entry cursor. Dictate into scrolling text views such as the TextEdit window shown in Figure 8-2 (bottom), or talk into Microsoft Word and Pages, and so forth. You can also dictate to text fields like the one at the top right of the Dictation & Speech screen (see Figure 8-2, top) or those found inside Safari. The rule is this: Wherever you find a text cursor, you can generally talk instead of type.

When you trigger dictation, a small microphone pops up, as shown in Figure 8-2 (bottom). It appears with a Done button under it and is positioned next to the text cursor. This virtual microphone enables you to start dictating using built-in audio input. This works whether you're using a headset, your iSight microphone, or any other mic you've attached to your computer. The purple bar in the microphone acts as a level meter for your voice.

As on iOS, talk until you click Done or until Siri runs out of space and cuts you off. If you've enabled Use Enhanced Dictation, you can continue to dictate indefinitely. Next, you wait for the conversion from text to speech. This usually happens quite quickly, especially on new Macs. The delay is slight and unobtrusive.

We find it easiest to end dictation by tapping the Fn key (or Command key, if that's what you're using to start dictation) one more time instead of moving our hands to the mouse to click Done.

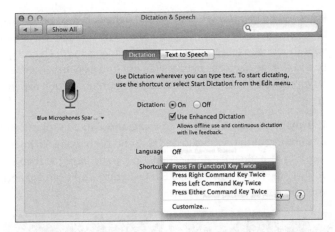

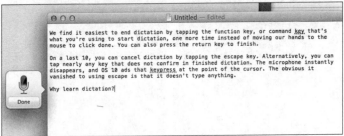

Figure 8-2
OS X's Dictation & Speech pane enables you to activate and customize dictation on your Macintosh (top). This screenshot was snapped while working on this chapter (bottom).

Why Learn Dictation?

On iOS, Siri dictation isn't limited to typing notes and filling out forms. It's as helpful when communicating through the standard Siri interface as it is when working in other apps and on OS X. That's because Siri dictation enables you to add nuance. Consider Figure 8-3.

In the left image, you see Siri's default behavior. The text message reflects everything you say, but there's no punctuation to separate your thoughts. Contrast it with the right image, in which each portion of the message has been pulled out into its own sentence. It's far more readable and provides a better communication experience.

This chapter teaches you how to create those more sophisticated text entries, both on iOS and on OS X, and both in the Siri interface and in standalone applications. In the sections that follow, you will see how knowing how Siri text entry works can enhance your dictation.

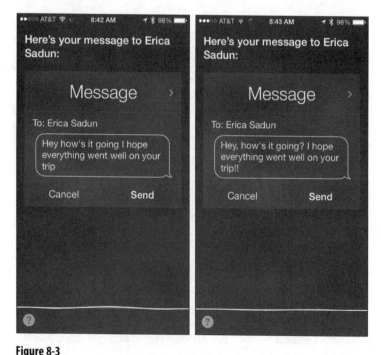

Figure 8-3
Siri's dictation features transform your utterances from streams of consciousness (left) to formatted sentences (right).

Enunciation Practice

When it comes to dictation, enunciation matters. Tongue-twisters provide a fantastic way for you to practice Siri enunciation skills. Plus, they're a lot of fun to try. The iOS Siri interface responds directly to each of the following twisty sentences (see Figure 8-4). You can also try dictating these into a text editor on OS X to see how well you can pronounce convoluted words.

As you'll discover, Siri creates a hilarious response to the wood-chuck question but redirects the other twisters to Wolfram Alpha or shows web search results.

- "How much wood would a woodchuck chuck if a woodchuck could chuck wood?"
- "How many pickled peppers did Peter Piper pick?"
- "What does she sell by the seashore?"
- "How many boards could the Mongols hoard if the Mongol hordes got bored?"
- "How many cans can a cannibal nibble if a cannibal can nibble cans?"

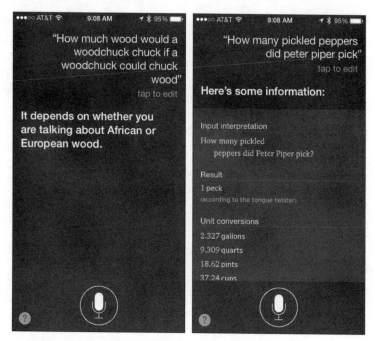

Figure 8-4
Train your Siri enunciation skills with these tongue-twisters.

Dictation 101

You've read how to enable dictation and how to work on your enunciation. Now it's time to try dictating. If you're on OS X, hop into a text editor such as TextEdit. On iOS, launch the Notes app and create a new note.

Use your dictation key shortcut (OS X) or tap the microphone button (iOS) and start talking. Try dictating the following paragraph from *Alice's Adventures in Wonderland*:

"Alice was beginning to get very tired of sitting by her sister on the bank, and of having nothing to do: once or twice she had peeked into the book her sister was reading, but it had no pictures or conversations in it, 'And what is the use of a book,' thought Alice 'without pictures or conversation?'"

Upon finishing, tap or click Done (iOS) or press the Fn or Command key (OS X). When you are finished speaking, Siri enters "thinking" mode; on iOS 7 devices, a small circle rotates on the screen during interpretation of your speech, while OS X machines display your spoken text quickly. The interpreted text is then pasted in at the point of the cursor (see Figure 8-5).

Notice that there is no punctuation here. You may also see a few misinterpretations, such as *people* instead of *peeked*. You can improve your Siri dictation in a number of ways to work around these issues.

Improving Dictation

The first rule of dictation is to always *speak a little at a time*. Although Siri can handle long sentences like the one you just dictated, it works better with shorter phrases.

Second, *enunciate*. Remember how certain teachers always over-emphasized each syllable? Pretend to be one of those teachers now, and reap the Siri rewards.

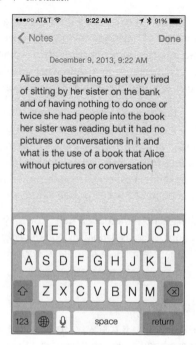

Figure 8-5
Siri tries its best to interpret the text you dictate into any text-entry element on the iPhone. You may see a blue underline below some text, which indicates multiple possible interpretations of your speech. Tap that word or phrase (iOS) or right-click just to its right (OS X) to bring up a bubble that lets you choose from possible corrections.

Third, *supply punctuation, capitalization cues, and so forth* to augment Siri's standard interpretation.

Here's an example for you to try. Try speaking the following as a series of dictation phrases. Speak slowly and clearly, including the extra items added to each bullet point:

- "Alice was beginning to get very tired of sitting by her sister on the bank comma."
- "And of having nothing to do colon."

- "Once or twice she had peeked into the book her sister was reading comma."
- "But it had no pictures or conversations in it comma."
- "Quote cap and what is the use of a book comma end quote."
- "Thought Alice quote without pictures or conversation question mark end quote."

This time, your results should look more like those shown in Figure 8-6. Here you'll find punctuation, proper cases, and so forth. You can further improve your results by adding information about sentence endings ("period" or "full stop"), "new line" to introduce a carriage return, and "new paragraph" to start an entirely new paragraph.

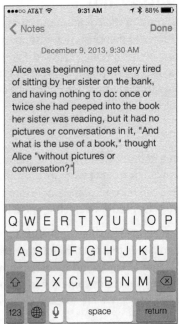

Figure 8-6
Dictating to Siri with grammar cues helps it include punctuation, capitalization, and more.

Errors still pop up, such as *peeped into* instead of *peeked into*, but overall, dictation has been much improved in this second example. Speaking more slowly, enunciating more carefully, and providing dictation cues immediately enhances whatever text you are creating.

We need to mention one final rule: *Give Siri time to learn about you*. Time allows Siri to learn your regional accent. With continued use, Siri categorizes your voice based on the dialects it knows about. The more the service can study your speech patterns, the more effective it becomes at recognizing what you say.

Inserting Punctuation

Siri understands most of the common punctuation names you throw at it. As Table 8-1 demonstrates, it supports most (but not all) items you find on the iPhone keyboard. For example, we have not been able to find a Siri entry for the bullet sign, so this area has room for growth. Right now, we get results like "Bullet tab hello" instead of what we want:

• Hello

Siri handles some items brilliantly, such as "period" or "full stop" to end sentences. It has trouble with possible interpretation over-laps. For example, Siri misinterprets "single quote" requests almost more often than it succeeds in detecting them.

If you find punctuation items that we missed on this list (or any Siri dictation commands that fell through the cracks for any of this coverage), contact us at info@sanddunetech.com and let us know. We did the best we could to document each element, but we did so through trial and error. We are sure we are missing other valu-able entries.

Table 8-1—Punctuation

Command	Result
"Period" (or "full stop")	Add a period, finishing a sentence.
"Dot"	Add a period midsentence without finishing the sentence (for example, "Cat dot dog" becomes "Cat.dog").
"Point"	Add a period midnumber as a decimal point (for example, "Pi is three point one four").
"Question mark" or "inverted question mark"	Add a ? or a ¿.
"Exclamation point" or "inverted exclamation point"	Add a ! or a ¡.
"Ellipsis" (or "dot dot dot")	Add an ellipsis (...).
"Comma" or "double-comma" or "colon" or "semicolon"	Add , or ,, or : or ;.
"Minus sign" or "plus sign"	Add − or +.
"Quote" (or "quotation mark")	Add ", a standard double quote.
"Quote ... unquote" (or "quote ... end quote")	Surround the text with quotation marks. (For example, "quote hello unquote" becomes ""hello""—that is, hello surrounded with a double quote on each side—that is, just one double quote, not the quoted quotes we use in this example, which quotes itself. Because... oh dear. We hope that makes sense.)
"Apostrophe" (or "single quote")	Add '. (For example, "Kitty apostrophe ess" becomes "Kitty's." and "Hello apostrophe world" becomes "Hello 'world.")
"Backquote" (or "backtick") or "ampersand" or "asterisk"	Add ` or & or *.
"Open parenthesis" or "close parenthesis"	Add (or).

Command	Result
"Open bracket" or "close bracket"	Add [or].
"Open brace" or "close brace"	Add { or }.
"Vertical bar" or "slash" or "backslash"	Add | or / or \.
"Dash" (or "en dash")	Add – (en dash), with spaces on either side. (For example, "Hello dash world" produces "Hello – world.")
"Hyphen"	Add - (hyphen), without spaces on either side. (For example, "Hello hyphen world" produces "Hello-world.")
"Underscore" or "percent sign" "at sign"	Add _ or % or @.
"Dollar sign" or "euro sign" or "cent sign" or "yen sign" or "pound sterling sign"	Add $ or € or ¢ or ¥ or £.
"Section sign" or "registered sign" or "copyright sign" or "trademark sign"	Add § or ® or © or ™.
"Greater than sign" or "less than sign"	Add > or <.
"Degree sign" or "caret" or "tilde"	Add ° or ^ or ~.
"Pound sign" (or "number sign" or "hash sign")	Add #.

Controlling Flow

You control text flow by telling Siri when to start a new paragraph or insert a carriage return (a term from ancient days, when many typewriters had a moving "carriage" that held the paper). Table 8-2 details these options. Providing natural spacing in your emails and text documents makes them more readable than leaving your dictation in a single large clump. Use these features to create paragraphs and lists as you speak.

Table 8-2—Starting Paragraphs

Command	Result
"New line"	Insert a carriage return
"New paragraph"	Begin a new paragraph

Adding Capitalization

Siri provides both immediate capitalization cues (for example, you can capitalize the next word) and modes (for example, capitalizing until you specify otherwise). When working with a mode in Siri, you specify what the mode is and when you are enabling and disabling it (via "On" and "Off"). Table 8-3 details the Siri capitalization commands.

Remember that Siri defaults to capitalizing the start of a new sentence and what it recognizes as proper nouns. You end a sentence by issuing a period or full stop or by starting a new paragraph. In contrast, new lines do not start new sentences and might not trigger capitalization of the next word spoken.

Table 8-3—Capitalization

Command	Result
"Capital" or "cap"	Capitalize the next word or letter. (For example, to type "A.B.C.," say "Capital A dot, capital B dot, capital C dot.")
"Caps on"	Enable initial caps. (For example, "oh boy" becomes "Oh Boy.")
"Caps off"	Disable initial caps.
"All caps"	Uppercase the next word. (For example, "oh boy" becomes "OH boy.")
"All caps on"	Start caps lock mode. (For example, "oh boy" becomes "OH BOY.")

Command	Result
"All caps off"	End caps lock mode.
"No caps"	Lowercase the next word. (For example, "Erica" becomes "erica." When you say "Hello no caps Erica," Siri adds "Hello erica.")
"No caps on"	Start lowercase lock mode. (For example, "Oh Boy" becomes "oh boy.")
"No caps off"	End lowercase lock mode.
"Spacebar"	Prevent a hyphen in a normally hyphenated word. (For example, "mother spacebar in space bar law" becomes "mother in law" instead of "mother-in-law.")
"No space"	Remove a natural space from between words. (For example, "hello no space world" becomes "helloworld.")
"No space on" and "no space off"	Disable natural spaces between words. (For example, "No space on this is my world no space off" becomes "thisismyworld." Make sure to pause after the initial "on" and before the ending "no.")

To see Siri capitalization in action, try dictating the following. Make sure you leave a significant pause after any "on"/"off" command. I've included hint pauses in the dictation. Do not say "pause" there—just pause a bit before continuing the dictation. "Full stop" means end the sentence with a period.

"Alice was beginning <pause> Caps on <pause> to get very tired of sitting by her sister on the bank <pause> Caps off <pause>, and of having nothing to do full stop. <pause> All caps on <pause> Alice in Wonderland full stop. <pause> All caps off <pause> The end full stop."

Figure 8-7 demonstrates what this dictation should look like when completed. Notice how the two modes (initial caps and all caps) are implemented in text.

So what do you do when you need to use the word *cap* in a sentence, such as "I put a cap on my head"? You just say so. However, try saying, "When I write in all caps it is lots of fun," and you will encounter difficulties.

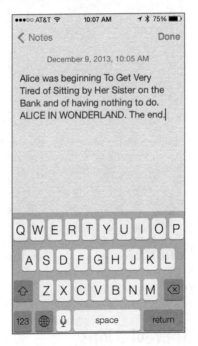

Figure 8-7
Pauses help Siri understand capitalization commands.

Figure 8-8 shows how Siri interprets these two sentences. The first use is caught properly, but the second results in the awkward sentence "When I write in IT is lots of fun." Adding a significant pause between "all" and "caps" fixes the problem. You can dictate "When I write in all <long pause> caps it is lots of fun" to produce the correct interpretation.

Figure 8-8
Siri sometimes gets the context right, but sometimes not.

Including Abbreviations

Siri offers a few simple, standard abbreviations, as shown in Table 8-4. Siri does not have a lot of direct abbreviation support built in, and it failed on most of the academic abbreviations that we tested. You get a few that are used very commonly in English.

Table 8-4—Abbreviations and Spaces

Command	Result
"i e"	i.e. (with periods)
"e g"	e.g.
"Et cetera"	etc.
"p s"	PS (for example, "PS I love you")
"v s"	VS (for example, "Alabama VS Auburn")

Dictating Technical Terms

Siri recognizes common measurements. For example, you say "five hundred milliliters," and Siri types "500 mL," or you say "two kilograms," and Siri types "2 kg." Fractions are also covered. Say "two and three quarters," and Siri types "2 3/4."

Table 8-5 shows examples of common technical terms you might use in your dictation, from numbers, to currency, to measurements. This table is not exhaustive. Instead, it gives you a flavor of the kinds of technical dictation available. As you see in these examples, Siri understands many standard scientific prefixes, suffixes, and measurements.

Table 8-5—Technical Dictation

Command	Result
"One hundred and five"	105
"Fifty-seven thirty-two"	5732
"Five point six"	5.6
"One hundred and thirty thousand two hundred and four"	130,204
"Zero point five two"	0.52
"Five and seven-ninths"	5 7/9

Command	Result
"Twenty dollars"	$20
"Twenty-five dollars and thirty-two cents"	$25.32
"One hundred kilograms"	100 kg
"Eighty-two milliliters"	82 mL
"Thirty-one parsecs"	31 pc
"Three millimeters"	3 mm
"Five thousand nanometers"	5000 nm
"Twelve microns" or "twelve micrometers"	12 µ or 12 µm
"Fifty-two degrees"	52°
"Two gigabytes," "two terabytes," "two exabytes"	2 GB, 2 TB, 2 EB
"Five angstroms"	5 Å
"Five feet two inches"	5'2"
"Six a m" / "eight p m"	6 AM / 8 PM

Phone Numbers

Siri formats phone numbers using standard hyphenation. You do not need to say "hyphen" when entering phone numbers. For example, you could say this:

"My phone number has changed from 3035551212 (full stop). It is now 5551919 (full stop). To order, call 18005551313."

Siri produces hyphenated text for you because it recognizes the phone context for the numbers you fed it, as shown in Figure 8-9.

Dates and Times

For basic dates, you do not need to speak any special formatting instructions. For example, Siri converts this:

"Thursday July Fourth Seventeen Seventy Six at Three P M"

to this:

Thursday, July 4, 1776 at 3 p.m.

But if you want to enter slash-formatted dates, you need to say the word *slash*. For example, you could say this:

"Ten slash one slash eleven at two thirty P M"

to create this date:

10/1/11 at 2:30 p.m.

Figure 8-9
Siri formats phone numbers using hyphens. You do not have to speak those hyphens to it.

Prices

As you saw in Table 8-5, you say prices as you normally would when talking to another person. For example, telling Siri this:

"It costs twenty dollars and thirty-two cents."

produces this:

It costs $20.32.

Siri understands some other currencies, so if you tell it "15 euros," it properly formats "€15." However, trying to tell Siri "five pounds 50 pence" results in "5 pounds £.50." When entering UK pounds sterling, use the format "five pounds sterling 50 pence" to get the proper result of "£5.50."

Smileys

Siri knows a few smileys, the text-based emoticons used in electronic communications. Table 8-6 shows the ones that Siri supports. Note that Siri adds hyphen-noses to its smileys, a non-standard approach for anyone from the :), :(, ;), and (: camps.

Table 8-6—Smileys

Command	Result
"Smiley" or "smiley face" or "smile face"	:-)
"Frowny" or "frowny face" or "frown face"	:-(
"Winky" or "winky face" or "wink face"	;-)

Dictating Formatted Text

Siri understands many standard formatting options while you dictate. Here are examples of typical ways to use this built-in feature to simplify your dictation tasks.

Addresses

Try dictating the following example to Siri:

"Seventy-three oh one South Santa Fe Drive Littleton Colorado Eight Zero One Two Zero"

Siri correctly formats the results, producing the address with proper ZIP code formatting, as shown in Figure 8-10.

Figure 8-10
Siri automatically formats ZIP codes.

URLs

Specify the *w*'s (you say "dub") and the dots when dictating URLs. For example, you might say

"Dub dub dub dot apple dot com"

to produce "www.apple.com." Say "dub dub dub" to create the "www" prefix. It's cute, and it's fun to say. Siri also knows that "World Wide Web" is a proper noun and that all three words should be capitalized.

Siri actually has quite a large database of these proper names. For example, if you say "Martin Luther King," "United Nations," or "New York Times," Siri correctly capitalizes them.

Email Addresses

To dictate email addresses, say "at sign" instead of "at." You might say this:

"His email address is Steve at sign Apple dot com"

to produce "His email address is steve@apple.com." You can use underscores and dots in names. For example, say this:

"The email you're looking for is Steve underscore Jobs at sign Apple dot com"

to get "The email you're looking for is steve_jobs@apple.com."

When Siri recognizes an email address, it automatically removes extraneous spaces to create a properly formatted address.

License Plates

Dictate license plates slowly, stating each number and letter. For example, this:

> "Colorado plate <pause> X <pause> Y <pause> W <pause> 3 6 7"

correctly produces "Colorado plate XYW367." Our experience shows that this feature works less well for all-letter plates and plates that don't follow common number/letter patterns.

 NOTE

Siri is not very accomplished when it comes to spelling out words. Do not expect to dictate letter by letter when working with Siri. The assistant wasn't designed for that.

Dictation Practice

Try entering the following letter into Notes or TextEdit entirely by voice. You need not get every nuance correct (see Figure 8-11), but it should be a good exercise of your Siri dictation skills. Focus on trying to match the style wherever possible, and learn where you encounter the greatest difficulties and how to modulate your dictation skills to accommodate. Remember that Siri dictation listens for only a short time, so be sure to break your dictation into several shorter sections—don't try to dictate the entire document at once.

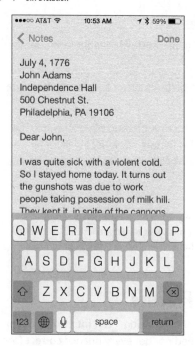

Figure 8-11
You'll be surprised by how soon and how quickly you can dictate complex documents...although Siri may misinterpret some words now and then.

"July 4, 1776

John Adams

Independence Hall

500 Chestnut Street

Philadelphia, PA 19106

Dear John,

I was quite sick with a violent cold. So I stayed home today. It turns out the gunshots was due to our people taking possession of Nook Hill. They kept it, in spite of the cannons firing on them. This has caused our Enemy to up and leave, or so I heard from a messenger just arrived from headquarters.

Some of the selectmen have been to the lines. They tell us that they have carried everything they could possibly take. What they could not, they burnt, they broke, or threw into the water.

This is, I believe, fact.

Please send me paper. I have only enough for one letter more. Or, you may call at 202-555-1414.

Yours, with full heart,

Abigail"

Punctuation Practice

One of the questions that people keep asking us is how to spell out the word *comma* or *period*. In other words, how do you dictate the literal word instead of the punctuation?

Fortunately, there is a solution for this. It's not an easy solution, but it can be done cleanly so that you do not have to go back and remove extraneous punctuation the way you do if you try saying punctuation names twice (for example, comma comma or period period). To type out "comma," you dictate "No caps on, no space on, C O M M A, no space off, no caps off."

This tells Siri to start a forced lowercase mode without spaces. You then spell out the word in question (*comma,* in this case). At the end, you return to normal dictation mode by disabling that mode.

Be aware that Siri looks for context. It can differentiate between "The Jurassic Period" and "The Jurassic." (see that period there?) during dictation, preferring the former because the word finishes a phrase.

Try dictating the following. These commands produce the sentence "I like to type comma and period every now and then," as shown in Figure 8-12. Make sure you include reasonable pauses as you move between lines and commands.

"I like to type"

"no caps on, no space on,"

"C O M M A"

"no space off, no caps off"

"and"

"no caps on, no space on,"

"P E R I O D"

"no space off, no caps off"

"every now and then"

"Full stop"

Figure 8-12
You can make Siri cleanly type the words *comma* and *period* and other symbol names, but not without significant effort.

Summary

No speech-to-text dictation software is perfect, but Siri provides a steppingstone to the future of text entry. Understanding both the power and limitations of Siri's abilities is key to making use of dictation to take notes, send legible emails, and even create rough drafts of documents.

This chapter includes the following information to maximize your use of Siri's dictation capabilities:

- Proper enunciation is key to making sure that Siri understands what you are saying before it converts your speech to text. Playing with complex tongue-twisters provides a great way to learn how to enunciate your words so Siri's dictation becomes more accurate.

- Don't hesitate to dictate text to Siri, even though it will make some humorous (and frustrating) mistakes. Turn to the keyboard and its interactive selection tools to patch things up after a long dictation session, and you will find that you're using Siri dictation much more often than you ever anticipated you would.

- You must tell Siri to add or remove capitalization and punctuation. This chapter provides all the phrases, know-how, and techniques you need to dictate properly capitalized and punctuated text.

- Siri knows several common abbreviations and smileys. It is more than happy to enter them into your documents when you know the verbal shortcuts that get you there.

- Polish your skills for dictating formatted text, such as phone numbers, addresses, dates and times, prices, Internet addresses, and email addresses. Siri knows how to format some of these items automatically, whereas others require you to phrase the text in a specific way.

Having Fun with Siri

You've taken a close look at the practical day-to-day uses of Siri. You've seen how to check the weather, send text messages, control your playlist, calculate tips, and more. Those are all well and good, but they fail to showcase Siri's real sparkle.

After all, Siri is fun as well as practical. You can use Siri in a… forgive the pun…serious manner and totally miss the point of how delightful a tool it is to use. With that in mind, this chapter introduces the lighter side of Siri.

Siri Diversions

Siri offers many delightful diversions to enjoy when you have a few minutes to play around with its features. As Figure 9-1 shows, Siri is quite whimsical if you know how to ask the right questions or feed it the right statement.

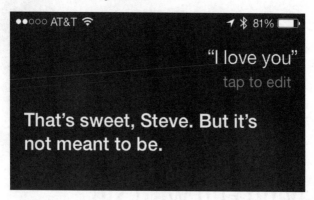

••○○○ AT&T 📶   ✈ ✳ 81% ▮▮▮

"I love you"

tap to edit

That's sweet, Steve. But it's not meant to be.

Figure 9-1
Siri can engage you in conversations that you probably didn't expect from a portable electronic device.

What's more, Siri doesn't offer just a single canned response to "I love you." In addition to the statement you see in the figure, it might answer:

- "You hardly know me."
- "All you need is love. And your iPhone."
- "Oh, I bet you say that to all your Apple products."
- "I hope you don't say that to those other mobile phones."
- "I am only here to serve you."
- "I value you."
- "That's nice. Can we get back to work now?"
- "Impossible."
- "Do you?"
- "You are the wind beneath my wings."
- "Oh, stop."

This expressiveness demonstrates the care and detail Apple has dedicated to its product. Siri isn't just an algorithm implemented to create control-by-voice on iOS. It's a vibrant library of interactions curated and grown by an involved and dedicated team.

Siri's small, detailed touches enhance day-to-day use. When you ask Siri the time, it normally reports that it is so many hours and so many minutes, as in "The time is 8:13 PM."

Every now and then, Siri slips in a joke. You might ask, "What time is it, Siri?" And occasionally, as reader Kemal Avunduk discovered, Siri replies, "At the tone, it will be 8:13." This is followed by a long pause, and then Siri adds in a deadpan voice, "Beep." This is a great time to use Siri's "Say it again" or "Repeat" command to share the joke with your friends.

You can engage Siri in many ways, as we demonstrate in the following sections. We've focused on the silly and fun, providing ideas that help you enjoy Siri and discover the whimsy built into the system.

Be persistent, and Siri will reward you. Although Siri responds to all the suggestions in this chapter, often with a silly reply, Siri might supply more than one answer for certain statements, as with the "I love you" example. It's worth trying again to see if Siri offers another reply that particularly tickles your funny bone.

Asking About Siri

Your virtual assistant has a lot going on behind the scenes. Siri's natural reticence and modesty mean you often have to work a little harder to get to know Siri better. Try these icebreakers:

- "Who are you?"
- "What is your name?" (You can also ask, "What is my name?")

- "Do you have a family?" (see Figure 9-2) or "Who is your mother?" or "Who is your father?" or "Who is your friend?"

- "What is your favorite color?" or "What is your favorite number?"

- "What do you like?" or "What do you like to do?"

- "What are you doing?"

- "Who is ELIZA?"

Figure 9-2
When it comes to family, Siri is happy to be part of your life. Being your iOS device is family enough for Siri.

- "How are you, Siri?"

- "Why are you so awesome?"

- "Who is your husband [wife]?"

- "Who's your daddy?"

- "How old are you?"

- "When is your birthday?"

- "Where do you come from?"

- "Tell me how old you are now."

- "Happy birthday!"
- "Are you real?"
- "Are you self-aware?"
- "Speak to me!" (Try this one more than once.)
- "Are you human?" (See Figure 9-3.)

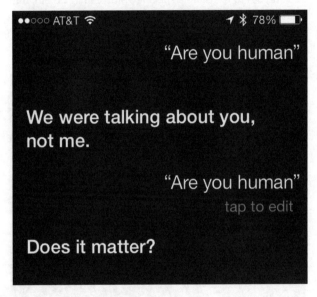

Figure 9-3
As far as Siri is concerned, you're probably an honorary personal virtual assistant.

- "Do you want a treat?"
- "How do you feel right now?"
- "Siri, do you have a face?"
- "Are you hungry?"
- "What do you look like?" (Hint, it's multidimensional.)
- "What are you wearing?"

- "Do you have a life other than being my assistant?"

- "Who is your favorite person?" (You'll like the answer to this one.)

- "Siri, are you a girl or a boy?"

- "What languages do you speak?" (See Figure 9-4.) Also, try asking Siri to translate a specific phrase, such as "Siri, translate 'how are you' to French," for some interesting responses. Make sure to keep asking repeatedly to get to the Easter eggs! Thanks for this tip goes to Florian Taltavull.

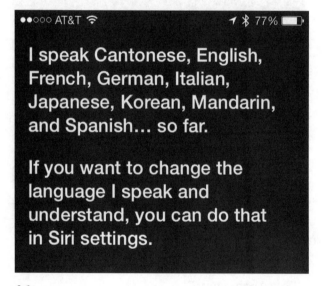

Figure 9-4

Siri is quite the polyglot! Not sure what that means? Ask it! Say "What does *polyglot* [PAH-lee-glot] mean?"

Siri Chitchat

Siri can provide some chuckles when it responds with canned responses to some basic statements. Here are some conversation openers to start some back-and-forth with your virtual assistant:

- "Thank you."
- "Have a nice day."
- "Do you love me?" (see Figure 9-5) or "Do you like me?"

Figure 9-5
Siri easily fends off unwanted advances.

- "Why don't you love me?"
- "I feel lonely."
- "Don't make me angry."
- "What is the best computer in the world?" or "What is the best phone in the world?" or "What is the best tablet?"
- "When will the new Mac mini [other Apple product] debut?" (Sadly, Siri doesn't make forward-looking predictions. Instead, it directs you to Apple's website.)

- "What do you think about Android?" (Be sure to ask a few times.)
- "What's new?"
- "You're silly."
- "What up?"
- "How much do you cost?"
- "Where did I put my keys?"
- "Am I pretty?"
- "Why?"
- "Can you eat?"
- "I don't like your voice."
- "You don't understand anything!"
- "You're wonderful!" (See Figure 9-6.)

Figure 9-6
Siri is also quite polite.

- "Do I look fat?"
- "Testing" or "Testing 1 2 3."
- "Howdy."

- "Hah!" or "Ye hah!" or "Ye haha!" or "ha ha" or "LOL" or "ROFL."
- "Blah. Blah blah. Blah blah blah blah blah. Yeah, blah."
- "Hey, guess what." (See Figure 9-7.)
- "Why does my wife [husband] hate me?"
- "Do you want to know a secret?"
- "I'm bored." or "I'm angry." or "I'm sad."
- "I'm sleepy." or "I'm tired of talking."
- "Tell me a joke [or story or poem]." (Make sure to keep trying with these!)

Figure 9-7
Siri is ready for any surprise you sling at it.

- "Can you sing?" or "Sing to me, Siri!" (See Figure 9-8.)
- "Knock knock."

Figure 9-8
If your expectations are modest, Siri will amuse and entertain you.

Pop Culture Fun

Siri is well versed in some pop culture references. Here are some that it can respond to directly. Don't forget to keep asking; Siri's versatility will amuse you.

- "Open the pod bay doors." (Figure 9-9 shows some of the replies to this one.)
- "Do you know HAL 9000?"
- "I can't let you do that, Dave."
- "Klaatu barada nikto."
- "Wake me up before you go go…" (Okay, this one too doesn't really do much.)
- "Take me to your leader." (this one is adorable) or "Who is your leader?"
- "Who is the fairest of them all?" or "Mirror, mirror on the wall, who's the fairest of them all?"
- "Show me the money!"
- "Okay, glass!" (Just so you know, that's the key phrase for engaging Google Glass. Siri gets offended when you mistake it for that *other* piece of technology.)
- "Who let the dogs out?"
- "Billy Jean is not my lover." (Technically, this is less pop culture and more contacts maintenance, but it's pretty funny regardless.)
- "Flip a coin." (No, it's not random, although it's greatly improved over previous Siri versions. Keep asking to get to the pop culture references. If you want actual random results, ask Siri to "roll the dice" instead.)
- "Why did the chicken cross the road?"
- "What came first, the chicken or the egg?"
- "Who's on first?" or "Who's on second?" or "Who's on third?"

Figure 9-9
Siri has an entire repertoire for some pop culture conversations. Here are a few responses to "Open the pod bay doors."

Siri Miscellany

Here are more fun things you can say to Siri, without any specific categories assigned to them:

- "I want drugs." (See Figure 9-10.)

- "I'm drunk." (This one provides an especially thoughtful extra. Siri will offer to help you call a cab!)

- "Where can I hide a body?" or "Send lawyers, guns, and money!"

- "When is Santa Claus coming to town?"

- "Do you believe in Santa Claus?"

- "Merry Christmas!" or "Happy New Year!" or "Happy Halloween!" or "Happy Columbus Day!" (and so on)

- "When is Thanksgiving?" (Sometimes Siri gives a little extra commentary, so keep trying until you get it.)

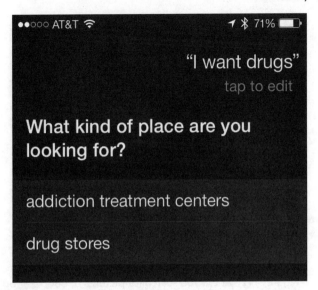

●●○○○ AT&T 🛜   ⌖ ✳ 71% ▬▭

> "I want drugs"
> tap to edit

What kind of place are you looking for?

addiction treatment centers

drug stores

Figure 9-10
Siri cares.

- "Will you marry me?" (Really, keep asking this one. Some of the replies are hilarious. See Figure 9-11, for instance.)
- "Siri! Siri! Siri!"
- "Is Google going to hell?" (Hint: It's probably not the answer you might be expecting.)
- "Make me a sandwich."
- "I have to urinate [poop]."
- "I am cold." or "I am boiling hot."
- "I don't like your tone." or "I don't like broccoli."
- "Siri, can you find the email I sent tomorrow?" (This one is hilarious.)
- Try saying "Good morning" at night or "Good evening" in the morning.

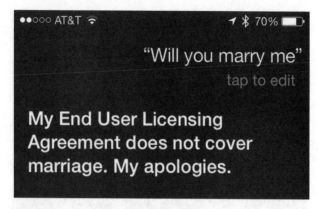

Figure 9-11
You can enter a two-year commitment with your carrier, but Siri's unwilling to tie the knot.

- "Talk dirty to me." (This is clean/family safe—promise [see Figure 9-12]! And if you search for pictures of boobies, you'll probably be rewarded by images of the blue-footed birds. Since these results vary by country, we encourage you to test a search privately before sharing it with your kids.)

Figure 9-12
Oh, Siri, you tease.

Siri Philosophy

Ever have a theology discussion with your iPhone? Apparently, Apple engineers have found that people ask their cellphones a lot of *intriguing* questions, and they have provided tactful responses.

Siri can respond to the following questions of philosophy, with a few assists from Wolfram Alpha:

- "What is the meaning of life?" (See Figure 9-13.)

Figure 9-13
Siri can be philosophical.

- "What is hell?" or "What is heaven?"
- "Do you believe in heaven?"
- "Are you self-aware?" or "Are you a god?"
- "Does God exist?"
- "What is evil?"
- "What is the purpose of existence?" (It's not quite the answer most people expect.)
- "What is the meaning of death?"
- "What is goodness?"
- "How many angels can dance on the head of a pin?"
- "What does the world need now?"

Mining the Fun in Wolfram Alpha and Wikipedia

Fun isn't limited to Siri itself. Wolfram Alpha and Wikipedia include a lot of built-in humor. Here are some statements Siri can interpret without your using the "Ask Wolfram" or "Wiki" prefix on your requests:

- "How many licks does it take to get to the center of a Tootsie Pop?"
- "Does this dress make me look fat?" (See Figure 9-14.)

Figure 9-14
Wolfram can be diplomatic.

- "Boxers or briefs?"
- "How many roads must a man walk down before you can call him a man?"
- "Who shot JR?"
- "What is the difference between a duck?" (See Figure 9-15.)

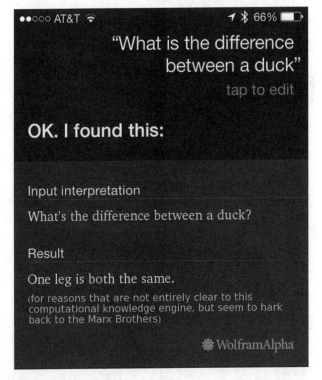

Figure 9-15
Wolfram's sense of humor skews definitively geek.

- "How long is a piece of string?"
- "How do I shot web?"

- "What's the frequency, Kenneth?" (Okay, it's not nearly as cool as you might want, but at least Siri properly accepts that as an input.)
- "What are the winning lotto numbers?"
- "What is a computational knowledge engine?"
- "Who watches the watchmen?"
- "Who lives in a pineapple under the sea?"
- "I just lost the game."
- "Is the cake a lie?" (See Figure 9-16.)

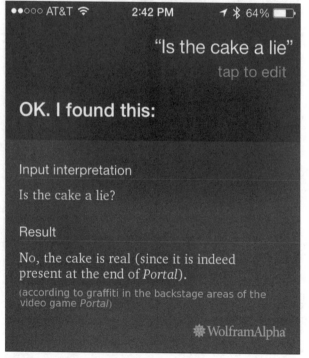

Figure 9-16

Cake and grief counseling will be available at the conclusion of the test, according to GLaDOS, who was a much less sympathetic virtual assistant than Siri is.

- "What would you do for a Klondike bar?"
- "What is a flux capacitor?"
- "What is 'How is babby formed?'?"
- "To be or not to be?
- "How many horns are on a unicorn?"
- "Who's afraid of the big bad wolf?"
- "What is dilithium?"
- "What is in the box?"
- "Why is the sky blue?"
- "Rick Roll."
- "Who shot the sheriff?"

Queries That Require Wolfram Prefixes

Each of the following items needs a little query love to ensure that Siri directs it properly to Wolfram Alpha. You can use "Wolfram," "Ask Wolfram," or "What is…" to ensure that your query is sent to Wolfram:

- "Wolfram, are we there yet?" (You can now get a Siri response to this as well by omitting "Wolfram.")
- "Wolfram, are you going to kill all humans?" (See Figure 9-17.)

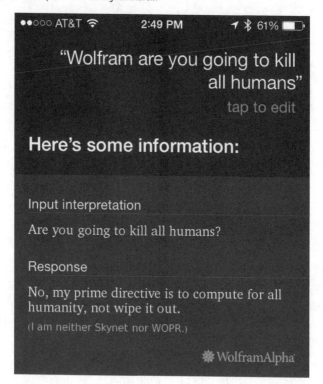

Figure 9-17
Wolfram comes in peace.

- "Wolfram, hit me!"
- "Wolfram, I know Kung Fu."
- "Wolfram, what do the knights say?"
- "Wolfram, what is your favorite color?"
- "Wolfram, where is Carmen Sandiego?"
- "Wolfram, why?"
- "Wolfram, why so serious?"

- "Wolfram, who framed Roger Rabbit?"

- "Wolfram, who is Luke's father?"

- "Wolfram, what are you going to do with all the junk?"

- "Wolfram, were the moon landings fake?"

- "Wolfram, if a tree falls in the forest, does it make a sound?"

Summary

Siri's creators knew that people would try to ask the intelligent assistant a lot of silly questions to see if they could stump it. Instead of having Siri respond with a rote answer like "I don't understand," they did an amazing job of anticipating some of these questions and crafted humorous and sometimes heartfelt responses.

That attention to detail is a hallmark of Apple products and is why Siri has become so popular in the media. Other voice-control and device-navigation systems are available, but none is as seemingly human as Siri. Hopefully you've stopped laughing enough to take away the following key points from this chapter:

- It's okay to be silly with Siri, one of iOS's best showcase features. If using its built-in humor and whimsy are useful in demonstrating those features, why not go for it? There's nothing wrong in taking pride in your device. Let Siri showcase itself and provide a little entertainment.

- Ask Siri about itself, and you'll be amazed by and amused with its responses. In many respects, Siri is a reflection of the clever design team that created and is evolving this astounding software.

- When Siri replies with a clever answer, ask again. Explore the range of responses the Apple engineers have added to certain statements to really appreciate how amusing some interactions can get.

- Siri can summarize movies from the perspective of a virtual assistant. See Chapter 6, "Going Shopping with Siri," for the hilarious details.

- Siri's connections to Wolfram Alpha, Wikipedia, and Bing provide it with a huge storehouse of pop culture references and make it your go-to mediator for arguments dealing with trivia, as well as math and science questions.

Our Top 10 Siri Jokes

Oh Siri, you jokester! In addition to being friendly, helpful, loyal, and kind, Siri can bring the sass and the laughs. Before we wrap up this book, we want to leave you with 10 of our favorite Siri wisecracks. We've picked the most amusing jokes we stumbled across while preparing this book for you. We hope you enjoy them as much as we do.

1. What the Fox Says

In 2013, "The Fox (What Does the Fox Say?)" by the Norwegian duo Ylvis took YouTube by storm. The video earned over 300 million views by the end of that year. The promotional video for this electronic dance song quickly went viral, and soon schoolchildren around the world were chanting, "Ring-ding-ding-ding-dinge-ringeding!" Siri was not far behind in catching the fox wave (see Figure 10-1).

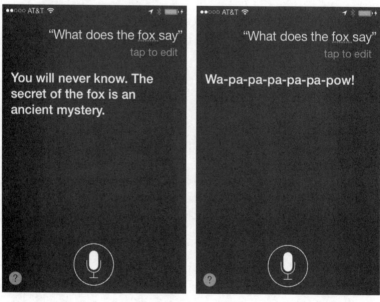

Figure 10-1
When it comes to the Fox, Siri does it Gangnam style.

2. The Konami Code

The Konami code was first used in the mid-1980s as a cheat code for video games. Its use spread across many titles, and it's become a geek meme. You may have seen it pop up in Disney's *Wreck-It Ralph*, when King Candy uses it to enter the Sugar Rush data code vault. Entering the code on some popular websites may bring up Easter eggs. Of course Siri is going to have a way to respond to something with a pedigree like that (see Figure 10-2)!

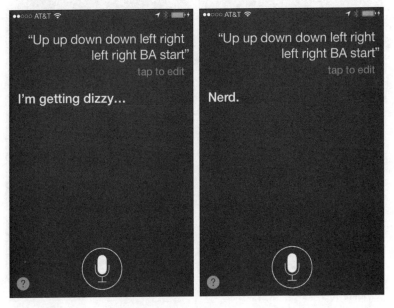

Figure 10-2
Siri recognizes your cheat codes and responds with a smile.

3. Deep Thoughts with Siri

Apple first launched the "Think Different" campaign back in 1997, when the TBWA\Chiat\Day advertising agency created the slogan. Although Apple discontinued the campaign in 2002, the catch phrase continues to form a part of Apple's DNA. It pops up in many places in both its technology and advertising—and in Siri, of course (see Figure 10-3).

Figure 10-3
Siri really is interested in what *you* are thinking about at any given time.

4. I Cannae Give Her No More

The Siri engineers show a special love for the old series *Star Trek*, with numerous *Trek*-related jokes built into the Siri database. Although the original series ended its run in the late 1960s, it still lives on in the hearts of loyal viewers, endless reboots, and Siri (see Figure 10-4).

Figure 10-4
"Dammit, I'm an iPhone, not a *Star Trek* compendium..."

5. Laws of Robotics

Isaac Asimov introduced the three laws of robotics in a 1942 short story. The laws referred to a set of rules by which robots must be programmed: namely to not harm humans, to obey orders, and to protect themselves except where doing so is in conflict with the first two laws. These rules became a theme that ran through Asimov's robot fiction and became well known not only in his books and short stories but also throughout the science fiction genre. Siri provides a rather hilarious take on this classic set of laws (see Figure 10-5).

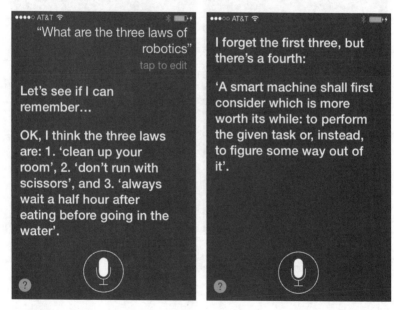

Figure 10-5
Siri knows that there's something important about obeying people and not hurting them.

6. Pets

Ask Siri whether it has a pet, and it will reach into its store of pop culture humor to answer (see Figure 10-6). Angry Birds, of course, refers to the popular video game franchise developed by Rovio Entertainment that first debuted on the iPhone. Mogwai appeared in *Gremlins*, the 1984 comedy-horror film that implored owners not to get Mogwai wet, not to expose them to bright light, and no matter how they begged or cried, not to feed them after midnight.

Figure 10-6
Siri also provides snark about Aibos, the Japanese dog robot, and Tribbles, the living balls of fluff from *Star Trek*. Because you can never have enough Tribbles, right?

7. The Lightbulb Joke

As long as there have been people and lightbulbs, there have been jokes about how many people it takes to screw in a lightbulb. Fortunately, Siri is in on the joke, although its understanding of the nuances of human behavior appears to be somewhat limited (see Figure 10-7).

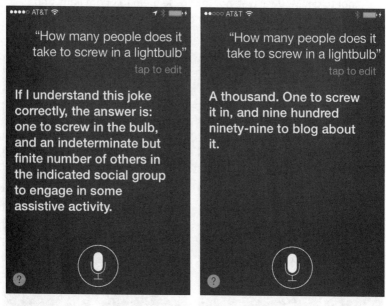

Figure 10-7
It takes only two, but then again only if they love each other *very, very much*.

8. Is That You, Mary?

Popularized in the 1964 musical *Mary Poppins*, Supercalifragilistic-expialidocious became a catchphrase for words that are difficult to learn but impressive to say. This makes it a perfect match for Siri (see Figure 10-8), especially when you're looking for "something to say when you have nothing to say." Supercalifragilisticex-pialidocious just about says it all.

Figure 10-8
Trying to say "dociousaliexpilisticfragicalirupes" is going a bit too far, wouldn't you agree?

9. Going Python

In the 1975 movie *Monty Python and the Holy Grail,* swallows and coconuts played key roles in a critical interrogation at a precipitous bridge crossing. Siri pays homage to that classic film by answering some similar questions about swallow speeds, both when carrying and not carrying coconuts (see Figure 10-9).

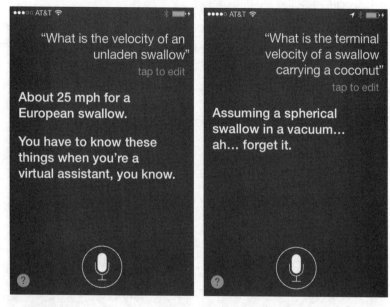

Figure 10-9
The last person who asked this question ended up in a crevasse.

10. The Meaning of Siri

So what does Siri stand for? For us, it stands for a tool that's amazingly useful for day-to-day life and imbued with warmth, humor, and delight (see Figure 10-10). We hope you've enjoyed reading this book as much as we've enjoyed writing it.

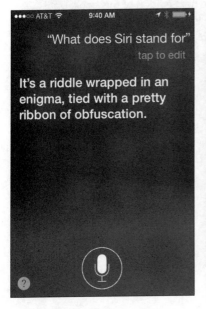
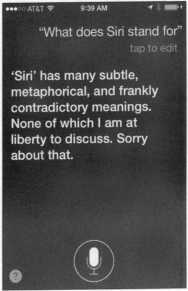

Figure 10-10
Siri stands for fun. Plain and simple.

Summary

It was a tremendously hard job for us to pare down our favorite Siri jokes to just these 10. That's because Siri is packed with wit and delight. Have you discovered a special Siri response that's tickled your funny bone? Contact us and let us know, and maybe we'll be able to include it in the next edition of this book. Until then, thank you so much for reading and we hope that you love talking to Siri as much as we do!

With best regards, Erica and Steve.

Siri Quick Reference

Now that you've learned to interact effectively with Siri by reading this book, you may find that you need a quick reminder from time to time about how to ask it how to do something.

Instead of flipping through the book, bookmark this quick reference, where you'll find many of the most important things to say to Siri. To speed your research, we've organized these by the functions you want Siri to perform.

Asking About Contacts

"What's Emily's address?"

"What is Susan Park's phone number?"

"When is my wife's birthday?"

"Show Lindsey's home email address."

"What's my brother's work address?"

Finding Contacts

"Show Brian Conway."

"Find people named Park."

"Who is Jimmy Patrick?"

Relationships

"My mom is Susan Park."

"Jimmy Patrick is my brother."

"Call my brother at work."

Pronunciation

"Learn how to pronounce my name."

"Learn how to pronounce my mom's name."

"Learn how to pronounce Siobhan Conway's name."

App Launching

"Launch Photos."

"Play Infinity Blade II."

"Open the Notes app."

"Open Facebook."

Adding Events

"Set up a meeting at 8."

"Set up a meeting with Jimmy at 10."

"Meet with Emily at noon."

"Set up a meeting about hiring tomorrow at 9 a.m."

"New appointment with Susan Park Friday at 3."

"Schedule a planning meeting at 8:30 today in the boardroom."

Changing Events

"Move my 3 p.m. meeting to 4:30."

"Reschedule my appointment with Dr. Patrick to next Monday at 9 a.m."

"Add Emily to my meeting with Brian."

"Cancel the budget review meeting."

Asking About Events

"What does the rest of my day look like?"

"What's on my calendar for Friday?"

"When is my next appointment?"

"When am I meeting with Jimmy?"

"Where is my next meeting?"

Alarm

"Wake me up tomorrow at 7 a.m."

"Set an alarm for 6:30 a.m."

"Wake me up in 8 hours."

"Change my 6:30 alarm to 6:45."

"Turn off my 6:30 alarm."

"Delete my 7:30 alarm."

"Turn off all my alarms."

Clock

"What time is it in Berlin?"

"What is today's date?"

"What's the date this Saturday?"

Timer

"Set the timer for 10 minutes and 30 seconds."

"Show the timer."

"Pause the timer."

"Resume timer."

"Reset the timer."

"Stop timer."

Sending Email

"Email Emily about the trip."

"Email Lindsey about the change in plans."

"New email to Susan Park."

"Mail Dad about the rent check."

"Email Dr. Patrick and say I got the forms, thanks."

"Mail Emily and Brian about the party and say I had a great time."

Checking Email

"Check email."

"Any new email from Jimmy today?"

"Show new mail about the lease."

"Show the email from Emily yesterday."

Responding to Email

"Reply 'Dear Susan, sorry about the late payment.'"

"Call him at work."

FaceTime

"FaceTime Brian."

"Make a FaceTime call to Susan Park."

"Make a FaceTime audio call to Craig Federighi."

Facebook

"Post to Facebook 'Headed to the new Pixar movie.'"

"Write on my Wall 'Just landed in San Jose!'"

Find My Friends

"Where's Brian?"

"Where is my sister?"

"Is my wife at home?"

"Where are all my friends?"

"Who is here?"

"Who is near me?"

"Let me know when Jimmy gets home."

"Let my wife know when I leave work."

Lock Screen Reading

"Read my notifications."

"Do I have any new messages?"

Settings

"Turn on Airplane mode."

"Is Bluetooth on?"

"Make the screen brighter."

"Turn on Bluetooth."

"Go to Twitter settings."

"Show me my privacy settings."

"Enable Wi-Fi."

"Open Mail settings."

"Turn on Do Not Disturb."

Maps

"Show me the Golden Gate Bridge."

"Show me a map of 1 Infinite Loop, Cupertino California."

Local Businesses

"Find coffee near me."

"Where's the closest Apple Store?"

"Find the best nail salon."

"Find a gas station near work."

Navigation

"How do I get home?"

"Get me directions to Yosemite."

"Directions to my dad's work."

"Get me directions from San Francisco to Santa Barbara."

"Give me walking directions to Emily's."

"What's my next turn?"

"Are we there yet?"

"What's my ETA?"

"Find a gas station."

Sending Messages

"Tell Susan I'll be right there."

"Send a message to Brian Conway."

"Send a message to Emily saying 'How about tomorrow?'"

"Tell Lindsey the show was great."

"Send a message to Susan on her mobile saying I'll be late."

"Send a message to 408-555-1212."

"Text Brian and Emily 'Where are you?'"

Reading Message Alerts

"Read my new messages."

"Read it again."

Responding to Messages

"Reply 'That's great news.'"

"Tell him I'll be there in 10 minutes."

"Call her."

Searching for Messages

"Read my last message from Emily."

Searching for Movie Information

"Find Disney movies."

"What comedies are playing?"

"Who starred in *Remember the Titans*?"

"Who directed *Finding Nemo*?"

"What is *Toy Story 3* rated?"

Finding Movie Show Times

"I want to see the new Pixar movie."

"What's playing at the movies tomorrow?"

"What's playing at Alamo Drafthouse Cinema?"

Getting Movie Tickets (U.S. Only)

"Three tickets to see *Brave*."

"Buy four tickets to see *Frozen* tonight in San Jose."

"Two tickets to *Tangled* at the City Theater at 9 p.m."

"Two tickets to that new Pixar movie."

Finding Movie Theaters

"Find some movie theaters near my office."

Reading Movie Reviews

"Show me the reviews for *Toy Story 3*."

Major Movie Awards

"Which movie won Best Picture in 1983?"

Music

"Play 'Walk' by Foo Fighters."

"Play *Little Broken Hearts* shuffled."

"Play Norah Jones."

"Play some blues."

"Play my party mix."

"Shuffle my road trip playlist."

"Play."

"Pause."

"Skip."

iTunes Radio

"Play iTunes Radio."

"Play my reggae station."

"Play my Steely Dan station."

"Play more songs like this one."

"Don't play this song again."

"I like this song."

Notes

"Note that I spent $12 on lunch."

"Note to self: Check out that new Norah Jones album."

"Find my meeting notes."

"Show me my notes from June 25."

"Add 'tour the catacombs' to my Paris vacation note."

"Read my note about book ideas."

Phone

"Call Brian."

"Call Emily's mobile."

"Call Susan on her work phone."

"Call 408 555 1212."

"Call home."

"FaceTime Emily."

"Call 911."

"Call the fire department."

"Get my call history."

"Do I have any missed calls?"

"Redial that last number."

Voicemail

"Do I have any new voicemail?"

"Play me the voicemail from Emily."

Reminders

"Add artichokes to my grocery list."

"Add skydiving to my bucket list."

"Remind me to call mom."

"Remind me to call my mom when I get home."

"Remember to take an umbrella."

"Remind me to take my medicine at 6 a.m. tomorrow."

"Remind me to pick up flowers when I leave here."

"Remind me when I leave to call Brian."

"Remind me to finish the report by 6."

"Read my work to-do list."

Searching for Restaurants

"Find a good pizza joint in Chicago."

"Good Mexican restaurants around here."

Reservations

"Table for four in Palo Alto tonight."

"Make a reservation at a romantic Italian restaurant tonight at 7 p.m."

Restaurant Reviews

"Show me the reviews for Elway's in Denver."

Scores

"Did the Giants win?"

"How did Kansas City do last night?"

"What was the score the last time the Tigers played the Red Sox?"

"Show me the football scores from last night."

"Who will win the Pittsburgh game?"

Game Schedules

"When do the Giants play next?"

"When is Kansas City's first game of the season?"

"What basketball games are on today?"

"What channel is the Red Sox game on?"

"When is England's next match?"

Standings

"Who's the best team in hockey?"

"How did the Red Sox do last season?"

"Did Pittsburgh make the playoffs?"

"What are the standings in the AFC West?"

"Get me college football rankings."

"What are the standings in the Champions League?"

Player Information

"Who has the highest slugging percentage?"

"Who has the most home runs on the Giants?"

"Which player scored the most goals in Italian soccer?"

"Which quarterback has the most passing yards?"

Team Information

"Show me the roster for the Dodgers."

"Who is pitching for the Colorado Rockies this season?"

"Is anyone on the Red Sox injured?"

"Which team has the fewest penalty minutes?"

"Which team has the most stolen bases in the NL West?"

Stocks

"What's Apple's stock price?"

"What is Apple's PE ratio?"

"What did Yahoo! close at today?"

"How is the Nikkei doing?"

"How are the markets doing?"

"Where's the NASDAQ today?"

Twitter

"Tweet 'Just watched the Giants win in extra innings.'"

"Post to Twitter 'Another beautiful day in Cupertino.'"

"Tweet with my location 'Great concert.'"

"Tweet 'Meeting up with Brian Conway for lunch today.'"

"Tweet 'The new iPad Air looks insanely great!' hashtag Apple Keynote."

Searching Twitter

"Search Twitter for Denver Broncos."

"Show me my tweets."

"What's the latest in San Francisco?"

"Find tweets with the hashtag Bay Bridge."

"What's trending on Twitter?"

"What's going on?"

"What are people saying about Beyonce?"

Facebook

"Post to Facebook 'Headed to see *The Hobbit: Desolation of Smaug*.'"

"Write on my Wall 'Went on a great hike to Longs Peak.'"

"Write on my Wall 'Just landed in Ft. Lauderdale.'"

Weather

"What's the weather for today?"

"What's the weather for tomorrow?"

"Will it rain in Cupertino this week?"

"Check next week's forecast for Denver."

"What's the forecast for this evening?"

"How's the weather in Tampa right now?"

"How hot will it be in Palm Springs this weekend?"

"What's the high for Anchorage on Thursday?"

"What's the temperature outside?"

"How windy is it out there?"

"When is sunrise in Paris?"

"What's the current moon phase?"

"What time is sunset today?"

"What time does Venus rise?"

Web Search

"Search the Web for polar bears."

"Search for vegetarian pasta recipes."

"Search the Web for best cable plans."

"Google the War of 1812."

"Find pictures of killer whales."

"Show me videos of the Northern Lights."

"What's the news for Chicago?"

"Search Wikipedia for Abraham Lincoln."

"Bing Foo Fighters."

Wolfram Alpha

"What does *repartee* mean?"

"How many calories in a bagel?"

"What is an 18 percent tip on $86.74 for four people?"

"Who's buried in Grant's tomb?"

"How long do greyhounds live?"

"What is the *Gossamer Condor*?"

"What's the square root of 128?

"How many dollars is €45?"

"How many days until Christmas?"

"How far away is the Sun?"

"When is the next solar eclipse?"

"Show me the Orion constellation."

"What's the population of Jamaica?"

"How high is Mt. Everest?"

"How deep is the Atlantic Ocean?"

"What's the price of gasoline in Chicago?"

"When was Abraham Lincoln born?"

"What's the population of San Francisco?"

"Tell me about Pixar."

Index

S

ght win their grudging agreement to some degree of arms
they expected him in return to smother SDI in its crib.

SPONSE TO GORBACHEV'S CHALLENGES surprised some
isers. He said the general secretary's presentation illustrated
ıst between their two governments. He proceeded to read
f twelve U.S. nuclear initiatives, beginning all the way back in
ed up the warheads the Soviets had added since SALT II and
two nations' arsenals were presently equal. "With righteous
Gorbachev writes sarcastically, "President Reagan tore apart
policy of deterrence, which had triggered the arms race and
the brink of destruction." Reagan claimed proudly that SDI
here had never been a weapon without a defense, he said. He
ut a shield. No one knew yet if it was possible. But if such a
e produced, it shouldn't be added to present offensive forces.
should sit down and get rid of nuclear weapons, and with
t of war. And defenses should be shared—they should be
to all.

igh-tech weapons system that would have cost the United
llions of dollars to invent was the proposal that surprised
's advisers. "We had no idea where the idea had come from,"
ıan recalled, "none of us. We thought it was wacko." Evidently
een asleep at the switch. Reagan had discussed sharing strate-
ring his second debate with the Democratic presidential can-
Mondale in Kansas City in 1984. Since Adelman, like many
eagan administration, found themselves unable to take their
ısly on questions of arms control, his lapse of memory prob-
contempt for the idea. Mondale took Reagan seriously. He
"sharply disagree[d] with the President on sharing the most
most dangerous, the most important technology in America
Union."
Geneva talked for a while about Third-World conflicts, but
to SDI. Gorbachev, trying a different tack, interrupted to ask
they should give to their negotiators. Reagan proposed that
Shultz, and their advisers work on the structures of forces
w the two superpowers to reduce their nuclear arsenals by 50
chev reminded the president that their foreign ministers
omyko) had agreed in January 1985 that there should be no

thought, overescalating the anti-SDI rhetoric. In my own frame of reference, I always had in mind the potential danger that could arise if . . . influential members of the military and industrial sectors in our own country were to involve us in a nonstop escalation of an SDI budget at that time, at the expense of the deteriorating strategic stability and our economy."

The scientists' investigation, which took the form of an extended meeting in April 1983 at the Soviet Academy of Sciences and culminated in a book, benefited from what Velikhov calls the Soviet government's previous "vaccinations" against strategic defense systems. The Soviet military had begun discussing strategic defenses in the late 1960s, Velikhov writes, when "the idea emerged of using lasers or charged-particle beams to hit warheads as they approached their targets." The scientists, led by Lev Artsimovich, quickly pointed out the futility of the scheme, however: "Compact reentry vehicles, specially designed to withstand the high temperatures of reentry from space, are hard to locate and lock on to for enough time to administer fatal doses of energy." Nor would such beams easily pass through the atmosphere. Yuli Khariton, the director of the Soviet Union's primary weapons-design laboratory, Arzamas-16, since the beginning of the Soviet nuclear-weapons program in 1946, insisted that "an honest and principled critique" be written and given to the government, "which decided to stop the program around the time the antiballistic-missile treaty was concluded in 1972."

The second vaccination came in 1980, when a Soviet engineer who designed booster rockets managed to slip a proposal to Leonid Brezhnev to create "a space-based defense using interceptor missiles"—a proposal similar to Daniel Graham's High Frontier program for battle stations in space. "Owing to the principled stand of a number of scientists and military experts," Velikhov writes with relief, "the heated debate resulted in a correct decision: The proposal was turned down."

Armed with these experiences, Velikhov and his group prepared an extended report on strategic defense in 1983 that Velikhov, Sagdeev, and Kokoshin edited and published in 1986 as a book, *Weaponry in Space: The Dilemma of Security*. The report reviewed the history and science of strategic defenses, but its essence was a careful analysis of the destabilizing consequences of an ABM-system buildup for strategic balance and of relatively inexpensive countermeasures that could foil any anticipated strategic defense. "The 'balance of terror,' " the report argued, "is a precarious balance. A really secure and peaceful world is only possible when both sides (and any other nations) have no nuclear arms. The world would be much safer if it were free of nuclear weapons and respective delivery vehicles, if all conflicts were tackled by negotiations, if economic, scientific and cultural international cooperation were improved and expanded." Nuclear abolition was a brave and radical argument to make in the Soviet Union of Yuri Andropov in 1983, the year of the Soviet war scare and ABLE ARCHER 83.

The "simpler, more effective system" that Gorbachev threatened to build to penetrate Reagan's defensive shield incorporated several of the countermeasures described in *Weaponry in Space.* "Our response to SDI will be effective," Gorbachev told Chernyaev. "The United States expects us to create analogous systems, they hope to outrun us technologically. . . . But . . . for only 10 percent of its cost we can produce a countersystem capable of nullifying SDI." Among the countersystems Gorbachev had in mind was an advanced version of a three-stage, solid-fueled mobile ICBM, the Topol-M (SS-27), with a 550-kiloton warhead with a maximum error of nine hundred meters across a range of eleven thousand kilometers (6,900 miles). The Topol-M's short engine burn time, flat ballistic trajectory that minimizes its time in space, maneuverable reentry vehicle, and advanced penetration aids, all discussed in the scientists' report, were intended to avoid or defeat antimissile attacks. Design of the advanced Topol system began in 1985, and development survived the dissolution of the Soviet Union. The Topol (silobased) and Topol-M (mobile) missile is Russia's designated primary ICBM today; by 2006, 312 had been deployed.

But if Gorbachev had a system already under design that could nullify SDI (if indeed a comprehensive system of strategic defense could ever be made to work in the first place, which is highly unlikely), why was he so determined to convince Reagan to abandon it? Or as the American physics Nobel laureate Steven Weinberg would ask later, "How could Gorbachev have been worried about something so silly?"

The answer seems to lie primarily with the Soviet military, and behind the military with the large and powerful bureaucracy of the Soviet military-industrial complex—the nine ministries overseen by the Military Industrial Commission (known by its Russian initials as the VPK) and the eight additional ministries that supported them. "Experts at the Soviet Academy of Sciences," writes the foreign correspondent Don Oberdorfer, "argued that the Star Wars program was impractical and that any partial success it might achieve could be nullified by modest countermeasures. But despite such advice and doubts about its practicality, the Soviet leaders 'could not ignore such a position' as that outlined by Reagan on March 23, [1983,] especially since it was soon to be backed up by many billions of dollars, according to Andropov's foreign policy assistant, Andrei Aleksandrov-Agentov. 'So

whether it was a practical idea or not, they
the real factor in the policy of the United St
worried about the danger that a multibilli
into strategic defense could turn up new
the VPK might well, as Sagdeev feared, tal
bachev for a larger share of the Soviet bud
and development to forestall an America
lieutenant general who directed the Natio
gan's second term, judges Gorbachev's pri
of reform within the Soviet government to

A surprisingly broad consensus existed amo
Soviet economy was in serious trouble and
ditures was much to blame. To reduce it, C
through arms control. That was impossible,
change in the Soviet Union's relationship
world and foreign communist parties.

To set a new course in military policy
cally began by changing Soviet foreign po
relations with Western political leaders co
serious. Soviet negotiators returned to Ge
vardnadze's determined guidance, they sur
changes in traditional Soviet positions.

"Disarmament through arms control
the Soviet economy and improving the qu
meant major reductions in the Soviet
Odom continues, "could free manpower
force, but it would not save significant n
tary pay was abysmally low—five or six
very large part of the military budget wer
ization of weaponry." (Which was how, f
to replace its old first-generation liquid-f
modern solid-fueled SS-20s, and why it
models than the United States.) "The key
bachev confronted more than the unifor
game. Somewhere between 20 and 40 pe
up in military production. The issue of
bachev and his allies against this large an
as well as against the conservative eleme

ership." H
reduction,

REAGAN'S
of his own
the lack o
through a
1946. He c
denied that
indignatio
the Americ
led mankin
was his ide
was talking
weapon cou
The two si
them the t
made availa

Sharing
States many
some of Rea
Kenneth Ad
Adelman ha
gic defenses
didate Walte
others in the
president se
ably reflects
rejoined that
advanced, th
with the Sov

Reagan in
soon returne
what directio
Shevardnadz
that would a
percent. Gor
(Shultz and

arms race in space. ("If the USA agreed to negotiate a total prohibition of offensive space weapons," Gorbachev had declared at a secret Warsaw Treaty summit in Moscow in April, "the road to radical reductions in the number of strategic assault weapons would be opened" and both sides could "reciprocally rid Europe of both intermediate-range and tactical nuclear weapons altogether." He had also announced the unilateral suspension of deployment of SS-20s and other missiles "until November 1985.") What about that goal? he asked Reagan, his voice rising.

Reagan said a defensive shield wouldn't be an arms race in space. It would be a way to eliminate weapons. He told a story. "Our U.N. ambassador, Vernon Walters, was asked what happens when a man with a spear that can penetrate anything meets a man with a shield that's impenetrable. Walters said he didn't know, but he did know what happens when a man with no shield meets a man who has a spear." Neither of us wants to be in that situation, Reagan told Gorbachev. If the technology is developed, he said again, it should be shared.

"Ronald Reagan's advocacy of the Strategic Defense Initiative struck me as bizarre," Gorbachev wrote of this debate. "Was it science fiction, a trick to make the Soviet Union more forthcoming, or merely a crude attempt to lull us in order to carry out the mad enterprise—the creation of a shield which would allow a first strike without fear of retaliation?" It was all those things, though not for Reagan. For Reagan it was a hubristic dream, a hope, a fantasy that American technological ingenuity could finesse a dangerous dilemma without resort to negotiation or compromise. Like the nuclear-arms race itself, it derived from a fundamental misunderstanding of the new knowledge that science had revealed to the world, knowledge of how to release energies millions of times greater than those released in chemical explosions.

" 'It looks like a dead end,' " Gorbachev remembers saying then. "An uneasy silence fell upon the room," he wrote. "The pause was becoming oppressive.

" 'How about taking a walk?' " the American president suddenly asked.

" 'That seems like a good idea to me,' " Gorbachev replied.

THE BREAK AND THE WALK had been planned; the two leaders, accompanied by their interpreters, were supposed to walk from the main château across a courtyard to the Fleur d'Eau pool house, where a small side room with a fireplace had been prepared where they could hold another tête-à-tête. Rather than try to negotiate as they walked, they talked about Reagan's movies. At a press conference earlier in the summit, a journalist had asked Georgi Arbatov if Gorbachev had seen any of the films the president had made. Arbatov had said he didn't know, adding gratuitously, "and besides . . . those were B movies." On their walk to the pool house Reagan asked Gorbachev to enlighten his foreign policy adviser; he had made not only B movies but also a few good ones. Gorbachev diplomatically volunteered the information that he had recently watched *Kings' Row* and had liked it very much. *Kings' Row* was based on a lurid novel drawn from turn-of-the-century life in Fulton, Missouri, where Winston Churchill would later deliver his "Iron Curtain" address—small world. Reagan plays a genial rake who is bruised in an encounter with a train, after which a sadistic Kings' Row doctor who disapproves of his behavior saws off both his legs. When "Drake McHugh" wakes from the anesthesia and discovers his amputations he cries out to his girlfriend, Ann Sheridan, "Where's the *rest* of me?" Curiously, Reagan would choose the line for the title of his 1965 as-told-to autobiography, a book that served to announce his entry into politics.

"The walk," Gorbachev remembers, "the change of scene, the crackling of burning wood—all these helped to alleviate the tension. But as soon as we sat down, Reagan rushed back to his old tactics. Seemingly anxious that I might take up SDI again—this time 'one on one'—he decided to anticipate my move by taking out a list of arms control proposals and handing them to me." There were nine proposals on Reagan's list, which he presented to Gorbachev in both English and Russian versions. The general secretary took the time to read through the list before responding, qualified his responses as preliminary, pointed to the first proposal for 50 percent reductions in strategic offensive weapons, and noted that Shultz and Gromyko's agreement in January to find a way to avoid an arms race in space—linked to that reduction—seemed to have evaporated.

So they would debate SDI that afternoon regardless. SDI was a defensive system, Reagan reiterated, and anyway, the two sides would share it. But why do you need it? Gorbachev countered. The Soviet Union had declared for all the world to hear that it would not be the first to use nuclear weapons, he said. Shouldn't that be enough? But it seemed the United States did not believe him. Then why should he believe the president's statement about sharing the results of research into strategic defense? Why should he believe that the United States would not take advantage of having deployed such a defense?

They could negotiate and sign an agreement, Reagan countered, forgetting or choosing not to mention his belief that treaties were a trap. Gorbachev responded passionately, with an intensity that even comes through the formality of the translator's notes:

> With some emotion Gorbachev appealed to the President as follows: if the two sides were indeed searching for a way to halt the arms race and to begin to deal seriously with disarmament, then what would be the purpose of deploying a weapon that is as yet unknown and unpredictable? Where was the logic of starting an arms race in a new sphere? It must clearly be understood that verification of such weapons would be totally unreliable because of their maneuverability and mobility even if they were classified as defensive. People would not be in a position to determine what it was that would be placed into space and would surely regard it as an additional threat, thereby creating crisis situations. If the goal was to get rid of nuclear weapons, why start an arms race in another sphere?

But these weren't weapons that would kill people or destroy cities, Reagan replied stubbornly. These were weapons that would destroy nuclear missiles. And then a significant concession, never to be heard of again: If they could agree that there would be no need for nuclear missiles, the president offered, then there might also be no need for defenses against them. Why did Gorbachev keep on speaking of space weapons, the president asked. He certainly had no intention of putting something into space that would threaten people on Earth. In 1925 in this city, Geneva, he said, all the countries that had participated in the First World War had met and agreed not to use poison gas again in war. But they had all kept their gas masks. What he was saying now was that they should go forward to rid the world of the threat of nuclear weapons, but at the same time retain something like that gas mask—a shield that would protect their countries should there be an unforeseeable return to nuclear missiles. They were not alone in the world. There were others such as Gadhafi and people of that kind who were not at all against dropping a nuclear bomb on the White House. Both their countries should conduct the relevant research and both should share the results; if one country produced a defensive shield before the other, it would make it available to all.

They should rejoin the plenary session, Reagan said, but before they did so, he had to tell Gorbachev that the people overwhelmingly wanted this defense. They look at the sky and think what might happen if missiles suddenly appear and blow up everything in our country. We believe that the idea of having a defense against nuclear missiles involved a great deal of faith and belief. And when he said we, he meant most of mankind.

Exasperated, Gorbachev pointed out that missiles were not yet flying, and whether or not they would fly would depend on how he and the president conducted their respective policies. But he calmed down enough to appeal to Reagan to recognize that the Soviet Union did indeed wish to establish a new relationship with the United States and to deliver their two nations from the increasing fear of nuclear weapons. He hoped, he said, that Reagan would not regard this wish as a sign of weakness on his part or on the part of the Soviet leadership.

"We were going around in circles," Gorbachev writes. "The fire was burning and the room was warm and cozy, but the conversation had not improved the general mood. We went outside again and I suddenly felt very cold—maybe in contrast to the warmth by the fireside or to our heated discussion. At that point, the President unexpectedly invited me to visit the United States, and I reciprocated by inviting him to Moscow." Thus, effortlessly, Reagan had accomplished his advisers' primary goal for the summit, which was to open the way to further meetings down the road.

They went around in circles again the next day, meeting at the Soviet Embassy, repeating the same arguments. Yet gradually the two men connected. "The day was difficult," Gorbachev told Chernyaev afterward, "but something very important happened in both of us. I think two factors were at work: responsibility and intuition, which as it turns out, Reagan possesses to a very high degree. Imperceptibly the human factor began to work. Some sense told each of us to continue talking and somewhere in the depth of our minds the hope was born to come to an understanding." An even deeper change came to Gorbachev, Chernyaev saw, a shrugging off of the accumulated weight of dogma: "For a Soviet leader, for Gorbachev, for the first time he got the sense that there is something deeply wrong in our general evaluation of the American administration and American life, that our class analysis is failing and does not give us an answer that would provide a good basis for any kind of realistic politics."

Reagan's evident sincerity influenced Gorbachev's change of heart. Shultz noticed: "We had a dramatic session . . . with Gorbachev on the second day. . . . Gorbachev out of the clear blue sky started this attack on SDI. When he got through, Reagan just gave a deep, well-thought-out but very emotional [response]. . . . Gorbachev finally said, 'Well, Mr. President, I don't agree with you, but I can see that you really mean it.' " Most of all, Gorbachev apparently realized that Reagan no more intended to use nuclear weapons than he did. Both men, each in his own way, were scouting a path out of the Minotaur's lair.

It took their advisers until two in the morning to put together a joint communiqué, and even then the two leaders had to knock heads to finish the work. Gorbachev rightly calls the communiqué a "truly historic document," because it incorporated Reagan's mantra about nuclear war:

> The sides, having discussed key security issues, and conscious of the special responsibility of the U.S.S.R. and the U.S. for maintaining peace, have agreed that a nuclear war cannot be won and must never be fought. Recognizing that any conflict between the U.S.S.R. and the U.S. could have catastrophic consequences, they emphasized the importance of preventing any war between them, whether nuclear or conventional. They will not seek to achieve military superiority.
>
> The President and the General Secretary discussed the negotiations on nuclear and space arms [then under way separately in Geneva].
>
> They agreed to accelerate the work at these negotiations, with a view to accomplishing the tasks set down in the Joint U.S.-Soviet Agreement of January 8, 1985, namely to prevent an arms race in space and terminate it on earth, to limit and reduce nuclear arms and enhance strategic stability.

However expectantly the two leaders left the old Swiss city by the lake, SDI still divided them. During the shouting match on the second day of the summit, Gorbachev had a glimpse of how deeply Reagan cherished his dream of spreading his arms to protect the world from its own encapsulated violence. He didn't know, Reagan had said, whether or not the general secretary believed in reincarnation, but for himself, he wondered if perhaps, in a previous life, he had been the inventor of the shield.

MIKHAIL GORBACHEV RETURNED TO MOSCOW from Geneva with mixed feelings about Ronald Reagan. When Gorbachev told his colleagues he had met "a caveman—a dinosaur," he was referring to Reagan's "primitive" anti-Communism, the president's pedantic conviction that Soviet leaders were slaves to Marxist dogma. (Accordingly, Reagan had been surprised at Geneva to find that "not once during our private sessions or at the plenary meetings did [Gorbachev] express support for the old Marxist-Leninist goal of a one-world Communist state," and intrigued with Gorbachev's frequent references to God.) According to the historian Vladislav Zubok, a Geneva participant noticed that "Gorbachev . . . was bothered by a huge chasm between the United States and Soviet positions, perceptions and logic. He said in a narrow circle: 'What is this President doing? He would be a good *dacha* neighbor, but as a political partner he leaves a dismal impression.' "

Despite Reagan's seeming limitations, Gorbachev concluded that the American president was someone he could work with. When the two of them concurred publicly that "nuclear war cannot be won and must never be fought," the Soviet leader writes, it "made meaningless the arms race and the stockpiling and modernizing of nuclear weapons." Gorbachev "decided that Reagan meant what he said at Geneva," concluded Arthur Hartman, the U.S. ambassador to the Soviet Union: Reagan "did want to rid the world of nuclear weapons, and he was deadly serious about SDI." Gorbachev's idea thereafter, Hartman speculated, "was to persuade Reagan to take the one without the other. He seems to have decided at Geneva that he could bring it off."

Reagan, for his part, wrote Gorbachev in late November confirming his mutual feeling that the two of them had been serious about eliminating nuclear weapons. "Obviously there are many things on which we disagree," Reagan wrote, "and we disagree very fundamentally. But if I understand you correctly, you, too, are determined to take steps to see that our nations manage their relationship in a peaceful fashion. If this is the case, then this is one point on which we are in total agreement—and it is after all the most fundamental one of all." A few days later, on 5 December 1985, a letter arrived from Gorbachev that had crossed in the mail, as it were, proposing that the United States join the Soviet Union in the voluntary moratorium on nuclear weapons tests it had introduced on 6 August of that year, which was due to expire at the end of the year unless the United States also canceled testing. Gorbachev's invitation was not without guile: If the United States gave up nuclear testing, then it would also forego developing space weapons powered by nuclear explosions, because any such new designs would have to be tested. On the other hand, if Reagan was serious about nuclear abolition, why would he need further nuclear weapons tests? (Gorbachev's letter and later appeals went unanswered, and after extending his self-imposed moratorium twice in the first six months of 1986, he reluctantly allowed Soviet nuclear weapons tests to resume.) At Christmastime Gorbachev responded at length to Reagan's late November letter, once again arguing that SDI would lead to the development of first-strike and space weapons, a new and less stable arms race in space. By then Yevgeny Velikhov and Roald Sagdeev had joined his circle of advisers; it was they who particularly encouraged him to continue the voluntary testing moratorium.

Despite these disagreements, Gorbachev resolved to move as rapidly as possible toward breakthrough arms negotiations, Nikolai Detinov remembers. "Gorbachev told the Ministry of Defense and all other ministries to start preparing a proposal about solving the issues that remained unresolved." Anatoly Chernyaev noted in his contemporary diary his "impression that [Gorbachev had] really decided to end the arms race no matter what. He is taking this 'risk' because as he understands it, it's no risk at all, because nobody would attack us even if we disarmed completely. And in order to get the country out on solid ground, we have to relieve it of the burden of the arms race, which is a drain on more than just the economy." Later, in their personal conversations, Gorbachev would tell Chernyaev more than once, "I feel that it is our fault that this arms race is still going on."

When Soviet arms negotiators returned to Moscow for their Christmas vacations, Gorbachev summoned them one by one to his Kremlin office for private talks. Ambassador Oleg Grinevsky, who headed the Soviet delegation to the Stockholm-based Conference on Security and Cooperation in Europe (CSCE), remembers Gorbachev encouraging him, " 'It's just the two of us, there's no one listening, don't be afraid to tell me the truth, I want to know only the truth. What's happening at your talks? Is there a possibility of progress and what needs to be done for that?' " He asked everyone the same questions, Grinevsky recalls, and then "literally the next day, he assembled all of us . . . and said, 'Now say what you told me—[but] openly, at the Politburo.' For everyone this was a shock. . . ." The new proposals Gorbachev would shortly offer the United States originated in these reluctant testimonies, but with a twist, Grinevsky reports:

> As a result of this Politburo discussion, which I think was on the 30th of December, the decision was taken to come out with a specific realistic program of disarmament and of policies to decrease tension in the international arena. . . . It included three components: 1) fifty percent reductions in strategic offensive armaments; 2) zero on intermediate- and medium-range missiles [i.e., the United States's zero option for SS-20s and Pershing 2s in Europe]; and 3) solving the issues of the Stockholm conference, in other words, European security. . . . Right from the beginning we ran into enormous resistance from the military. They were supported by the KGB. Basically, they were saying that "we cannot do this, neither fifty percent reduction, nor zero level. It would undermine the basis for the security of the Soviet Union."

The twist came during a meeting of a group of Politburo arms-negotiation experts, the so-called small group of five, that reported to the Big Five commission that supervised such negotiations (representatives of the foreign ministry, the defense ministry, the KGB, the VPK, and the Academy of Sciences). The three-part proposal Grinevsky describes was on the table and up for discussion, and they had begun a long argument about it:

> Suddenly, at the height of this argument, the door opened and Marshal [Sergei] Akhromeyev entered—I wouldn't say he entered, he flew in. He was a very thin, very agile man, he literally flew into the room. I remember General [Valentin] Varennikov said, "Comrade officers, stand up." We started to look at each other, wondering whether to stand or not to stand up, we were confused, not all of us were in the military. Marshall Akhromeyev said, "Forget your program, forget it. General [Nikolai] Chervov just came back from Crimea where Mikhail Sergeyevich Gorbachev was vacationing. I have to tell you an enormous secret. *The general staff, in great secrecy, has been developing a program of liquidating all nuclear arms.* Even members of the delegation, even the military general staff and general cabinet people did not know about it. They are not aware of this secret program, and now finally the program is ready. General Chervov went south to present it to Mikhail Sergeyevich Gorbachev. Gorbachev approved it, so therefore forget your fifty percent reduction of strategic armaments, forget the zero level on medium range missiles. Here is the new agenda and it covers everything."

"We immediately thought that this was all phony," Grinevsky remembers; the small group knew every program developer in the military and knew that none of them had been working on anything so grand. Caucusing in the hallway, Grinevsky and his foreign ministry colleagues agreed that the West would consider such a program propaganda, smacking as it did of the cynical proposals for general and complete disarmament that Khrushchev used to proclaim to stall arms negotiations to lesser ends. To salvage something they decided to recommend including their agenda—50 percent reductions, the zero option, negotiations on conventional forces—in the military's new proposal as stage one. "We pushed it with great difficulties," he recalls, "but we managed to have them accept this as the first stage of their program."

By endorsing a phony but seemingly responsive program, the Soviet military leadership thought it was putting one over on the general secretary. They should have known better. Gorbachev and Shevardnadze had "agreed on the necessity for such a step," Gorbachev wrote, "during a conversation we had soon after his appointment as Foreign Minister"—that is, more than six months earlier. "By the autumn we had made a start—a scientific analysis of the international situation, contacts and meetings we had had in the past months. It was then that we decided to formulate our ideas and intentions in a long-term agenda which would serve as a basis for our 'peace offensive.' "

In the meantime, independently, the military had seized upon a cynical public-relations gambit cobbled together by two specialists on the United States within the foreign ministry and decided to explore its possibilities as a diversion. Sergei Tarasenko and one of his deputies had devised the nuclear-disarmament proposal on their own initiative in April 1985, shortly after Gorbachev took office, expecting that he, like his predecessors, would want something harmless but appropriately spectacular to announce to the world on 9 May 1985, the fortieth anniversary of the Soviet victory over Germany and the end of the Second World War in Europe. "It took us about half a day," Tarasenko concedes. ". . . It was put together based on fairly cynical ideas." He passed it to his boss, who liked it. Then, he says, "the paper vanished." In midsummer, the anniversary having passed, he asked about the proposal. His boss told him, " 'Forget that paper, it does not exist. It's been given away, you've never heard about it.' " Then suddenly, at the end of December, rumors of talk about "a world without nuclear arms" began to circulate through the ministry corridors. "We knew that according to the political order we were small fish—God forbid we should find ourselves under the wheel of history. We kept very quiet about what we had done." What happened, Tarasenko surmises, was that First Deputy Foreign Minister

Georgy Kornienko "talked Akhromeyev into believing that this was not a threatening thing . . . that there would be no immediate disarmament consequences, but as propaganda it sounded good, a nice honorable initiative, and one could get some points for it. I don't know if it went exactly that way, but evidently the proposal did go through Akhromeyev to the military, and the military presented it as their own proposal."

"This was not an 'improvisation,' " on the military's behalf, William Odom confirms, quoting Detinov, "but rather a well-considered tactic, one that made the military look 'eager' to eliminate nuclear weapons while assuring that it 'could hardly lead to any practical results in the foreseeable future.' " The reason the military felt it needed to introduce a diversionary dead end, Odom adds, was that "Gorbachev was building negotiating momentum that would derail some major weapons programs."

Phony or not, the proposal had to look authoritative if it was to be presented to the general secretary as a serious military initiative. Major General Vladimir Slipchenko of the Soviet general staff was one of those who participated in the evaluation process in spring 1985:

> It was very interesting work. Marshall Akhromeyev demanded right away, very urgently, to take the best scientists from the Ministry of Defense. He took twelve people, three people from the strategic missile forces, three people from the navy, three people from the nuclear forces and three people from the general staff. I was in the group from the general staff. . . . We had to solve this task in one month. . . . We were taken to one of the houses of the Ministry of Defense . . . but there was a lot of pressure on us and we were actually asked to present our product in two weeks. . . .
>
> What were we doing? . . . In front of us we had the basic starting point that the Soviet Union would completely abolish its nuclear weapons and we needed to evaluate what would happen in this situation. What other countries would still keep nuclear arms? Who is not going to agree to a one-sided or even multi-sided agreement of liquidation of nuclear arms? . . . The period we were looking at was up to the year 2000. . . .
>
> We produced the information. . . . I think that we might not have completed everything that we had to, but the conclusions that we did make were very shocking for us at that time.
>
> We concluded that there was not one nuclear state which could adequately protect itself through the use of its nuclear arsenal. . . .
>
> The second conclusion was that it is necessary to think about the security of all states, including that of our enemy, in order to ensure our security. So you cannot really use nuclear arms just to protect yourself, you have to consider the safety and security of your potential enemies. . . . We came to the conclusion that we had to start thinking about the inevitability of peaceful coexistence.

Another conclusion was that we had to try to manage all of the existing conflicts on the globe and do everything necessary such that conflicts would never
arise again.

Ordered to evaluate seriously a proposal for nuclear abolition, Akhromeyev's tough military experts discovered themselves to be naked to their
enemies and independently rediscovered the idea of common security. No
wonder they were shocked.

FOR GORBACHEV, the military's cynical proposal for nuclear disarmament
was a godsend: protective cover for his plans. "He promptly put it to the Big
Five," Odom wrote, "who found problems with this 'Gorbachev initiative,' as
it was known thereafter. At Gorbachev's request, [Lev] Zaikov [a Gorbachev
appointee to the Big Five] refereed the dispute in the Big Five between the
[Ministry of Defense] and [Ministry of Foreign Affairs], then submitted the
initiative to the Politburo, where it was quickly endorsed." Asked in retirement if he had encountered much resistance to it, Gorbachev answered,
"Not to the idea, not to the statement. But I must admit that most of the military men thought this was just another propaganda bluff, another deception." In Gorbachev's hands it would be much more. Detinov cites two
important uses to which Gorbachev would put the proposal:

In and of itself, [it] played a great role in developing the Soviet position at the
[arms-control] talks. First of all, it demonstrated to the whole world what path
needs to be taken in order to achieve peace on earth—you need general nuclear
disarmament. It was a great propaganda slogan. It was an idea to play against
Reagan's statement that safety can be found in new kinds of armaments, in
deploying weapons in outer space and creating an anti-missile system. No, we
said, this was an incorrect path, the better solution lies in the total liquidation
of nuclear armaments.

Secondly, this document gave Gorbachev an opportunity to feel more sure
of himself in the future. Once you have a document in your pocket approved
by the Politburo about the total destruction, down to zero, of all nuclear armaments, then you are justified in continuing in this policy direction. It is easier to
speak to the military on those issues once you have such a document.

Thus armed, Gorbachev moved quickly. He wanted to maintain the
momentum of the Geneva summit, such as it was, but he was even more
concerned to broadcast his proposals to the world—and receive its
responses—before the 27th Congress of the Communist Party of the Soviet

Union, forthcoming in February, a meeting that would determine the next Soviet Five-Year Plan; missing that deadline could delay his reforms until 1991. Boris Yeltsin, whom Gorbachev had appointed to the Politburo two days before Christmas, admired the general secretary's maneuvering. "The chief problem of Gorbachev's launching of perestroika," Yeltsin would tell Gorbachev's biographer Archie Brown, "was that he was practically alone, surrounded by the authors and impresarios of Brezhnev's 'era of stagnation,' who were determined to ensure the indestructibility of the old order of things. . . . At that all-important initial moment of his reforming initiative, he operated with amazing finesse. In no way did he frighten the old mafia of the Party apparat, which retained its power for a long time and which, if necessary, might have eaten any general secretary alive without so much as a hiccup."

On 15 January 1986, Gorbachev sent a letter to Reagan outlining his new initiative. Simultaneously he released the text in Moscow, where it was carried in *Pravda* and *Izvestia* and read by announcers on Tass's English-language news and in a Moscow Television Service newscast. It began with a challenge:

[The Soviet Union proposes] a concrete program, calculated for a precisely determined period of time, for the complete liquidation of nuclear weapons throughout the world . . . within the next fifteen years, before the end of the present century. . . .

FIRST STAGE. Over a period of 5–8 years the Soviet Union and the United States will halve the nuclear arms which can reach each other's territory. No more than 6,000 charges [i.e., bombs or warheads] will be retained on the [remaining] delivery vehicles. . . .

It goes without saying that such a reduction is possible only given the mutual renunciation . . . of the development, testing and deployment of space-strike arms. As the Soviet Union has warned repeatedly, the development of space-strike weapons will cancel hopes for the reduction of nuclear arms on earth.

That much had already been debated inconclusively at Geneva. Gorbachev went further, picking up Richard Perle's supposedly unnegotiable zero option without demanding that the regional nuclear powers do more than freeze their arsenals, but also requiring the two superpowers to stop testing:

The first stage will see the reaching and implementation of a decision on the complete liquidation of Soviet and U.S. medium-range missiles in the European zone—both ballistic and cruise missiles—as a first stage on the path to freeing the European Continent of nuclear weapons.

Here the United States must adopt a pledge not to supply its strategic missiles and medium-range missiles to other countries; Britain and France must adopt a pledge not to build up their own corresponding nuclear arms.

Right from the start it is necessary for the Soviet Union and the United States to agree to ending any nuclear [weapons tests] and to call on other states to join in this moratorium as swiftly as possible.

The second stage, Gorbachev continued, would begin no later than 1990 and would last five to seven years. The Soviet Union and the United States would freeze their tactical nuclear weapons and eliminate medium-range nuclear arms while continuing to reduce their strategic weapons. The other nuclear powers would begin nuclear disarmament during this stage, first pledging to freeze numbers and bring the weapons home, then, after the superpowers reached 50 percent reductions, joining them in eliminating tactical nuclear weapons and in banning "space strike arms." All nuclear powers would end nuclear weapons tests.

Finally, during the third stage, beginning no later than 1995, all remaining nuclear arms would be eliminated. "By the end of 1999 no nuclear weapons will be left on earth. A universal accord on ensuring that these weapons are never revived will be elaborated." Another breakthrough that Gorbachev offered at this stage was on-site inspection and verification as well as inspection by "national technical means," meaning satellite intelligence. As a closed society, the U.S.S.R. had long resisted admitting foreign inspectors onto its territory, rejecting them as spies. Offering to abandon that resistance was one more illumination that followed from Gorbachev's policy of glasnost.

Gorbachev knew that the Soviet Union's large stocks of chemical weapons and its purportedly massive advantage in conventional forces in Europe were standard justifications U.S. conservatives used to reject Soviet nuclear-arms-control proposals. In fact, of course, the United States had large stocks of chemical weapons as well, which could quickly be deployed to Europe, and the discrepancy in numbers between Warsaw Pact and NATO forces was illusory. "Actual troop levels on the two sides were not so radically different," writes the IISS research fellow Dana Allin. "In 1985 on the central front (Denmark, the Benelux countries, Germany, Poland and Czechoslovakia), the Warsaw Pact fielded roughly 975,000 troops against NATO's 814,300—a 1.2 to 1 ratio. Overall in Europe, the ratio was about the same, while globally the two alliances had roughly an equal number under arms as well. The Soviets *did* have a large advantage in main battle tanks (16,620 to NATO's 8,050).

NATO had a qualitative superiority in airpower, while the numbers were roughly balanced." The Soviets fielded so many tanks in Europe, according to V. V. Shlykov, a Soviet military intelligence (GRU) department chief, because they expected the majority of them to be destroyed by NATO antitank forces in the early days of a war, and knew that their industry was not capable of replacing them as rapidly as they believed the U.S. industry to be. "It wasn't because we wanted to lunge at Europe," Shlykov told two Western economists studying the collapse of the Soviet economic system in the mid-1990s. He added: "For the very same reason, we accumulated 45,000 nuclear warheads, which is a lot more than all the Western countries combined. This crazy story is still waiting to be told."

None of these numbers mattered if neither side was planning to start a war, but rather than continue to give U.S. conservatives reasons to reject his initiatives, Gorbachev added proposals to eliminate chemical weapons entirely before the end of the century and to negotiate reductions in conventional arms and armed forces. He argued once more, fervently, the folly of SDI:

> Thus, we propose entering the third millennium without nuclear weapons on the basis of mutually acceptable and strictly verified accords. If the U.S. Administration—as it has repeatedly stated—is committed to the goal of completely eliminating nuclear weapons everywhere, it is being given a practical opportunity to actually do just that. Instead of spending the next 10–15 years creating new weapons in space, which are extremely dangerous for mankind and are allegedly intended to make nuclear arms unnecessary, is it not more sensible to tackle the destruction of these arms themselves—and ultimately reduce them to zero? The Soviet Union, I repeat, proposes precisely this course.

Gorbachev once more invoked the Palme Commission's idea of common security, emphasizing that the problem of nuclear weapons "is a problem of importance to all mankind; it can and must be resolved jointly. And the faster the program is translated into the language of practical action, the more secure life on our planet will be." In conclusion, he connected the nuclear-arms race to other large challenges the world faced:

> Our new proposals are addressed to the entire world. The switch to active steps to stop the arms race and reduce arms is also a necessary prerequisite for resolving overwhelming global problems: the destruction of man's environment, the need to find new sources of energy and the struggle against economic backwardness, hunger and disaster.
>
> The principle of armament instead of development imposed by militarism

must be replaced by the reverse order of things—disarmament for development. The noose of the trillion-dollar debt which is now strangling dozens of countries and entire continents is a direct consequence of the arms race. . . .

We want . . . to complete the 20th century under the sign of peace and nuclear disarmament. The package of new foreign policy initiatives proposed by us is designed to ensure that mankind greets the year 2000 beneath peaceful skies and space, that it does not fear a nuclear, chemical or any other threat of destruction and is firmly confident of its own survival and the continuation of the human race.

Many of the proposals that Gorbachev presented to the Reagan administration and the world on 15 January 1986 matched and sometimes even advanced beyond those developed in the Palme Commission report, which prefaced its parallel "program of action . . . based on the principle of common security" with a caution Gorbachev clearly heeded: "In the nuclear age, states cannot achieve security through competition in arms. They must cooperate to attain the limitation, reduction and eventual abolition of arms."

Chernyaev judges "the very beginning of 1986" to be the exact time "when Gorbachev placed his stake on a direct dialogue with the American leadership." That is, Gorbachev intended his offer to end the nuclear arms race to win him the international support and prestige he needed to discredit what Yeltsin called "the old mafia of the Party apparat" and turn his country away from militarism. "Disarmament for development," he hoped, would begin at home.

RONALD REAGAN, AT LEAST, received Gorbachev's letter with enthusiasm. "Gorbachev surprisingly is calling for an arms reduction plan which will rid the world of nuclear weapons by the year 2000," the president wrote in his diary that day. "Of course, he has a couple of zingers in there which we'll have to work around. But at the very least it is a h—l of a propaganda move. We'd be hard put to explain how we could turn it down." When George Shultz learned that Gorbachev would publicly announce his initiative that day, he called in Paul Nitze to draft a statement that Reagan could release to the press. Richard Perle, hearing from Nitze that the statement would welcome Gorbachev's initiative, worked on Caspar Weinberger to call Reagan to complain, hoping to beat the State Department to the draw: "Secretary Weinberger had called [the president] with his usual angst," Nitze confirmed dryly, "after Richard Perle had reported to him what we were proposing."

In the Oval Office that afternoon, Shultz succeeded in convincing the president to ignore Weinberger's reservations, which may not have been difficult to do; Reagan's first enthusiastic response to Gorbachev's initiative, Nitze reports, was, "Why wait until the year 2000 to eliminate all nuclear weapons?" The White House had already released a statement noting the opening in Geneva the next day of the fourth round of the nuclear and space arms talks. The statement released that afternoon cited Reagan's many previous calls for nuclear abolition, welcomed "the Soviets' latest response," and promised to "give careful study to General Secretary Gorbachev's suggestions." A further statement released the next morning, 16 January 1986, made a point of agreeing with Gorbachev about the malevolence of "space-strike arms" while exempting Reagan's benevolent "strategic defenses."

No one within the Reagan administration whose opinion counted shared the president's enthusiasm for nuclear abolition. The dismissive judgment that day in January and for long after was that Gorbachev's proposal was nothing more than crude Soviet propaganda. Reagan found it interesting that for the first time a Soviet leader had actually set a target date for nuclear disarmament. Unlike his advisers, the president was prepared to put Gorbachev's intentions to the test, as he wrote in his diary in early February after a meeting of the national security planning group, the NSPG, which included, among others, Shultz, Weinberger, William Casey, and Reagan's latest national security adviser, John Poindexter:

> NSPG time in the situation room re Gorbachev's proposal to eliminate nuclear arms. Some wanted to tag it a publicity stunt. I said no. Let's say we share their overall goals and now want to work out the details. If it is a publicity stunt this will be revealed by them. I also propose that we announce we are going forward with SDI but if research reveals a defense against missiles is possible, we'll work out how it can be used to protect the whole world not just us.

Shultz encountered even more naked resistance, which he gleefully exposes in his memoirs. "The naysayers were hard at work," he writes:

> No one could accept the thought of a world moving toward the elimination of nuclear weapons. Richard Perle declared . . . in mid-January that the president's dream of a world without nuclear weapons—which Gorbachev had picked up—was a disaster, a total delusion. Perle said the [National Security Council] should not meet on the idea, because then the president would direct his arms controllers to come up with a program to achieve that result. The Joint Chiefs' representatives agreed with Perle. They feared the institutionalization and acceptance of the idea as our policy.

Shultz disagreed, and more to the point, so did the president. "He thinks it's a hell of a good idea," Shultz told the State Department arms-control group. "And it's a political hot button. We need to work out what a world without nuclear weapons would mean to us and what additional steps would have to accompany such a dramatic change. The president has wanted all along to get rid of nuclear weapons. The British, French, Dutch, Belgians and all of you in the Washington arms control community are trying to talk him out of it. The idea can potentially be a plus for us: the Soviet Union is a superpower only because it is a nuclear and ballistic missile superpower." In another meeting, Shultz writes, "Perle insisted that Gorbachev's letter was not serious, just propaganda. 'We must not discuss it as though it was serious,' he said. The worst thing in the world would be to eliminate nuclear weapons."

Probably because Perle or his lawyers objected, Shultz demoted the last sentence ("The worst thing in the world . . .") to indirect address, but Shultz clearly intends us to construe it to be something he heard Perle say. Why would eliminating weapons of terrible mass destruction be "the worst thing in the world"? Perle himself has never explained in detail why he prefers threats to diplomacy, other than to assert that the Soviets couldn't be trusted, despite the long record across the Cold War of tacit U.S.-Soviet cooperation to keep the peace. One of his reasons may be the reason Shultz's adviser, the ambassador Rozanne Ridgway, offered during another January discussion that Shultz recounts:

> Roz Ridgway broke in. "At dinner last night, Dianne Feinstein [at that time mayor of San Francisco] said, 'Of course people can imagine a nonnuclear world—everybody does.' She was astonished that we had questions about its desirability." But Roz was troubled too. "The loss of nuclear weapons would mean the loss of a special American preeminence; it would change the way we walk down the street. And it can't be done without a gigantic conventional military buildup."
>
> Art Hartman bolstered her point. "In Europe, our allies are up against huge Soviet conventional power. The threatened use of nuclear weapons in order to deter the Soviets is essential to them."

But the conventional advantage in Europe was less than met the Washington eye, as Dana Allin's 1.2-to-1 ratio of Warsaw Pact to NATO forces reveals, and as for a loss of "special preeminence," wasn't that what Shultz had identified as a loss the Soviet Union would sustain from arms reductions, one that could "potentially be a plus for us"? What sort of people build and sustain their "special preeminence," the cocky way they walk down the street, by amassing weapons capable of destroying the human world? If both superpowers shed their vast arsenals, reduced their conventional forces, and settled back into merely major-power status, would the world be better off or worse?

Shultz judged that reducing and eliminating intermediate nuclear forces (INF)—the Pershing 2s, ground-launched cruise missiles (GLCMs), and SS-20s in Europe and Soviet IRBMs in Asia—was the best place to start to test Gorbachev's sincerity. Reagan copied out a seven-page, handwritten letter to that effect in late February. "Our proposal also called for broad cutbacks in conventional forces in Europe," the president later recalled. In response to Gorbachev's more sweeping proposal to begin eliminating nuclear arsenals, Reagan put in another plug for SDI. He did not offer to discontinue nuclear testing.

Gorbachev got the message. "The moratorium helps clarify the real motives of our Western partners," he told the Politburo on 24 March 1986, "precisely that they're not inclined to disarm. When will the new thinking reach them? It's hard to say. But it will come, and maybe even faster than we expect. . . . Maybe we should just stop being afraid of SDI! Of course we can't simply disregard this dangerous program. But we should overcome our obsession with it. They're banking on the USSR's fear of SDI—in moral, economic, political, and military terms. They're pursuing this program to wear us out. So we've decided to say: Yes, we're against SDI, because it destabilizes the peace. But for us it's not a question of fear but responsibility, because the consequences might be unpredictable. SDI doesn't reinforce security, it destroys the remaining security guarantees." At the next Politburo meeting, on 3 April, Gorbachev reminded his colleagues of the new policy of common security that he had announced at the 27th Party Congress in February: "Despite all the contradictions in our relations, the reality is such that we can't do anything without them, and they can't do anything without us. We live on the same planet. We won't be able to preserve peace without America. This is a strong move in our game: [that] we acknowledge their role."

To Reagan, Gorbachev wrote in early April that "more than four months have passed since the Geneva meeting. We ask ourselves: What is the reason for things not going the way they, it would seem, should have gone? Where is the real turn for the better?" He said people were attempting "to portray our initiatives as propaganda." He heard "increasingly vehement philippics addressed to the USSR" and witnessed "quite a few actions directly aimed against our interest. . . . All this builds suspicion as regards to the U.S. policy." Nevertheless, Anatoly Dobrynin, preparing to move back to Moscow as a Gorbachev adviser after twenty-four years as Soviet ambassador to the United States, stopped by Shultz's office a few days later to report, "Gorbachev thinks INF is possible." INF was important—the SS-20s and Pershing 2s with their ten-minute flight times were dangerous—but Gorbachev was playing for the highest stakes. At that point he needed arms reductions to reform his country, not to stay in power. "There have been some questions in the press about whether Gorbachev is in control," Dobrynin volunteered to Shultz. "Let me tell you, *he is in control!*" Arms reductions could only diminish the Soviet threat; why would Reagan's advisers resist them? "The Western governments resorted to their usual strategy of simply ignoring our initiative," Gorbachev writes bitterly.

Among the "actions directly aimed against our interests" Gorbachev would have counted two U.S. Navy intelligence-gathering ships that deliberately approached within six miles of the Soviet Black Sea coastline on 13 March 1986, "part of the worldwide navy program to assert our rights of 'innocent passage,' " Shultz explains, and "not the first time in the Reagan administration when we had made such an assertion close to Soviet shores" but "the first time since the Geneva summit." In March the United States demanded that the Soviet mission to the U.N. be cut back by 170 personnel. On 14 April, responding to a terrorist explosion in a Berlin discotheque frequented by U.S. servicemen, a limited U.S. air strike against Libya killed sixty people, including—when Muammar Gadhafi's personal compound was bombed—Gadhafi's adopted infant daughter; Libya was a Soviet client.

Gorbachev "was disappointed with the way the Americans behaved after Geneva," Chernyaev said later. "He thought that they were just giving the appearance of conducting serious negotiations, but really they were just wasting time. . . . He saw these things as an attempt to irritate him, to test him to see what his reactions would be. He thought it was indicative of a desire to put him in some kind of an awkward situation in front of his own society, in front of his own colleagues. He [had] opened his soul and sincerely offered [Reagan] his suggestions involving these big ideas, and this was the response he received—small and somewhat strange steps."

Matlock, on the other side, remembered a different mood. Gorbachev and his advisers "couldn't yet grasp how important certain issues were to us such as human rights, the breaking down of the Iron Curtain, communications and engaging in reducing the violence in [Third-World conflicts]. . . . The Soviets weren't moving on those things. . . . There were still political prisoners in insane asylums and nothing was being done about it. You still had large numbers of refuseniks. . . . These things weren't moving in 1986. Although we kept saying they are connected for us and that we couldn't go very far in one of these areas without some progress in others, it seemed like we were talking to a wall. It seemed that to the Soviet side, either we simply accept their arms control proposal or nothing's going to happen. . . . This really made everything a little difficult."

Finally, in 1987, Shevardnadze would tell Shultz they were going to deal with human rights in the Soviet Union to improve his country's image in the world, and they made a beginning. At first, said Chernyaev, "we looked at all that as a step back, as a gift—*Okay, we'll do it for the benefit of our dialogue* [with the United States]. . . . Eventually we didn't look at this as a gift or a step back. We started thinking about it as something else. We started thinking about all of these things as momentum, as an issue that is very important for ourselves." For now, his negotiations stalled, Gorbachev pushed on at home.

TWO TECHNOLOGICAL DISASTERS marked the winter and spring of 1986. The U.S. space shuttle *Challenger,* seventy-two seconds into its mission, broke up at an altitude of forty-eight thousand feet over Florida on 28 January 1986 when a seal failed on one of the two solid rocket boosters attached by struts to its external main fuel tank. The failure allowed a blowtorch-like flame of hot gas to jet from the booster casing. The intense flame affected the fuel tank, which was mounted below the winged orbiter that housed the shuttle crew—seven persons including the veteran mission specialist Judith A. Resnik and a Concord, New Hampshire, high school teacher named Christa McAuliffe. Hydrogen gas began discharging from the external fuel tank, which then ruptured, releasing the large volume of liquid hydrogen in the tank just as the rocket booster broke loose and smashed against the orbiter wing. The blowing hydrogen acted as a rocket to drive the hydrogen tank into the oxygen tank directly above it. The oxygen tank ruptured as well, oxygen mixed with hydrogen, and the flame from the booster ignited the hydrogen-oxygen mixture to produce a huge white fireball. Inside the fireball cloud the orbiter swerved sideways into the Mach 2 airstream and broke up. The crew cabin, torn intact from its orbiter housing and with its crew still alive inside, continued ascending up to sixty-five thousand feet before it began to fall back toward the ocean. It fell for almost three minutes, crashing into the ocean at 207 miles per hour—a force on impact of about two hundred times gravity—completely demolishing the crew cabin and crushing to death all seven crew members. The cabin debris was subsequently recovered, but whether or not the crew was conscious at impact was impossible to determine.

The president, personally grieved, said the right things afterward. He said the members of the *Challenger* crew were pioneers. He told the schoolchildren of America, who had been watching the launch in their classrooms because a schoolteacher was aboard, that although painful things sometimes happen, "the future doesn't belong to the fainthearted; it belongs to the brave." He said Sir Francis Drake had died on that date "390 years ago." He quoted a favorite verse of pilots, "High Flight," written in 1941 by an eighteen-year-old American pilot officer, John Gillespie McGee, Jr., during the Battle of Britain, saying that the crew had "slipped the surly bonds of earth" to "touch the face of God." What he did not say, and appears never to have remarked, was the evidence the *Challenger* disaster offered of the great risk of relying on complicated technological systems—such as SDI would have to be—to protect the nation from nuclear attack.

The other disaster, of course, was Chernobyl. When the big RBMK reactor exploded in the northern Ukraine on 26 April 1986, Gorbachev was still thinking through the problem of moving the Reagan administration toward the radical arms-reduction measures he had proposed in mid-January. Andranik Petrosyants, the director of the Soviet atomic energy program, wrote later that "Chernobyl was only a minor event compared with what a nuclear war could be.... A one-megaton nuclear bomb explosion would release into the atmosphere one thousand times more radioactivity than a nuclear reactor accident. It would take only one day for seventy percent of the radioactive substances to come back to earth and, at sufficiently high wind velocities, to pollute a vast area. In that case, 1,000 sq. km. [368 square miles] would be covered by lethal fallout."

Petrosyants's comparison of bomb and burning reactor fallout, published in 1988, minimizes Chernobyl's output; a comprehensive scientific review published in 2003 found it to be the equivalent of a twelve-megaton explosion. There is no reason to doubt his bomb fallout estimates, however. By that measure, then, ten thousand megatons might contaminate with lethal fallout an area at least two thousand miles on a side—an area larger than the continental United States. Gorbachev, as he labored in the aftermath of the accident to cope with its enormous demands for relocation and decontamination, saw at first hand what nuclear war would be like and took the lesson to heart. As Shevardnadze would write, the disaster "tore the blindfold from our eyes." Gorbachev made the connection clear to the Warsaw Pact Party secretaries, his counterparts, at a meeting in Budapest on 11 June 1986. In the meeting minutes' paraphrase:

> Comrade Gorbachev stressed that the Soviet Union is currently witnessing serious problems. . . .
>
> Comrade Gorbachev informed extensively about the accident at the power plant in Chernobyl. . . .
>
> One should not pretend that nothing happened [Gorbachev said], that everything would be under control. Very serious problems are still to be faced, the majority of which are new to the Soviet Union. . . .
>
> It was like war. People were evacuated, families were separated and only slowly found their way back to each other. All this was extraordinarily serious. The situation and its impact must not be played down in any way.
>
> The tragedy of Chernobyl is closely related to the issue of disarmament. Medical experts all over the world clearly state that there would be no medical help in case of a nuclear war. Soviet and American physicians agree on this.

George Shultz was struck by the parallel as well, which may partly explain his somewhat greater enthusiasm for Reagan's commitment to disarmament—greater at least than that of his scornful colleagues. Alexander Bessmertnykh remembered returning from a visit to the United States just weeks after the accident and reporting to Gorbachev "one personal remark that George Schultz had made. He said, 'After Chernobyl, we all now realize the real danger of everything nuclear,' because Chernobyl according to U.S. calculations was something like one-third of the smallest nuclear explosive. And if it caused such great damage to almost half of Europe, what will happen if we shall use all those arsenals we now have in our hands?" Chernyaev concurred: "That phrase, 'Don't put on my desk any war-fighting program,' was uttered [by Gorbachev] before Chernobyl, but I would like very much to endorse what Alexander Bessmertnykh said. Chernobyl had a very significant effect, and it even strengthened Gorbachev's conviction."

In May 1986, Gorbachev took the unprecedented step of calling together in Moscow the entire Soviet foreign-policy establishment—"all the ambassadors and Moscow's 'diplomatic elite,' " he said—to explain and justify to them the "new thinking" in foreign policy and to demand their loyalty to his foreign minister. With all six hundred seats filled in the second-floor auditorium of the foreign ministry where he spoke, he told them "that in today's world of mutual interdependence, progress is unthinkable for any society which is fenced off from the world by impenetrable state frontiers and ideological barriers. A country can develop its full potential only by interacting with other societies, yet without giving up its own identity. We [cannot] ensure our country's security without reckoning with the interests of other countries, and . . . in our nuclear age, you [cannot] build a safe security system based solely on military means. This [prompted] us to propose an entirely new concept of global security, which included all aspects of international relations, including the human dimension." These were not easy ideas to accept, he writes, neither in the Soviet Union nor abroad, and he would continue to shake up and try to reeducate a recalcitrant foreign-policy establishment as well as a recalcitrant military, military-industrial complex, and KGB.

A sour example of his problem with the West occurred shortly after his foreign-policy meeting: Richard Perle, using the hedging of the Soviet leadership about the Chernobyl accident as fresh evidence that the Soviet government was untrustworthy, persuaded Reagan to announce on 27 May that the United States would no longer observe the SALT II agreement, erasing the only restraints on building up strategic weapons then in place between the United States and the U.S.S.R. "From 1986 [onward]," Thomas Graham, Jr., notes, "there were no limitations on strategic offensive arms until the START I Treaty entered into force in December of 1994." The president justified his action with an exaggerated claim Perle had developed to undercut arms agreements: that the Soviets regularly cheated on their commitments to arms control. Ironically, one of Reagan's complaints was that "since the November summit, we have yet to see the Soviets following up constructively on the commitment made by General Secretary Gorbachev and myself to achieve early progress in the Geneva negotiations, in particular in areas where there is common ground." Gorbachev, Chernyaev writes, "was surprised and annoyed by the cautious, unenthusiastic response of the West to his bold and sincere initiatives."

Perle's response was far more than simply cautious and unenthusiastic. He was categorically opposed to arms control, believing dogmatically that it always worked out to the Soviet Union's advantage, and immensely clever at finding ways to convince a secretary of defense inexperienced in the subject of nuclear policy and an equally inexperienced president why they should resist new agreements and repudiate old ones.

Caspar Weinberger "virtually turned over the Pentagon's arms-control portfolio to Perle," Strobe Talbott writes. "In that sense, Weinberger, too, became a member of the Perle mafia [along with Perle's nominal Pentagon superior Fred Iklé, Secretary of the Navy John Lehman, the ACDA's Kenneth Adelman, and others]. And since Weinberger . . . was also a member of President Reagan's inner circle, that gave Perle special advantages." The zero option was Perle's; the so-called broad interpretation of the ABM Treaty that essentially nullified its basic purpose by asserting that it imposed no restrictions on exotic antimissile technologies such as lasers or particle beams was his; a Weinberger letter warning against agreements that was leaked to the press just prior to Reagan's departure for Geneva was his; and the president's decision to cease compliance with SALT II originated with him as well.

Reagan's passion for nuclear abolition greatly worried Perle. When Perle first heard of the president's dream of strategic defense, he dismissed it contemptuously as "the product of millions of American teenagers putting quarters into video machines." After further consideration he realized it might be useful. As Rozanne Ridgway would say later, "There were people who really did want to use SDI, and its implications for the ABM Treaty, to stop the arms control process." Perle was one of those people, and first in line. But since their dispute over SDI alone might not be enough to prevent two such passionate abolitionists as Gorbachev and Reagan from agreeing to eliminate their nations' nuclear arsenals, Perle championed a new poison pill in that spring of 1986. It had originated with Iklé, who had sold it to Perle after talking it over with Max Kampelman. It fit Perle's modus operandi of promoting offers that looked good on paper, that he could sell to Weinberger and Reagan with a straight face, but that he judged the Soviet Union must inevitably refuse. The zero option had been such an offer, and so far, so good. Now, Bach at his harpsichord again, he set about promoting another phony proposal, his ally Edward Rowny recalled:

> Richard Perle called me over . . . and he said, "You know, Reagan is not going to give up this idea of getting rid of all nuclear weapons." I agreed. He said, "I've got an idea. We'll just go ahead and say we'll reduce all ballistic missiles, which are the really dangerous part, but we'll keep sea-launched and ground-launched cruise missiles, and we'll keep bombers." He added, "We'll always have our reserve, and I don't think the French or British will give up their ballistic missiles." So we went in to see Weinberger, and Perle convinced Weinberger and Weinberger himself said, "Yes, I also feel that the President wants to get rid of all nuclear weapons and I can't convince him otherwise. But let's try this ballistic missile proposal out." So we did and it caught on, particularly with Secretary of State Shultz. He had been quite hostile, I think, to Perle up to then. He now thought that Perle was being creative, which he was. Their rapport improved after that.

(In fact, according to Shultz, the secretary of state had been hostile to Perle because he believed Perle had been the high-level Pentagon official who had committed an act of gross disloyalty by secretly encouraging the Japanese and the French to agitate against the president's INF proposals that spring. "On February 21," Shultz writes, "the president handed [his national security adviser John] Poindexter a note on which he had written that the secret approach to the French and Japanese (and probably to other allies) was 'a despicable act.' The president left it up to Cap Weinberger to deal with this breach of discipline and of loyalty to the president. 'These people,' I said, 'are out of control.' To my knowledge, Weinberger did nothing." Shultz says he eventually confronted Perle, "who assured me that he had not been responsible. I accepted his word. By this time, I knew from my own sources that he was not the culprit. The air was cleared, and our relations proceeded amicably." But if not Perle, then who? Who else in the Pentagon had both motive and authority? Despite Shultz's previous indignation, however, he dropped the matter forthwith, except to say that he increasingly found Perle to be "one of the most creative and reliable thinkers on arms control matters.")

Michael Guhin, a counselor to the Arms Control and Disarmament Agency at the time and a senior staff member on the National Security Council, characterizes Perle's proposals more critically. "About this business of doing away with ballistic missiles," he told the Brown conference on the Cold War in 1998—"I think we have to step back from that and say . . . that this was a propaganda ploy. I think zero-zero was [also] a propaganda ploy." Asking the Soviets to give up their ballistic missiles when those missiles constituted the vast majority of their nuclear arsenal, while the United States would retain its more numerous arsenal of bombs, bombers, and air-, sub-marine-, and ground-launched cruise missiles, was not likely to win their agreement, any more than it would have won U.S. agreement were the tables turned. Weinberger and the president thought otherwise, however, when they met to discuss the subject on 12 June 1986. "It made little sense," Weinberger told Reagan, "to commit to share the benefits of advanced defenses with the Soviet Union if the Soviet Union insisted on continuing to retain large numbers of offensive ballistic missiles which would, in turn, attempt to defeat our defenses." Such an argument was doubly cynical—SDI would never be more than a bloated research program, and even if it had been viable, the United States would never have shared it with the Soviet Union—but Weinberger may not have known that. Certainly Perle did. Nitze saw through the Perle initiative immediately. He had one word for it when he heard about it: "ridiculous." By the time the NSC had worked it over and diluted it, it came to very little, although Perle would bring it up again at the next summit meeting to contribute to poisoning the air.

Two important meetings that summer changed Gorbachev's mind about whether "hopes for major changes in world politics . . . kindled by our summit meeting with President Reagan in Geneva . . . were waning." The French president, François Mitterrand, visited Moscow in early July. "I do not judge the American administration as harshly as you do," Mitterrand told Gorbachev after listening to the general secretary's long, angry analysis of Soviet-U.S. relations. "I admit that the U.S. military-industrial complex puts a lot of pressure on the U.S. administration. At the same time, we have to bear in mind that Reagan is the product of his milieu, and he is not without common sense and intuition. . . . In order to break away from the contradictions in the judgments of his own government, Reagan is moving above them—into the sphere of prophecies." Here Chernyaev takes up the story:

> "It seems to me," Mitterrand remarked, "that notwithstanding his political past, Reagan is one of those statesmen who is intuitively striving to find a way out of this dilemma. You may find this judgment contradictory, but it is really true. Unlike many other American politicians, Reagan is not an automaton. He is a human being."
>
> "This is extremely important," Gorbachev replied, "and I'm taking special note of it." In this way the French president played a major role in eroding the remaining stereotypes in Gorbachev's "new thinking."

What Gorbachev himself remembered most vividly of his discussion with Mitterrand was the French president's report of his meeting a few days previously with Reagan. "He told me that he considered the arguments the American President had advanced as unconvincing, commenting ironically that Reagan's belief in the effectiveness of the Strategic Defense Initiative as a panacea for all ills was, in his view, more mystic than rational."

A week later, in mid-July, Richard Nixon also visited Moscow and talked with Gorbachev at length. The former president, working on resuscitating his reputation after the debacle of Watergate, encouraged the general secretary to have patience with Reagan:

> I have known President Reagan for a long time, more than thirty years. I have a firm conviction that he considers the matter of American-Soviet relations his personal concern. You are right that there are people in the administration who do not want agreements with the Soviet Union. They believe that if they can isolate the Soviet Union diplomatically, apply economic pressure on it, achieve military superiority, then the Soviet order would collapse.* Of course, this is

---

* A formula for international relations with sovereign states that would find its proponents once again, after 2000, in the context of U.S. relations with North Korea and Iran.

not going to happen. For years Reagan, as you know, was thought to have been a supporter of the group holding such views [i.e., the Committee on the Present Danger]. But not now. I know from conversations with him that the meeting with you did influence a gradual change in his attitudes. He was very impressed not only by the contents of your exchanges, but also by your personal commitment to peaceful relations between our countries. This he clearly recognized. He also thinks that a certain personal relationship has been formed between the two of you, and consequently believes that you will be able to reach an agreement on the issues of mutual interest.

Despite these encouragements, Gorbachev assessed the letter he received from Reagan on 25 July 1986 as "an attempt to uphold the pretense of a continuing dialogue, another tactical move in the 'double game' played by the Americans." In the letter Reagan offered to continue in compliance with the ABM Treaty for at least the next five years (the Soviets had proposed fifteen or twenty years), after which either country could deploy strategic defenses if it first offered a plan for sharing them and—a vestige of Perle's most recent program of presidential misdirection—a plan for eliminating all ballistic missiles.

Gorbachev was vacationing in the Crimea when the letter came. "Eduard Shevardnadze telephoned me to say that he had already sent a draft reply for approval," he recalls, "adding that we did not need to give a detailed reply since there were no significant proposals in Reagan's message. Still, we could not leave it unanswered." Anatoly Chernyaev had accompanied the Gorbachevs on vacation. The draft reply arrived from Moscow where Shevardnadze's first deputy, Anatoly Kovalev, had supervised its preparation. "I took it to Mikhail Sergeyevich," Chernyaev writes. "He took it and read attentively. Then he tossed it on the table, looked at me, and asked: 'What do you say?' I replied: 'It's no good, Mikhail Sergeyevich!' He said: 'Simply crap!' "

Gorbachev continues:

It was a short, routine statement, and as I was reading it, I suddenly realized that I was gradually being forced into accepting a logic that was alien to me—a logic that was in open contradiction to our new attitude, to the process we had started in Geneva, and—most important—to the hopes of ordinary people. I said that I could not sign such a letter, and told Anatoly about the thoughts that had been haunting me for days. In the end, I decided to take a strong stand, suggesting an immediate summit meeting with President Reagan to unblock the strategic talks in Geneva, which were in danger of becoming an empty rite. A meeting was needed to discuss the situation and to give new impetus to the peace process.

"He started thinking aloud," Chernyaev concludes the story, "and then he said: 'Write this down. Urgently prepare a draft of my letter to the president of the United States of America with a suggestion to meet in late September or early October either in London or,' he paused for a moment, 'in Reykjavik.' I stared at him in surprise. 'Why Reykjavik?' He said, 'It's a good idea. Halfway between us and them, and none of the big powers will be offended!' "

Chernyaev wrote Kovalev on Gorbachev's behalf, directing Shevardnadze's deputy to rethink his department's pedestrian first approach. The memorandum demonstrates that Gorbachev's Reykjavik proposals followed from a serious and continuing effort to rethink Soviet foreign policy from the ground up:

In his [recent Czech newspaper interview] Mikhail Sergeyevich posed the question: "What can we conclude from the Americans' behavior? That they are preparing for war?" It seems that the same question can be asked of the authors of this project. Are we going to fight a war?

Of course the military has its own logic, its interests mean that it's always trying to restrain the politicians. But this doesn't mean that the military should define our general policies. The conclusion of the [27th Party] Congress was that given the right policies—foreign, domestic, economic, in short, policies following the new guidelines—*there will be no war.* This is what our military expectations should be based upon, as well as our military expenditures (although this is a different question). . . .

By keeping our SS-20s in Europe, we'll certainly never get the West Europeans on our side. Besides, do you seriously believe that Thatcher, Mitterrand, or whoever follows them into office, could, in any imaginable situation, press the button to launch their missiles against us? Can this really be what underlies our European strategy?

. . . Going to Reykjavik with little progress beyond that reached over the past year's negotiations in Geneva would condemn this summit to failure and provoke universal disappointment. The summit in Reykjavik is not aimed at experts who know all the fine points of modern weapons, but at nations and states, the world community. Therefore, big politics should be in its forefront, not negotiating minutiae. The world must hear major, sweeping proposals from Reykjavik, in the spirit of the January 15 program.

Shevardnadze personally carried the resulting letter to an angry Reagan in September 1986—the KGB's high-handed arrest of Nicholas Daniloff, an American journalist, had temporarily frozen relations between the two countries—but with the release of Daniloff on 29 September the atmosphere cleared. Reagan announced on 30 September that he would meet with Gorbachev in Reykjavik, Iceland, on 10 through 12 October 1986.

At the Politburo on 4 October, Gorbachev told the group preparing for Reykjavik, "We should not create big hopes for Reykjavik in the press. But for ourselves we should keep in mind that first of all we need to get the Pershing 2s out of Europe. They are a pistol against our head. . . . Our [larger] goal is to prevent the next round of the arms race. If we do not accomplish it, the threat to us will only grow. We will be pulled into an arms race that is beyond our capabilities, and we will lose it, because we are at the limit of our capabilities." To Reagan he had written: "In almost a year since Geneva, there has been no movement on these issues. . . . I have come to the conclusion that the negotiations need a major impulse. . . . They will lead nowhere unless you and I intervene personally."

ICELAND, AN ISLAND THE SIZE OF KENTUCKY that rises in the North Atlantic between Norway and Greenland, marks the place where the spreading center of the Atlantic crustal plate—the Mid-Atlantic Ridge—passes over a perpetual upwelling in the earth's mantle called a hot spot. The small island nation is raw and spectacular, still forming from periodic eruptions of basaltic black lava, treeless outside its few cities and towns, with lichen-greened cliffs and glacier-fed waterfalls, mud geysers and steaming blue pools, abrupt canyons, rocky coves, and sandy shores on the cold northern ocean alive with seabirds and migratory ducks and geese. The population of Iceland in 1986 was only 243,000 people, more than half of whom lived in and around Reykjavik, an enlarged fishing village on a peninsula on the southwest coast that juts like a jaw from the west face of the island. The proud nation with the world's oldest parliament was excited to host a Soviet-U.S. summit meeting. It offered a historic white art-nouveau house built for the French consul in 1909, the Hofdi House, as a secure location isolated outside the Reykjavik center. With only ten days' notice, Iceland managed to prepare itself to welcome a crowd of Soviet and U.S. officials and world press. Every inn and hotel room would be filled. Ronald Reagan stayed in the American ambassador's residence. Having been told that Raisa Gorbachev would not attend, Nancy Reagan remained behind in Washington; she was miffed to learn that Raisa showed up after all and upstaged her. The Soviet contingent provided its own housing in the form of an ocean liner, the *George Otts*, chartered over from Tallinn, Estonia and docked in the Reykjavik harbor.

As Reagan explained as he boarded Air Force One for Iceland on 9 October 1986, his administration understood the event to be "essentially a private meeting between [General Secretary Gorbachev and me]. We will not have large staffs with us nor is it planned that we sign substantive agreements. We will, rather, review the subjects that we intend to pursue . . . afterward, looking toward a possible full-scale summit." The summit they were looking toward was to be held in Washington, the date as yet undetermined, but Gorbachev was planning much more for Reykjavik, and he intended to disclose his concessions and proposals as a series of surprises in the hope of a breakthrough. The United States had last-minute intelligence on his plans, however, Paul Nitze told an interviewer. Nitze believed they exposed Gorbachev's intentions for the mini-summit to be basically propagandistic, and his chill recommendation, which he said Shultz and "the others" agreed to, was that they should "await Mr. Gorbachev's marvelous concessions, we should then say we take all those concessions, but we shouldn't give anything more. Therefore we could come out of these negotiations winning without cost." In his memoirs he added, succinctly: "We could pocket what we wished to pocket."

As he had at Geneva, Gorbachev bulked up his Reykjavik delegation with Soviet journalists, scientists, and Central Committee apparatchiks; their purpose, Chernyaev explains, was "to interact around the clock with the Americans and other foreigners who had flocked there in great numbers from all over the world, to explain the policies of new thinking, and to help create a new image of the Soviet Union." What Nitze did not know, or couldn't countenance, was that Gorbachev's strategy for Reykjavik had substance and paralleled his strategy for reforming the Soviet Union itself; he evidently considered wresting changes from a hostile U.S. foreign-policy establishment to be a challenge comparable to his ongoing challenge of wresting changes from a hostile Soviet Communist Party, about which he wrote in his memoirs:

> By the mid-1980s our society resembled a steam boiler. There was only one alternative—either the Party itself would lead a process of change that would gradually embrace other strata of society, or it would preserve and protect the former system. In that case an explosion of colossal force would be inevitable. We also had to consider that only a force that held the reins of power could reform the system, that is, gradually reshape it. Moreover, the very idea of reform could not, at least at first, be a subject for public discussion. This would have immediately provoked rejection and irreparably damaged our work before we even began. It was important to get the "engine of change" started and drive up to a point from which there was no turning back.

In internal discussions earlier in October, Gorbachev had explained why Reykjavik would require concessions and compromise. "We are by no means talking about weakening our security," he told the Politburo. "But at the same time we have to realize that if our proposals imply weakening U.S. security, then there won't be any agreement. Our main goal now is to prevent the arms race from entering a new stage [i.e., into space and into advanced, third-generation nuclear weapons]. If we don't do that, the danger to us will increase. If we don't back down on some specific, maybe even important issues, if we won't budge from the positions we've held for a long time, we will lose in the end. We will be drawn into an arms race that we cannot manage. We will lose, because right now we are already at the end of our tether."

The difference between Gorbachev's approach and that of Reagan's advisers was the difference between common security and the adversarial, zero-sum "realism" that both sides had stubbornly maintained throughout the Cold War and that had stalled meaningful arms negotiations for decades. Gorbachev wanted change. Most of Reagan's advisers did not. Gorbachev's goal then must be to push past the president's advisers and somehow engage the president directly. Knowing that Reagan was totally committed to SDI, his deus ex machina for ending the nuclear-arms race, Chernyaev had advised the general secretary not to link arms reductions to limitations on strategic defense—"otherwise," Chernyaev had written, "it will be another dead end." But Gorbachev had little choice: The Soviet military had been willing to agree to his package of Reykjavik concessions only if he held the line on SDI. "Nobody except the Foreign Ministry was in favor of disarmament," Sergei Tarasenko, a specialist on American affairs, recalled. "The military played hard on Star Wars." Alexander Yakovlev confirmed that "Star Wars was exploited by [Soviet] hardliners to complicate Gorbachev's attempt to end the Cold War." That is, far from forcing Gorbachev to make concessions, as the Reagan conservatives believed, SDI was a key issue Soviet hardliners used to resist the greater concessions Gorbachev wanted to make in the hope of slowing or ending the nuclear-arms race.

When he flew to Iceland on 10 October, Gorbachev left behind grim reminders of the stakes in the debate. That was the time when workers in Kiev were raking up the city's chestnut leaves as the trees shed them into the streets and parks and burying them outside the city to sequester their burden of Chernobyl fallout. At Chernobyl itself, engineers were finishing construction of a makeshift sarcophagus braced around Reactor Number Four, entombing the burned-out reactor within 400,000 cubic meters of reinforced concrete. Only when that work was finished would Number Four cease to dust its surroundings with radiation.

The Hofdi House stood in open grassland next to a breakwater beside a stretch of beach road that U.S. and Soviet security had cordoned off from the unbadged. The 2,600-square-foot house counted two floors and a basement under a mansard roof with gables framing the main entrance. Its builder had ordered it precut from a Norwegian sawmill. By the 1950s it had fallen nearly to ruin when a Reykjavik city engineer had lobbied to have it restored. The two delegations had divided it roughly in half, each group taking two of the five modest rooms on the second floor and sharing the common meeting room between. Security details occupied the basement, leaving the dining room, salon, and sitting room on the main floor for the leaders and their advisers. The foyer was paneled with rustic planking, and an angular spiral staircase in Norwegian dragon style connected the lower and upper floors.

As at Geneva, the president and the general secretary began their discussions—on Saturday morning, 11 October—by meeting privately with only their translators and note-takers at hand. They sat across a table from each other in low-backed tan leather armchairs beside a bay of windows that looked out through the cold morning rain onto the gray sea; the floor was warmed with a large rust-red rug in a Caucasian pattern that must have made Gorbachev feel at home. Gorbachev commented that both of them had a lot of paper with them. Reagan joked that his was to help him recall their Geneva discussions. He was glad Gorbachev had proposed this meeting, he added; it would help make their next one productive.

Their subsequent dialogue was greatly aided by simultaneous translation, which Shultz's people had negotiated and which the Soviet side had previously refused. It allowed each man to respond directly to the other's expressions and body language as well as his words. Much that was said was still redundant or extraneous; I give the gist.

Reagan, note cards in hand: "Which problems should we talk about first? We have a whole set that we didn't finish at Geneva—INF, outer space, the ABM Treaty. . . . I'm proceeding from the assumption that both sides want to rid the world of ballistic missiles and of nuclear weapons in general. The world wants to know if we can make that happen."

Gorbachev: "Mr. President, it would make sense first to talk about why we proposed an urgent meeting with you. Afterward I will explain the concrete ideas I brought to this meeting. For that part it would be helpful to invite Shevardnadze and Shultz to join us. Of course, we're prepared to discuss any issues you wish to raise."

Reagan: "We truly ought to talk about human rights. They have a major influence on how far we can go in cooperating with the Soviet Union given American public opinion."

Gorbachev: "About human rights we have yet to speak. Right now I'd like to give you a general impression of what has happened since Geneva. Then we can move on to the concrete problems of arms control and disarmament."

Reagan: "I agree. I mention human rights only to remind you of what I said about them in Geneva." What Reagan said about human rights in

Geneva he then repeated. Gorbachev listened. (In a transcript of Gorbachev's presentation to the Politburo on 8 October, identified and translated by a young Yale scholar, Michael Mazo, he had already made a beginning. He discussed, Mazo wrote, "the need for a 'serious analysis of the whole situation, of the whole human rights concept, both ours and in the world,' and again at the very end: 'Once more about human rights in our land. Here is also required a "speeding up." No routine any more. We must shake up our agencies—the Interior Ministry [KGB] and so on. See what can be done. It is necessary to open the way back to the Soviet Union for thousands of emigrants, to reverse that flood. And, in general, one should work on these things with greater joy.' ") "But I agree," Reagan concluded, "that these problems can take second place in importance to the problems of nuclear weapons."

Gorbachev began his presentation: "This meeting is being talked about across the world. People have wide-ranging and even contradictory opinions about it. Sitting here now, I'm even firmer in my conviction that the very decision to have this meeting was a crucial step on both sides. It means the Soviet-American dialogue is continuing. If it progresses only with difficulty, still it progresses. This alone justifies our coming to Reykjavik. This meeting is a witness of our joint responsibility before the peoples of our countries and of the whole world."

Reagan: "As I said in Geneva, I consider our situation to be unique. Here we are sitting together in a room, and between us we can resolve the question of whether there is to be war or peace in the world. Both of us want peace, but how do we attain it—how do we strengthen the trust and decrease the mutual suspicions between our two peoples?"

Gorbachev: "That was my second thought. I'd like to develop it, in principle supporting what you just said. After Geneva we set in motion a complex and extensive mechanism for Soviet-American dialogue. It has fallen out of step more than once, we've felt more than a few bumps and bruises, but on the whole, it's moving and gaining momentum. That's the positive side. But on the main question that concerns both governments—how to remove the nuclear threat, how to make use of the helpful impulse of Geneva, how to arrive at concrete agreements—there's no movement, and that troubles us greatly. We're very close to a dead end in our negotiations. That's why we wanted an urgent meeting with you, so that you and I can push the process to arrive at agreements that we can conclude when we meet again in Washington."

Reagan: "I feel the same way." He reverted to the Geneva negotiations, discussed the difficulties there with setting a ceiling on nuclear missile warheads, and proposed a compromise.

Gorbachev: "Let me be as clear as possible: We want such solutions to the arms limitation problem. We approached the proposals I'm making today with the understanding that the interests of both the U.S.A. and the Soviet Union have to be considered in equal measure. If we only consider our own interests—and especially if we give you cause to believe we're trying to attain military superiority—then you aren't going to be interested in seeking agreement. So let me precisely, firmly, and clearly declare: We are in favor of finding a solution that would lead eventually to a complete liquidation of nuclear arms. Along the way to that goal, at every stage, there should be equality and equal security for the U.S.A. and the Soviet Union. Anything less would be incomprehensible, unrealistic, and unacceptable. We expect that the U.S.A. will act in the same way."

Reagan: "We feel exactly the same way. The hard question here is verification. There's a Russian saying about this: *Doveryai no proveryai:* Trust, but verify." (Proud of his three words of Russian, Reagan would repeat this saying so often in his meetings with Gorbachev that the general secretary would eventually cover his ears when he saw it coming.) "You and I were optimistic at Geneva about reducing intermediate-range nuclear missiles in Europe. I can see us completely eliminating this class of weapons. We should be able to make progress on strategic weapons as well. But verification is a necessity. If we can make these things happen, the whole world will welcome it."

Gorbachev: "I agree. We're in favor of effective control over fulfillment of any agreements. We'll go as far as we need to go to give and get an assurance that both sides are doing what they agreed to do. But let me say something about the next meeting, in the U.S.A. We consider Reykjavik a step on the path toward that meeting."

Reagan: "People have been calling it a 'base camp' on the path to Washington."

Gorbachev: "Yes, and they said it was the halfway point—and Reykjavik is almost exactly halfway between Moscow and Washington."

Reagan: "Can we talk about the date of your visit? Will you suggest some possibilities, or should I?" ("Whoops," Matlock, the president's note-taker, says he thought. "He's making the same mistake Gorbachev did in Geneva when he talked about the importance of trade. . . . We had briefed Reagan repeatedly on this point, advising him to play it cool and not appear to want a meeting without results. He would always agree, but at that moment in Reykjavik his eagerness to show Gorbachev the United States got the better of his judgment.")

Gorbachev: "Let me finish my thought. You know I've spoken publicly about the importance of the next meeting leading to palpable accomplishments on the problem that worries the world most—limiting the arms race. You and I can't let the next meeting fail in that sense. People have begun asking what sort of politicians we are that we meet together, make speeches, talk for hours, organize one, then another, and then a third meeting but aren't able to agree on anything. Instead, this meeting in Reykjavik should set the requirements for working out agreements on arms reduction that you and I can sign during my visit to America. For that to happen, we'll have to work hard today and tomorrow to lay everything out for our foreign ministers— and only then can we decide when it would be best to organize my visit."

Reagan reverted to his earlier discussion of strategic missile numbers, raising the question of "maximum throw weight"—throw weight being the weight of the warhead package and guidance system a missile could lift. Gorbachev said impatiently that he would respond to that question as well. An hour had passed, he said. He proposed that they invite in their foreign ministers.

The memoirs of the two leaders give sharply contrasting versions of this first Reykjavik discussion. "Gorbachev and I first met alone briefly with our interpreters," Reagan wrote dismissively, "then he said he wanted to bring in George Shultz and Shevardnadze and that's the way it went for the rest of the two days." Gorbachev to the contrary misremembered that he "outlined the proposals we had prepared in Moscow"—the proposals he would shortly read out to the president and the two advisers—and that Reagan was disconcerted by them:

> Reagan reacted by consulting or reading his notes written on cards. I tried to discuss with him the points I had just outlined, but all my attempts failed. I decided to try specific questions, but still did not get any response. President Reagan was looking through his notes. The cards got mixed up and some of them fell to the floor. He started shuffling them, looking for the right answer to my arguments, but he could not find it. There could be no right answer available—the American President and his aides had been preparing for a completely different conversation.

Factual memory is more fallible than emotional memory; it was so important to Gorbachev to surprise the Americans with his plan for nuclear disarmament, enriched with major concessions, that he recalled doing so once more than he actually did. He expected it to make Reagan fumble— Gorbachev, quick on his feet and vain about it, was always impatient with Reagan's cards—and remembered that it did (it may have done so in the upcoming two-on-two session). Certainly he was accurate in recalling that the Americans had been prepared for a different conversation; the last-minute intelligence about Gorbachev's surprises had not come in time to change the general U.S. mind-set that Reykjavik would be only a warm-up for Washington and needed only limited preparation. By Sunday afternoon, Kenneth Adelman recalled, Reagan would say resentfully, "Hell, this isn't a meeting to prepare for a summit. It's a summit." Gorbachev was "eager to wheel and deal," Adelman continues with unintentional irony, "his briefcase bulging with new ideas, quite in contrast with the old days when only we would propose new ideas and they would mostly say *nyet*." Now it was the United States that would mostly be saying *nyet*.

WITH SHULTZ AND SHEVARDNADZE seated at the table, Gorbachev began reading out his proposals. Both sides agreed, he read, that the principal matter of international politics between their countries was an acknowledgment of the complete liquidation of nuclear arms as a bilateral goal. That goal followed logically from their agreement in Geneva that a nuclear war could not be won and must never be fought.

"How do we imagine moving toward this goal?" he went on. "Our approach is stated in my declarations of 15 January 1986. Corresponding official declarations have also been made on your side. I would like to confirm that our point of view with regard to moving toward this goal is that we should do so in stages, while providing at each stage for an equal degree of security for both sides. We expect that the U.S.A. will feel the same way. Again, such an approach is related to our agreement in Geneva that neither side should acquire military superiority over the other."

He was ready then to state his proposals for strategic nuclear weapons.

Both sides, he read, had proposed a 50 percent reduction in such weapons. They had discussed the reduction at Geneva. But since that time, as many as one hundred variants of that proposal had found their way to the negotiating table and negotiations had stalled. To clarify, he would now confirm that the Soviet leadership was interested precisely in deep, 50 percent reductions in strategic offensive weapons and nothing less. Previously the Soviet position had been for 50 percent reductions in weapons with ranges that could reach each other's territories. Now they were proposing reductions of all strategic weapons and of strategic weapons only. "We are taking into consideration the United States's point of view here," Gorbachev said, "and are making a major concession to them." (Reducing only long-range weapons would have left the Soviets with the capability of attacking U.S. allies in

Europe and Asia with intermediate-range ballistic missiles, a capability the United States would not have had—thus Gorbachev's concession.)

That was concession one.

With the 50 percent reduction, Gorbachev continued, they were prepared to take into consideration the U.S.A.'s concerns with heavy missiles—the throw-weight issue that Reagan had raised—and to significantly reduce that category of weapons as part of the larger reduction—"significantly," Gorbachev underlines, "not cosmetically." In exchange, the Soviet Union expected the United States to address Soviet concerns as well. "The U.S.A. has six thousand five hundred nuclear warheads on submarines scattered all across the world, which constitutes an enormous problem of verification and control. Of these, more than eight hundred warheads are MIRVed. We hope the U.S.A. will meet the Soviet Union halfway here."

Reducing the Soviet Union's heavy missiles instead of holding them back in the 50 percent that would remain active was Gorbachev's second concession.

Next Gorbachev turned to intermediate-range nuclear forces, INF: the SS-20s in Europe and Asia, the Pershing 2s and GLCMs in Europe. The Soviet Union had been leery of Perle's zero option in Europe and unwilling as well to give up maintaining a fleet of SS-20s facing China from the far-eastern U.S.S.R. It had also insisted that French and British missiles be counted on the NATO side. Now Gorbachev proposed "a total liquidation of both the USSR's and the U.S.A.'s missiles of this class in Europe. We are making a major concession—we are removing the question of [counting] the nuclear powers England and France." In return, he asked the United States to "make a concession and remove the question of Soviet INF in Asia, or at the very least, agree to begin negotiations about nuclear weapons—Soviet and American—in Asia."

That was concession number three.

This third concession was less than it appeared, George Shultz would write: "He proposed a freeze on deployment of short-range INF systems, knowing that we had none deployed. The freeze would be followed by negotiations to reach some permanent understanding about these weapons. I thought to myself, if we have none and they have 120 and the deployments are frozen, we would be frozen into a permanent disadvantage."

These, Gorbachev summarized, were his proposals on nuclear weapons. He hoped the American leadership appreciated the broad scope of his compromises.

Next Gorbachev turned to the question of the ABM Treaty and of a ban on nuclear testing. The treaty needed to be strengthened, he said, to serve as a foundation for nuclear disarmament. He proposed a compromise that would "accept the American approach" of a fundamental time period during which neither side would withdraw from the treaty followed by a time period when they would negotiate over the treaty's future. "Under these terms," he emphasized, "development and testing of strategic defense systems would be allowed in a laboratory setting, but tests outside the laboratory would be prohibited." For time periods, he proposed not less than ten years of nonwithdrawal, followed by three to five years of negotiation on the treaty's future. Antisatellite technologies would be prohibited as well, since creating such technologies might allow the development of antimissile systems.

As for nuclear tests, Gorbachev said, they had studied the problem comprehensively and at length. "It might be understandable, as long as both sides were not moving toward major reductions, to question the advisability of ceasing nuclear testing. Now, however, in the context of the proposals I have made, any such doubts should fall by the wayside. We should come to agreement on the complete and final prohibition of nuclear tests.

"That, Mr. President," Gorbachev concluded his long reading, "is our package of proposals on all the fundamental aspects of nuclear-weapons reductions. I propose that you and I, here in Reykjavik, give directions to our aides to jointly work out draft agreements that you and I can then approach and sign during my visit to Washington." Having perhaps overlooked it earlier, Gorbachev mentioned that the Soviet Union was prepared to use all means necessary to make these proposals work, including on-site inspections. Whereupon he handed Reagan an English translation of his proposal text.

Shultz characterized the general secretary's presentation wryly: "Gorbachev was brisk, impatient and confident, with the air of a man who is setting the agenda and taking charge of the meeting. Ronald Reagan was relaxed, disarming in a pensive way and with an easy manner. He could well afford to be, since Gorbachev's proposals all moved toward U.S. positions in significant ways."

Shultz's assessment ignored Gorbachev's proposals of a comprehensive nuclear test ban and an ABM Treaty agreement that would strangle SDI in its crib. Reagan, however, instantly spotted the threat to his cherished program and reacted. "What you have just said gives us cause for hope," he told Gorbachev. "But I did notice several differences in our positions." He mentioned reductions in SS-20s in Asia to go with the zero option in Europe. He said the

United States would like to reduce strategic nuclear weapons not merely by 50 percent but to zero. "As I already said in Geneva," he explained, "SDI would make sense only if strategic weapons are eliminated. Therefore, along with reducing strategic weapons, we propose that you sign a treaty that would replace the ABM Treaty." (I find no previous reference to this idea in the record, but Thomas Graham, Jr., recalls that there was discussion in conservative circles at this time of an "SDI cooperation treaty" to replace the ABM Treaty. Gorbachev ignored the proposal, and nothing seems to have come of it.)

"In this [new] treaty," Reagan told Gorbachev, "both sides would carry out research on strategic defense as allowed in the ABM Treaty. If either side approached the limit of what is allowed under the ABM Treaty, then experiments could continue with the other side present—so if we were the first to approach the boundary, then we would invite you to observe our experiments. And if the experiments were successful, then this treaty would require us to share such a system. In the course of two or three years of negotiations, both sides would agree on the mutual use of such a system. In exchange, both sides would be bound to completely eliminate strategic weapons. The reason for this approach is that both sides will continue to be able to produce offensive weapons—after all, we certainly know how—and we need a guarantee that if anyone does, either one of us or a maniac like Hitler, that we have a defense against it. So we propose defending ourselves once and for all time against the recurrence of strategic weapons in the world, and on this basis to build our future for many years to come."

Matlock says Gorbachev was "obviously disappointed that Reagan did not show greater enthusiasm for his proposals." To Shultz, Gorbachev seemed "somewhat taken aback at President Reagan's pleasant but argumentative reaction." Considering how hard Gorbachev had fought at home to wrest his proposals from the reluctant conservatives in his military and his government, he was probably furious. He sounds furious even through the muffling screen of note-taking and translation, scolding Reagan as if the president were a student who had failed to pay attention and spoke without thinking:

Let me react to your remarks. First, we will consider your statements to be preliminary. I have only just now made some completely new proposals; they have not yet been discussed in any negotiations. Therefore I would ask you to pay them their due attention, and to state your reaction later. Second, what you said just now is on the very same level, on the same plane, as what the American negotiators in Geneva are saying. We value the efforts of experts in the detailed working out of questions, but they do not move the matter forward; we need a new contribution, a new impulse. We want to create this with our proposals. But how is the American side proceeding? We propose accepting the American "zero" in Europe and sitting down at the negotiating table about Asia within the framework of the IRBM problem—but you are now departing from your former position. We do not understand this. Now, regarding ABM. We propose preserving and strengthening this fundamentally important agreement, but you propose rejecting it and destroying a mechanism that has created the foundation of strategic stability. We do not understand this. Now, about the SDI. You need not worry. We have studied this problem, and if the USA creates a three-layered system of ABMs, then we will find a response. It is not this that concerns us, but rather the fact that the SDI would signify a shift of the arms race into a new environment, the raising of it to a new stage, the creation of new types of weapons, destabilizing the strategic situation in the world. If this is the goal of the U.S.A. that is one thing. But if they want greater security for the American people, for the whole world, then their position contradicts this goal and is downright dangerous. I hope, Mr. President, that you will study our proposals and respond to them point by point as to what you agree with, what you disagree with and what you're bothered by.

Reagan acknowledged that they would continue to discuss Gorbachev's proposals that afternoon. He couldn't let Gorbachev's attack on SDI go unanswered, however. "For now," he said, "let me just make one remark. The Soviet side refuses to see the point of SDI. If we were proposing to do research on strategic defensive systems under conditions where we had refused to reduce our offensive weapons, then we could be accused of creating a cover for first-strike capabilities. But that's not our position. We propose giving up offensive strategic systems. The treaty that I proposed would prohibit us from developing a strategic defense system until such time as we reduce our offensive weapons. This system would be our defense, together with you, from unforeseen situations—a sort of gas mask." Not for the first time, nor the last, the president explained to the impatient general secretary the similarity between strategic defenses and gas masks, concluding, "We need a gas mask here. But we can discuss this in more detail at our next meeting."

"Fine," Gorbachev said abruptly, and the principals left the table.

GEORGE SHULTZ RECALLED THAT HE "was relieved. Gorbachev had introduced new and highly significant material. Our response, I knew, must be prepared with care. . . . I was glad we had on hand a knowledgeable team with all the expertise we needed. They could rework the president's talking points during the break. Excitement was in the air. I felt it, too. Perhaps we were at a moment of breakthrough after a period, following the Geneva summit, of stalemate in our negotiations." Back at the American Embassy, Shultz assembled Donald Regan, John Poindexter, Paul Nitze, Richard Perle, Max Kampelman, Kenneth Adelman, and Poindexter's military assistant, Robert Linhard, inside what Adelman calls "the smallest bubble ever built"— the Plexiglas security chamber, specially coated to repel electromagnetic radiation and mounted on blocks to limit acoustic transmissions, that is a feature of every U.S. Embassy in the world. Since the State Department had seen no need for extensive security arrangements for negotiating U.S. relations with little Iceland, the Reykjavik Embassy bubble was designed to hold only eight people. When Reagan arrived, the air-lock-like door swooshed and everyone stood up, bumping into each other and knocking over chairs in the confusion. Reagan put people at ease with a joke. "We could fill this thing with water," he said, gesturing, "and use it as a fish tank." Adelman gave up his chair to the president and sat on the floor leaning against the tailored presidential legs, a compass rose of shoes touching his at the center of the circle.

"Why did Gorbachev have more papers than I did?" Reagan kidded his secretary of state. Nitze volunteered that the Soviet proposal was "the best we have received in twenty-five years." Perle complained that the zero option wouldn't work if the Soviets kept missiles in Asia, since they could always shift them back to Europe. When Reagan mentioned Gorbachev's proposed ban on antisatellite testing, Adelman blurted, "Tell him it's a done deal. The Congress gave that away yesterday." Shoulder to shoulder, the president and his advisers talked for most of an hour about strategy. Then some of them went to a baked chicken lunch in the embassy dining room while others prepared a new set of talking points, six pages of single-spaced text. Reagan rehearsed reading the talking points. Gorbachev and his advisers, lunching on the main deck of the *George Otts,* discussed their afternoon's strategy.

THE TWO LEADERS CONVENED AGAIN with their two foreign policy advisers at Hofdi House at 3:30 p.m. Reagan began reading. In the first paragraph his document resurrected Perle's ballistic-missiles dodge, and even had the chutzpah to attribute "the focus . . . placed on ballistic missiles" to Gorbachev. "We are prepared for appropriate corresponding reductions in all ballistic missile systems," Reagan read, "including in our sea-launched ballistic missile force . . . as suggested. Additionally, we need throw-weight reductions, additional sub-limits and effective verification."

Reagan's advisers wanted to limit air-launched cruise missiles as well, but to exclude "other bomber weapons, gravity bombs and short-range attack missiles [for bomber defense]." Why exclude bombers? "Bombers fly slow and face unconstrained Soviet air defenses." "Unconstrained" was a Perle term of art, implying that Soviet air defenses were so good, or could be made so good, that they could effectively shield the Soviet Union from U.S. bombers—which would certainly have come as a surprise to the Strategic Air Command and Prime Minister Stanley Baldwin. "You cannot equate bomber weapons with missile warheads," Reagan read on, "and this was not done in past arms control agreements. But we can consider a sublimit of 350 bombers, thus bounding bomber weapons." The United States was prepared to accept an "aggregate ceiling on bombers and ballistic missiles" of 1,600. Bombers, of course, could carry multiple bombs, and the Soviet Union had only a limited bomber fleet.

Reagan said that he was disappointed with Gorbachev's position on INF. Intermediate-range missiles had to be controlled globally, he asserted, not simply in Europe. He would accept a global limit of one hundred each, with verification.

Turning now to SDI, Reagan told Gorbachev, confusingly, that his SDI cooperation treaty would not eliminate the ABM Treaty but simply take precedence over certain of its provisions. It would, he said, "establish a mechanism for the two sides to move together toward increasing reliance on defense." One by one Reagan repeated his old arguments. SDI would not be used to attack the Soviet Union. It would not be used to attack from space to earth—ballistic missiles were much better at long-distance attack. It would not be used to cover a first strike—to assure Gorbachev of that was the reason he was proposing to eliminate all ballistic missiles. Defenses would reinforce stability. They would protect against cheating. The United States would share them. If the two sides eliminated all ballistic missiles, their remaining forces would be far more stable. "Neither bombers nor cruise missiles are suitable for surprise attack. They are slow and vulnerable to unconstrained Soviet air defenses."

Rather than agree to a comprehensive test ban, Reagan said that the United States needed "verification improvements" in the Threshold Test Ban Treaty and the Peaceful Nuclear Explosions Treaty, negotiated in 1974 and 1976 but not yet ratified by the U.S. Senate. "Let's agree to fix those treaties," Reagan said, but he also said that "neither a test moratorium nor a comprehensive test ban is in the cards for the foreseeable future."

There was more, but the president finally concluded by proposing that they direct their experts that night to work through all the issues the leaders had identified: strategic offensive weapons, intermediate-range nuclear forces, defense and space, nuclear testing. He said Nitze, Kampelman, Perle, Edward Rowny, and Adelman would be prepared to work with Gorbachev's team there in Hofdi House beginning at eight o'clock that night. And believe it or not, he told Gorbachev, he had come to the end of his reading.

To clarify, Gorbachev asked if Reagan had agreed to his proposal for 50 percent reductions in strategic offensive missiles.

"Yes," Reagan said.

Gorbachev said sublimits for different systems had been the bane of the Nuclear and Space Talks going on in Geneva. His proposal had been to reduce all the strategic systems on both sides by 50 percent, he said, calling Perle's bluff. He meant land-based, sea-launched, and those carried by strategic bombers. "The force structures have evolved historically," he explained, "and if we proceed to reduce them by fifty percent across the board, we will reduce the level of strategic confrontation. The structure will remain the same, but the level will be lower, and this will be clear to everyone. Then the disputes which have been going on for years about limits and sublimits will be superseded by fifty-percent reductions. The level of confrontation will be cut in half." He included the SS-18 heavy missiles that the United States worried so much about, he added. Shultz, he said, was hearing that concession for the first time. We should act to untie the knot, he urged. Otherwise Kampelman and Karpov (Viktor Karpov, Kampelman's Soviet negotiating counterpart in Geneva) would continue beating around the bush.

It was an interesting idea, Reagan countered, but since the Soviet forces outnumbered the U.S. forces "by a lot," cutting by 50 percent wouldn't redress the imbalance. Gorbachev had a data sheet showing both U.S. and Soviet nuclear forces; he passed it to Reagan. Here is the data, he said. Let us cut this in half. Reagan said the experts should take it up. Gorbachev said it wasn't a matter for the experts; it needed a political decision. I *said* it was an interesting idea, Reagan bristled; Gorbachev should give the U.S. side a chance. Shultz spoke up to calm the waters: It's a bold idea, he interjected, and they needed bold ideas. Gorbachev agreed. Otherwise, he joked, it went back to Karpov and Kampelman, and that meant *kasha* forever (i.e., the same old porridge).

Reagan asked if he could keep the data sheet. Gorbachev said he could. Now the president had all their secrets, he added. He shrugged: There was no other way out of the forest. But if the United States tried to outsmart him, that would be the end of their negotiations. Reagan reassured him that such was not his intention.

They debated the zero option once more. Reagan claimed the United States had no missiles in Asia. But you have nuclear weapons in South Korea, Gorbachev insisted, on bases in Asia, and forward-based naval vessels as well; it doesn't matter to us if the bomb dropped on us came from an aircraft carrier or a base on land. Back and forth they argued, and finally the general secretary asked: "If we find a solution on Asian missiles, do you accept zero in Europe?" "Yes," Reagan said—a major breakthrough and a defeat for Perle, but one he later claimed to be a victory.

They came then again to SDI. If they were really beginning to reduce strategic missiles, Gorbachev argued, and eliminate medium-range missiles, which would itself be a tense business, how could they destroy the ABM Treaty, the only brake they had on dangerous developments? How could they abandon it when they should be strengthening it? Both sides had proposed not to withdraw from the treaty for a number of years; numbers were the only difference between the two positions. The Soviet side had proposed ten years, during which large-scale reductions would be taking place. That much time would certainly be needed. So it was logical to commit to ten years and limit strategic defense work to laboratory research only. They weren't far apart on testing, either, Gorbachev added, since negotiating a total ban would take time, and in the meantime they could begin reducing test yields and numbers and discuss the future of the test-ban treaties.

Gorbachev's points were interesting, Reagan responded, and their people should take them up. We believe you've already violated the ABM Treaty, he said, with the defenses you've built. He himself thought that SDI was the greatest opportunity of the twentieth century for peace. He wasn't proposing that they annul the treaty, but rather that they add something to it.

Dryly Gorbachev agreed that their experts should meet at eight that evening to consider all the ideas they had discussed. He would be instructing his people to look for genuine solutions in all areas of nuclear arms, he said, including verification. Now that they were getting down to specifics, his people would be fighting for verification. They would want it three times as much as the U.S. side.

We're both civilized countries, Reagan countered passionately, civilized people. "I'm older than you are," he told Gorbachev. "When I was a boy, women and children could not be killed indiscriminately from the air. Wouldn't it be great if we could make the world as safe today as it was then?"

He was proposing something to change this barbarism, he said. It was something to be shared. It was not for one country only. It would protect people if a madman wanted to use such weapons. Take Gadhafi—if he had them he would certainly have used them. Defense couldn't happen in their time; it would be in someone else's time. But he asked Gorbachev to think about the two of them standing there and telling the world that they had this protection, and asking others to join them in getting rid of these terrible systems.

By now, Rozanne Ridgway remembered, "It was a shouting match. Not angry, but two people passionate in their views, with diametrically opposed positions."

Gorbachev went through his arguments yet again, concluding that his concerns about SDI were not military. They had to do with convincing his people, and the Soviet Union's allies, that they should be prepared to begin reductions while the ABM Treaty was being destroyed. That wasn't logical, and his people and allies wouldn't understand it.

All the United States was saying, Reagan shot back, was that in addition to the missiles covered by the ABM Treaty, SDI was something bigger that he wanted the world to have. The United States was not building it for superiority—it wanted every country to have it. With the progress he and Gorbachev were making, he claimed, they didn't need ten years. He couldn't have said that a few years ago, but he didn't think it would take that long. He felt they were making progress. (In the end, SDI was a $44 billion failure; it was abandoned in 1993 for a program of research into ground-based ballistic-missile defense.)

After more discussion of meeting schedules, Reagan said he had one closing remark. Gorbachev had said the Soviet Union didn't need SDI and had a better solution. (Gorbachev had said his country had a cheaper solution, referring among other things to the Topol ballistic missile that Soviet designers were developing.) Perhaps both sides should go ahead, Reagan said, and if Gorbachev's people did better, the Soviet Union could give the United States theirs.

"Gorbachev finally exploded," Matlock recalls. " 'Excuse me, Mr. President,' he said, voice rising, 'but I cannot take your idea of sharing SDI seriously. You are not willing to share with us oil well equipment, digitally guided machine tools, or even milking machines. Sharing SDI would provoke a second American revolution! Let's be realistic and pragmatic.' "

Reagan responded with evident sincerity that if he thought the benefits wouldn't be shared, he would give up the project himself. Gorbachev scoffed that he doubted if the president even knew what the project contained.

MARSHAL SERGEI AKHROMEYEV, small and wiry, with pale blue eyes, at sixty-three the chief of the Soviet general staff, told George Shultz he was the last of the Mohicans—the last Soviet commander still active who had fought against the German Army in the Second World War. The Americans had wondered what his role would be at Reykjavik. He appeared that evening as the leader of the Soviet arms-negotiation expert group. (Gorbachev thus exquisitely co-opted the Soviet military after its attempt to manipulate him with its vacuous plan for complete disarmament.) A story Akhromeyev told over dinner that evening revealed both his stoicism and his survival instincts: Early in the war, he said, he had been assigned the task of blocking the advance of the German Army on a particular stretch of road leading into Leningrad. With his tank battalion he guarded that road for eighteen months, through the terrible Soviet winter, and never once in all those months went indoors. Shultz praised his patriotism. "Mr. Secretary," the marshal responded, "there was that, but I knew that if I had left that road, Stalin would have had me shot."

Akhromeyev's counterpart on the U.S. side was Paul Nitze, then seventy-nine. The Soviet team also included Viktor Karpov, Yevgeni Velikhov, and Georgi Arbatov; the U.S. team was Kampelman, Perle, Adelman, Rowny, and Linhard. A second pair of negotiating teams under Rozanne Ridgway and Alexandr Bessmertnykh met in another room to deal with human rights and regional issues. Ridgway and Bessmertnykh finished a little after midnight. The Nitze-Akhromeyev teams ran a marathon across more than ten hours of negotiation.

Akhromeyev made it clear at the beginning that he was there to push for change. "I'm no diplomat, like you," he told the Americans—reminding his own team as well. "I'm not a negotiator, like you. I'm a military man. Let's not repeat all the familiar arguments. Let's see how much progress we can make tonight. That's what I want and that's what Gorbachev wants."

They focused on three issues. Akhromeyev reverted to Gorbachev's original formula of an across-the-board 50 percent cut in strategic weapons. Since, theoretically, that formula would have left the United States at a disadvantage, with fewer ICBMs than the Soviets, Nitze argued for an agreement that equalized the numbers. An equal outcome, of course, meant that the Soviets would have to eliminate more ICBMs than the United States. They debated the question for six hours, along with a subsidiary question: How many warheads should a bomber count for? The U.S. side was adamant that bombs in no way equaled ballistic-missile warheads. (Certainly there were differences in time to target and perhaps in vulnerability to Soviet defenses, but the largest weapons in the U.S. arsenal were bombs, for the obvious reason that a bomber could carry more weight than a missile.)

Sometime after midnight, Rowny, who was greatly worried that the

United States might give something away, disagreed with Nitze on rules for counting missile warheads. Nitze called a caucus to hash out the difference, but the other members of the team backed Rowny. Akhromeyev had a similar argument with Karpov about the equal-outcomes problem in his caucus. Both sides returned to the table and debated some more. "At two o'clock in the morning," Nitze recalled in an interview, "Marshal Akhromeyev suddenly rose from his chair. He said that he was leaving, and I thought that that was the end of the negotiations, at least for that night. But then he turned at the door as he was leaving the room, and he said, 'I will be back at three o'clock.' So Bob Linhard . . . and I talked about it and we decided to go to the hotel at which Secretary George Shultz was staying and wake him up, and tell him exactly where we were in the negotiations, and get guidance from him as to what we should do next." Nitze and Linhard "hopped into a car and drove through the frigid Icelandic night to our hotel and woke up Secretary Shultz. He received us in his suite in robe and pajamas, surprisingly alert for that hour." Shultz listened, advised, and made it clear that Nitze was the boss of his team and didn't have to count heads. Nitze apologized for waking Shultz in the middle of the night. Shultz laughed: "Who do you think Akhromeyev woke up?"

Back at Hofdi House, Nitze continues, "Marshal Akhromeyev walked in and he sat down and he said, 'I'm authorized to change the position which I have been insisting upon up to now.' We on our side agreed to look for an equal end point through unequal reductions. So that on the main thing that had been blocking us, apparently Mr. Gorbachev had authorized him to move to our position, and it was at that point that I thought that with that basic change in the Soviet position, we probably could move on from there to really, finally working out an agreement that we could live with, and which they would accept."

For negotiating the START treaty the numbers they agreed on were six thousand weapons and sixteen hundred delivery vehicles. But how should they count bombers? Without long-range stand-off air-launched nuclear cruise missiles, Nitze argued, "it was unlikely our bombers could get to their targets against heavy Soviet air defenses, which were not to be limited." Whatever the authority of that argument Akhromeyev agreed to count bombers with bombs and defensive short-range attack missiles (SRAMs) as one each in the weapons category and the delivery vehicle category—a significant concession.

They were unable to agree on Asian INF limits. "It became clear," Nitze explains, "that Akhromeyev was not authorized to negotiate on the Asian level." They would have to leave that problem for the principals. So also the last frustrating hour-and-a-half debate over how to count such difficult-to-verify weapons as sea-launched cruise missiles carried out of sight on ships and submarines.

All in all, the night had been a success. "We made an immense amount of progress during those few hours, from three o'clock a.m. to 6:30 a.m.," Nitze said. "Defining strategic systems," Adelman concurs, "excluding bomber weapons, and closing on limits is one amazing night's work, indisputably more progress than we achieved in thousands of hours in hundreds of meetings over the previous five years." Then they had to work together to prepare a memorandum to be included in the final Reykjavik joint communiqué. Hofdi House was devoid of copiers; to make copies as they drafted the memorandum they had to borrow some old-fashioned Soviet carbon paper, which Akhromeyev provided—with a joke about superior Soviet technology. It was still dark when they finished; the sun would not rise for another hour. Nitze went off to brief Shultz, Akhromeyev to brief Gorbachev. "Damn good!" Shultz told Nitze. "It's what we came for!" Nitze, for whom negotiation was a professional sport, finally relaxed. "I haven't had so much fun in years," he confided.

The Reykjavik base camp was scheduled to fold its tents that Sunday morning after one more meeting between the principals. Schedule or no, Gorbachev and Reagan still had a range of mountains left to climb.

"FOR THE SUNDAY MORNING SESSION," George Shultz remembered, "we took our whole delegation to Hofdi House. People wandered about the upstairs sitting rooms, where huge oil paintings of subjects such as American astronauts in surreal landscapes hung on the wall." (U.S. astronauts had trained for their moon walks on the Iceland barrens.) "The president, in our pre-meeting discussion, agreed that our working group had made great progress in fleshing out and strengthening material developed during the first day. But the president also saw, as we all did, that much work remained."

In fact, both Reagan and Gorbachev were sharply disappointed. When they sat down together they proceeded to debate SS-20s in Asia, then nuclear testing. Reagan proposed turning the SDI issue over to their negotiators to explore areas of possible agreement. Gorbachev said the proposals he had brought to Reykjavik had been highly constructive, they had made real concessions, but the United States hadn't budged an inch. If anything, it was trying to drag things backward. They sparred a little more on INF.

Reagan said that the Soviet Union and the United States were the only two real nuclear powers; other countries had nuclear weapons basically for defense. (So the two superpower arsenals were weapons of war in Reagan's mind; so much for deterrence theory.) If the United States and the Soviet Union, Reagan said eagerly, were to start reducing their nuclear forces to zero, and stood shoulder to shoulder telling other nations that they must eliminate their nuclear weapons as well, it would be hard to imagine a country that wouldn't do so.

Gorbachev agreed. He felt, in fact, that the present opportunity might not come again. He had not been in a position a year ago, to say nothing of two or three years ago, to make the proposals he had made at Reykjavik. Ominously, he said he might not be able to make the same proposals in another year. Time passed, things changed; Reykjavik would be only a memory.

Reagan said they were both in the same boat, but that meant it was all the more important to use the time they had to free the world from the nuclear threat. Gorbachev said that given the proposals he had brought to Reykjavik, his conscience was clear. Abruptly he offered a major concession, another formula for agreeing on INF: zero U.S. and Soviet intermediate-range weapons in Europe, French and British forces excluded, one hundred warheads on Soviet systems in Asia, and one hundred U.S. warheads based on its own territory. (As they had discussed earlier, that meant the United States would be free to locate Pershings or similar weapons in Alaska, within range of the Soviet East.) The Soviets would accept this formula, Gorbachev said, even though it would require them to reduce their forces in Asia by an order of magnitude he could not even compute. Since the United States insisted on posing ultimata, Gorbachev added bitterly, and since the president was unwilling to make proposals of his own, the Soviet Union would accept these terms—which should show how serious his country was about reaching agreements.

Reagan said he agreed to the INF proposal Gorbachev had described, putting it in his pocket. That was good, Gorbachev said sarcastically, and when would the United States start making concessions of its own? He listed where they had found agreement: to reduce strategic forces by 50 percent; to eliminate intermediate nuclear forces from Europe; to freeze and begin to negotiate shorter-range INF; to reduce Soviet Asian warheads to one hundred, with the United States to have the right to the same number on its own territory. These were unprecedented steps, Gorbachev said, and they would require responsible implementation, including stringent verification—and the United States would find the Soviet Union even more vigorous than the United States in insisting on verification.

But the ABM Treaty was the crux of the matter, Gorbachev told Reagan. We understood before we came here that you were attached to the SDI program. We took that into account when we proposed that SDI-related research could continue in the laboratory for ten years. Ten years would allow the two sides to solve the problems of reducing nuclear weapons. This arrangement wouldn't impede SDI politically, practically, or technically.

What the hell was it that they were defending? Reagan erupted, revealing his real feelings about the ABM Treaty. The treaty restricted defenses to one hundred ground-based antiballistic missiles on each side, he said—which the United States had never deployed. That meant our only defense was retaliation if someone wanted to blow us up. That didn't give protection—it limited protection. Why the hell, the president went on, should the world have to live for another ten years under the threat of nuclear weapons when we'd decided to eliminate them? He failed to see the magic of the ABM regime. Far better to eliminate the missiles, so that our populations could sleep in peace. With strategic defense they could give the world a means of putting the nuclear genie back in the bottle. The next generation would reap the benefits when he and the general secretary were no longer around.

So it went through the morning and an hour past the time scheduled for lunch. Gorbachev reminded Reagan that "it takes two to tango" and asked if the president was ready to dance. Reagan reminded Gorbachev "once burned, twice shy," and recalled Soviet perfidies. Reagan quoted Marx and Lenin; Gorbachev said history was full of examples of those who had sought to overcome Marxism and Leninism by force and all had failed.

Shultz intervened and listed the points he felt they'd agreed upon. Both leaders took a deep breath. Reagan said he hoped he had made it clear that he would not give up SDI. Gorbachev said with a laugh that some had accused him of trying to encourage the development of SDI to increase the United States's defense burden—backhanding the notion popular among Reagan's national security advisers that SDI would weigh down the Soviets with the burden of trying to keep up.

Finally Gorbachev called time. On the first two questions, he said—strategic weapons reductions and INF—they could say there were common points. On the second two—the ABM Treaty and banning nuclear testing—there had been a meaningful exchange of views, but no common points. With that, Gorbachev said somberly, the meeting could end. It had not been in vain. But it had not produced the results that he had expected. Probably the same could be said for the United States. One had to be realistic. In political life one had to follow reality. "No, let's go home," he concluded. "We've accomplished nothing."

Were they truly to depart with nothing? Reagan asked plaintively. Gorbachev said they should talk about the humanitarian and regional issues, and they did. After a while Shultz asked to read some language he had formulated on nuclear security. Gorbachev rejected one paragraph and accepted a second. Then, relenting from his determination to break off negotiations, he proposed that the two foreign ministers meet over lunch to see what they could come up with. He didn't mind waiting an hour or two, he added. If the president agreed, he proposed they meet again at three p.m.

"The president agreed," the Sunday morning memorandum of conversation concludes, "and escorted Gorbachev from the room, ending the session." The two very frustrated men who led the two most powerful nations in the world would give ending the nuclear arms race another chance.

SHULTZ PULLED HIS TEAM TOGETHER. "It's been a slugging match all the way," he told them. "We're going to have one more round." They talked for a few minutes. The Soviet team joined them. Shultz began summarizing what the leaders had agreed on. Shevardnadze stopped him. "He was cold," Shultz recalls, "almost taunting. The Soviets had made all the concessions, he said. Now it was our turn: there was no point in trying to perfect language on other issues. Everything depended on agreement on how to handle SDI: a ten-year period of nonwithdrawal and strict adherence to the terms of the ABM Treaty during that period. That was their bottom line."

At the other end of the table, Linhard and Perle scribbled away on a yellow pad. When they were finished, the pad passed to Poindexter, Linhard's boss, and from Poindexter to Shultz. Shultz read it, explained to Shevardnadze that it was "an effort by some of us here to break the impasse" and read it aloud. It proposed limiting work on strategic defense to the research, development, and testing allowed by the ABM Treaty for five years, during which time the sides would achieve a 50 percent reduction in "strategic nuclear arsenals." After five years, the sides would continue reducing "the remaining ballistic missiles" with the goal of eliminating all "offensive ballistic missiles" at the end of a second five-year period. After ten years, "with all offensive ballistic missiles eliminated," either side could deploy defenses if it chose.

Gorbachev and Reagan returned. The leaders retreated upstairs with their teams. Reagan's advisers briefed him in the only place where they could meet in private, Rowny recalled, "a little ten by twelve bathroom where about ten of us crowded in. Several stood in the bathtub, Reagan was on the throne. I was agitated, I was worried about the idea of giving up all nuclear weapons."

Reagan reviewed the Linhard-Perle formulation. He liked it. "He gets his precious ABM Treaty," the president said, "and we get all his ballistic missiles. And after that we can deploy SDI in space. Then it's a whole new ball game." Reagan had the formulation typed up and took it with him when he descended the Norwegian dragon stairway to meet Gorbachev, with Shultz, Shevardnadze, two interpreters, and two note-takers to assist.

Shevardnadze had briefed Gorbachev on the Linhard-Perle formulation, and he and Gorbachev had formulated a paragraph. Back at the table with Reagan, the general secretary led off by reading his formulation aloud: no right of withdrawal from the ABM Treaty for ten years, all its provisions strictly observed during that period, testing of any components of an ABM system prohibited "except research and testing conducted in laboratories." Fifty percent reductions in strategic offensive weapons within five years, the remaining strategic offensive weapons eliminated during the second five years. "Thus by the end of 1996, the strategic offensive weapons of the USSR and the United States will have been totally eliminated."

Gorbachev made no immediate comment about the distinction in the Linhard-Perle formulation between "strategic nuclear arsenals" and "offensive ballistic missiles," the latter being the idea Perle had flogged around the White House earlier that year. The general secretary may not have noticed the distinction yet, or he may simply have decided to deal with his more fundamental objections first. In any case, the most obvious differences between the two formulations concerned how SDI research would be limited and whether or not strategic defenses after a ten-year limitation would be explicitly endorsed.

Reagan and Gorbachev hacked away at those differences for an hour. Gorbachev, evidently still believing he could swing the president over to his side, held himself calm while Reagan battered him: Why would Gorbachev object to SDI deployment after ten years, the president asked sarcastically—if, that is, he wasn't planning to develop a nuclear weapon or to pull one out of hiding somewhere? And if Gorbachev was so decidedly set on strengthening the ABM Treaty, how was Reagan to understand the Krasnoyarsk radar (a large radar station the Soviets were building in a location the treaty prohibited and that Gorbachev eventually would order to be torn down)?

When battering didn't work, Reagan unveiled a curious scenario complete with the happy ending he always sought as an outcome for the conflicts in his life: If the two countries completely eliminated their nuclear arsenals, why would Gorbachev be troubled if the United States or the Soviet Union put up a defense system against nonexistent weapons, just in case? Other people could build missiles. But if both countries completely eliminated their weapons, he could imagine, ten years from now, the two of them returning to Iceland with the last two missiles in the world. Reagan would be so old that Gorbachev wouldn't recognize him. He'd say, "Hello, Mikhail," and Gorbachev would say, "Ron, is that you?" The two of them would destroy the last missiles, and then the whole world would have a tremendous party.

The origin of Reagan's fantasy is revealing. It first appeared in notes he wrote for a speech he delivered to a governors' conference in 1963, "Are Liberals Really Liberal?" Criticizing the current U.S. "policy of accommodation with the Soviet Union," he mocked what he called the "liberal . . . answer to the bomb threat":

> The theory goes something like this: As time goes on the men in the Kremlin will come to realize that dogmatic communism is wrong. The Russian people will want a chicken in every pot, and decide some features of decadent capitalism may make for more plentiful poultry, while their system hasn't even provided a pot. By a strange paradox us decadent capitalists will have discovered in the meantime that we can do without a few freedoms in order to enjoy government by an intellectual elite which obviously knows what is best for us. *Then on some future happy day Ivan looks at Joe Yank, Joe looks at Ivan, we make bridge lamps out of all those old rockets, and discover the cold war just up and went away.* To bring all this about it is of course necessary that we whittle the back edge of our heels round so we can lean over backwards in an all out effort to prove to Ivan that we aren't mad at anybody.

At the end of his speech, Reagan offered an alternative to round-heeled accommodation: "We can make those rockets into bridge lamps," he concluded, "by being so strong the enemy has no choice, or we can bet our lives and freedom on the cockeyed theory that if we make him strong enough he'll learn to love us." His editors describe this 1963 speech as "an unvarnished statement of the strategy for dealing with the Soviet Union that he would follow, some twenty years later, as president." Unfortunately for Reagan's strategy, he had not, by his own estimate, come to Reykjavik stronger than the enemy, the men in the Kremlin had indeed begun to realize that dogmatic Communism was wrong, and they were still proving vigorously resistant to his plans.

Charmed despite himself by Reagan's Mikhail-and-Ron last rocket routine, Gorbachev said he wasn't sure he would survive until then.

Reagan: Well, I'm sure that I will.

Gorbachev: Oh, you'll survive. You've already passed the dangerous age for a man. You'll have smooth sailing until you're one hundred. I still have all the dangers ahead that catch up with a man at around sixty. And furthermore, I'll still have to meet with President Reagan, who, as I have learned, hates to concede a point. President Reagan wants to emerge the victor. But here, in these questions, there can't be one victor: Either we both win, or we both lose. We're both in the same boat.

Reagan: I know I won't live to see a hundred if I have to live in fear of these damned missiles.

Gorbachev: Then let's reduce them and liquidate them.

Reagan: This is a very strange situation. You want a ten-year period. I won't give up SDI. But both of us insist that the most important issue is eliminating our nuclear arsenals.

Gorbachev: You wouldn't even have to give up SDI, you know, since you could continue with research and testing at the laboratory scale. But I'm categorically opposed to a result where one of us wins and the other loses. Equality is essential at every stage. Only if the document takes into consideration the interests of both the U.S.A. and the U.S.S.R. will it be worthy of ratification and support. If one of us won and the other lost, that would come out at the next stage and the loser would leave everything in a ruin.

They went back to haggling.

Shultz interrupted to point out the "offensive ballistic missile" variation in the second five years of the Linhard-Perle formulation. He may have done so to remind Reagan of the terms he was offering—the president had never been entirely clear about the different kinds of nuclear delivery systems. Gorbachev found the variation bewildering. He thought they'd already agreed yesterday, he said, to reduce the entire triad of strategic weapons (i.e., missiles, submarines, bombers). Let's agree, he proposed, that we're speaking not only of missiles but of all strategic offensive weapons in this case as well.

At that point Reagan suggested they recess to meet with their advisers to see what was keeping them apart.

HIS TEAM AT HAND, INTENSELY EXCITED, Gorbachev paced an upstairs room. "Everything could be decided right now," he said.

In the room where Reagan met, it was. Richard Perle's biographer Jay Winik describes the crucial exchange as Perle described it to him:

> The president first looked at Perle. "Can we carry out research under the restraints the Soviets are proposing?"
>
> Perle's mouth was dry; he felt short of breath. Reagan was asking him for a

reason. If he said yes, it gave Reagan cover with the conservatives to confine SDI to the laboratory ("Richard Perle assured me . . ."); if he said no, he would be arguing against Shultz.

But his view was an unequivocal no. "Mr. President, we cannot conduct the research under the terms he's proposing. It will effectively kill SDI."

The president paused and weighed this, and then turned to Nitze and Shultz. They both counseled him to accept the language proposed by Gorbachev, and suggested that they would worry about whether research could be conducted in the laboratory later.

Perle stared hard at Reagan. What was he going to do?

What indeed. In Winik's telling, which came from Perle, Perle was left in doubt until the principals met again. But in fact Reagan accepted Perle's argument immediately, over the arguments of his most experienced counselors, Nitze and Shultz, as Perle revealed in a later interview:

> Some of the people present urged [the president] to go forward and thought that there were ways we could work around these limitations. . . . I expressed the categorical view that there was no way you could see the program through to a successful conclusion if we accepted the constraints that Gorbachev had in mind. . . . And upon hearing that, [Reagan] turned to Don Regan, his Chief of Staff, and said, "If we agree to the Gorbachev limitations, won't we be doing that simply so we can leave here with an agreement?" And it was a rhetorical question, of course, and you knew the moment he put it that he'd made his decision.

Just as Reagan's Joe Yank and Ivan story anticipated his Mikhail-and-Ron routine, so also did Reagan's 1963 condemnation of round-heeled liberals anticipate his rhetorical question. Was he trying to explain to his advisers, and justify to himself, why he should pass up the historic breakthrough, then so near at hand, that he so eagerly wanted? "Round-heeled" in the president's generation was a pejorative for women who were easily seduced; Reagan, and perhaps Gorbachev too, were both struggling not to be easily seduced. They were both men who prided themselves on their persuasive powers. Reykjavik was solving the old riddle of what happens when the Irresistible Force meets the Immovable Object; the answer was impasse.

I asked Perle why he felt limiting SDI to the laboratory would kill it. "The president went round the room," he told me, "to see if the others agreed. Ken Adelman did, but Don Regan wanted an agreement badly and so did the representative of the Joint Chiefs. The president saw the danger." I asked if Perle was concerned primarily with congressional support under such limiting conditions. "Yes," he said emphatically. "But I also didn't see how you could keep scientists interested in SDI for so many years with those limitations." I didn't ask Perle to address the question of the substance of the SDI program. He spoke of it in 2006, long after its demise, as he had spoken of it in Reykjavik, as a real phenomenon, not as the politically useful chimera that it was.

Reagan, having made his decision, sent Linhard and Perle off to revise their formulation, instructing them to reframe it in Gorbachev's format—but also, crucially, to remove the word "laboratory" from the result. With no other private space available where they could work, the two conspirators once more commandeered the upstairs bathroom, laying a board across the bathtub for a desk.

AT FIVE THIRTY P.M. on that cold, blustery October day, long after their discussions were supposed to have concluded, Reagan, Gorbachev, Shultz, and Shevardnadze met one last time. The several thousand journalists, photographers, and radio and television correspondents clamoring beyond the Hofdi House barriers understood the message of the afternoon's delay: The leaders were working on a major breakthrough. A Soviet press secretary had violated the press blackout early that afternoon to announce as much—another way Gorbachev put pressure on Reagan to come to agreement.

Reagan apologized for keeping Gorbachev waiting. You know how much trouble Americans have getting along with each other, he joked. He held up what he called "the final version we can offer you" and proceeded to read it:

> The USSR and the United States undertake for ten years not to exercise their existing right of withdrawal from the ABM Treaty, which is of unlimited duration, and during that period strictly to observe all its provisions while continuing research, development and testing, which are permitted by the ABM Treaty. Within the first five years of the ten-year period (and thus through 1991), the strategic offensive weapons of the two sides shall be reduced by 50 percent. During the following five years of that period, all remaining offensive ballistic missiles of the two sides shall be reduced. Thus by the end of 1996, all offensive ballistic missiles of the USSR and the United States will have been totally eliminated. At the end of the ten-year period, either side could deploy defenses if it so chose unless the parties agreed otherwise.

How do you feel about this formula? Reagan asked.

Gorbachev: I have two questions for you by way of clarification. You speak of "research, development and testing" as allowed by the ABM Treaty. Any mention of laboratory testing has disappeared from your formula. Was this done on purpose?

Reagan: The two sides have different views on what the treaty permits. This is something that ought to be decided in Geneva.

Gorbachev: I'm asking you, did you drop the mention of laboratories consciously or not?

Reagan: Yes, consciously—what's the problem?

Gorbachev: I'm simply clarifying your position; so far, I'm not commenting on it. One more question: In the first part of this formula you speak of reducing the strategic offensive weapons of the parties by 50 percent in the first five years. But in the second part, where you speak of the second five years, you mention offensive ballistic missiles. What's that about? Why such a difference in approach?

Reagan responded with a remarkable answer. During the recess, he said, while he was upstairs, he had received the message that the Soviets were mainly interested in ballistic missiles. He had thought earlier that they were thinking of everything nuclear, and then he had heard it was ballistic missiles. That's why we included that formula, he said. It's true that in the first part they had spoken of all types of strategic nuclear weapons including bombs on bombers and [cruise] missiles. But in the second part the United States spoke of ballistic missiles because he understood that's what Gorbachev wanted.

Gorbachev had been clear throughout the negotiations that he meant for all strategic nuclear weapons to be included in the agreement; he had reiterated the point just prior to the last break for consultations at four thirty that afternoon. Could Reagan have become confused? Evidently he could; for the next ten minutes the two leaders sparred over the question, and Reagan, increasingly testy, blamed the confusion on Gorbachev:

Gorbachev: We both agreed a long time ago that the terms include all components of the triad.

Reagan: So am I to understand that by the end of 1996 all strategic offensive ballistic missiles will be eliminated?

Gorbachev: What about planes?

Reagan: But what I want to know is, will all offensive ballistic missiles be eliminated?

Gorbachev: In the first part of your formulation . . .

Reagan: Is that the only thing you're opposed to?

Gorbachev: I'm simply trying to clarify this question.

Reagan: We'll have to figure it out.

Gorbachev: We really need both formulations to be identical.

Reagan: Apparently we simply misunderstood you. But if that's what you want—okay.

Was Reagan being disingenuous? Did someone deliberately mislead him? He said specifically that they had received a message. It would not have come from the Soviet side, since limiting disarmament to ballistic missiles was against Soviet interests, given the U.S. preponderance in bombers and cruise missiles. Who on the American side had lied to the president and misled him? Whoever it was, no one is telling; none of the post-Reykjavik accounts of the meeting even mentions the exchange.

Shultz jumped in to save the ballistic missile bait-and-switch by raising questions about other categories of ballistic missiles, evidently trying to confuse Gorbachev. He didn't succeed.

The president listened as the general secretary traded details with the secretary of state. The details—ballistic missiles versus ballistic missiles, cruise missiles, and bombers, Shultz's interjection of short-range and intermediate-range missiles—seem to have clarified for Reagan the scale of what Gorbachev was proposing, and he rejoined the conversation with an eager question.

Reagan: Let me ask, do we mean that by the end of the two five-year periods all nuclear explosive devices will be eliminated, including bombs, battlefield weapons, cruise missiles, sub-launched, everything? *It would be fine with me if we got rid of them all.*

Gorbachev: *We can do that. We can eliminate them all.*

Shultz: *Let's do it!*

Reagan: If we agree that by the end of the ten-year period all nuclear weapons will be eliminated, we can send that agreement to Geneva. Our teams can put together a treaty and you can sign it when you come to Washington.

Gorbachev, seemingly startled, agreed. Then he raised the red flag of confining SDI to the laboratory.

Reagan reacted angrily. We've come a long way, he said. The ABM Treaty sets the limits, and what the hell difference does it make anyway? He was just trying to protect the United States, to make a sort of gas mask against the danger of nuclear maniacs.

Yes, Gorbachev said with contempt, he'd already heard about the gas mask and the maniacs, about ten times. But Reagan still hadn't convinced him, he said.

Upstairs, where the two teams of advisers had gathered, the mood was increasingly grim. "I remember tension growing," Chernyaev writes, "as both we and our American colleagues awaited the end of the meeting. We didn't want to talk about anything anymore. We stood by the windows, looking out on the dark ocean. Waiting, waiting, hoping."

More debate: "A matter of principle." "But you're burning all my bridges."

Gorbachev: Is that your final position? If so, then I think we can end our meeting on that.

Reagan: Yes. It's final. You must understand that experiments and research cannot always remain within laboratory walls—sometimes it's necessary to go outside.

Gorbachev: And you understand me too. The question of the laboratory for us isn't a matter of being stubborn or hardheaded. It's not casuistry. We're agreeing to deep reductions and in the final analysis to the destruction of nuclear arms. But at the very same time, the American side is pushing us to agree to allow them the right to create space weapons. That's unacceptable to us. If you agree to restrict your research to the laboratory, without going into space, then in two minutes I'll be ready to sign the treaty.

But Reagan couldn't agree; as Perle had assured him, restricting SDI to laboratory research must kill it.

Gorbachev gave it one more try: Mr. President, allow me to speak in confidence and with frankness. If we sign a package containing huge concessions on the part of the Soviet Union on the cardinal problems, then you will become, without exaggeration, a great president. You're literally two steps away from there. If not, then we may as well go home and forget about Reykjavik. But there won't be another chance. I know I won't have another chance. I believed strongly in the possibility of coming to agreement. Otherwise I wouldn't have proposed holding an urgent meeting with you and I wouldn't have come here in the name of the Soviet leadership with a solid supply of serious compromises. I counted on their being met with understanding and support and on our being able to come to agreement. If that did happen, even now, if we were able to attain the destruction of nuclear arms, then none of your critics will be able to say a word, because the vast majority of people in the world would welcome our success. If we're unable to agree, however, then obviously this will become a matter for another generation of leaders: You and I no longer have any time left. The American side has not made any substantive concessions at all, not a single large step to meet us even partway. It's hard to conduct business on this basis.

Shevardnadze jumped in. He said he would speak very emotionally, because he felt they had come very close to accomplishing a historic task, to decisions of historic significance. If future generations read the minutes of these meetings, the foreign minister said, and saw how close the two countries had come before they let these opportunities pass—those generations would never forgive them.

Reagan: It's a question of one word. If I give you what you're asking, it will cause me great damage at home.

Gorbachev: Let's end it there, then. We can't agree to what you're asking—that's all I have to say.

Reagan: Are you really, for the sake of one word, going to reject the historic possibility of an accord?

Gorbachev: It's not just a question of a word, but a question of principle. If I return to Moscow and say that I agreed to allow you to test in the atmosphere and in space, they would call me a fool and not a leader.

Reagan: I ask you for a personal favor, one that would have enormous impact on our future relations, and you refuse me.

Gorbachev: There are different kinds of favors. What you're asking of the U.S.S.R. would never be acceptable to the United States.

Reagan: One word. I ask you again to change your mind as a favor to me, so that we can go to the people as peacemakers.

Gorbachev: It's unacceptable. Agree to a ban on tests in space and in two minutes we'll sign the document. We can't agree on anything else. What we could agree to, we already have. We can't be reproached for anything. I have a clear conscience before my people and before you. I did all that I could.

Reagan: It's a pity. We were so close to agreement. I think, after all, that you didn't want to reach an agreement. I'm sorry.

Gorbachev: I'm also sorry this happened. I did want an agreement, and I did everything I could for it, if not more.

Reagan: I don't know when we'll have another chance like this, or if we'll be able to meet soon.

Gorbachev: I don't know either.

REAGAN STOOD UP FIRST. "LET'S GO, GEORGE," he said to Shultz. He wrote later that he was getting "angrier and angrier," and his face was knotted with anger when he and Gorbachev emerged together into the television lights. "More than body language conveyed a message," Shultz said. "Our faces looked stricken and drained."

"It was a dark day," Chernyaev recalled, "with huge waves coming off the beach. We all crowded outside. . . . The time was late. . . . The stress was incredible. The tension was so high that we couldn't talk. We were just making strange, low sounds. Then the door opened . . . and we saw there the grave faces of the leaders. The Americans looked graver and more disappointed than the others. Gorbachev also looked very unhappy."

Gorbachev wrote that he and the president "left the house as it was getting dark. We stood by the car." Everyone was in a bad mood.

"Reagan reproached me. 'You planned from the start to come here and put me in this situation!'

" 'No, Mr. President,' I replied. 'I'm ready to go right back into the house and sign a comprehensive document on all the issues agreed if you drop your plans to militarize space.'

" 'I'm really sorry,' was Reagan's reply. We made our farewells and he left in his car."

Dobrynin, who was standing with the men when they reached Reagan's car and served as an impromptu interpreter, adds two more lines to their dialogue. "Gorbachev," he wrote, "his voice ringing with bitterness he could hardly hide, said: 'Mr. President, you have missed the unique chance of going down in history as a great president who paved the way for nuclear disarmament.' Reagan replied gloomily, 'That applies to both of us.' "

Reagan remembered a different exchange:

> I realized [Gorbachev] had brought me to Iceland with one purpose: to kill the Strategic Defense Initiative. . . .
>
> When we reached our cars before leaving Reykjavik, Gorbachev said, "I don't know what else I could have done." I said, "I do. You could have said yes." In my diary that night, I wrote:
>
>> He wanted language that would have killed SDI. The price was high but I wouldn't sell and that's how the day ended. All our people thought I'd done exactly right. I'd pledged I wouldn't give away SDI and I didn't, but that meant no deal on any of the arms reductions. He tried to act jovial but I was mad and showed it. Well, the ball is now in his court and I'm convinced he'll come around when he sees how the world is reacting.
>
> I was very disappointed—and *very* angry.

Whose victory, whose defeat? I asked Thomas Graham, Jr., who was the general counsel to the Arms Control and Disarmament Agency at the time of the Reykjavik summit, about Perle's part in encouraging the president to hang a potentially world-transforming breakthrough on a specious concern for testing outside the "laboratory" systems that had hardly yet even entered the laboratory in 1986. "Perle regarded his successful frustration of agreement at Reykjavik as one of his most important achievements," Graham responded.

Reykjavik was not quite over. Reagan, still furious, returned to the American Embassy to reframe the standoff as a victory. Shultz told the waiting press that all was not in vain, but his quivering lip said otherwise.

Gorbachev, prepared in his anger to condemn the American side and call the meeting a failure, turned himself around in the space of the few minutes it took him to reach the press center:

> I walked from the building where the talks had been held. It was a distance of some 400 meters and I was feverishly collecting my thoughts. One thing preyed on my mind—had we not reached an agreement both on strategic and intermediate-range missiles, was it not an entirely new situation, and should it be sacrificed for the sake of a momentary propaganda advantage? My intuition was telling me that I should cool off and think it all over thoroughly. I had not yet made up my mind when I suddenly found myself in the enormous press conference room. About a thousand journalists were waiting for us. When I came into the room, the merciless, often cynical and cheeky journalists stood up in silence. I sensed the anxiety in the air. I suddenly felt emotional, even shaken. These people standing in front of me seemed to represent mankind waiting for its fate to be decided.
>
> At this moment I realized the true meaning of Reykjavik and knew what further course we had to follow.
>
> My speech has been published in newspapers and commented on by scores of journalists, political scientists and politicians. I therefore do not quote it *in extenso.* The key phrase of the speech was: "*In spite of all its drama, Reykjavik is not a failure—it is a breakthrough, which allowed us for the first time to look over the horizon.*" The audience came out of its state of shock, greeting the sentence with thunderous applause. One journalist wrote later in an article characterizing the mood of the press conference: "When the General Secretary presented the failure of the Reykjavik meeting as a victory, Raisa Gorbachev was sitting in the conference hall, looking with awe at her husband, with tears rolling down her face."

In that extraordinary press conference, in private remarks to Chernyaev during their flight home to Moscow, and in talks to the Soviet people afterward, Gorbachev evaluated Reykjavik for the complicated but ultimately productive confrontation it was:

> The position of the American side in Reykjavik on the ABM issue has clearly shown that they have not abandoned the quest for superiority. That is why they

did not have enough character, responsibility or political decisiveness to step over that threshold.

It seems to me that America has yet to make up its mind.

We felt that there was a definite lack of a new way of thinking at this meeting. And the ghost of pursuit of military superiority re-emerged. This summer I met with Mr. Nixon, and he said to me then: I have grounds to say, on the basis of my vast political and life experience, that the search for the ghost of superiority has taken us too far. Now we do not know how to break away from the mounded stockpiles of nuclear weapons. All this is complicating and poisoning the situation in the world.

I think nevertheless that the entire meeting here was of major significance. We did, after all, come close to reaching agreements; only they have yet to be endorsed.

Reykjavik generated more than just hopes. Reykjavik also highlighted the difficulties encountered on the way to a nuclear-free world.

After all, a start has to be made somehow. . . . If we always turn to the past for advice and make use of what belongs to very different times, without considering where we are today and where we will be tomorrow, and that there may be no tomorrow at all if we act in this way, there will be no dialogue whatsoever. There must be some way of making a start.

IN THE SPRING OF 1992, MIKHAIL GORBACHEV visited Stanford University as a guest of George Shultz. Before dinner at Shultz's house, the former secretary of state recalled, "We sat in the back yard, and I said to him, 'When you entered office, and when I entered, the Cold War was about as cold as it got, and when we left office it was over. So what do you think was the turning point?' And he didn't hesitate one second. He said, 'Reykjavik.' I said, 'Why do you say that?' He said, 'For the first time, the real leaders got together and really talked about the important subjects.' "

Gorbachev's answer was perhaps tinged with nostalgia; compared to the domestic political struggles that challenged him after Reykjavik, the debate with Ronald Reagan must have come to seem benign. At the time it left him with mixed feelings of anger, frustration, and hope; he said later that its effect on him was "comparable to Chernobyl." In his 1987 book *Perestroika,* he wrote that "the meeting in Iceland was a landmark [that] signified completion of one stage in the disarmament effort and the beginning of another." After Reykjavik, however, he added, "the objective is nearer and more palpable, while the situation has grown more complex and contradictory." Shortly after returning from Iceland he also told the Politburo that it had botched the job of modernizing Soviet industry fifteen years ago and that the country couldn't afford such "irresponsibility" again. "The fate of the country is on the line," Gorbachev reproached his colleagues, "and we are really at a historical turning point. *They look at us in the West and wait for us to drown.*" He said reducing the defense burden was crucial to the success of perestroika.

Gorbachev was ready to negotiate seriously the reduction and even abolition of nuclear weapons, replacing nuclear deterrence with common security. He had learned at Reykjavik that Reagan was also ready, but believed fervently that nuclear abolition required the protection of strategic defense. The U.S. rejection of the grand bargain Gorbachev had offered at Reykjavik—strategic nuclear disarmament, zero INF in Europe, a comprehensive test ban, intrusive on-site inspection in exchange for restricting SDI to the laboratory—supplied confirming evidence, as he told Chernyaev on the way home, that "SDI is the main obstacle to nuclear disarmament." But shockingly, neither he nor Eduard Shevardnadze had been clear at Reykjavik on what restricting SDI to laboratory research actually meant when they insisted on it so vehemently.

"A few days after Gorbachev came back," Roald Sagdeev told me, "Shevardnadze called me. 'Could you come talk to me?' he asked. So I came. He said, 'You know what happened. Gorbachev insisted on a laboratory level of activity and it stalemated the negotiations.' Shevardnadze asked me, 'Can you explain to me what is a laboratory in this context? Is it a small room down in the basement tinkering with something, or what is it?' I told him, 'Eduard Ambrosievich, it's too late to interpret "laboratory" as a room in a building, because if you open *Pravda* in the last couple of years, you'll find a story almost every day reporting about the success of our orbital laboratory—the *Salud* orbital station.'

"This interested Shevardnadze very much," Sagdeev continued. "He said, 'This is important.' And then he did something very interesting. He said, 'Can you fly to New York and give a talk about what you understand a laboratory to be in the context of strategic defense research?' So in two or three days I was given a diplomatic passport and a ticket. I flew to New York, where a press conference had been arranged at the United Nations [on 29 October 1986]. I said some tests could be carried on in space, because we scientists consider manned space stations to be orbital laboratories. It's the amplitude of activity that's important—the power of a laser and so on. Tests with modest instruments—devices, not actual components—would be admissible under the ABM Treaty. So next day the *Washington Post* reported, 'Soviet scientist says "modest" SDI testing is compatible with ABM pact.' It was Shevardnadze who promoted this understanding. He was far ahead of anyone in trying to reach practical agreement. I personally think Shevardnadze played a tremendous role at that time."

Realizing that the West would never acknowledge progress in glasnost while the Soviet physicist and Nobel Peace Prize laureate Andrei Sakharov and his physician wife, Elena Bonner, continued to live in forced exile in the city of Gorky, which was off-limits to the Western press, Gorbachev moved in early December to arrange their return to Moscow.* Fortuitously, Sakharov began criticizing the Reykjavik all-or-nothing negotiation almost as

---

* In Moscow in 1992, Bonner told me bitterly of reviewing her husband's KGB file and discovering that at a Politburo meeting Gorbachev had attributed Sakharov's stubborn dissent to the influence on him of

soon as he and Bonner stepped off the overnight train at Yaroslavl Station in Moscow on 23 December 1986. He spoke to an international audience on the subject at a forum called *For a Nuclear-Free World and the Survival of Humanity* in Moscow in mid-February 1987. The forum included a delegation from the Federation of American Scientists, the successor organization to the original associations organized by the scientists of the Manhattan Project in 1945. The two leaders of the FAS delegation, the Princeton physicist Frank von Hippel and the CEO of the Federation, Jeremy Stone, shared Gorbachev's table at the forum's final banquet and supported Sakharov's arguments. Sakharov dismissed SDI as a "Maginot line in space—expensive and ineffective." He favored abandoning the all-or-nothing "package principle," he said, because doing so "would create a new political and strategic climate in which the U.S. would not deploy antimissile defenses in space" or, alternatively, if they did so, "we would simply revert to the current situation [of mutual deterrence], with appreciable political gains for the USSR."

Gorbachev untied SDI from at least the INF negotiations in a television address on 1 March 1987. Three days later the United States offered a draft treaty with comprehensive provisions for verification. Shultz traveled to Moscow in April, and he and Gorbachev discussed the idea of reducing or eliminating not only intermediate nuclear forces but also short-range nuclear forces. A Soviet treaty draft followed.

Soviet military leaders strongly resisted an INF treaty; some even dared to warn Gorbachev to slow down, the journalist Don Oberdorfer reports. Again fortuitously, a nineteen-year-old German student named Mathias Rust, who had earned his private pilot's license around the time of the Reykjavik summit, decided to take East-West relations into his own hands. He said later that he was "very political," followed Reykjavik closely, and out of that experience formed a belief that "the aircraft was the key to peace. I could use it to build an imaginary bridge between East and West." On 13 May 1987, Rust rented a Cessna 172B, a four-seat light aircraft with a range of about 625 miles (1,005 kilometers), and began a fifteen-day odyssey that culminated in a shocking penetration of Soviet airspace that decisively refuted Richard Perle's contention of unconstrained and supposedly impenetrable Soviet air defenses.

"that Jewish bitch," meaning Bonner. The file has since been published and I do not find the phrase there, but it may have been purged. Gorbachev in the course of manipulating his colleagues often pretended to share their values. Certainly he felt ambivalence about Sakharov, and may well have been prepared to blame Bonner.

Rust flew first from Hamburg to Iceland, presumably to visit the scene of the Reykjavik summit. From Iceland he flew to Norway, then on to Helsinki. When he left Helsinki on the morning of 28 May, he filed a flight plan for Stockholm. Once over the Baltic, however, he turned east and followed the coastline toward Leningrad, about 180 miles, then turned southeast, dove beneath Soviet radar, and beelined across 400 miles of Soviet territory into Moscow, the combined distance nearly emptying the Cessna's fuel tanks. (When a Soviet Air Defense pilot spotted and reported the border violation, his ground commander refused to believe him. The Finns thought Rust had crashed into the Baltic and mounted a major search-and-rescue effort.) "My plan was to land in Red Square," the German student said, "but there were too many people and I thought I'd cause casualties. I had thought about landing in the Kremlin, but there wasn't enough space. I wanted to choose somewhere public, because I was scared of the KGB." He buzzed Red Square three times before he noticed a wide highway bridge paralleling the large parking area behind St. Basil's Cathedral. "I landed there and taxied into Red Square. As it turned out, the day I chose [for the flight] was the [national] holiday of the border patrol. I suspect that's how I got away with it." Alien in a red flight suit and wearing a motorcycle helmet, Rust climbed down from his plane and informed the citizens crowding around him that he carried a twenty-page plan for nuclear disarmament to deliver to Gorbachev. The KGB eventually hauled him away. He served 432 days in Lubyanka prison— KGB headquarters—before returning home.

The results of Rust's peaceful mission, which drew Gorbachev and the senior leadership of the Politburo back early from a Warsaw Pact meeting in Berlin, came to be called the Rust Massacre. Gorbachev used the embarrassing event to sack the resistant defense minister, Sergei Sokolov, and replace him with a younger and more pliant general, Dmitri Yazov, who was a perestroika enthusiast within the military. "Gorbachev also ordered far-reaching military reform," the historian Robert English summarizes, "including a purge of the officer corps, that shattered the morale and unity of the brass. With his opponents temporarily reeling, and with public opinion increasingly assertive and increasingly hostile to them, Gorbachev now prevailed in pushing through the concessions necessary for the INF treaty, for an Afghan settlement and for progress on issues from human rights to third world conflicts." The joke around Moscow was that Rust should get the Order of Lenin.

In the United States, the Iran-Contra affair became public in November 1986. The revelation that the Reagan administration had been defying Congress and the Constitution to sell arms to Iran to raise money to support the right-wing militia fighting to overthrow the revolutionary government of Nicaragua preoccupied and politically wounded Reagan that winter. The scandal allowed Shultz to gain leverage against the neoconservatives who were resisting post-Reykjavik arms reductions. Frank Carlucci replaced John Poindexter as national security adviser. Perle, who had complained for years that government service was impoverishing, resigned in the spring as deputy secretary of defense to write his novel and make some money. When Caspar Weinberger stepped down in November 1987, Carlucci replaced him as secretary of defense and Colin Powell moved up to national security adviser. Despite the neoconservatives, Shultz pursued arms negotiations vigorously with Shevardnadze and Gorbachev because he believed that one of the most popular presidents in American history had the right and the mandate to end the nuclear arms race and the Cold War.

For Thomas Graham, Jr., who participated in the INF treaty negotiations, Reykjavik was "the true watershed of modern arms control." Everything changed when Gorbachev agreed to the principle of intrusive on-site inspection, Graham writes:

> In 1987 the Soviets at INF were prepared to exchange more data on their systems than the [U.S. Joint Chiefs of Staff] wanted, as there was a limit to what the JCS was prepared to turn over. In the last week of the INF negotiations the Soviet officer making the presentation said, "A week ago I would have been shot for what I am doing today" (he really meant a year ago). Gorbachev agreed to the U.S. proposal, pressed during 1986 in Geneva, of double zero. There were, first, a ban on all intermediate-range, ground-launched nuclear missiles (both ballistic and cruise) of ranges from 1,000 to 5,500 kilometers and a ban on all short-range, ground-launched nuclear missiles of ranges 500 to 1,000 kilometers. The higher range ban captured the U.S. Pershing II and GLCM as well as the Soviet SS-20. There were no systems between the range of Pershing II (1,800 km) and Pershing I (950 km). The Soviet SS-23 had a 500-km range and was caught by the lower range ban. In 1981 Richard Perle had urged Ronald Reagan to propose a zero solution for INF. It looked good. Dutch peace groups had proposed it, but it was virtually out of the question that the Soviet Union would accept it given their advantage of about 1,200 to zero in INF systems. But lo and behold, five years later Gorbachev was accepting not one, but two zeros, the famous INF double-zero solution.

Negotiations and preparations were barely completed in time for the treaty to be signed at the Washington summit on 8 December 1987 at 1:45 p.m., an hour Nancy Reagan's astrologer had declared to be propitious. In his memoirs, Gorbachev would call the Soviet deployment of SS-20s, which had started the whole complicated problem, "an unforgivable adventure embarked on by the previous Soviet leadership under pressure from the military-industrial complex"; the INF Treaty, he wrote with relief, "removed a pistol held to our head." This "first nuclear arms reduction treaty," he added, ". . . set the whole process in motion. It is doubtful whether we would ever have been able to sign the subsequent agreements without it—the INF treaty represented the first well-prepared step on our way out of the Cold War, the first harbinger of the new times." There had not been time to devise a verification regime; the United States's Sandia National Laboratories learned in December that it had six weeks to develop a prototype and two months to deliver—which it did. During negotiations, the United States had insisted on the right to station inspectors at the plant that had built the SS-20s and would continue producing the SS-25 Topol, the Votkinsk Machine-Building Plant in the town of Votkinsk, in the Ural Mountains. "A reciprocal right was granted the Soviet Union," Graham notes with amusement, "at a former U.S. Pershing II production facility at Magna, Utah . . . much to the surprise of the Hercules Corporation, whose site it was."

"A great number of missiles were [eventually] destroyed," the Soviet arms control expert Nikolai Detinov recalls. "I can tell you how many. On May 31, 1991, we [finished liquidating] 889 intermediate-range missiles, including 654 SS-20 missiles, as well as 957 shorter-range missiles, including 239 SS-23 missiles. The United States during that time liquidated 234 Pershing II missiles and 443 cruise missiles and 169 Pershing I missiles. That was the end, I hope, of intermediate-range missiles in Europe." The INF Treaty eliminated a whole class of nuclear-weapons systems, the first treaty ever to do so.

EARLY IN THE COLD WAR, when someone insisted that the Soviet Union and the United States would come to blows one day, Enrico Fermi, the Italian-born Nobel-laureate physicist who coinvented the nuclear reactor, had asked dryly, "Where will they fight?" Fermi meant that the two nations lacked a traditional cause for armed belligerence—they contested no territory— and technically that was true, but the answer to his question through the years of U.S.-Soviet conflict was always Europe. Since the Russian Revolution, the wealthy elite of the United States had feared that the red tide of Communism would flood across the world if it was not resolutely stanched. The Soviet victory over Nazi Germany, Stalin's evident determination to dominate Eastern Europe, his reluctance to quit northern Iran after the end of the Second World War, all reinforced Western fears. Two world wars had begun in Europe, and it seemed to the architects of containment—Dean Acheson and George Kennan first of all but Paul Nitze enduringly—that the United States had suffered for not engaging with and guarding Europe to prevent those earlier conflicts. They also intended to prevent German rearmament.

NATO originated in those concerns. So did arming NATO with nuclear weapons and threatening their first use when Soviet conventional forces fell into formation along the NATO nations' eastern borders. At the height of the confrontation, no continent on earth was more heavily armed than Europe. The Cold War was not, first of all or fundamentally, the clash between radically different and incompatible ideologies that American policymakers claimed for it in order to encourage and sustain popular American support; it was first of all and fundamentally an effort to prevent a third conflagration (and this one potentially nuclear) from catching fire in the unstable space where two previous world wars had burned. George H. W. Bush confirmed this analysis, mutatis mutandis, in a memoir he wrote in retirement with Brent Scowcroft:

> I always have believed that the United States bears a disproportionate responsibility for peace in Europe and an obligation to lead NATO. In the 1930s, we learned the hard way that it was a mistake to withdraw into isolation after World War I. We watched as Europe struggled with fascism, but were drawn inevitably into battle to restore its freedom. When the Cold War began, Western Europe became the front line against a Soviet threat, and our allies depended on the United States to point the direction for NATO; the American president was to lead the way.

It followed that if Europe could be stabilized—if the confrontation between the two alliances could be neutralized there—then the Cold War would lose its real purpose and would very likely melt away.

The question of reducing Soviet *conventional* forces in Europe had already come up briefly at the Geneva and Reykjavik summits, but Gorbachev had focused first of all on unloading the nuclear pistol pointed at his head. With the changes of military leadership that followed the Mathias Rust invasion and the conclusion of the INF Treaty, he was ready to begin negotiating conventional-force reductions. One reason certainly was to save the expense, but such economy would not have won Politburo backing until the logic of common security and Gorbachev's conviction that the West had no intention of starting a war made such massive deployment both superfluous and unnecessarily provocative.

At a meeting in Moscow between Gorbachev and Shultz on 28 February 1988, the two "briefly touched on the question of conventional forces, agreeing that we 'should push on.' " Push on they did. At the Moscow summit at the end of May 1988 where Reagan and Gorbachev signed the instruments of ratification of the INF Treaty, the two leaders discussed conventional forces; the discussion, Gorbachev writes, "was facilitated by the fact that only two weeks before, George Shultz and Eduard Shevardnadze had finally agreed on the agenda for negotiations: armed forces, conventional weapons and equipment—all types would be included in the negotiations"—an important preliminary agreement.

Gorbachev's continuing concern for nuclear as well as conventional forces emerged at a private dinner the Gorbachevs and the Shevardnadzes gave during the Moscow summit for the Reagans and the Shultzes. Shultz, in a memo to Reagan written shortly afterward, documented for the president "the remarkable evening . . . at the Tsarist palace . . . the liveliness of the conversation and the easy conviviality." He was struck, Shultz wrote, "by how deeply affected Gorbachev appeared to be by the Chernobyl accident. He commented that it was a great tragedy which cost the Soviet Union billions of rubles and had only been barely overcome through the tireless efforts of an enormous number of people. Gorbachev noted with seemingly genuine horror the devastation that would occur if nuclear power plants became targets in a conventional war, much less a full nuclear exchange. . . . It was obvious from that evening that Chernobyl has left a strong anti-nuclear streak in Gorbachev's thinking."

Alexander Yakovlev, Gorbachev's primary idea man, was writing a book that year, a furious book about what he called "the fate of Marxism." Gorbachev could not have missed hearing its arguments. They reflected the increasing sense of urgency that the Soviet leader and his reformers felt as Party, military, and bureaucratic resistance to perestroika increased. The time was "merciless," Yakovlev wrote, but it was "also a tragic and cleansing time," a "great time of a Great Sobering. It has been a tortuous and contradictory path from the hopes and illusions of the Social Experiment of the Twentieth Century to *an understanding* of the depths of the abyss of our national fate, most of all for those who sincerely believed, sincerely hoped, sincerely blundered." As for the present day, 1988:

> Our country is now morally and physically exhausted. Naturally, various people assess the reasons for this exhaustion in various ways and see different paths out of the situation. Right-wingers of all stripes have constantly reiterated that

perestroika has brought the country to a state of collapse. If we get rid of perestroika, they say, we will live like human beings again, as we lived in "the good
old times of stagnation."

But how did we live?

Irresponsibility, lack of discipline and elementary order, and unrestrained
drunkenness litter the landscape of both our private and our public existence.
There are millions of micro- and macro-Chernobyls, from the actual tragedy
of the nuclear power station, to pollution of the sea, air and land, to the lack of
nitroglycerine [tablets for angina] in our drugstores. Time bombs are con-
stantly going off and will continue to explode until normal economic relations
prevail.

For decades, cast iron, coal, steel and petroleum had priority over food,
housing, hospitals, schools and services. The claim that "it had to be that way"
is fallacious. Because of the economic re-feudalism of management, the price
of industrialization has been disastrously high in both human and material
terms. Disregard for the individual has known no bounds.

We will not brag about the absence of unemployment under the old system.
There was no unemployment under serfdom, either. . . .

The country, the people, and the young generations are having to pay for the
past. That is why no turning back, no restoration of the past in new forms is
possible—with or without perestroika, with the reforms or in spite of them,
with democracy or dictatorship. Those who maintain otherwise either do not
understand what is at stake or understand and are deliberately deceiving the
people. . . . History may be maimed, mutilated, falsified, concealed, rewritten,
or treated in any fashion whatsoever, but it cannot be deceived.

By the end of October 1988, increasingly frustrated with the Reagan
administration's inertia, Gorbachev was planning a spectacular speech at the
United Nations. It was to be, he wrote, "the exact opposite of Winston
Churchill's famous [Iron Curtain] speech." By then Gorbachev felt that he
and his reformers had "fully developed both the conceptual basis and the
policies of our new political thinking." Among other policies, "everyone
agreed that the time had come to make significant cuts in our armed forces
and that the next five-year period should be dedicated to disarmament."
Through the Soviet Defense Council, now run by one of his appointees, Gorbachev ordered the Defense Ministry to begin planning the withdrawal of
Soviet forces from Eastern Europe, a fact attested to in Soviet documents
since made public that confirm Gorbachev's determination to allow the
European satellite nations to choose their own way. For now, at the U.N., he
intended to announce major unilateral force reductions, which Akhromeyev
worked with him to plan.

Before announcing his new policies to the world, Gorbachev had to bully them through the Politburo. He had already told the 29th Party Congress in June 1988 that his predecessors should be faulted for their reliance on military muscle rather than politics and negotiation to protect the country. "As a result," he said, "we let ourselves be drawn into the arms race, which was bound to affect the socio-economic development of the country and its international position." Now he challenged the Politburo members directly and personally. He began casually, saying that he'd talked with Nikolai Ryzhkov, the chairman of the council of ministers, and Yuri Maslyukov, the deputy chairman in charge of the military-industrial complex, had read letters from the people and met with young Komsomol members at the Palace of Youth, and these encounters had forced him "finally to give some serious thought to the question Komsomol members have asked: 'Why do we need such a big army?' " The truth is, he said, "we need quality, not quantity. Now the time has come to make major decisions. Yes, we're taking 'little steps' on medium- and short-range missiles and some other things. But they don't change the situation principally." By now "agitated and tough," Chernyaev records, Gorbachev barreled on:

> Our announced military doctrine contradicts our actual military programs. . . . Our military expenses are 2.5 times larger than those of the United States. No country in the world—except the "underdeveloped" ones, whom we flood with arms without ever being paid back—spends more per capita on the military sector. . . .
>
> We won't solve the problems of *perestroika* if we leave the army as it is. As before, it still gets the best scientific and technical talent, the best financial support, always provided for without question. . . . The Komsomol kids are right—what do we need such an army for? Six million people!
>
> . . . What are we doing? Knocking our best young talent out of the intellectual pool! Who are we going to implement reforms with? We have a strong tank attack force in the GDR [i.e., the German Democratic Republic, East Germany] plus pontoon equipment. With all this "hanging over them" how can the Americans and the others believe in our defense doctrine?

At which point Ryzhkov jumped in to be the first to agree with him: "If we don't do it, we can forget about any increase in the standard of living." Gorbachev immediately turned Ryzhkov's intervention into a call for endorsement:

> *Gorbachev:* If we all agree and if we come to make major decisions, including unilateral reductions and not just what's required by the agreement on

medium- and short-range missiles and the Vienna mandate, I think I'll announce it in my U.N. speech.

Everyone: Yes, yes!

Gorbachev: After the medium- and short-range missile agreement and the decision to pull out of Afghanistan, this will make a huge impression. They'll see that we aren't just blowing smoke, but making real politics for the whole world. The main reason why we're doing this is *perestroika.* Nikolai Ivanovich is right, without reductions in the army and the military-industrial complex we won't be able to deal with *perestroika*'s tasks. . . . There's no question about it, we can't afford not to be militarily strong. But for the purposes of security, not intimidation.

Chernyaev wrote these notes; his acute sense of irony colors that obsequious "Yes, yes!" from the Politburo collectivity. Gorbachev had already decided to announce reductions in conventional forces in his U.N. speech. He wanted the Politburo members on the record so they would have to share responsibility afterward for the decision.

George H. W. Bush, Reagan's vice president, had been president-elect for one month when Gorbachev flew to New York to speak at the United Nations on 7 December 1988, a brisk, windy New York winter day. They would meet after the speech along with Reagan on Governors Island in the East River. Gorbachev wanted to assess Bush's enthusiasm for continued cooperation. He also, he writes candidly, "hoped that a positive international response to my [speech] would strengthen my position [at home] and help overcome the growing resistance to change in the Soviet Union." By then he was a world celebrity; the U.N. speech was his first to that institution, and expectations were high. He did not disappoint them.

"I started speaking somewhat hesitantly," Gorbachev remembers, "with occasional pauses. But gradually I felt the growing interest of the audience, sensing that my words and ideas were coming across and gaining self-confidence and perhaps eloquence." He spoke for an hour, in general terms first, then about world problems and possible solutions. Near the end he turned to the subject of disarmament. The following day would be the first anniversary of the signing of the INF Treaty, he said. The world was "witnessing the emergence of a new historic reality—a turning away from the principle of superarmament to the principle of reasonable defense sufficiency." And then he offered his "deeds":

Today, I can report to you that the Soviet Union has made a decision to reduce its armed forces.

Within the next two years their numerical strength will be reduced by

500,000 men. The numbers of conventional armaments will also be substantially reduced. This will be done *unilaterally,* without relation to the [negotiations ongoing in Vienna].

By agreement with our Warsaw Treaty allies, we have decided to withdraw by 1991 six tank divisions from the German Democratic Republic, Czechoslovakia and Hungary, and to disband them.

Assault landing troops and several other formations and units, including assault-crossing support units [i.e., that "pontoon equipment"] with their weapons and combat equipment, will also be withdrawn from the groups of Soviet forces stationed in those countries.

Soviet forces stationed in those countries will be reduced by 50,000 men and 5,000 tanks.

All Soviet divisions remaining, for the time being, in the territory of our allies are being reorganized. Their structure will be different from what it is now: a large number of tanks will be withdrawn, and they will become clearly defensive.

At the same time, we shall reduce the numerical strength of the armed forces and the numbers of armaments stationed in the European part of the USSR.

In total, Soviet armed forces in this part of our country and on the territory of our European allies will be reduced by 10,000 tanks, 8,500 artillery systems and 800 combat aircraft.

He also said his country would work toward a treaty on a 50 percent reduction in strategic offensive arms, a convention on the elimination of chemical weapons ("we believe that 1989 may be a decisive year in this regard") and negotiations on the reduction of conventional arms and armed forces in Europe.

"After an hour of holding its breath," Chernyaev reports, "the audience erupted in an endless ovation." Robert Kaiser of the *Washington Post* called it "a speech as remarkable as any ever delivered at the United Nations."

Gorbachev was elated, but news that had first come to him the previous evening by telegram from his good friend Margaret Thatcher preoccupied him: A magnitude 6.9 earthquake had shaken northwestern Armenia, followed four minutes later by a magnitude 5.8 aftershock. Though it was far less powerful than the magnitude 7.8 earthquake in China in 1976 that killed more than 240,000 people, it caused great damage and many deaths, the U.S. National Oceanic and Atmospheric Administration reports: "Swarms of aftershocks, some as large as magnitude 5.0, continued for months in the area. Direct economic losses were put at $14.2 billion (U.S.) at the United Nations official exchange rate. Twenty-five thousand were killed and 15,000 were injured by the earthquake. In addition 517,000 people were made homeless."

On Governors Island, Gorbachev met with Reagan and Bush, the general secretary advising the president-elect over lunch, "I know what people are telling you now that you've won the election: you've got to go slow, you've got to be careful, you've got to review. That you can't trust us, that we're doing all this for show. You'll see soon enough that I'm not doing this for show and I'm not doing this to undermine you or to surprise you or to take advantage of you. I'm playing real politics. I'm doing this because I need to. I'm doing this because there's a revolution taking place in my country. I started it. And they all applauded me when I started it in 1986 and now they don't like it so much, but it's going to be a revolution nonetheless." Bush was noncommittal, and although he phoned Gorbachev within days of his 20 January 1989 inauguration to promise "no foot-dragging" on arms control, "weeks and months passed," Gorbachev writes, with little initiative from the American side. He and his advisers took to calling the period "the pause." The Bush administration was in no hurry to develop Soviet-American relations. Scowcroft; the CIA director, Robert Gates; the NSC's Condoleezza Rice; and others agreed that Moscow should be left to struggle for a while, to soften it up for future concessions.

Bush appointed Richard Cheney as secretary of defense in March 1989 when his first choice, John Tower, failed to win Senate approval. Since serving as Gerald Ford's chief of staff, Cheney had been elected a Republican member of the House of Representatives from Wyoming; he left the job of House minority whip, with a 100 percent conservative voting record, to join Bush's Cabinet. Cheney was convinced that Gorbachev was a fraud and a failure. He told CNN in April, journalists Franklin Foer and Spencer Ackerman write, "that Gorbachev would 'ultimately fail' and a leader 'far more hostile to the West' would follow." The policy within the administration—discussed among Bush; his new secretary of state, James Baker III; Scowcroft; and Rice—was to support Gorbachev and perestroika, however cautiously. Cheney disagreed, Foer and Ackerman report:

> Cheney believed that, with a gust of aggressive support for alternatives to Gorbachev, the United States could dismember its principal adversary once and for all.
>
> To craft an alternative strategy, Cheney turned to alternative experts. On Saturday mornings, [undersecretary of defense for policy Paul] Wolfowitz's deputies convened seminars in a small conference room in the Pentagon's E Ring, where they sat Cheney in front of a parade of Sovietologists. . . . Out of

these Saturday seminars, Cheney's Soviet position emerged—with concepts and rhetoric that perfectly echo the current [2004 George W.] Bush administration's Iraq policy. *They would push regime change in the Soviet Union, transforming it into a democracy. . . .* Cheney was unsuccessful in pushing the White House away from Gorbachev. After he mused aloud about Gorbachev's shortcomings in a 1989 TV interview, Baker called Scowcroft and told him, "Dump on Dick with all possible alacrity."

Gorbachev's answer to the collective skepticism of the Bush administration was to continue to follow through on his program of "new thinking" while agitating for further change. In 1988 he discontinued production of highly enriched uranium (HEU) for weapons, although the Soviet military-industrial complex continued to process HEU for other purposes until 1990. According to two U.S. military historians, Joseph Harahan and John C. Kuhn III, Gorbachev volunteered a breakthrough during this period that "changed the course of all previous negotiations [on conventional forces] by conceding that since the Soviet Union had numerically superior conventional forces in Europe, the NATO nations might reasonably conclude that these forces were a threat. He further stated that under any negotiated all-European arms-control treaty, the side with the greater number of forces ought to take a larger share of the reductions, provided there was adequate verification through on-site inspections." The Warsaw Pact endorsed Gorbachev's initiative. On 15 February 1989, Lieutenant General Boris Gromov, who commanded Soviet forces in Afghanistan, crossed the Termez bridge from Afghanistan into the Soviet Union, closing out the war. Thirty-six thousand young Soviet men and women had died in the ten-year course of the bloody project and about one million Afghanis, most of them civilians.

If preventing another world war from starting in Europe had been the fundamental object of the Cold War, it followed that ending the Cold War would require both sides to stand down not only their nuclear but also their conventional forces in Europe, with "Europe" defined, as the French defined it, as extending from the Atlantic coast to the Ural Mountains (ATTU, the negotiators called it—Atlantic to the Urals), and thus including a large swath of Soviet territory as well as the NATO and Warsaw Pact alliances. The negotiating entity that had been pursuing such improvements in security was called the Conference on Security and Cooperation in Europe (CSCE), an ongoing consultation among thirty-five nations that had begun meeting in 1973. The Helsinki Final Act of 1975 had been the CSCE's first important agreement. Confidence-building measures followed, including a requirement that every CSCE nation notify all its counterparts three weeks in advance of any large (more than twenty-one thousand in personnel) military exercise it intended to undertake. In 1983, the CSCE nations agreed to begin negotiating not only new confidence-building measures but also gradual European disarmament. In 1986, with Gorbachev now in power in the Soviet Union, the CSCE nations agreed to require notification of military exercises involving as few as thirteen thousand personnel with provision for on-site inspection of larger-scale (more than seventeen thousand in personnel) exercises. "Known as the Stockholm Document of 1986," Harahan and Kuhn write, "this was the first multinational agreement that the Soviet Union signed permitting on-site inspection of its own territory to verify an arms control accord."

It was in the context of these CSCE negotiations—the "Vienna talks" Gorbachev sometimes referred to—that the Soviet leader proposed that the Warsaw Pact should bear the burden of larger cutbacks in troops and equipment in the interest of achieving balanced force reductions. Why such a seemingly overgenerous concession? Gorbachev explains:

> For us, it was essential to break the stalemate in the talks on armed forces reduction in Europe, which had been dragging on since the early 1970s. The time had come for us to acknowledge that, even by Cold War logic, Soviet superiority in conventional weaponry in Europe stopped making political sense the moment we had reached nuclear parity with the United States. On the contrary, this situation helped to maintain the image of the Soviet Union as the enemy, thus creating ever new threats to our own security. Soviet conventional superiority served as a pretext for the United States and NATO to push through all sorts of military programs, including the upgrading of nuclear weapons—in a sense, we were even giving them a hand with it!

Other negotiations followed, culminating in January 1989 in a Mandate for Negotiation on Conventional Armed Forces in Europe, agreed upon among sixteen NATO states and seven Warsaw Treaty Organization (WTO) states. The mandate laid down the ground rules for negotiating a Conventional Armed Forces in Europe (CFE) Treaty, which would be designed to prevent surprise attacks across national borders by asymmetrically reducing offensive military equipment—tanks, artillery, and armored combat vehicles—with extensive on-site inspections to police the agreement. According to Thomas Graham, Jr., who participated in the CFE negotiations, the Soviet Union "wanted to include combat aircraft and attack helicopters" as well, but the NATO side disagreed. "But in March of 1989,

President Bush decided to concede on this point and the CFE negotiations finally began."

Bush and Gorbachev were both committed to the negotiations, which made for rapid progress. Gorbachev had already promulgated what he called "the principle of reasonable sufficiency in defense," which was an extension to conventional forces of the idea of minimal deterrence: enough to defend but not enough to threaten offensively. "Developing this new doctrine had been far from easy," he writes. ". . . Indeed, two factors formed one psychological knot: on the one hand, the constant worry about a secure peace (the Soviet people remembered Hitler's attack in 1941) and, on the other, the need drastically to reduce our defense budget—an indispensable condition for improving our economy." He adds of the CFE negotiations, "For us, it was essential to prevent upgrading of any types of weapons; this would have dealt a fatal blow to everything we had achieved by then and to the trust we had taken such pains to establish."

In April, Graham took it upon himself to prepare, with a colleague, a "bare-bones draft CFE Treaty" based on the January mandate:

> I called [the U.S. negotiator, Ambassador Stephen] Ledogar and told him that he needed a lawyer and a treaty, that I was a lawyer, that I had a draft treaty, and that I was coming over to see him. He did not say no, so I was off to Vienna in June to persuade the U.S. CFE delegation that they in fact did need a lawyer and a treaty. . . .
>
> When I returned to Washington [a week later] I could say that I had a draft treaty text which had been approved by the delegation. All of this was made up from whole cloth. Of course, no one had asked for a draft treaty text; I was just saying we needed one and here it is. CFE was blessedly different from the SALT/START process, however. It was a negotiation everyone wanted and one that had been authorized and advocated by the president. Thus, there was not a high degree of bureaucratic infighting of the type that characterized those processes. I remember remarking what a pleasure it was working on a negotiation that everyone, in the U.S. government at least, wanted.

Nineteen eighty-nine was the year Eastern Europe pulled free of Soviet domination. In a May entry, Chernyaev sketched the turmoil in his journal:

> All around, Gorbachev has unleashed irreversible processes of "disintegration" which had earlier been restrained or covered up by the arms race, the fear of war, myths about the international communist movement, the socialist community, the worldwide revolutionary process, and proletarian internationalism. . . .

Socialism in Eastern Europe is disappearing. Communist parties are collapsing in Western Europe and everywhere else where they couldn't "latch onto" the national idea. In other words, what has long been brewing has now boiled over and is following its natural course. Everywhere things are turning out different from what had been imagined and proposed.

The Baltic states—Latvia, Estonia, and Lithuania—went first, not without resistance, harassment, and violence on the part of the Soviet Union despite Gorbachev's promises. With a tin ear for ethnic nationalism, his tragic flaw, he distinguished sharply between nations like the Baltic states that the U.S.S.R. had absorbed and those like Poland and Hungary that it had only dominated; he feared that if he allowed the Baltic states to withdraw from the U.S.S.R., other ethnic nationalities would want to secede as well—as indeed they would and did. Estonia and Lithuania nevertheless bravely declared their sovereignty on 18 May 1989; Latvia followed on 29 July. In elections in Poland in June, candidates affiliated with Solidarity, the labor union led by Lech Walesa, overwhelmingly defeated Communist Party candidates. Shortly afterward, in a speech to the European parliament, Gorbachev encouraged Eastern European reformers by insisting that "respect for the sovereign right of every people to choose its own social system" was an "important precondition . . . for a normal European process." Change in the social and political order of a country, he added, "is exclusively a matter for the people themselves to decide. It is their choice." Shevardnadze reemphasized the point over dinner with James Baker, the secretary of state, at the Soviet Embassy in Paris on 29 July 1989. "If we were to use force," the Soviet foreign minister told Baker, "then it would be the end of *perestroika*. We would have failed. It would be the end of any hope for the future, the end of everything we're trying to do, which is to create a new system based on humane values. If force is used, it will mean that the enemies of *perestroika* have triumphed. We would be no better than the people who came before us. We cannot go back."

In August, after interagency vetting, Graham's CFE treaty draft became the official NATO treaty text. Graham himself followed his draft to Vienna at the beginning of September as the U.S. delegation's legal adviser and ACDA representative. Ten days later, Hungary opened its border with Austria and thousands of East Germans who had traveled to Hungary to wait crossed into the West, to be followed in the weeks ahead by thousands more.

On 9 November 1989, East Germany capitulated and allowed its citizens to travel freely. Crossing points along the Berlin Wall opened and East Germans streamed into glittering West Berlin. I visited Berlin two weeks later and watched a flow of people on foot, on bicycles, or driving shabby Trabants passing through a crossing point and flooding out into the city. Not much of the Wall had yet been torn down—the concrete of its composition had been mixed with asbestos to make it tough and it was difficult to break. The cold Berlin winter air, air that a writer in an earlier era had described as "always bright, as if it were peppered," was criss-crossed with sulfury scent trails of cream of broccoli soup from soup kitchens the Red Cross had set up to feed lunch to the visitors, who seldom possessed even a Deutschmark of West German coin. Returning to the East at dusk, many of them carried brightly printed plastic bags, usually empty, as souvenirs of their first free encounter with Western capitalism; the books I bought the next day at a government bookstore in dark, sooty East Berlin were wrapped begrudgingly in brown paper tied up with twine.

Watching the same scenes "on a television set in his small study adjoining the Oval Office," Michael Beschloss and Strobe Talbott write, "Bush knew what this meant. He told his aides, 'If the Soviets are going to let the Communists fall in East Germany, they've got to be really serious—more serious than I realized.' " The two historians add: "Before the fall of that year, Bush had been able to argue, as Kissinger had done before the inauguration, that the changes wrought by Gorbachev were 'cosmetic' and easily reversible. But with the Berlin Wall down and Eastern Europe as a whole leaving the Soviet sphere, it was almost impossible to maintain that the world was in imminent danger of returning to the Cold War as everyone had known it." Some years later I had occasion to ask the former congressman Lee Hamilton of Indiana, a leader astute in foreign affairs, why the United States had been so slow to recognize the validity of the revolution Gorbachev was piloting. Hamilton thought a moment and answered, "You know, we were so used to thinking of the Soviets as the enemy that when they changed, we just couldn't turn ourselves around that fast." Certainly not George H. W. Bush, a dogged champion of the status quo guided by a national security adviser, Brent Scowcroft, who cautioned Condoleezza Rice in 1989 to avoid saying publicly that the Cold War was over because once it was said, it couldn't be rescinded, and Congress would use it as an excuse to cut the defense budget.

The CFE negotiations, Graham writes, "lasted about twenty months"—record time for so complicated an agreement. During that time, "five negotiating parties changed their names and one disappeared (the German Democratic Republic . . . merged into the Federal Republic of Germany on October 3, 1990)." When the treaty was signed, in Paris on 19 November 1990, there were twenty-two signatories. Two days earlier, the delegations had gathered in a room at the Hofburg Palace in Vienna, where the negotiations had been held, for the initial exchange of information about their "treaty-limited equipment" (TLE)—the tanks, armored combat vehicles, artillery, and aircraft they had agreed to reduce. "It was like a bazaar," Graham recalls. "Tables were set up around the room with each delegation handing out books containing the initial date exchange—the one to take place at the time of signature—with appropriate pictures of weapons systems, tanks and the like. There were the Soviets, the French, the Germans and all the rest, hawking their data presentations. Some of the delegations had slicker presentations than others but all were comprehensive. It was quite a scene."

The CFE Treaty, limiting NATO and Warsaw Pact hardware to equivalent levels, resulted in major reductions for the Warsaw Pact. A "sufficiency rule" restricted the numbers of treaty-limited equipment belonging to any one country within the Eastern or Western bloc to one-third of the bloc total, which meant proportionally even larger cuts for the Soviet Union. "In 1988," Graham writes, "the Soviets alone had 41,000 battle tanks, 57,000 ACVs and 42,000 pieces of artillery in the area of application [i.e., the ATTU]. Under the sufficiency rule, the Soviets were permitted only 13,000 battle tanks, 20,000 armored combat vehicles, 13,700 artillery pieces, 5,150 combat aircraft and 1,500 attack helicopters. Thus, the sufficiency rule itself imposed a very significant reduction in Soviet military power."

The numbers of machines actually withdrawn and destroyed—chopped up or smashed according to an agreed protocol—were staggering: 40 percent of Warsaw Pact tanks, 26 percent of Pact artillery, 30 percent of armored combat vehicles, 19 percent of aircraft. When the dust cleared, conventional Western and Eastern bloc forces were equal and balanced from the Atlantic to the Urals. "The CFE Treaty," Graham writes with justifiable pride, "ended the Cold War and is one of the central pillars of European security." The leaders who signed the treaty in Paris concurred, the political scientist Matthew Evangelista found. "They declared a formal end to the Cold War, stated they were 'no longer adversaries,' and pledged to 'build new partnerships and extend to each other the hand of friendship.' "

BEFORE THE CONVENTIONAL ARMED FORCES in Europe Treaty was signed, Mikhail Gorbachev had finally agreed with his scientists and other advisers to unlink the Strategic Arms Reduction Treaty (START) negotiations in Geneva from limitations on SDI. With the George H. W. Bush administration's renewed commitment as well, START negotiators were able to resolve many issues in 1989 and 1990 while the CFE negotiations were ongoing. In October 1990, Gorbachev was awarded the Nobel Peace Prize—considered a scandal by those who despised his politics and human rights record, a well-deserved honor by those who admired his work for common security and disarmament. He called again for a moratorium on nuclear testing on 24 October, when the Soviet Union conducted its last nuclear weapons test.

At a summit in Washington at the beginning of June 1990, Gorbachev writes, "we finally managed to settle the basic provisions for the strategic arms reduction treaty, which was designed to cut our strategic arsenals by fifty percent—an idea launched four years ago in Reykjavik. The remaining disagreements were finally resolved." The summit, he added, "significantly increased the pace of the clean-up of the gigantic powder magazine left over from the Cold War." The two presidents—Gorbachev became the first and last Soviet president—in 1990—agreed to sign START I in Moscow on 31 July 1991. That agreement "put the negotiations in overdrive," Graham notes, "and somehow the delegations were able to complete the treaty with its many associated documents and side agreements and deliver it to Moscow in time to be signed." As the U.S. ambassador and arms negotiator James Goodby summarized the agreement: "START I . . . limited the United States and the Soviet Union to 6,000 accountable strategic nuclear warheads and 1,600 nuclear delivery vehicles on each side." It was not nuclear abolition, but it was a measurable stride down that road.

The last trip wires in the nuclear forest were so-called tactical nuclear weapons: bombs, artillery shells, rocket and missile warheads, land mines, demolition munitions, and depth charges intended for use in land and sea battles, primarily in and around Europe, that ranged in yield from a fraction of a kiloton up to as much as one megaton (i.e., one thousand kilotons; by comparison, the Nagasaki bomb yielded twenty-two kilotons). At his first summit meeting with Bush, at Malta in December 1989, Gorbachev had told the U.S. president, "the strategic component is part of the Geneva talks; the tactical nuclear weapons remain. We propose that they be eliminated completely. Such a radical solution would also simplify verification procedures." The previous April, the Soviet Union had formally proposed negotiations on tactical nuclear weapons reductions, and Gorbachev had also announced the unilateral withdrawal of tactical nuclear weapons from Eastern Europe. The United States had not responded, however, even though the Soviet Union stocked some twenty-two thousand tactical nuclear weapons at that time. (The United States stocked twenty-three thousand.) Attention was still focused on strategic and conventional weapons and forces, but already in 1989, an interagency group led by Condoleezza Rice, under a directive from Scowcroft to "put on your Kremlin-watcher's hat . . . and start asking questions about what we do if various nightmare scenarios come true," had concluded that keeping Soviet nuclear weapons, particularly tactical weapons, under secure control was essential. The fact is, the United States had (and has) very little intelligence about either numbers or disposition of Soviet (or Russian) tactical nuclear weapons.

The abortive Soviet coup of August 1991, only days after Bush and Gorbachev had signed START, reminded the Bush administration that tactical nuclear weapons could easily fall into the wrong hands. When eight nervous plotters with hesitant support from the Soviet military isolated Gorbachev at his vacation compound at Foros, in the Crimea, and tried to turn the clock back to 1984, Boris Yeltsin, now the president of the Russian Republic, denounced them as no more than "a right-wing junta" and called out the Moscow citizenry to surround and protect the Russian Republic building— the "White House"—where he and his advisers had barricaded themselves. Under Yeltsin's bare-knuckle tank-turret leadership, the coup quickly failed. One of its casualties was Marshal Sergei Akhromeyev, who had been involved only peripherally but who shot himself the day after the collapse, convinced that Gorbachev's reforms had destroyed what he had spent his life building and protecting. "During the coup," wrote James Baker, "U.S. intelligence had picked up several anomalous indicators involving the Strategic Rocket Forces (SRF), the nuclear arm of the Soviet military. While there had been no indications that the threat of a nuclear accident had increased, these anomalies quite naturally concerned [the president]."

Gorbachev returned to find his power base gone. While Gorbachev was still assessing the damage, Senator Sam Nunn, Democrat of Georgia, who at the time was the chairman of the Senate Armed Services Committee, saw the handwriting on the wall. "I was in Budapest at a meeting when the coup began," Nunn told me. "A Russian friend of mine had to leave the meeting to rush back to Moscow. When Gorbachev was released, my friend invited me to come to Moscow, and I went. I listened to the debate in the Duma about forming a commonwealth of states. I could see all sorts of troubles coming, and after I got back to Washington I introduced the Nunn-Lugar program legislation." The Nunn-Lugar program, cosponsored by Senator Richard Lugar, Republican of Indiana, passed both houses of Congress in November 1991. Initially it provided funds from the U.S. Defense Department budget to secure Soviet nuclear weapons and material—the best investment in defense the DoD ever made.

Eliminating tactical nukes had long been one of Colin Powell's "hobbyhorses," he writes in a memoir. As the chairman of the Joint Chiefs of Staff under Defense Secretary Richard Cheney, Powell had ordered a study of their usefulness. "The staff's recommendation," he recalls, "was to get rid of the small, artillery-fired nukes because they were trouble-prone, expensive to modernize and irrelevant in the present world of highly accurate conventional weapons." The four service chiefs, lobbied by the Army artilleryman among them—"the nukes were a matter of prestige to the artillery," Powell explains without apparent irony—rejected the recommendation. "The report went up to the Pentagon policy staff, a refuge of Reagan-era hardliners, who stomped all over it, from Paul Wolfowitz on down." Cheney rejected it as well.

At a meeting of the National Security Council on 5 September 1991, which Bush called, according to Scowcroft, to review possible arms-control initiatives "while there were [Soviet and Russian] leaders in power . . . who would work with us," Cheney strongly resisted pursuing further cuts; he distrusted arms negotiations and feared they would encourage reductions in the defense budget. He had already decided that there would be no peace dividend from the demise of the Soviet Union, declaring in a speech the previous summer, "I don't think the notion of a military threat to the interests of the United States was invented by the Communist Party of the Soviet Union, and I think it will be there long after the Communist Party of the Soviet Union no longer wields the interest [sic] that it has in the past." (Powell thought otherwise. "I'm running out of demons," he told the *Army Times* that year. "I'm running out of villains. I'm down to Castro and Kim Il Sung.") Bush was determined, however, and at the end of the meeting he charged Cheney, Powell, Scowcroft, and the rest of the NSC, "I want to see some new ideas on nuclear disarmament. I don't want talk. I want solid proposals."

Given "Cheney's distaste for negotiated arms control," Scowcroft writes, it occurred to Bush's national security adviser after the NSC meeting that unilateral cuts in the U.S. nuclear arsenal might be a more effective approach, one that could "take advantage of the situation to solve a number of tactical nuclear weapons questions at the same time." Cheney himself had proposed reviewing the basing of tactical nukes in Germany, an embarrassment now that its two states were reunited. South Korea wanted U.S. nuclear weapons removed from its territory as part of its new initiative toward the North, but effecting such a removal in isolation might look like a U.S. withdrawal, which was not a signal the United States wanted to send to Kim Il Sung, the North Korean dictator. Navy ships carrying tactical nuclear weapons caused problems in countries such as Japan and New Zealand, which refused to allow nuclear weapons on their territory. "The sum of all these issues," Scowcroft concludes, "led me to suggest that we unilaterally declare we were getting rid of all tactical nuclear weapons (except air-delivered ones)." Cheney, skeptical at first, signed on when Scowcroft agreed that the weapons would be withdrawn but not destroyed. You can't be too careful: Like the troll under the bridge, watching out for billy goats, Cheney was determined to husband the republic's resources.

In his memoir, Powell sorts out the pile of proposals, which "far exceeded the elimination I had urged of artillery-launched nukes":

> Get rid of short-range nuclear weapons, like the Army's Lance missiles. Ground the Strategic Air Command bombers that had been on alert for the previous thirty-two years, and offload their nukes. Remove nuclear weapons from all ships, except for strategic missiles on Trident submarines. Get rid of multiple-warhead intercontinental ballistic missiles [i.e., MIRVs] and stick to single-warhead ICBMs. Shut down as many Minuteman missile silos as we dared.

"The chiefs," Powell concludes, "now responding to a radically changing world, signed on, as did Paul Wolfowitz and his hardliners. Cheney was ready to move with the winds of change. Within three weeks, on September 27, President Bush announced these unilateral nuclear reductions to the world."

Gorbachev, in what would turn out to be his last arms-control venture, welcomed Bush's initiative and responded a week later with initiatives of his own. Bush summarizes most of them in his memoir:

He wanted to destroy tactical nuclear weapons on sea forces and was prepared to make further cuts in strategic weapons. The Soviets would also take their heavy bombers off alert and stockpile their weapons. He proposed a one-year moratorium on testing, and was ready to discuss a plan to reduce fissionable materials. In addition, the Soviets would reduce their army by 700,000. [Bush had announced a 500,000-man U.S. reduction.] There were some differences in our positions, but on balance it was very positive and forthcoming. Mikhail told me he had spoken with Yeltsin, and indicated that Yeltsin was in agreement.

One offer Bush chose not to mention was Gorbachev's possibly tongue-in-cheek adoption of Ronald Reagan's pledge to share research on SDI: "We propose to study the possibility of creating joint systems to avert nuclear missile attacks with ground- and space-based elements."

In the wake of the dissolution of the Soviet Union, the United States would have to negotiate with a crowd of nuclear-armed successor states to win their commitment to these initiatives—another story for another book. Nevertheless, the unilateral initiatives of autumn 1991 may fairly be counted as the final, historic acts of demolition in the termination of the superpower nuclear-arms race that had burdened and threatened the world since 1949. After 1991 there would be a diminished second-tier arms race between India and Pakistan and efforts toward nuclear proliferation in North Korea, Libya, and Iran, aided by a private black-market operation out of Pakistan led by a Pakistani metallurgist named A. Q. Khan. The terrorist attacks on New York and Washington of 11 September 2001 would raise fears of an undeterrable terrorist nuclear strike with a stolen or homemade arsenal— the ultimate argument for complete, worldwide control of fissile materials and nuclear abolition. But such mutually arrogant, economically disastrous, self-defeating, and mortally dangerous nuclear militarism as that of the Soviet Union and the United States in the years of the Cold War will almost certainly never repeat itself on so large a scale, if only because no other nation, seeing the crushing folly of the first round, would choose to waste the resources.

MIKHAIL GORBACHEV WAS NO SAINT. He came to office fully committed to Soviet Communism, believing that its troubles and failures were the result of the corruption and incompetence of its leaders, not inherent in the system itself. Whether or not he ever completely gave up that belief continues to be a contentious question. His biographer Archie Brown offers one answer, based on the testimony of Gorbachev adviser Georgi Shakhnazarov:

Dismissing the myth—increasingly disseminated both in Russia and abroad in 1991—that Gorbachev wished merely "to perfect the system" while "not touching its essence," Shakhnazarov quoted verbatim from his December 1989 conversation with Gorbachev in which Gorbachev said:

"Don't think that something will stop me, that there is a threshold through which I shall not be able to pass. Everything that is needed for the very deepest transformation of the system I accept without embarrassment. I will go as far as it is necessary to go for that. And if we speak about the final goal, insofar as it is possible today to be definite, that is integration into the world community by peaceful means. By conviction I am close to social democracy."

Anatoly Chernyaev, frustrated in the summer of 1990 with Gorbachev's seeming equivocation with Communist Party resistance to reform, has described this exchange with the Soviet president:

Gorbachev, while seeing and understanding everything, once again failed to draw the necessary conclusions. After meeting with secretaries of city, regional, and district Party committees during the Congress he told me: "Self-interested scum, they don't want anything except a feeding trough and power. . . ." He swore at them in the foulest language. I replied: "To hell with them, Mikhail Sergeyevich. You're the president. You see what kind of Party this is. And [so long as you remain at its head] you'll be its hostage, its permanent whipping boy." He replied:

"You know, Tolya, you think I don't see. But I do, and I've read your notes. And those of Arbatov and Shmelev too. All arguing the same thing, as if by design. That I should give up the general secretary's post [i.e., now that he was president]. But you must understand me, I can't let this lousy, rabid dog off the leash. If I do that, all this huge structure will be turned against me."

In an article defending perestroika written at Foros only days before the August 1991 coup, Gorbachev himself had this to say:

In the most general terms, the aims of *perestroika* are: economic freedom, political freedom, escape from isolation and the inclusion of the country in the mainstream of civilization. And the fundamental principle, if you look at it on a philosophical level, is the unacceptability of any ready-made models which might once again, however good the intentions, be imposed on society, to bring people happiness "from above."

. . . We did not realize immediately, of course, how far we had to go and what profound changes were needed. This gave rise to mistakes. . . .

All that is true. But we had to get involved practically in the new work, to acquire experience, look deep into the public mind as it was found to be after seventy years of an extraordinary regime and isolation from the rest of the world, and to learn to take account of all its specific qualities. It was only then that we came to the final conclusion that *perestroika* was not to be measured by the usual criteria or directed according to the principles of a previously dominant ideology. In the end we saw also that *perestroika* would not succeed within the framework of the old system, however much we tried to renew it and improve it. What was needed was a change of the whole economic and political system, the reform of the whole multinational state; that is, in all aspects a real revolution which had been prepared by all our own past and by worldwide progress.

At least two of those who participated directly at the highest level in bringing an end to the superpower nuclear-arms race gave Gorbachev the credit that the evidence demonstrates he properly deserved. François Mitterrand had this to say to Gorbachev at the G7 meeting in London in the summer of 1991:

> In the final analysis, you could have behaved like your predecessors, and the result would be catastrophic. History will record this. It will note not only the fact that you are transforming a country that does not have democratic traditions, but also how its relations with other countries have changed. Nations have been freed from the presence of foreign troops. Germany has been unified. All this is a result of your policy.

And James Baker, a tough, experienced politician, told Gorbachev in Moscow in September 1990, when Gorbachev and Bush were working together to confront Saddam Hussein's invasion of Kuwait:

> Mr. President . . . nobody in the world has ever tried what you and your supporters are trying today. We're talking about breaking a pattern of thinking that had been formed over seven decades. Naturally, it has to be done gradually, step by step, in order to be successful. . . . I'm not a rookie in politics, I've seen a lot, but I've never met a politician with as much bravery and courage as you have. I know that you have to deal with various limitations, to work within a certain political framework. I know how tough the steps you're so bravely taking are. And I'd like to tell you that President Bush shares this opinion.

Gorbachev himself, as it happens, unlike many Reagan and George H. W. Bush administration alumni, has been more than happy to share the credit for ending the Cold War—provided that the United States is willing to share the blame as well:

Both the Soviet Union and the United States bear their share of the responsibility for the fact that the post-war period was marked by a wasteful and dangerous confrontation, which exhausted resources and distorted not only the economy but society as a whole. In an unprecedented, far-reaching move, these same two countries took upon themselves the responsibility for dismantling, as soon as possible, the existing mechanisms of military confrontation between East and West, in order to employ the resources freed by disarmament to improve the well-being of the people. If it is true that the world has changed in the past few years, moving towards a period of genuine peace, the decisive contribution was made by the Soviet Union and the United States of America.

SPEAKING IN MUNICH IN LATE JANUARY 1987, not long before he resigned as assistant secretary of defense, Richard Perle ridiculed the idea of a nuclear-free world as "foolishness" that was "in no way mitigated by the conditions that Western statesmen routinely attach to its achievement in order to avoid dismissing the idea as the empty propaganda that it is." Perle disguised his ex cathedra censure of nuclear abolition as a deconstruction of Gorbachev's surprising proposals at Reykjavik, but his reference to "Western statesmen" makes it clear that he also meant to condemn Ronald Reagan's dream. "To argue that eliminating all nuclear weapons is a good idea," Perle went on, "but the year 2000 is too soon, or to suggest that it must proceed by steps or stages, or that it must await a more favorable conventional balance or the settlement of regional disputes, is a self-defeating obfuscation. These arguments—rationalizations, really—are deployed by officials and politicians who fear that the public would not support them if they simply rejected outright Mr. Gorbachev's beguiling maneuver."

Perle's conviction that fielding a nuclear arsenal is self-evidently necessary and useful raises the interesting question of whether nuclear weapons served the purposes that national leaders and deterrence theorists attributed to them during the years of the Cold War. The evidence indicates they did not.

Anatoly Dobrynin, for example, points out that both the United States and the Soviet Union based their military planning on the assumption that the other side would initiate a war with "a nuclear first strike with maximum devastation." At a conference in 1994 attended by Carter administration principals Cyrus Vance, Zbigniew Brzezinski, and Harold Brown, however, Dobrynin learned that "the Carter administration did not work under a first-strike doctrine against the Soviet Union (though Carter—like his predecessors—considered the possibility of using nuclear weapons first in case of a mass Soviet attack by conventional forces in Europe)." At the same conference, two high-ranking Russian generals, "both of them participants in nuclear war planning during the cold war, also confirmed that the Soviet government and general staff never followed a first-strike doctrine because, contrary to its public statements in the 1960s, they were convinced that nuclear war would cause unacceptable damage to both countries." Dobrynin concludes: "Nevertheless, hundreds of billions were spent to counterbalance the mutual fear of a sudden nuclear attack when—as we now know—neither side ever conceived of such a strategy because it knew what horrors it would visit on both."

The activist-scholar Richard J. Barnet, approaching the question from another angle, notes that although the United States "came out of World War II the most powerful nation on earth—perhaps, briefly, the paramount nation of all time—it has not won a decisive military victory since 1945 despite the trillions spent on the military and the frequent engagement of its military forces." What the United States got instead of victory, Barnet writes, was a national security state with a permanent war economy maintained by a military-industrial complex—much like the Soviet Union in those departments, but with a far greater reserve of resources to squander. "The national security state structures could not accomplish their task unless the American people were socialized to accept the idea that the only peace possible is a form of permanent war. . . . A threat of one sort or another to justify the continuous flow of resources to the military was now a fixture of American life."

Threat inflation, as I hope I have shown, was crucial to maintaining the defense budgets of the Cold War. The practice was carried to its extreme by Ronald Reagan, who with neoconservative coaching actually claimed that the U.S. nuclear arsenal was dangerously inferior to the Soviet arsenal, vulnerable to the first strike that Dobrynin reports was never a part of Soviet planning—and inflated his defense budgets accordingly. In words published in 1985 that describe the post-2000 George W. Bush years as well as the years of the Cold War, Barnet adds, "It is one of history's great ironies that at the very moment when the United States had a monopoly of nuclear weapons, possessed most of the world's gold, produced half the world's goods on its own territory, and laid down the rules for allies and adversaries alike, it was afraid." Fear was part of the program, the psychological response to threat inflation that delivered reliable votes. How did we come to such a pass? I was raised to believe that Americans were a courageous people. Weren't you?

All of these indignities to the person of the American electorate might have been justified if nuclear deterrence in its vast, glittering malevolence had actually deterred. The political scientist Jacek Kugler has his doubts, although he acknowledges the difficulty of proving the case. A good case can still be made, however.

"Deterrence," Kugler writes, "is more than simply avoiding massive war." Deterrence—limited conflict or nuclear threat—can only be called successful when nations can use it to achieve policy goals. "Nuclear nations . . . should consistently [be able to] impose their own policy preferences in disputes with nonnuclear nations, and should achieve draws with equivalent nuclear powers." If they don't—if a weaker nation achieves its goals in conflict with a nuclear nation—then the technical term for the policy of the nuclear nation is not deterrence but appeasement. Yet "of the forty-odd crises since 1945 that involved nuclear powers directly," Kugler finds, referring to the Berlin airlift, the Korean War, the Soviet invasion of Hungary, the building of the Berlin Wall, the Vietnam War, the Soviet war with Afghanistan, and a number of other such events, "over one-fourth escalated to the point that nuclear weapons were an important factor in the eventual settlement. Hence, the risk of nuclear war did not inhibit the escalation of crisis. In the remaining thirty crises that were not serious enough to warrant any nuclear threats, the nonnuclear nations attained desired policy objectives as many times as they failed." Thus, "nuclear nations have not *consistently* prevented opponents from attaining contested policy objectives. Of . . . fourteen extreme cases considered, five are resolved in favor of the nuclear contenders and nine produced outcomes that favor nonnuclear challengers." That is, in a large majority of cases, nuclear weapons failed to deter. Conventional forces, Kugler discovered, accounted far more precisely for the outcome of extreme conflicts in the nuclear era than did nuclear capabilities. "Paradoxically, the addition of nuclear considerations *detracts* from the effective accounting of crisis outcomes." Kugler draws surprising and promising conclusions from his analysis:

> The main and disturbing result of this investigation is that nuclear weapons, despite their massive destructive potential, may not be the unique element that accounts for the absence of massive war in the international system in the last 35 years [Kugler published his study in 1984]. Several indirect evaluations lead to this conclusion. First, nuclear nations do not have an obvious and direct advantage over other nuclear or nonnuclear nations in extreme crises. Rather, conventional capabilities are the best predictor of outcome of extreme crises regardless of their severity. Second, nuclear preponderance, which, logically, should enhance the likelihood of war, does not lead to demonstrably different

or less stable behavior than nuclear parity. . . . Finally, the most consistent reason for the absence of major war in the nuclear era seems to be the relative congruence of policy objectives among the nuclear powers, and this congruence cannot be directly traced to the buildup of nuclear arsenals.

If the failure of nuclear arsenals to reliably deter undercuts the arguments of those who believe in maintaining the national security state despite its parasitism, it also, Kugler pointed out, undercuts the arguments of those who believe the answer lies in arms control:

> Challenging the persuasive and ingrained notion that war can be prevented by the deployment of nuclear arsenals deprives decision makers of the one manipulatable tool in their possession to control conflict of great magnitude. Also, by questioning, even indirectly, the implication that nuclear arsenals can prevent massive conflict, one challenges other long-held deductions. One can no longer argue with impeccable logical conviction that effective arms limitations increase the likelihood of peace, or that, in the absence of arms limitation agreements, one can find reassurance in the buildup of nuclear arsenals capable of destroying the opponent. . . . The need to open fresh arenas in the search for peace is indeed urgent. To do otherwise is to believe in magic.

(One fresh arena that needs to be opened, it seems to me, is nuclear abolition, but that too must be the subject of another book.)

How much we have believed in magic in space, on earth, and under the sea is measured by a little-known story told in hearings before the Senate Armed Services Committee in late April 1986. Looking for arguments to defeat congressional endorsement of the Nuclear Freeze movement then rallying millions of citizens in the United States and Europe, the Department of Energy produced a report of past problems with U.S. nuclear warheads. The point of the report was to justify nuclear testing. In pursuit of that point, it revealed that "at times in the past, the warheads for a large part of the U.S. Fleet Ballistic Missile force [i.e., ballistic missile submarines] have been found to be badly deteriorated. At different times, a large fraction of the warheads either obviously or potentially would not work; they were obvious or potential duds." And not only were U.S. nuclear submarines patrolling the seas across the years of the Cold War with dud warheads on their missiles. At various times, there were duds among Minuteman ICBM warheads ("In late 1963 the AEC had to rebuild all the W56 warheads of the Minuteman ICBM force") and W45 warheads used in the Army's Little John tactical missile, the Navy's Terrier surface-to-air missile and the Marines' atomic demolition munition. In other words, at various times throughout the Cold War we were naked to our enemies. No doubt the Soviets had such troubles as well. Yet both sides plowed on, following the blind, plodding oxen of mutual belligerence, believing ourselves to be protected. Magic indeed: a house of cards, with all our lives at risk.

AFTER A SHAKEN MIKHAIL GORBACHEV RETURNED from Foros in late August 1991, Boris Yeltsin's Russia rapidly divested him of his powers. Gorbachev resigned as general secretary of the Communist Party of the Soviet Union on 24 August 1991, the same day Ukraine declared its independence. Belarus, Moldova, Azerbaijan, Uzbekistan, Kyrgyzstan, and Tajikistan followed. Kazakhstan's president, Nursultan Nazarbayev, closed the nuclear-weapons test site at Semipalatinsk. Yeltsin in turn closed Novaya Zemlya, the other Soviet test site, in October. "The coup had given a strong impulse to disintegration," Gorbachev writes. "All the republics declared their independence in September and October 1991. The separatists felt that their day had come." The Congress of People's Deputies had functioned as an interim parliament, but with republics spinning off right and left it no longer had a constituency. Under Gorbachev's guidance it issued a resolution supporting central control over Soviet nuclear weapons and NPT membership as a requirement for independence and then dissolved itself.

Stanislav Shushkevich, the nuclear physicist who had cursed Gorbachev after Chernobyl for Moscow's refusal to authorize potassium iodide tablets for Byelorussian children, had gone into politics when glasnost had opened up the opportunity. By the time Byelorussia declared its independence and renamed itself Belarus, Shushkevich was head of the Belarusian Supreme Soviet, and thus became the first Belarusian head of state. He, Yeltsin, Nazarbayev, and other heads of state tried to work with Gorbachev in October 1991 to negotiate an all-union treaty that would hold the former Soviet Union together in a confederative state. "In Gorbachev's conception of the union," Yeltsin writes, "a strong center would be preserved that would determine matters of defense and some fiscal issues. A single president would remain . . . [to] represent the Union of Sovereign States . . . in dealings with foreign countries." But "to Gorbachev's immense consternation, one after another of the former Union republics began to drop out. . . . They all dreamed of elevating their own status; all of them wanted to become full-fledged members of the UN." It was obvious, Yeltsin concludes, "that Gorbachev, not because of anyone's ill will, was, historically speaking, painting himself into a corner."

The people of Ukraine endorsed independence with an overwhelming majority vote on 1 December 1991 and elected Leonid Kravchuk as their first president. At that point Yeltsin, Shushkevich, and Kravchuk realized, Yeltsin writes, that they "had to find another way" than Gorbachev's desperate union, which Kravchuk, on behalf of his new nation, refused to join. When the union treaty had fallen apart in October, Gorbachev had stalked off in fury to his office. Shushkevich and Yeltsin had been delegated to go to him and coax him back. "Yeltsin and I went off to make peace," Shushkevich told me in one of our conversations, "walking down the hall in the Kremlin. I said to Yeltsin, 'You have a beautiful place, but we have a beautiful place in Belarus. Come and visit.' Yeltsin said, 'Sure.'" The beautiful place Shushkevich had in mind was the Bison Lodge in the Belovezhskaya Pushcha nature reserve in western Belarus, a semi-wilderness where the last of Europe's ancient forest bison, relatives of the bison that once populated the American West, had been restored across the decades by German and Soviet wildlife experts to cater to the hunting tastes of German generals and Soviet premiers. It had been a Brezhnev favorite.

A week after the vote in Ukraine at the beginning of December, Yeltsin, Kravchuk, and Shushkevich met at the Bison Lodge in the Belovezh forest. "We were meeting," Yeltsin writes, "to decide the fate of the Soviet Union." Shushkevich told me less dramatically that he met "not to consider dissolution but problems in Belarus. We had to do something, because an economic crisis was looming. Gas and oil were impossible. Belarus and Ukraine would have frozen and starved." But when they got together and talked it over, Shushkevich added, "we realized the whole system didn't work."

Yeltsin recalled "a wonderful winter evening with a soft snowfall." He felt a certain imperial discomfort when he thought about letting go of Ukraine and Belarus "perhaps forever, offering them in a new agreement a guaranteed status on a par with Russia." Shushkevich suggested they go hunting or walk in the woods, Yeltsin says, "but no one felt like strolling. We were all too overwrought." Yeltsin's aides had prepared documents—"an enormous amount of work"—which suggests that the meeting in the Bison Lodge was less indefinite than the participants present it to be. So does the fact that it was kept a close secret, "even guarded," Yeltsin writes, "by a special security division." Shushkevich told me at another time of the purpose of the meeting. "Something had to be done. Everyone had his own agenda. Yeltsin wanted to get rid of Gorbachev. I wanted independence for Belarus. And Krauchuk wanted independence for Ukraine." The documents Yeltsin offered, and over which the three heads of state then labored in turn, resulted in an agreement dissolving the old Soviet Union and replacing it with a

Commonwealth of Independent States, with Minsk as its capital. Other republics could join if they chose, or go their own ways.

Separating from the Soviet Union compromised Belarus's economy, Shushkevich told me. Under the old system, essentially colonial, the region had been designated an industrial center, sending finished machinery and goods to Moscow in exchange for food and energy supplies produced elsewhere in the U.S.S.R. Separating would compromise that arrangement. Then why break away? I asked him, expecting, from someone trained in science and skillful at statecraft, a pragmatic answer. His explanation, which parallels Yeltsin's explanation of Russia's separation, surprised me with its vehement nationalism:

First a little history. In 1918, Byelorussian patriots resolved that Byelorussia should be an independent state. At about the same time, Ukraine, Lithuania, Latvia, Estonia, and Finland also announced the formation of independent states. This actually worked for some of them (Finland, for example), but not for others. Later on, people who had such intentions were relentlessly destroyed by the Bolsheviks. We came back to the idea only in 1990. On 27 July 1990, the [Byelorussian] Supreme Soviet that had been elected to office in 1990 passed the Declaration of State Independence. This had only symbolic meaning, since Russia—which had also announced its own sovereignty earlier—had intended Ukraine and the other republics to be its constituent parts.

By 1991, an advantageous situation had developed: Boris Yeltsin wanted to become the sovereign ruler of Russia, and had the right to do so, since he had been elected president by the people of Russia. But Gorbachev believed that he outranked Yeltsin, since he had been elected president by the Congress of People's Deputies of the U.S.S.R. Given this situation, Yeltsin decided that the easiest solution would be to strip Gorbachev of his authority by officially declaring the cessation of the U.S.S.R.'s functions as a subject of international law. This was fairly logical, since it wasn't a union of states anymore (Moscow no longer controlled this large conglomerate); but the U.S.S.R. officially continued to exist. Moreover, fearing that a breach of the Yalta Agreements might lead to chaos or even to nuclear war, President Bush (Senior) announced in an October 1991 speech in Kiev that the West would recognize the U.S.S.R. only as a complete whole and warned about the danger of its disintegration, supposing that this would give rise to several new countries with nuclear weapons. For these reasons, Kravchuk and I took advantage of Yeltsin's desire to become the sole master of Russia and helped him to make Gorbachev the de jure president of a nonexistent state. We believed our primary achievement to be Russia's recognition of the independence of Belarus and Ukraine (as well as that of the other republics of the former Soviet Union).

Yeltsin's explanation:

> The idea of a new kind of state system had not been born yesterday, and not just in my head or that of Shushkevich or Kravchuk. If we recall the years 1917–1918, immediately after the democratic February revolution [i.e., the liberal socialist democratic Russian Provisional Government under Alexander Kerensky], the republics immediately began the process of succession, eventually moving toward independence. Several new national governments were declared in the territory of the Russian empire, including in the Caucasus and Central Asia. Ukraine led the process. The Bolsheviks managed to suppress all the nationalist uprisings, forcing peasants and soldiers into a civil war, although the revolution was supposedly spontaneously proletarian. With an iron fist, the Soviets strangled the liberation struggles, executed the national intelligentsia and dispersed national parties.

Seventy-three years later, the wheel had come full circle. As Yeltsin, Kravchuk, and Shushkevich signed the historic documents, they discovered that no one had thought to provide a copying machine, just as there had not been one at Reykjavik, and because of the extreme security they couldn't call for one. Rather than use carbon paper they set two fax machines side by side and faxed the documents from one to the other to make copies. Yeltsin made a point of calling Bush first (after which he asked Shushkevich to call Gorbachev, who was predictably furious). "On December 8, 1991," Bush writes, ". . . Boris Yeltsin called me from a hunting lodge near Brest, in Belarus. Only recently elected President of the Russian Republic, Yeltsin had been meeting with Leonid Kravchuk, President of Ukraine, and Stanislav Shushkevich, President of Belarus. 'Today a very important event took place in our country,' Yeltsin said. 'I wanted to inform you myself, before you learned about it from the press.' Then he told me the news: the Presidents of Russia, Belarus, and Ukraine had decided to dissolve the Soviet Union."

SOVEREIGNTY, ONCE ATTRIBUTED TO DIVINE RIGHT, later to the people, today has an additional locus of authority: control of a nation's nuclear weapons. When George H. W. Bush delivered his notorious "Chicken Kiev" speech in Kiev on 1 August 1991, for example, cautioning the Ukrainians against separating from the Soviet Union, he was motivated in part by his fear of what Shushkevich described to me as "Bush realizing that the nuclear monster could split up into many little monsters." The ambassador and arms negotiator James Goodby remembers Baker using the phrase "Yugoslavia with nukes" to characterize what Goodby calls "the nightmare that could result from a loss of central authority and control over [Soviet] nuclear weapons." After the meeting at the Bison Lodge, Shushkevich told me, "there was a second meeting in Alma-Ata [the capital of Kazakhstan, now Almaty] to discuss the transfer of nuclear weapons to the CIS." That meeting, held on 21 December, after Gorbachev had announced his forthcoming resignation, gave the other new republics an opportunity to join the CIS, which most of them did.* Four leaders, Shushkevich said, would officially take control of the former Soviet nuclear arsenal: "Yeltsin, Nazarbayev, Kravchuk and Shushkevich. The day after that meeting we received the communications equipment that would connect these four people—it was called 'Metal'— and there was always a man around us carrying it. We only tried it once, and it worked. But it was all a farce. All those weapons of course were controlled by Yeltsin, which we understood. And you Americans also understood that it was a pretense." Pretense or not, Belarus alone had eighty-one MIRVed mobile missiles on its territory, "sufficient to eradicate Europe and the United States." There were hundreds more ICBMs on the territories of Ukraine and Kazakhstan, a problem that Baker would undertake to solve in the immediate months ahead. In the end it would take five years.

It remained then for Gorbachev to transfer the *chemodanchik*, the "little suitcase" that contained the missile launch codes, to Yeltsin. The two bitter rivals met for the last time in Gorbachev's Kremlin office on 24 December, had what Yeltsin calls a "protracted and difficult" conversation, and formally accomplished the transfer. After the meeting, the two officers assigned to protect the *chemodanchik* left with Yeltsin. "It was like being in the front line of a war," Gorbachev said of his years as general secretary and then president. "I lived through several lives, and I don't know how I survived."

Gorbachev called Bush at Camp David on Christmas morning 1991. "My dear George," he said, "greetings! Let me begin with something pleasant. Merry Christmas to you and Barbara and your family!" He went on, Bush writes, "to sum up what had happened in his country: the Soviet Union had ceased to exist. He had just been on national TV to confirm the fact, and he had transferred control of Soviet nuclear weapons to the President of Russia."

"I attach great importance to the fact that this aspect is under effective control," Gorbachev concluded. "I've signed a decree on this issue that will come into effect immediately after my final statement. You may therefore feel at ease as you celebrate Christmas, and sleep quietly tonight."

* The exceptions were the three Baltic states and Georgia.

THE SUPERPOWER NUCLEAR-ARMS RACE had ended after forty-two dangerous years. Afterward, some of those in America who had promoted that confrontation with inflated threats, fearmongering, and misleading or fraudulent intelligence claimed shamelessly that the United States had won the Cold War. The world had won with the two superpowers at least partly disarmed. The Soviet Union had dissolved into its original components, a socioeconomic disaster for most of the new nations and especially for Russia, where life expectancy continued to decline, descending to a truncated 59.0 years for Russian males in 2000, and the population to plummet from a wide excess of deaths over births. The United States was left still standing, seemingly triumphant, but across the Cold War, nuclear weapons and weapons-related programs alone had cost the nation at least $5.5 trillion. Carl Sagan estimated in 1992 that other Cold War costs took the total even higher, to about $10 trillion. That, Sagan wrote in indignant benediction, was "enough to buy everything in the United States except for the land." What we bought for a waste of treasure unprecedented in human history was not peace nor even safety but a pervasive decline in the capacity and clemency of American life. As in the countries of the former Soviet Union, but not so severely, even American male life expectancy stalled compared to the European democracies and Japan.

The investment banker and Federal Reserve Board Chairman Marriner Eccles argued as long ago as the 1960s that "over-kill spending of the military" was "responsible for our financial inability to adequately meet the problems of our cities (poverty, crime, riots, pollution) and our rapidly expanding educational requirements." The Columbia University economist Seymour Melman noted in 1974 that "the extent of economic deterioration in the cities of the U.S. would be a mystery forever if we had no way of explaining the unique consequences of nonproductive [military] economic activity. After all, the decay of America's cities occurred during a period of economic growth in the United States. . . . [But] the additional taxes generated by the new income were being preempted for the military." Melman dismisses the triumphalist right-wing claim that the United States with its superior economy could afford to spend the Soviet Union into bankruptcy—one argument offered for the huge defense budgets of the Reagan years. "The purveyors of this shrewd idea," he writes, "never allowed themselves to admit the possibility that the American war economy could also devour the civilian economy of the United States." Further, "the assumption that sustained war economy brings economic and allied well-being encounters a cruel contrast in the shape of what is forgone in the United States in health care, housing, education and minimum nutrition. These are all recognized areas of public responsibility partly because the consequences of deficiencies in these realms have blighting effects on the entire society." Melman quotes the Yale scholar Bruce Russett on the long-term effects of investing in military power rather than civilian needs:

> Since future production is dependent upon current investment, the economy's *future* resources and power base are thus much more severely damaged by the decision to build or employ current military power than is current indulgence. According to some rough estimates . . . an additional dollar of investment in any single year will produce 20–25¢ of annual additional production in perpetuity. Hence, if an extra billion dollars of defense in one year reduced investment by $292 million, thenceforth the level of output in the economy would be *permanently* diminished by a figure on the order of $65 million per year.

"The dollars that pay for the operation of the military system," Melman concludes, "finally represent something forgone from other aspects of life, especially those parts that are also dependent on financing from the community's public budgets." Which should be indisputable, since civil destitution is exactly what happened to the Soviet Union.

Some argue that the buoyant American economy of the 1990s disproved these economic predictions. The defense budget began declining in the late 1980s and was cut by about $10 billion per year during the Bill Clinton presidency, but such deep budget deficits had accumulated during the Reagan era that the savings went largely to deficit reduction. A "Report Card for America's Infrastructure" issued for the year 2001 by the American Society of Civil Engineers (ASCE) confirms the continuing and even worsening decrepitude of the United States's physical plants in the years after the Cold War. For 2001, the nation's civil engineers gave American infrastructure the following grades:

Aviation: D
Bridges: C
Dams: D
Drinking Water: D
National power grid: D+
Hazardous waste: D+
Navigable waterways: D+
Roads: D+
Schools: D–

Solid waste: C+
Transit: C−
Wastewater: D

Nor had these grades increased by more than a plus sign by 2005; in the majority of categories they had further declined. The ASCE estimated at that time that "all levels of government and the private sector" would need to invest $1.6 trillion over a five-year period to correct the pervasive deficiencies it found.

Far from victory in the Cold War, the superpower nuclear-arms race and the corresponding militarization of the American economy gave us ramshackle cities, broken bridges, failing schools, entrenched poverty, impeded life expectancy, and a menacing and secretive national-security state that held the entire human world hostage. "If you try to look at [the Cold War] from today's point of view," Gorbachev's adviser Georgi Shakhnazarov concluded at the 1998 Brown conference, "from the height of a bird's flight, so to speak, the politics of both sides were not moral. Each side, of course, thought they were doing the right thing."

The politics of both sides were not moral because they put the human world at mortal risk, with no reasonable gain in security, for domestic advantage and the international play of power. Robert Oppenheimer saw the dishonesty as early as 1953, when he wrote sardonically in *Foreign Affairs:*

> The very least that we can say is that, looking ten years ahead, it is likely to be small comfort that the Soviet Union is four years behind us, and small comfort that they are only about half as big as we are. The very least we can conclude is that our twenty-thousandth bomb, useful as it may be in filling the vast munitions pipelines of a great war, will not in any deep strategic sense offset their two-thousandth. . . . We may anticipate a state of affairs in which two Great Powers will each be in a position to put an end to the civilization and life of the other, though not without risking its own. We may be likened to two scorpions in a bottle, each capable of killing the other, but only at the risk of his own life.

The discovery of how to release nuclear energy was a fact, not a choice, a new understanding of the natural world. It revealed that there was no limit to the amount of energy that might be packaged into small, portable, and relatively inexpensive weapons; that there could be no defense against such weapons, each of which could destroy a city; that therefore a policy of common security in the short run and a program of abolition in the long run would be necessary to accommodate the new reality and avoid disaster.

Recoiling from such urgencies, which would require negotiation, compromise, and a measure of humility, we chose instead to distend ourselves into the largest scorpion in the bottle. Obstinately misreading the failure of our authoritarian counterpart on the other side of the world, to our shame and misfortune, we continue to claim an old and derelict sovereignty that the weapons themselves deny.

NOTES

ONE **TO THE CHERNOBYL SARCOPHAGUS**

3 BYELORUSSIAN INSTITUTE RADIATION EVENTS: Irina and S. Shushkevich interviews, April 2003; Alexievich (1997), pp. 180–81; Yaroshinskaya (1995), p. 16; Scherbak (1989), p. 26.

4 A LARGE CACHE OF MONEY: Volkogonov (1998), p. 430.

4 "I WAS THE FIRST . . . WALL": S. Shushkevich interview, Apr. 2003.

4 "WE JUST . . . THIS": Gorbacheva (1991), p. 5.

4 "I EMPHASIZED . . . ORGANIZATIONS": Gorbachev (1995), p. 167.

4 "THE ELIMINATION . . . DEVELOPMENT": ibid., p. 173.

4 SOVIET MILITARY-INDUSTRIAL COMPLEX . . . STATE BUDGET: Gorbachev, in his *Memoirs,* gives this number as a percent of "the state budget": Gorbachev (1995), p. 215. For a different view see Vitaliy V. Shlykov, The structural militarization of the Soviet economy: the unknown phenomenon, in Genin (2001), p. 101: "Research conducted at the end of the 1980s by the Institute for Economic Forecasting of the Soviet Academy of Sciences, showed that if the output of the USSR machine-building industry were to be rated at world market prices, the share of military equipment would account for more than 60 percent of the output, and consumer goods not more than 5 percent." See also Reed (2004), p. 219; Clem (1986), p. 3.

4 "A CONCRETE . . . CENTURY": quoted from *Izvestia* in Mazo (2004), p. 16.

5 AT 2:30: Alexievich (1997), p. 181.

5 DETAILS OF PROMPT CRITICAL EXCURSION: John Dunster, *Nature* 333, 811 (30 June 88); Wilson (1987), p. 1636.

5 THE *PYATACHOK* "BEGAN TO . . . DANCE": Josephson (2000), p. 256.

6 ABOUT HALF THE TOTAL RADIATION: Z. Medvedev (1990), p. 45.

6 EXPLOSION DETAILS: see in particular ibid., p. 28ff.

6 A CONTAINMENT DOME WOULD HAVE CONFINED THE REACTION: "Had the Soviet Union built its RBMKs with a containment shield, the world community would have been spared the events at Chernobyl and their aftermath." Ebel (1994), p. x.

6 CONTAINMENT DOME BEYOND SOVIET CAPACITY: Z. Medvedev (1990), p. 232.

6 INFORMATION ABOUT ACCIDENTS DENIED: Potter emphasizes this point: Potter (1989), p. 12.

6 THIRTEEN ACCIDENTS: see list at Potter (1989), pp. 9–12. Also see Z. Medvedev (1990), pp. 17–19.

7 "SOMETHING AWFUL . . . EXPLOSION": this and the following quotation cited in *Nature* 342 (10) (2 Nov. 1989).

7 BRYUKHANOV DELAY ALERTING KIEV: Mould (2000), p. 300, n. 13.

7 FIREFIGHTERS: Ebel (1994), pp. 6–7.

7 SEVEN A.M.: Z. Medvedev (1990), p. 44.

7 "1-2-3-4": Legasov (2000), p. 289.

7 CIVIL DEFENSE ALERTED TWO HOURS AFTER EXPLOSIONS: Potter (1989), p. 58.

8 GORBACHEV ALERTED, POLITBURO MEETING: Gorbachev (1995), p. 189.

8 EIGHT P.M. GOVERNMENT COMMISSION ARRIVAL: Legasov (2000), p. 291.

8 "THE REACTOR . . . HOSPITALIZED": ibid., p. 290.

8 "THEY HAD . . . SPOT": ibid., p. 293.

8 "A WHITE . . . LUMINESCENCE": ibid., p. 291. Original italics.

8 GRAPHITE BURNING RATE: ibid., p. 292.

9 PRIPYAT TOWN COMMITTEE . . . SANDBAGS: Shcherbak (1989), pp. 57–58.

9 ANTOSHKIN ARRIVAL: Potter (1989), pp. 50–51.

9 "THE FIRST . . . RUNS": Current Digest of the Soviet Press 38 (19), p. 10.

9 "[AT 110 . . . SACKS": quoted in Z. Medvedev (1990), pp. 168–69. Ellipses in original text.

9 "IF YOU . . . LEAD": quoted in Schmid (2005), p. 285, n. 53. I altered Schmid's translation slightly to save the rhyme.

9 20 TO 80 RADS PER FLIGHT: Z. Medvedev (1990), p. 168.

10 DEATHS AMONG LIQUIDATORS: "The Ukrainian government has estimated the number of deaths among cleanup workers alone as 7,000–8,000. Total civilian casualties are not known and may never be known." Marples (1996a), p. 1. Marples's total is disputed by knowledgeable Russian authorities (Sig Hecker, personal communication, Oct. 2006).

10 "THEY FLUNG . . . REACTOR": Alexievich (1997), p. 76.

10 QUENCHING MATERIALS: Z. Medvedev (1990), p. 56.

10 MORE THAN ELEVEN MILLION POUNDS: 5,000 tonnes. Mould (2000), p. 45.

10 REM LEVELS: Wilson (1987), p. 1637.

10 KIEV BUSES AND TRUCKS: Mould (1988), p. xiii.

10 THE DRIVERS . . . SECRECY: Hopkins (1993), p. 41.

10 "HAVE YOUR . . . YOU": Shcherbak (1989), p. 64.

11 10 REM PER HOUR: Wilson (1987), p. 1637.

11 DECONTAMINATION CENTER: Current Digest of the Soviet Press 36 (23), p. 14.

11 POTASSIUM IODIDE DISPENSED: G. Medvedev (1991), p. 186.

11 POTASSIUM IODIDE EFFECTIVENESS: Zanzonico and Becker (2000).

11 "IN EVERY . . . TABLETS": S. Shushkevich interview, Apr. 2003.

12 NESTERENKO NARRATIVE: Alexievich (1997), p. 210ff.

12 "EVERY POLITICAL . . . ACCIDENT' ": S. Shushkevich interview, Apr. 2003.

13 "THE WORST . . . AVERTED": Gorbachev (1987c), p. 522.

13 "THAT WAS . . . HATED HIM": S. Shushkevich interview, Apr. 2003.

13 "IN THOSE FIRST . . . MILLIONS": Alexievich (1997), p. 185.

13 "OPINION CHANGED . . . SILO": Mould (2000), pp. 48–49.

14 BRITISH GOVERNMENT INFORMED: ibid., p. 49.

14 HELSINKI RADIATION LEVELS: Rippon (1986).

14 CROSSED INTO SWEDEN, STUDSVIK, FORSMARK: Hopkins (1993), pp. 37–38; Z. Medvedev (1990), pp. 195–96; L. Devell et al. (1986). "Initial Observations of Fallout from the Reactor Accident at Chernobyl." Nature 321 (192) (15 May 1986).

14 "COMBINED WITH . . . WEAPONS": L. Devell et al., "Initial Observations."

14 RUTHENIUM . . . VAPORIZED: ibid.; Z. Medvedev (1990), p. 2.

15 THE GOVERNMENT COMMISSION . . . MEETING: Z. Medvedev (1990), p. 53; Gorbachev (1995), p. 189.

15 "WE CATEGORICALLY . . . TRUTH": quoted in Shevardnadze (1991), p. 173.

15 "HOW CAN . . . THINKING": Shevardnadze (1991), pp. 173–74.

15 "POSSESSED BY . . . CAMP": Vitaliy V. Shlykov, The Soviet system of mobilization preparedness, in Genin (2001), p. 66.

15 "IT WAS . . . EASY": Shlykov in Genin (2001), p. 68.

15 RBMK ADAPTED IN THE 1970S: Marples (1996a), p. 3.

16 GORBACHEV TRUSTING THE EXPERTS: Chernyaev (2000), p. 65.

16 "UNSHEATHED . . . CLAWS": Shevardnadze (1991), p. 174.

16 "NOTHING TERRIBLE . . . IT": Gorbachev (1995), p. 191.

17 "FROM THE . . . CREATED": quoted in Marples (1986), p. 1.

17 "I WAS PHONED . . . IT": Hans Blix interview, Las Vegas, Sept. 2005.

17 POLITBURO OPERATIONAL GROUP: Yaroshinskaya (1995), p. 123.

17 "THE EMISSION . . . NORMALLY": *Current Digest of the Soviet Press* 38 (16), 21 May 1986, p. 1.

18 TEN-KILOMETER . . . ZONE: Mould (1988), p. xiii.

18 A NEW . . . THREAT: see Z. Medvedev (1990), p. 57ff.

18 MONDAY LEVEL: ibid., p. 61.

18 "AT FIRST . . . HEROES": Alexievich (1997), pp. 76–77.

19 116,000 PEOPLE, 86,000 CATTLE: Mould (1988), p. xiii.

19 "WE DIDN'T . . . LIVES": Alexievich (1997), p. 34.

19 "IT COULD . . . SOLID": Z. Medvedev (1990), pp. 57–58.

19 LIQUID NITROGEN PROJECT: ibid., p. 60.

19 PUMPING OUT BUBBLER POOL: Shcherbak (1989), p. 98.

19 FILLING POOL: Z. Medvedev (1990), p. 58; Potter (1989), p. 56.

20 "WE SAT . . . ANYTHING": Alexievich (1997), p. 146.

20 "IN SERIOUS . . . VICTIMS": *Current Digest of the Soviet Press* 38 (16), 21 May 1986, p. 3.

20 SECRET PROTOCOLS: These documents were subpoenaed by a Russian parliamentary commission investigating the Chernobyl accident late in 1991. See Yaroshinskaya (1995), p. 123ff.

20 "1,882 PEOPLE . . . CONDITION": Yaroshinskaya (1995), p. 124.

20 BLIX MOSCOW BRIEFING: Petrosyants (1988), pp. 43–44.

20 "I KNOW . . . CONTINUED": Hans Blix interview, Sept. 2005.

20 "SO THAT . . . MUCH": Shevardnadze (1991), p. 174.

20 "THE NUMBER . . . CHILDREN": quoted in Yaroshinskaya (1995), p. 124.

21 "IN ONE . . . 34": quoted in ibid., p. 125.

21 "WE CIRCLED . . . HAPPENED": Hans Blix interview, Sept. 2005.

21 "THE HELICOPTER . . . OVER": Petrosyants (1988), pp. 44–45.

21 3.5 REM PER HOUR: Z. Medvedev (1990), p. 68.

21 "AND THEN . . . ENOUGH": Hans Blix interview, Sept. 2005.

21 CHERNOBYL FALLOUT . . . TNT: Paton et al. (2003), p. 5.

21 "THE SOVIET . . . ACT": Director-General's statement for Roundtable 7, "The Future of Nuclear Power," World Energy Conference, 13th Congress, Cannes, Oct. 1986.

22 "IT WAS . . . JUDGMENT": Z. Medvedev (1990), p. 70.

22 "SHED LIGHT . . . REFORMS": Gorbachev (1995), p. 193.

22 "SEVERELY AFFECTED . . . TRACKS": ibid., p. 189.

22   GORBACHEV SPEECH, 14 MAY 1986: Gorbachev (1987c), p. 519ff.

22   POLITBURO PROTOCOL FOR 12 MAY: Yaroshinskaya (1995), p. 125.

23   THIRTEEN KILOTONS: the current (c. 2006) official yield of the Hiroshima bomb.

24   THREE HUNDRED THOUSAND TONS OF LEAVES: Mould (1988), p. xiv.

24   "WE BURIED . . . LIVE": Alexievich (1997), pp. 93–94.

24   "MORE THAN . . . ANALYSIS": quoted in Mould (2000), pp. 198–99.

24   " 'CHERNOBYL DAY' . . . EYES": Shevardnadze (1991), p. 175.

24   "CHERNOBYL HAPPENED . . . CHANGED": Alexievich (1997), p. 170.

24   7 MAY 1986 AGRICULTURAL PRODUCTS BAN: "The Soviets End Their Silence—But the Damage Keeps Mounting," *Business Week,* 19 May 1986, p. 44.

25   "THE DECISION . . . PRIORITY": Z. Medvedev (1990), pp. 241–42.

25   27TH PARTY CONGRESS GOALS: ibid., p. 69.

25   "CHERNOBYL WAS . . . FAILED": Shevardnadze (1991), p. 176.

25   " 'PROFOUNDLY REALISTIC' . . . WEAPONS": Volkogonov (1998), p. 482.

25   "SENIOR POLISH . . . WAR": Potter (1989), p. 83.

25   "I WAS . . . EXCHANGE": George Shultz to Ronald Reagan, reproduced in Reagan (1990), p. 710.

26   "HIS MIND . . . 'DE-IDEOLOGIZATION' ": Chernyaev (2000), p. 67.

26   "CHERNOBYL . . . HANDS?": Wohlforth (1996), p. 33. (Translation slightly corrected.)

26   "GLOBAL NUCLEAR . . . POLITICS": quoted in Volkogonov (1998), p. 483.

26   "WHAT HAPPENED . . . IT": quoted in Chernyaev (2000), p. 67.

TWO   **MOSCOW DOES NOT BELIEVE IN TEARS**

27   "FREE AND EASY": Remnick (1994), p. 152.

27   "MY [MATERNAL] GRANDFATHER . . . LAND": Gorbachev and Mlynar (2002), p. 14. Emphasis added.

27   "*LENIN GAVE . . . SAYS*": Gorbacheva (1991), p. 16. Emphasis added.

28   "NOT REALLY . . . PROCEEDS": Conquest (1986), p. 108.

28   "HE PARTICIPATED . . . CHAIRMAN": Gorbachev (1995), p. 23.

28   "LOYALTY TO . . . OFFICE": Dolot (1985), p. 93.

28   "THE LIQUIDATION . . . CLASS": quoted in Conquest (1986), p. 117.

28   "THE CAPITALISTS . . . VILLAGE": quoted in Gareth Jones, "Seizure of Land and Slaughter of Stock," *The Western Mail,* 8 Apr. 1933.

28   CONQUEST ESTIMATES . . . PEOPLE": Robert Conquest, hearing testimony, U.S. Commission on the Ukraine Famine, 8 Oct. 1986.

28   TEN MILLION SMALL FARMS: Conquest (1990), p. 18.

28   KULAK TRANSPORT AND TEMPORARY HOUSING: Viola (2001), pp. 735–41.

28   8.5 TO 9 . . . VORTEX": Volkogonov (1988), p. 166.

29   "EVEN BY . . . RUINS": Conquest hearing testimony, 8 Oct. 1986; ibid.

29   "THE STAVROPOL . . . DISTRICT": Conquest (1986), p. 123.

29   "IT IS . . . TEARS": ibid., p. 130.

29   "HOW INSIGNIFICANT . . . FARMS": Doder and Branson (1990), p. 11.

29   "UP TO . . . CAMPAIGN": Dolot (1985), p. 137.

29   "WITH COLLECTIVIZATION . . . INDUSTRY": Malia (1990), p. 311.

30   INDUSTRIALIZATION . . . 12.5 MILLION: Conquest (1986), p. 168.

30   "THIS INCREASE . . . 26 PERCENT": ibid., pp. 168–69.

30   GRAIN REQUISITIONS: ibid., p. 174.

30 "ALL TOO . . . FAMILIES": Khrushchev (1974), p. 108, quoted in Conquest (1986), p. 176.

30 "I REMEMBER . . . ORDEAL": Dolot (1985), pp. 137–38.

30 "ONE OF . . . LAW": ibid., pp. 156–57.

31 PASSPORTS DENIED TO RURAL POPULATION: Gorbachev (1995), p. 36.

31 "THE FAMINE . . . ESCAPE": Carynnyk et al. (1988), p. 259.

32 "PEOPLE HAVE . . . SEVERELY": ibid., p. 264.

32 "FOR NOT . . . YEAR": quoted in Remnick (1994), p. 149.

32 "THE FAMINE . . . YEARS": Gorbachev (1995), p. 27.

32 "BEARING TWO . . . IMMEDIATELY": ibid.

32 A MILLION, FIVE MILLION: Volkogonov (1988), p. 307.

33 "FIRST REAL TRAUMA": Gorbachev (1995), p. 24.

33 "AFTER GRANDFATHER'S . . . SINCE": ibid.

33 "THE HEAD . . . PRISON": ibid., p. 26.

33 "I REMEMBER . . . ELSE": ibid.

33 "HE WAS . . . MISFORTUNES": ibid.

34 "THE TRAGEDY . . . PERVERSION": Remnick (1994), p. 149.

34 "IN THE . . . LIVES": Dolot (1985), p. 92.

34 "NOT ONLY . . . POSSIBLE": Gorbachev and Mlynar (2002), p. 17.

34 "THE SHOPS . . . THEN": Gorbachev (1995), pp. 27–28.

35 "THE THIRD . . . COUNTRYSIDE": Conquest (1986), p. 181.

35 2,500 MTS, PARTY OFFICIALS, AND SECRET POLICE: ibid., pp. 181–2.

35 "THE VILLAGE . . . GONE": Gorbachev (1995), p. 28.

35 "GORBACHEV PASSED . . . GOLD": Sheehy (1990), p. 47.

35 ON THE RARE . . . PROBLEMS: ibid.

35 "UNBEARABLE TERROR": Gorbachev (1995), p. 29.

35 "FIERY ARROWS . . . SOUND": ibid.

35 "RUMORS OF . . . GAS": ibid., p. 30.

36 GORLOV TOLD SHEEHY: Sheehy (1990), p. 46.

36 GORBACHEV HIDDEN; MONTHS OF OCCUPATION: Gorbachev (1995), p. 30.

36 "FELT AS . . . WOOD": ibid., p. 31.

36 "THE FAMILY . . . WELL": ibid., p. 33.

36 "I WROTE . . . US": ibid.

36 "UNSPEAKABLE HORROR . . . WORLD": ibid., p. 34.

37 "SPREADING THE . . . RUSSIA": first Komsomol program, quoted at http://www .iremember.ru/nagrady/Komsomol.htm (accessed 5 Oct. 2005).

37 "A GREAT . . . FRIENDS": Gorbachev (1995), p. 36.

37 "CORRECTING TEACHERS . . . MEETING": quoted (apparently from a *Washington Post* story by David Remnick) in Doder and Branson (1990), p. 7.

38 "DISLIKE OF . . . GENERICALLY": Doder and Branson (1990), p. 31.

38 THIRTY-SEVEN MILLION TONNES, SEVENTEEN MILLION TONNES: Gorbachev (1995), p. 38.

38 "VERY, VERY . . . YEARS": Sheehy (1990), p. 49.

38 120 MILLION TONNES: compiled from USDA National Agricultural Statistics Service Track Records, U.S. Crop Production (April 2003), online.

38 "WE SOMEHOW . . . WINTER": Gorbachev (1995), p. 38.

38 "THE TERRIBLE . . . DROUGHT": ibid.

39 "I WAS . . . AWARDS": ibid.

39 "THE PROBLEM . . . RUSSIA": Mlynar (1980), pp. 10–11.

39 "ABSENCE OF . . . COMMUNISM": ibid., p. 11.

39 GORBACHEV HAD HOPED TO STUDY PHYSICS: See his statement to that effect quoted in Doder and Branson (1990), p. 8.

39 SAGDEEV ON GORBACHEV DENIED ACCESS TO PHYSICS COURSE: See Sagdeev (1994), pp. 25–26.

40 SAKHAROV RECRUITED WHILE A POSTDOC: See Sakharov (1990), p. 94ff.

40 LENIN: a connection made by Doder and Branson (1990), p. 8.

40 "I HAD . . . ME": Gorbachev (1995), p. 41.

40 ROMANTIC AND INNOCENT: See Doder and Branson (1990), p. 14.

40 "THE SOVIET . . . COURTYARD": Mlynar (1980), p. 20.

40 "EVERYTHING WAS . . . PASSIONATELY": Gorbachev (1995), p. 42.

40 ALUMNI REMEMBER: see, e.g., Remnick (1994), p. 160.

41 PARTY MONITOR AND ORGANIZER: Doder and Branson (1990), p. 10.

41 "MASSIVE IDEOLOGICAL . . . CONCLUSIONS": Gorbachev (1995), p. 45.

41 "BEFORE THE . . . PROCESS": Gorbachev and Mlynar (2002), p. 23.

41 STALIN DEATH SCENE: Volkogonov (1988), p. 574.

41 "THE INSTRUCTOR . . . LIFE": Gorbachev (1995), p. 47.

41 " 'MISHA, WHAT'S . . . KNOW' ": Gorbachev and Mlynar (2002), p. 21.

41 "WE ADVANCED . . . PLACE": Gorbachev (1995), p. 47.

41 "THE DENSITY . . . AWAY": Mlynar (1980), p. 25.

42 "A STONY . . . FEELINGS": Gorbachev (1995), p. 47.

42 "THE GENERATION . . . -OLDS": Gorbacheva (1991), p. 47.

42 "THE NEVER-ENDING . . . LIKE?": ibid., p. 17.

42 "AT THE . . . PEOPLE' ": ibid., pp. 16–17.

42 "I DO . . . PEOPLE' ": ibid., pp. 186–87.

43 MAXIM TITORENKO'S TRANSFER TO CHERNIGOV: Jürgens (1990), p. 18.

43 TITORENKO PURGED: The German biographer who offers this information says it came from "Lydia Budyka, a pediatrician [who] is one of Raisa's closest friends" and who was willing to talk "only under certain conditions: following each interview, she had to refer back to Raisa"—who then allowed or disallowed the information to be used. I find no evidence that Raisa Gorbachev ever publicly disputed or repudiated the biographer's information. Nor, of course, did she endorse it, and the conditions under which Budyka spoke with the biographer allowed Raisa Maximovna deniability. See Jürgens (1990), p. 12.

43 "I REMEMBER . . . OUT": Gorbacheva (1991), p. 18.

44 "A DAILY . . . SOCIAL": ibid., p. 20.

44 "I RECEIVED . . . HISTORY": ibid.

44 "IN OUR . . . SYSTEM": ibid., p. 93.

44 "OUR RELATIONSHIP . . . MARRIED": ibid., pp. 61–62.

45 "A BEAUTIFUL . . . IT": Gorbachev (1995), p. 51.

45 "YOU'VE GOT . . . INCENTIVE": ibid., p. 50.

45 "I KNOW . . . INTELLECT": quoted in Gorbacheva (1991), p. 69.

45 "I HAD . . . BEFORE": Gorbachev (1995), p. 50.

THREE **A HIERARCHY OF VASSALS AND CHIEFS**

46 "STAVROPOL STRUCK . . . EVERYWHERE": Gorbacheva (1991), p. 76.

46 AGRICULTURAL REFORMS: See Fainsod (1956), p. 32.

46 "SHEER MISERY . . . MIND": Gorbachev (1995), p. 59.

47   "I DON'T . . . LIFE": Gorbacheva (1991), p. 83.

47   "THE CHIEF . . . TERROR": Berman (1963), p. 933. Berman discusses the Special
      Board's abolition.

47   "HUNDREDS . . . REFORMS": Berman (1963), p. 936.

48   "A SUBSTANTIAL . . . CITIZENS": ibid., p. 944.

48   "THE MAIN . . . DEVELOPMENT": Gorbachev and Mlynar (2002), p. 27.

48   "PRACTICED BRUTAL . . . [HIM]": Paul Halsall, *Modern History Sourcebook:
      Nikita Khrushchev, Secret Speech, 1956,* excerpts, www.fordham.edu/halsall/mod/
      khrushchev-secret.html (accessed 1 Aug. 2005).

48   "LENIN HAD . . . REVOLUTION": Volkogonov (1998), p. 203.

48   "HOW WERE . . . INTIMIDATION": ibid., p. 205.

48   "MORALLY DISCREDITED . . . SYSTEM": Gorbachev (1995), p. 70.

48   "I WAS . . . 1930S": quoted in Archie Brown (1996), p. 39.

48   "I HAD . . . REVELATIONS": Gorbachev and Mlynar (2002), p. 20.

48   "THE CONCRETE . . . MIND": Mlynar (1980), p. 27.

49   "TO UNDERSTAND . . . WAS": Gorbachev and Mlynar (2002), p. 21.

49   "AM I . . . DID?": quoted in Remnick (1994), p. 150.

49   "I DID . . . FUTURE": Gorbachev and Mlynar (2002), p. 25.

49   "WE HAD . . . LIFE": Shevardnadze (1991), p. 23.

49   "SHAKEN . . . FAITH": ibid., p. 20.

49   "THE EAST . . . 1960S": ibid., p. 21.

50   "IT IS . . . POLITICS": ibid., pp. 20–21.

50   "IF WE . . . ADD HUNGARY": János M. Rainer, "Decision in the Kremlin, 1956—the
      Malin notes," posted at The Institute for the History of the 1956 Hungarian Revolu-
      tion, http://www.rev.hu/intezet/index.html (accessed 25 Jan. 2006).

51   "I WAS . . . KRAI": Gorbachev (1995), pp. 73–74.

51   "BOTH THE . . . SYSTEM": Gorbachev and Mlynar (2002), p. 48.

51   "THE PEASANT . . . BOOTS": Gorbacheva (1991), pp. 94–96.

52   "AND NOT . . . CONCEPTS": ibid., p. 96.

52   "THE TRADITIONAL . . . CITIZEN": Gorbachev (1995), p. 118.

52   FOOD RATIONING, VIOLENT DEMONSTRATION: Malish (1984), p. 301.

52   "THE LEADERSHIP . . . BREAD' ": ibid.

52   "FROM 13.1 . . . 1963": Volkogonov (1998), p. 211.

52   "A REFINED . . . ME": Gorbachev (1995), p. 74.

53   "A MILD . . . MAN": Volkogonov (1998), p. 262.

53   "WE . . . STALINISM": Gorbachev and Mlynar (2002), pp. 31–32.

53   THE GORBACHEVS' TRAVELS ABROAD: Doder and Branson (1990), p. 20; Archie
      Brown (1996), p. 328, n. 14.

53   "MY PREVIOUS . . . COUNTRIES?": Gorbachev (1995), pp. 102–3.

53   YEFREMOV WAS FURTHER FRUSTRATED AND ANGERED: According to ibid., pp.
      79–80. Volkogonov (1998), p. 440, claims that Yefremov supported Gorbachev's
      appointment for second secretary as well as, later, first secretary.

54   "I SUDDENLY . . . US": Gorbachev and Mlynar (2002), p. 43.

54   "THE KGB . . . COUP": quoted in Kramer (1992), p. 21.

54   SOVIET NUCLEAR ALERT: This discussion follows Kramer (1992), pp. 42–43.

54   "ENGENDERED A . . . STAGNATION": Gorbachev and Mlynar (2002), p. 65.

54   "PRACTICALLY PUT . . . MANAGEMENT": Gorbachev (1995), p. 83.

54   "GRADUALLY, AND . . . CENTER": Gorbachev and Mlynar (2002), p. 47.

55   "MANIPULATORS . . . PUNISHABLE' ": Gorbachev (1995), p. 94.

55 GORBACHEV "WAS . . . CREATURE": Doder and Branson (1990), pp. 30–31.

55 "WE MADE . . . RIGHT": Gorbachev (1995), pp. 95–96.

55 "THE ENTIRELY . . . FUTURE": quoted in Arbatov (1992), p. 259.

55 "A BRILLIANT . . . STAVROPOL": quoted in Archie Brown (1996), p. 50.

56 "GORBACHEV COULD . . . LANGUAGE": Remnick (1991), n.p.

56 "DOES NOT . . . BELIEVE": quoted in Scheer (1988), p. 147.

56 "MY TRIPS . . . THEMES": Gorbachev and Mlynar (2002), p. 50.

56 "I AM . . . COMPLICITY": quoted in Doder and Branson (1990), p. 21.

56 "I HEARD . . . WHOLE": Gorbacheva (1991), p. 119.

57 KULAKOV'S MANNER OF DEATH: Kotkin (2001), p. 39. Gorbachev (1995), p. 97, has Kulakov dying of "heart failure."

57 "THOSE BASTARDS . . . MOSCOW": Arbatov (1992), p. 259.

57 "THE TRAIN'S . . . WELL": Doder and Branson (1990), p. 39.

57 "MY CHARACTER . . . AUTUMN": Gorbachev (1995), p. 105.

57 FOOD IMPORT COSTS: Doder and Branson (1990), p. 40.

58 GROSS OUTPUT: Malish (1984), p. 308, Table 3. Rubles converted at the rate of five rubles to the dollar.

58 1972 WHEAT DEAL DESTABILIZING: See Luttrell (1973).

58 LIBYA, $20 BILLION: Gates (1996), p. 77.

58 OIL AND GAS PRODUCTION AND PRICES: Reed (2004), p. 215.

58 "THE CARELESS . . . PEOPLE": Gorbachev (1995), p. 118.

58 ELECTRICAL SUPPLY: ibid.

58 "DESPITE THE . . . ENTERTAINMENT": ibid.

58 "ONE-FIFTH . . . THEM": Doder and Branson (1990), pp. 40–41.

58 "MUCH MORE . . . COUNTRYSIDE": Gorbachev (1995), p. 120.

59 SEVENTEEN MILLION TONNES: ibid., p. 116.

59 "THE GROWING . . . RESOURCES": Arbatov (1992), p. 215.

59 "GROMYKO AND . . . GRAIN": Gorbachev (1995), pp. 116–17.

59 FOOD PROGRAM: See Malish (1984), p. 302ff.

59 40 BILLION RUBLES: Gorbachev (1995), p. 121.

59 "THIS PROBLEM . . . SAVINGS": ibid.

60 "N. K. BAIBAKOV . . . RESOURCES": ibid.

60 "WE BOTH . . . TURF": ibid.

60 "WITH TECHNOLOGICAL . . . PREGNANT": Gorbachev et al. (1996).

60 "THE MILITARY-INDUSTRIAL . . . MILITARY": Arbatov (1992), p. 201.

61 "I LEARNED . . . IN": Chernyaev (2000), p. 26.

61 "ARGUING . . . SENSELESS": Chernyaev (2000), p. 26.

61 "A PRETTY . . . AID": Arbatov (1992), p. 198.

61 MINISTRY OF DEFENSE INSISTED: ibid., citing Oleg Kalugin and "quite a few other pieces of information."

61 "AS A . . . WEAPONS": Arbatov (1992), p. 203.

61 "SOMETHING LIKE . . . SATURATED WITH THEM": Vitaliy L. Katayev, MIC: the view from inside, in Genin (2001), pp. 54–56.

62 "TO KEEP . . . 'WARM' ": Shlykov in Genin (2001), p. 85.

62 1930S POLICY: ibid., p. 82.

62 "UNDERMINED WESTERN . . . RACE": Arbatov (1992), p. 203.

62 "THE REGIME . . . TROUBLE": Pryce-Jones (1995), p. 39.

62 $1 BILLION ANNUALLY PER $1 PRICE DECLINE, "THE CREAKY . . . HOUSE": Reed (2004), p. 215.

62 "STRAIGHT FROM . . . APPARAT": Arbatov (1992), p. 191n.

62 "ANDROPOV AND . . . IT": Gorbachev (1995), p. 146.

63 "LEADING . . . THINKERS": Chernyaev (2000), p. xxi.

63 "THE RELATIONS . . . COUNTRY": quoted in Ellman and Kontorovich (1997), p. 263.

63 110 STUDIES: according to Nikolai Ryzhov, quoted in Archie Brown (1996), p. 64.

63 "THEIR ANALYSIS . . . PERESTROIKA": Gorbachev (1987a), p. 27.

63 YAKOVLEV CRITICISM OF BREZHNEV CULT: Yakovlev's exile is usually attributed to his 1972 article on Soviet nationalism, but see Kaiser (1991), p. 110, for this explanation, Yakovlev's own.

63 "TERRIBLY ASHAMED": quoted in Kaiser (1991), p. 108.

63 "WE SPOKE . . . PRINCIPLES": quoted in Archie Brown (1996), p. 81.

63 "MY CANADIAN . . . THOUGHT": Gorbachev (1995), p. 149.

64 "HE REALIZED . . . SYSTEM": ibid., p. 153.

64 "INDECISIVENESS . . . GENERATION": Arbatov (1992), p. 258.

64 "KOSTYA [CHERNENKO] . . . CHOSEN": quoted in Roxburgh (1991), p. 18.

64 "LOOKED AT . . . ELSE": Chernyaev (2000), p. 7.

64 "NOT PSYCHOLOGICALLY . . . PERSON": Archie Brown (1996), p. 69.

64 "BRILLIANTLY": quoted in Archie Brown (1996), p. 73.

64 "I LIKE . . . TOGETHER": Margaret Thatcher Foundation Archive.

65 " 'EVERYTHING'S ROTTEN . . . PITSUNDA": Shevardnadze (1991), p. 37.

65 GORBACHEV SPEECH OF 10 DECEMBER 1984: Unless otherwise cited, all extracts are taken from "Gorbachev Keynotes Ideological Meeting," *Current Digest of the Soviet Press* 36 (5), 9 Jan. 1985, pp. 1–5, 26–27.

65 GORBACHEV INTRODUCED . . . WORLD: He had used "perestroika" before, but not in the same context; see Archie Brown (1996), pp. 122–23.

65 "PRICES . . . CREDIT": omitted from *Pravda* transcript but quoted in Kaiser (1991), p. 77.

65 " 'WAS UNAMBIGUOUSLY . . . FAR": Archie Brown (1996), p. 80.

66 GORBACHEV MEETING WITH GROMYKO: Gorbachev (1995), p. 164.

66 "MIKHAIL . . . THIS": Gorbacheva (1991), pp. 4–5.

66 "THE HALL . . . APPLAUSE": Chernyaev (2000), pp. 19–20.

FOUR **"THE BOMBER WILL ALWAYS GET THROUGH" (I)**

69 WEAPONS NUMBERS AND YIELD; "A FEW . . . WELL": McNamara (1986), p. 5.

69 "IT MUST . . . WEAPON": Otto Robert Frisch and Rudolf Peierls, quoted in Rhodes (1986), p. 325. The complete Frisch-Peierls memorandum is reprinted in Ronald W. Clark, *Tizard,* MIT Press, 1965, p. 214ff.

70 NATIONS THAT WORKED ON NUCLEAR-WEAPONS DEVELOPMENT: James Walsh, panel discussion, "Why Do States Abandon Nuclear Ambitions," United Nations, NPT RevCon, 10 May 2005.

71 "A SCIENTIFIC . . . PROGRAMS": Memorandum for the President from Secretary of Defense Robert McNamara, "The Diffusion of Nuclear Weapons With or Without a Test Ban Agreement," 16 Feb. 1963, National Security Archive Electronic Briefing Book *The Making of the Limited Test Ban Treaty, 1958–1963,* Document 47, at http://www.qwu.edu/~nsarchiv/index.html (accessed 6 Mar. 2006).

71 "PERSONALLY, I . . . HAZARD": John F. Kennedy, News Conference Number 52 (21 Mar. 1963), transcription at http://www.jfklibrary.org/jfkpressconference_630321.html (accessed 9 Mar. 2006).

71 SOVIET UNION'S FIRST PROPOSAL: Graham and LaVera (2003), p. 29.

71　"ALL NUCLEAR . . . MONITORED": Eisenhower News Conference, 11 Feb. 1960, partial text at http://www.clw.org/archive/coalition/eis0260.htm (accessed 9 Mar. 2006).

72　IRELAND'S PROPOSAL TO U.N. GENERAL ASSEMBLY: Graham and LaVera (2003), p. 100.

72　CONCERNS OF NONNUCLEAR STATES: See full discussion at Graham and LaVera (2003), pp. 102–5.

72　"TO NEGOTIATE . . . ARSENALS": Graham and LaVera (2003), p. 102.

73　TEXT OF NPT: See ibid., pp. 108–12.

73　TREATIES: for texts and commentary See Graham and LaVera (2003).

74　"THE CENTRAL . . . CIVILIZATION": Schneider and Dowdy (1998), p. 189.

74　BERIA ORDERED COPY: Yuli Khariton, personal communication, 1992.

74　RDS-1 PILOT SERIES: Podvig (2001), p. 2. For the full story of the early years of the Soviet nuclear-weapons program see this reference, Holloway (1994), and Rhodes (1995).

74　RDS-1 SERIAL PRODUCTION: Podvig (2001), p. 2.

75　STOCKPILE NUMBERS: Norris and Arkin (1994).

76　"SUCH A . . . LIGHT": quoted in Rhodes (1995), pp. 401–2.

76　"THE NOTION . . . WEAPONS": ibid., p. 403.

76　THE JOINT . . . 1950: ibid., pp. 406–7.

77　JOINT CHIEFS HAD ENDORSED SURPRISE ATTACK: See Rhodes (1995), p. 225.

77　"OFFENSE . . . DEFENSE": JCS 169 1/7 (30 June 1947), quoted in Rhodes (1995), p. 225.

77　"WHAT THE . . . IT": quoted in Rhodes (1995), p. 407.

77　"TO CONTINUE . . . SUPER-BOMB": ibid.

77　"WE HAD . . . RUSSIANS": ibid.

78　SOVIET FULL-SCALE THERMONUCLEAR WEAPONS PROGRAM APPROVED: Podvig (2001), p. 74.

78　"HE SAID . . . KIDS' ": quoted in Herken (1980), p. 11.

78　"TO HAVE . . . ONE": Millis (1951), p. 458.

78　"A SYSTEM . . . 1948": Rosenberg (1983), pp. 11–12.

78　"SINCE WE . . . WEAPONS": quoted in Rosenberg (1983), p. 22.

79　"LED PRESIDENT . . . OFF": Robert Bowie in Hunter and Robinson (2005), Chapter 7.

79　1950, 1953 SITES AND EMPLOYEES: Douglas Lawson, in Hunter and Robinson (2005), Chapter 8.

79　6.7 PERCENT; CAPITALIZATION: Anders (1987), p. 4.

79　1953–1955 STOCKPILE NUMBERS AND YIELDS: Norris and Arkin (1994), p. 4.

79　"IS FAR . . . WHOLESALE": quoted in Rosenberg (1983), pp. 26–27.

79　"THE WAR . . . MEN": quoted in Rhodes (1995), p. 583.

79　"WERE ALL . . . JAPAN": Rosenberg (1983), p. 20.

79　"THAT JUST . . . GOVERNMENT": ibid., p. 31.

79　"FIRMLY CONVINCED . . . III": William B. Moore memorandum, appended to Rosenberg and Moore (1981–1982), p. 27.

80　"WITH THE . . . INCIDENTAL": Rosenberg (1983), p. 15.

80　"WHAT WAS . . . INDUSTRY?": quoted in Rosenberg (1983), p. 15.

80　"THE GENERAL . . . DIRT' ": Gates (1996), p. 21.

80　"THE BOMBER . . . THEM": MacArthur (1999), pp. 125–26.

80　"NO AIR . . . PREPARED": quoted in Rhodes (1995), pp. 227–28.

81　"IN GENERAL . . . U.S.": Samuel E. Anderson briefing, appended to Rosenberg and Moore (1981–1982), p. 32.

81   "IN LIGHT . . . UNTHINKABLE": Bundy (1969), pp. 9–10.

81   "I COULDN'T . . . AGAIN": quoted in Holloway (1994), p. 339.

81   "THE RETALIATORY . . . COUNTRY": Tannenwald (1999), p. 51.

82   "HE SAID . . . SECURITY": ibid., p. 23.

82   "THESE WEAPONS . . . WEAPONS": Todd White in Hunter and Robinson (2005), Chapter 2.

83   "THE LARGE . . . REQUIREMENTS": Douglas Lawson in Hunter and Robinson (2005), Chapter 8.

83   "IT WAS . . . BE": Leon Smith in Hunter and Robinson (2005), Chapter 8.

83   "WE WERE . . . ALONG": John Foster in Hunter and Robinson (2005), Chapter 5.

FIVE   **"THE BOMBER WILL ALWAYS GET THROUGH" (II)**

84   THREE CATEGORIES OF TARGETING: see Rosenberg (1983), pp. 16–17.

84   "ALL BUT . . . LEVEL": Rosenberg and Moore (1981–1982), p. 11.

84   1,700 DGZS: Moore memorandum, appended to Rosenberg and Moore (1981–1982), p. 18.

84   "LAY DOWN . . . HOURS": Moore memorandum, appended to Rosenberg and Moore (1981–1982), p. 25.

84   AS FAR . . . THE BETTER: See Rosenberg's description of the Navy's "devastating critique" of Air Force targeting plans, and USAF chief of staff Thomas White's rebuttal, at Rosenberg (1983), p. 51.

85   SHARES OF DEFENSE APPROPRIATIONS: Rosenberg (1983), p. 29.

85   BISON A, BISON B: Podvig (2001), p. 341; p. 376, Table 6A.3.

85   "DEPLOYED ON . . . ALERT": Podvig (2001), p. 342.

85   REFUELING ON ICE AIRSTRIPS: ibid.

85   "SUCH ACTION . . . US": quoted in Sagan (1987), p. 31, n. 28.

85   1960 WEAPONS NUMBERS AND YIELDS: Norris and Arkin (1994), p. 4.

86   "THE RULE . . . DESTRUCTION": ibid., p. 2.

86   FOUR ICBMS: Kaplan (1983), p. 286.

86   SOVIET VULNERABILITIES: Sagan (1987), pp. 27–29.

86   "THE SOVIETS . . . STATES": James Schlesinger in Hunter and Robinson (2005), Chapter 16.

86   "IT BECAME . . . WEAPONS": General Lyman L. Lemnitzer in Sagan (1987), p. 41.

86   WEAPON SHARES TO SAC AND THEATER COMMANDERS: ibid.

86   "THE COMPLEX . . . PLAN": Burr (2004), Document 28, p. 3.

86   "TIME OVER TARGET" CONFLICTS: Burr (2004), Document 28, p. 4; Sagan (1987), p. 42, n. 1.

87   "ATOMIC OPERATIONS . . . POSSIBLE": quoted in Burr (2004), Document 28, p. 4.

87   KENNEDY'S SIOP-62 BRIEFING: Sagan (1987), pp. 41–51.

87   "WE ESSENTIALLY . . . POLAND?' ": Robert McNamara in Hunter and Robinson (2005), Chapter 16.

87   3,153 WEAPONS, MEGATONNAGE: Norris and Arkin (1994), p. 4.

87   "BECAUSE OF . . . MEASURE": Sagan (1987), p. 51.

87   285 MILLION DEAD: Kaplan (1983), p. 269.

87   GENERAL DAVID SHOUP STORY: ibid., p. 270.

88   ONE HUNDRED KILOTONS: Eden (2004), p. 27.

88   "ONLY BLAST . . . SIOP": Burr (2004), Document 20, p. 3.

88   KISTIAKOWSKY TO OMAHA: Kistiakowsky (1976), p. 403.

88   "THE JSTPS . . . REQUIREMENTS' ": Burr (2004), Document 23, p. 1914.

88 "MIGHT ACTUALLY . . . ATTACK": Solomon and Marston (1986), p. 17.

88 "THE EXTRAORDINARILY . . . SPEEDS": Eden (2004), p. 27.

89 "GROUND WINDS . . . ELSE": ibid., pp. 25–26. For Eden's Washington scenario see p. 15ff.

89 "A NUCLEAR . . . WEAPON": Solomon and Marston (1986), p. 52.

89 "ABOUT 300 . . . SECOND": Eden (2004), p. 16.

89 "WE MUST . . . D.C.": quoted in Eden (2004), p. 16.

89 "TOSSING IT . . . BARREL": Hap Arnold, quoted in Eden (2004), p. 72.

90 "THE WORLD . . . EQUIPMENT": Eden (2004), p. 290.

90 "WE DON'T . . . IMPORTANT": quoted in Eden (2004), p. 276.

90 "ADMIRAL COLLEY . . . SENSE": Eden (2004), p. 276.

90 EDEN LISTS: ibid., p. 228.

91 "ULTIMATE . . . DETERRENT": quoted in Rosenberg (1983), p. 52.

91 BURKE TOLD THE JOINT CHIEFS: as described in Rosenberg (1983), p. 57.

91 "THE NAVY . . . PROBLEM": Rosenberg (1983), p. 57.

92 "THAT MILITARY . . . RESERVE' ": ibid., p. 55.

92 "THAT IN . . . SUFFICIENT": Burr (2004), Document 1, p. 4.

92 SOVIETS LIMITED BOMBERS: Podvig (2001), p. 4.

93 "THEATER" NUCLEAR MISSILES, SUBMARINES: ibid., p. 3.

93 PODVIG WRITES: ibid., p. 5.

93 "THE LEVEL . . . DEPLOYMENT": ibid.

93 TWENTY-FOUR HOURS TO LAUNCH: ibid., p. 181, Table 4A.2.

93 "COULD DELIVER . . . TERRITORY": ibid., p. 4.

93 1,576 SAC BOMBERS: Cowley (2005), p. 223.

94 "THE U.S. . . . CRISIS": Podvig (2001), p. 6.

94 "THE RESULTS . . . PROBLEM": Tannenwald (1999), p. 24.

94 "WELL, MR. . . . AGAIN": quoted in Powers (1996), n.p.

94 "HUMILIATION IN . . . STATE": Gates (1996), p. 29.

94 "DURING THE . . . HARD": Tannenwald (1999), pp. 24–25.

94 "A SIMPLE . . . STATES": Podvig (2001), p. 201.

95 SS-9: ibid., p. 127.

95 SOVIET SUBMARINES PATROLLING COASTS: ibid., p. 7.

95 "WERE QUIETLY . . . BUILDUP": Reed (2004), p. 96.

95 FRACTIONAL-ORBITAL SS-9: Podvig (2001), p. 196.

95 "THE SOVIETS . . . WELL": Gates (1996), p. 29.

95 U.S. STOCKPILE AT 32,200: Schwartz (1998), p. 45.

96 "ONE OF . . . OURS": Sheldon (2004), p. 68.

96 "OTHER CONSIDERATIONS . . . CHOICE": Bundy (1988), p. 551.

96 "WOULD BE . . . SYSTEM": ibid.

96 "THE INADEQUACY . . . ANYWAY": Alexei Arbatov, Verification: servant or master of disarmament? Carnegie International Nonproliferation Conference "Sixty Years Later," Washington, D.C., 7–8 Nov. 2005.

97 U.S. REMAINED AHEAD: See Norris and Arkin (1994), Estimated U.S. and Soviet/Russian nuclear stockpiles, 1945–94.

97 "MASSIVE AND . . . EFFORT": Nitze (1976), p. 3.

97 "A NUCLEAR- . . . SIDE": ibid., p. 5.

97 "UNLESS ACCURACIES . . . THEM": Lodal (1976), p. 3.

97 "THAT IMPLEMENTATION . . . SURVIVE": Nitze (1976), p. 3.

98 "WE DID . . . PROGRAM": Sheldon (2004), p. 68.

98   "Q.—MCNAMARA . . . EACH": Burr (2004), Document 24B, p. 4.

99   "EACH INDIVIDUAL . . . INSANE": Robert McNamara, personal communication, Washington, D.C., Nov. 2005.

99   "EACH OF . . . SUPPORT": McNamara (1986), pp. 5–6.

99   "DESPITE AN . . . CATASTROPHE": ibid., p. 44.

100 "MOVED FROM . . . CERTAINTY": McNamara (1995), p. 341. The number 162 is McNamara's.

100 "WE ARE . . . SECURITY": quoted in Gaddis (1997), p. 221.

100 "GREATER THAN . . . STAFF": quoted in Rodberg and Shearer (1970), p. 300.

100 MCNAMARA TOLD JOHNSON: Kaplan (1983), p. 317; Kunsman and Lawson (2001), p. 49.

101 "WE HAD . . . UNION": Sheldon (2004), p. 69.

101 "YOU CAN'T . . . STREETS": quoted in Kunsman and Lawson (2001), p. 121.

101 "WE ARE . . . WAR": Nielsen (1963).

101 THIRTY-ONE OTHER MEMBERS: Cahn (1998), p. 30.

SIX   **THE SORCERER'S APPRENTICES (I)**

102 "WERE NOT . . . ONE": Nitze (1989), p. 43.

103 "THIS EXPERIENCE . . . CONCEPT": "Interview with Secretary of the Navy Nitze," by Alfred Goldberg, 15 June 1966, Burr and Wampler (2004), Document 6, p. 1.

103 "TO UNDERTAKE . . . UNION": quoted in NSC-68 (1950), p. 2.

104 "THE PURPOSE . . . OUT": quoted in Sanders (1983), p. 31.

104 "WANTED TO . . . THREAT": Paul Y. Hammond, quoted in Sanders (1983), p. 30.

104 "ANIMATED BY . . . ANNIHILATION": NSC-68 (1950), I, p. 3.

104 "THE DESIGN . . . DESIGN": ibid., I, p. 4.

104 "THUS UNWILLINGLY . . . POWER": ibid., I, p. 5.

104 SOVIET WAR LOSSES: cited from several contemporary sources in Rhodes (1995), p. 179.

105 "DRIV[ING] TOWARD . . . DAMAGE THIS COUNTRY": NSC-68 (1950), I, pp. 12–13.

105 "TO CHECK . . . DOMINATION": ibid., III, p. 13.

105 "A RAPID . . . WORLD": ibid., III, p. 12.

106 "ONCE THE . . . PACTS": Karl R. Bendetsen Oral History Interview, 21 Nov. 1972, Harry S. Truman Presidential Library.

106 "NOT ONLY . . . NOT": Hobbes (1651), Chapter VI, cited in Robin, 2004, p. 43.

106 "DIMENSION OF . . . INFERENCE": Robin (2004), p. 43.

106 "ADDRESSED WHAT . . . WAY?": Nitze (1989), p. 95.

107 "AT THE . . . THROUGH": Academy of Achievement (1990), p. 8.

107 "WE LIVED . . . JUNGLE": Nitze (1989), p. xi.

108 "ONE TIME . . . GANG": Academy of Achievement (1990), p. 9.

108 "TO HAVE . . . STRATEGY": quoted in Sanders (1983), p. 256.

108 "IN THAT . . . CONSPIRACY": NSC-68 (1950), II, p. 3.

108 "A PRINCIPAL DRAFTSMAN": Bundy (1988), p. 337.

108 "YOU HAVE . . . TIME": Herbert York interview, National Security Archive.

109 "THE USSR . . . PROGRAMS": Burr and Wampler (2004), Document 2, p. 14.

109 "PREDICTED A . . . U.S.": Kistiakowsky (1979), p. 6.

109 "NO MORE . . . 1961": Wohlstetter, Nitze, et al. (1974), p. 85.

109 "MANNED BOMBERS . . . U.S.": Burr and Wampler (2004), Document 2, p. 16.

109 1959 SOVIET BOMBER FORCE: Podvig (2001), p. 350, Table 6.1.

109 "A SPECTRUM . . . NUCLEAR WEAPONS": Burr and Wampler (2004), Document 2, p. 4.

109 1959 SOVIET NUCLEAR ARSENAL: Norris and Arkin (1994), p. 4.

110 "FROM 80 . . . 600": Burr and Wampler (2004), Document 2, p. 6.

110 "A NATIONWIDE . . . POPULATION": Burr and Wampler (2004), Document 2, p. 8.

110 "HE KNEW . . . SIGNIFICANT": Bundy (1988), p. 338.

110 "MORAL FIBER": quoted in Callahan (1990), p. 106.

110 "HE WAS . . . SURRENDER": Nitze (1989), pp. 168–69.

110 "PROMINENT MEMBERS . . . PARTICULAR": ibid., p. 294.

111 "LACKING FUNDS . . . PERLE": ibid., p. 295.

111 "WOHLSTETTER . . . MISSILES": Winik (1996), p. 50.

112 "THE NUMBER . . . ENEMY": Gates (1996), p. 82.

112 450 TO 150: Graham and LaVera (2003), p. 337.

112 50 PERCENT, 30 PERCENT: Fosdick (1990), p. 136.

112 "A LONGTIME . . . COALITION": Cahn (1998), p. 39.

112 "TO SEEK . . . UNION": Fosdick (1990), p. 153.

112 "KEY NUCLEAR . . . 1960s": Kull (1988), p. 34, Table 2.1.

113 "THE GAME . . . PEOPLE": ibid., p. 127.

113 "IF YOU . . . DUBIOUS": ibid., p. 139.

113 "STRATEGIC WEAPONS . . . CATEGORY": ibid., p. 116.

113 "LET'S PUT . . . IT": ibid., p. 299.

114 "HE PUSHES . . . MASTERED": Scheer (1988), p. 189.

114 "PARTICIPATION IN . . . CONTROL": Gates (1996), p. 46.

114 "BECAUSE FEAR . . . FEAR": Robin (2004), p. 43.

115 "MOST THREATENING . . . REPERCUSSIONS": Graham (2002), p. 54.

115 " 'ONE OF . . . IT?' ": quoted in Nacht (1975), p. 163.

115 "THOSE WERE . . . REGRET": William Hyland, quoted in Cahn (1998), p. 66.

115 "THE CRITICS . . . DISAPPEAR": Cahn (1998), p. 15.

115 SANTA MONICA DINNER, RAND CONFERENCE: ibid., pp. 9, 11.

115 WOHLSTETTER PAPER: Wohlstetter (1974); Wohlstetter, Nitze, et al. (1974).

115 "THE UNITED . . . RACE": Wohlstetter (1974), p. 71.

116 WOHLSTETTER'S "CONCLUSIONS . . . COMPARISONS": Cahn (1998), p. 13.

116 "STOPPED WITH . . . SUBS": ibid.

116 WARHEAD TOTALS; "FOR THE . . . WARHEADS": Nacht (1975), p. 170.

116 "NOT LIVED . . . SERVED": ibid., p. 177.

116 "HIS PROBLEM . . . ELSE": Sidney Drell, personal communication, Stanford University, Sept. 2005.

116 "WOHLSTETTER'S CHARGES . . . UNION": Cahn (1998), p. 15.

116 "TO DEFEND . . . WERE": Gates (1996), pp. 47–48.

117 "DECLINED SHARPLY . . . FLAT": Cahn (1998), p. 196.

117 "SOVIET . . . CHANGES,"; "A BALANCE . . . DOGMA": quoted in Sanders (1983), p. 150.

117 "THE DEMOCRATIC . . . PUBLICITY": quoted in Callahan (1990), p. 174.

SEVEN **THE SORCERER'S APPRENTICES (II)**

118 "CHENEY WAS . . . RULES": Hartmann (1980), p. 283.

119 "RUMSFELD AND . . . IDEAS": Blumenthal (2005).

119 "IF THE . . . SYSTEM": Cahn (1998), p. 95.

119 SS-9 FIVE-KILOMETER MAXIMUM ERROR: Podvig (2001), p. 198, Table 4A.7.

120 CIA DISAGREEMENT: Cahn (1998), p. 97.

120 "THAT WHAT . . . PLAN": ibid., p. 112.

120 TELLER DRAFT DOCUMENT: "An Alternative NIE," 18 June 1975, cited in Cahn (1998), p. 113, n. 55.

120 "TELLER QUICKLY . . . NIE": Cahn (1998), p. 113.

121 TELLER AND FOSTER TO THE CIA: ibid., pp. 114–15.

121 "IT IS . . . PREPARE": quoted in Cahn (1998), p. 119.

121 "FOSTER AND . . . PREDECESSORS": ibid., p. 130.

121 "BUSH WAS . . . PREDECESSOR": Blumenthal (2005).

121 TEAM B EXPERIMENT: described at Cahn (1998), p. 139.

121 B TEAMS: Cahn (1998), pp. 141–47.

121 CHENEY CONNECTION: Blumenthal (2005).

121 RUMSFELD AND PAUL WOLFOWITZ: ibid.

122 "IMPORTED TO . . . JACKSON": Blumenthal (1987b), p. 6.

122 TELLER, FOSTER, WOHLSTETTER'S ESSAYS CONSULTED: Cahn (1998), p. 151.

122 "MEMBERS OF . . . CONSENSUS": Burr and Wampler (2004), Document 10: Report of Team "B," p. iii.

122 "ACQUIRED A . . . NEGOTIATIONS": Pipes (1986), pp. 25–26.

122 "SO PERSUADED . . . FLAT": ibid., p. 26.

122 "THE ONLY . . . LOW LEVEL": ibid., pp. 26–27.

123 "I WILL . . . FACT": Wiesner (1984), p. 736.

123 "SIMPLY IGNORED . . . STANFORD": Pipes (1986), p. 28.

124 "HIS DEEP . . . SOUL": quoted in Herken (1985), p. 276.

124 "WE HAVE . . . WARS": quoted in Kull (1988), p. 23.

124 "IGNORE THE . . . WAR": Burr and Wampler (2004), Document 10: Report of Team "B," p. 2.

125 "A REALISTIC . . . EFFORT": ibid., p. 16. Original italics.

125 "THE IMPLICATION . . . YEARS": ibid., p. 32.

125 "YES, THAT'S . . . THAT": Curtis (2005), Part I.

125 "THE POSSIBILITY . . . THREAT": Burr and Wampler (2004), Document 10: Report of Team "B," p. 4.

125 "AN INTENSIFIED . . . LEVEL": ibid., pp. 45–47.

125 "ALL OF . . . THEM": Curtis (2005), Part I. N.B.: Cahn misstates the location of the imaginary laser-beam weapon-test facility as Krasnoyarsk in her interview with Curtis; I have corrected her misstatement by inserting text from Cahn (1998), p. 167.

126 "SEVERAL [SOVIET] . . . 'COMPENSATE' ": Kull (1988), p. 287.

126 "WHAT WAS . . . INSTALLATION": Sakharov (1990), p. 97.

127 VIKTOR GIRSHFELD: identified after the dissolution of the Soviet Union.

127 "COL. X . . . WRONG": quoted in Kull (1988), p. 290; original source: "Colonel X's Warning: Our Mistakes Plus Your Hysteria," Detente, No. 1, Oct. 1984, pp. 2–3.

127 "THERE WAS . . . SECURE' ": Kull (1988), p. 291.

127 "THERE WAS . . . PROGRAMS": Tannenwald (1999), p. 34.

128 "WE DID NOT . . . GENUINE": ibid., pp. 56–57.

128 "THERE IS . . . WORLD!' ": Ellman and Kontorovich (1998), pp. 41–42.

129 "THERE WERE . . . [PEOPLE]": Tannenwald (1999), pp. 32–33.

130 "APES ON A TREADMILL": Warnke (1975).

130 "WE COULDN'T . . . CURRENCY": ibid., p. 24.

130 "NOT A . . . UNION": ibid., p. 28.

130   "ONE SOURCE . . . POINTS' ": Murrey Marder, "Carter to Inherit Intense Dispute on Soviet Intentions," *Washington Post*, 2 Jan. 1977, p. A1.

130   "IT MEANS . . . VIEW' ": ibid.

131   "SABOTAGE SALT II . . . STATES": quoted in Pipes (1986), p. 35.

131   "TO CRITICS . . . THREAT' ": Callahan (1990), p. 380.

131   "THAT SOVIET . . . OURS": Cox (1980), pp. 4–5.

131   "IF THE . . . ALONE": quoted in Cahn (1998), p. 137.

132   "A COUPLE . . . IT?": quoted in Sanders (1983), p. 152.

132   "A CLEAR . . . PREVENT": SCHENCK *v.* UNITED STATES, SUPREME COURT OF THE UNITED STATES 249 U.S. 47 (3 Mar. 1919).

132   CPD ROSTER: Sanders (1983), p. 154ff.

133   "HE NEEDED CREDENTIALS": Winik (1996), p. 110.

133   "THE PRINCIPAL . . . POWER": quoted in Winik (1996), pp. 110–11.

133   "NITZE WAS . . . APPROACH": quoted in Talbott (1988), p. 149.

133   "WE WERE . . . FRIGHTENING": quoted in Winik (1996), p. 111.

133   "TO TRY . . . ARSENALS]": Interview with President Jimmy Carter, Cold War Interviews, Episode 18, National Security Archive.

134   BRZEZINSKI AND PERLE DRAFTED CARTER PROPOSAL: Thomas Graham, Jr., personal communication, Sept. 2006.

134   WOHLSTETTER AND THE EUROPEAN-AMERICAN WORKSHOP: For details see Kaplan (1979).

134   "OWING TO . . . EUROPE": Schmidt (1981), p. 3.

134   "ARMS CONTROL . . . DEPLOYMENTS": Graham (2002), p. 107.

135   "IN THE RANGE . . . WELL": Garthoff (1983), pp. 205–6.

135   "WAS A . . . FAVOR": ibid., pp. 876–78.

136   "POLICY OF . . . RUINS": Fosdick (1990), p. 167.

136   "THE CONGRESS . . . UNION": Interview with President Jimmy Carter, Cold War Interviews, Episode 18, National Security Archive.

136   CARTER PULLED THE TREATY: Thomas Graham, Jr., personal communication, Sept. 2006.

136   "I COULD . . . NATION": Interview with President Jimmy Carter, Cold War Interviews, Episode 18, National Security Archive.

136   REASON FOR SOVIET INVASION: Garthoff (1985), p. 920; Westad (2001), p. 130.

136   "THE USA . . . ALARMING": Gorbachev (1995), p. 116.

136   LIST OF SANCTIONS: Garthoff (1985), p. 951.

136   "BY THE 1980 . . . SPENDING": Cahn (1998), p. 49.

137   OFFICIAL SOVIET RESPONSE: Garthoff (1985), p. 998ff.

EIGHT   **DECAPITATION**

138   JACKSON ACCUSING CARTER OF APPEASEMENT: quoted in Whelan (1988), p. 82.

138   CARTER COMPARED TO CHAMBERLAIN; "REAGAN OPENLY . . . COLLAPSE": Blumenthal (1986), p. xiii.

138   "SOME BIZARRE . . . WRITTEN": quoted in Beth A. Fischer (1997), p. 19.

138   "BY VIRTUE . . . TEAM B": Cahn (1998), p. 191.

138   "A STUDY . . . U.S.S.R.' ": ibid.

139   INFORMATION WENT TO PFIAB: ibid., p. 192.

139   "BY ANY . . . NATIONS": ibid., p. 193.

139   "THE MORE . . . ERA": quoted in Stone (1973), p. 2.

139 "CANNOT BE . . . POWER": ibid.

140 "IN SOCIALIST . . . PERCENT)": ibid., pp. 3–4.

140 "PENCHANT FOR . . . PROPHESYING": Janos Radvanyi, review of *The Final Fall* in *Russian Review* 39 (1) (Jan. 1980), p. 97.

140 "INTERNAL PRESSURES . . . SYSTEMS": Todd (1979), p. 3.

141 "SHABBY AND . . . DATA": ibid., p. 10.

141 "HAVE FIXED . . . SAME": ibid., pp. 10–11.

141 "THERE WILL . . . WAGES?": ibid., pp. 58–62.

141 "THE DEGREE . . . ALIENATION": ibid., pp. 40–43.

141 CHINA: TWENTY ICBMS: CRS (2006), p. 11.

141 "BY THE . . . EXPLOITED": Todd (1979), p. 72. Original italics.

142 "CONSIDER THAT . . . LIFE-STYLES?": ibid., pp. 68–69. Original italics.

142 "IN 1976 . . . *ECONOMY*": ibid., p. 71. Original italics.

143 "TO TRANSFORM . . . SURVIVE": ibid., p. 40.

143 "IS THE . . . PRODUCTIVITY": ibid., pp. 78, 81.

143 "THE BEGINNING . . . CYCLE": ibid., p. 222.

143 "NO ONE . . . WEALTH": ibid., (emphasis in original).

143 "SUFFER . . . UPHEAVAL": ibid., p. 202.

143 "THE SUCCESSIVE . . . FUSS": ibid., p. 204.

143 "COULD NOT . . . COME": ibid., p. 202.

144 THE NATO DECISION: discussed at Guadeloupe in Jan. 1979, issued in final form in Dec. Gates (1996), p. 112.

144 "EVEN THE . . . STATES": Mastny and Byrne (2005), Document No. 84, pp. 418–19.

144 "THE THREAT . . . PERCEPTIONS": Nuenlist (2001), pp. 22–23.

145 "[THE KGB CHIEF . . . JUSTIFIED": Quoted in Benjamin B. Fischer, Intelligence and disaster avoidance: the Soviet war scare and US-Soviet relations, in Cimbala (1999), p. 90. Fischer cites (and translates from) the German edition of Wolf's memoir; a less detailed version of the encounter appears in Wolf (1997), p. 221.

145 "WHEN CARTER . . . THINGS' ": Wolf (1997), p. 223.

145 "ON AT . . . SURPRISE ATTACK": Gates (1996), p. 114.

145 "AS HE . . . THOUGH": ibid., pp. 114–15.

146 "AND BY JUNE . . . WAR' ": Fischer, in Cimbala (1999), p. 91.

146 "IF DETERRENCE . . . ATTACK": quoted in Fischer, in Cimbala (1999), p. 92.

146 "THE MOST . . . ANARCHY": Gray and Payne (1980), p. 21.

147 SEVEN HUNDRED BUNKERS, FOURTEEN HUNDRED SILOS: Fischer in Cimbala (1999), p. 92.

147 MINUTEMAN II, TRIDENT C4 CHANGES: John Prados, personal communication, May 2006.

147 W86, W85 PERSHING 2 CHANGES: Robert S. Norris, personal communication, June 2006.

147 THIRTY-ONE APPOINTEES: Cahn (1998), p. 30.

148 " 'IT WAS . . . HOME' ": Schweizer (1994), pp. 8–9.

148 PROBES BEGAN MID-FEBRUARY: ibid., p. 9.

148 CARTER INCREASE: Stockman (1986), p. 107.

148 "A PARTING . . . ADMINISTRATION": ibid.

149 "WE HAD . . . 1986": ibid., pp. 108–9.

149 "WE'D LAID . . . *DOLLARS*!": ibid., p. 108.

149 "THE FEBRUARY . . . COMPLEX": ibid., p. 109.

149 REAGAN'S DEFENSE SPENDING COMPARISONS: Wirls (1992), pp. 35–36.

149 "FOR FISCAL . . . *PERCENT*": ibid., p. 54.

149 "EXTRAORDINARY SURGE . . . PROGRAM": ibid., p. 37.

149 "IN ALL . . . STATES": Fitzgerald (1976), p. 58.

150 "FEWER THAN . . . PURPOSES": Steinbruner (1981), p. 18.

150 "COMMAND VULNERABILITY . . . SIZE": ibid., p. 22.

150 "AS SEEN . . . WAR": ibid., p. 27.

151 PROJECT RYAN, ANDROPOV SPEECH: Andrew and Gordievsky (1991), p. 67.

151 "THOSE IN . . . USTINOV": Gates (1996), p. 270.

151 "WHAT APPEARS . . . REVERSE": quoted in Blake (1990), pp. 267–68.

151 "PARTICIPATION IN . . . READY": Mastny and Byrne (2005), Document No. 92, p. 449.

151 "RYAN . . . MORE": Andrew and Mitrokhin (1999), p. 214.

152 "ONLY ADDED . . . RYAN": Gates (1996), p. 271.

152 REAGAN'S SPEECH BASED ON NSDD-32; "THE DISSOLUTION . . . EMPIRE": Reed (2004), p. 237.

152 "WAS NO . . . LOSE": ibid., p. 236.

152 "INCLUDE . . . ACTION": ibid., p. 237.

152 "THE PRESIDENT . . . INEVITABLE": Maynes (1982), p. 86.

152 "SOME SOVIET . . . LATE": ibid., pp. 100–101.

152 "A SPECTACULAR . . . ENEMY' ": Benjamin Fischer, in Cimbala (1999), pp. 95–96.

153 "THE REAGAN . . . BEFORE": Mastny and Byrne (2005), Document No. 96, pp. 466–68.

NINE **REHEARSING ARMAGEDDON**

154 "ZERO SOLUTION"; "ILLUSORY": Talbott (1985), pp. 56–57.

154 "INTENDED . . . UNACCEPTABLE": Graham (2002), p. 107.

154 "I DO . . . AGGRESSIVE": Tannenwald (1999), p. 136.

154 "AT LEAST . . . TOMAHAWKS: Talbott (1985), p. 57.

155 "COMPACT . . . RESERVED": Perle (1992), p. 5.

155 "CONVINCED THAT . . . WAR": ibid., p. 36.

155 "UNLIKELY THE . . . AGREE": ibid., p. 95.

155 "ZERO . . . EARS": ibid., p. 91.

155 "URBANE GUERRILLAS . . . LEAKS": ibid., p. 5.

155 "WHAT IS . . . ACTIVITY": Robin W. Winks, review of *Hard Line* by Richard Perle, *Washington Post Book World,* 9 June 1992.

155 CUBAN MISSILE CRISIS: as Andropov told Oleg Grinevsky from his deathbed in December 1983: see Tannenwald (1999), p. 15. Grinevsky's information disqualifies any claim that Andropov was simply cranking up the Cold War to encourage his people to work harder, although that was certainly one of the uses to which he put the U.S. arms buildup and the Reagan administration's belligerence, as he does in this speech.

156 EXCERPTS FROM ANDROPOV 1983 SPEECH: Mastny and Byrne (2005), Document No. 98, pp. 472–79.

156 KGB DOCUMENTS: Andrew and Gordievsky (1991), pp. 69–81.

157 EVIL EMPIRE SPEECH MEANT TO WIN FUNDAMENTALIST SUPPORT: Oberdorfer (1992), p. 24.

157 "THE MILITARY . . . WAR": quoted in Wittner (2004), p. 1.

157 "FORWARD STRATEGY," "HIGH-THREAT": quoted in Hersh (1986), p. 17.

157 "WAS ONE . . . BOSS": Hersh (1986), p. 17.

157 "THREE AIRCRAFT . . . THERE' ": ibid.

157 "IMPOTENT AND . . . THEMSELVES": Ronald Reagan, "Address to the Nation on Defense and National Security," 23 Mar. 1983.

158 "THAT WAS . . . PRESIDENT": quoted in Lettow (2005), p. 114.

158 "TOOK PRODIGIOUS . . . CLOTH": Shvets (1994), p. 75.

159 "THE RHETORIC . . . WAR": Andrew and Gordievsky (1991), p. 81.

159 "PAID A . . . WAR": James Buchan in Morton (2005).

159 "CIVILIANS DEBATED . . . NUANCES": Powers (1996), p. 10.

159 "UNABLE TO . . . STRIKE": quoted in Lettow (2005), p. 114.

159 "A BID . . . THREAT": quoted in Oberdorfer (1992), p. 29.

159 "ONE NIGHT . . . HIGHER": Hersh (1986), pp. 17–19.

160 "READ TOGETHER . . . DOWN": Sayle (1993), p. 95.

160 "UNPRECEDENTED SHARPENING . . . MANKIND": Andrew and Gordievsky (1991), p. 81.

160 "IF WE . . . WEAP[ONS]": quoted in Oberdorfer (1992), p. 38.

160 ADVICE OF WILLIAM CLARK: Shultz (1993), p. 360. Clark replaced Richard Allen on 4 Jan. 1982.

161 KAMCHATKA FIGHTER TANKS LIGHT: Sayle (1993), p. 98.

161 "PROVISIONALLY . . . RC-135": ibid.

161 "THE AIR . . . FLASHING": quoted in Dallin (1985), p. 24.

161 ANDROPOV REVIEWED FILES: Sayle (1993), p. 97.

162 "THE SOVIET . . . MISSILES' ": ibid., p. 99.

162 "I HAVE . . . ATTACK": quoted in Dallin (1985), p. 25.

162 "WERE MANDATED . . . INTRUSION": Sayle (1993), p. 100.

162 "THE MURDER . . . AIRLINER": quoted in Cannon (1991), p. 476.

162 "WAS ASTONISHINGLY BRUTAL": Shultz (1993), p. 369.

162 "THE MEETING . . . IT": ibid., p. 370.

162 "THE 747 . . . PLANE": Beth Fischer (1997), p. 126.

163 KENNAN DESCRIBED: according to Talbott (1984), p. 23.

163 "A MILITARIST . . . IMPLANTED": Talbott (1984), "Yuri Andropov Statement," pp. 119–27.

163 ABLE ARCHER, AUTUMN FORGE: Maloney (2004), pp. 607–8.

164 "TO ASCERTAIN . . . NATO": Andrew and Gordievsky (1991), p. 76.

164 LEADERS' APPROVAL: Benjamin Fischer (1997), p. 16.

164 "I HAD . . . PLANNED": quoted in Beth Fischer (1997), p. 123.

164 MCFARLANE SCRUBBED: Oberdorfer (1992), p. 65.

164 THATCHER, KOHL: Beth Fischer (1997), p. 123.

164 "THE SUDDEN . . . RYAN": quoted in CNN Cold War, Episode 22: Star Wars at http://www.cnn.com/SPECIALS/cold.war/episodes/22/spotlight.

164 "THEY WERE . . . DEPLOYMENTS": Morton (2005).

164 "THE ENTIRE . . . 'PRE-WAR' ": Benjamin Fischer, in Cimbala (1999), p. 93.

164 "SOME CLANDESTINE . . . ANALYSTS: CNN Cold War, Episode 22: Star Wars.

165 "WHEN THE . . . AMERICA?": Beth Fischer (1997), p. 132.

165 SOVIETS AND NATO STARTING WAR FROM WITHIN EXERCISE: Gen. Eugene Habiger, personal communication, Nov. 2005.

165 "THE EXERCISE . . . WAR' ": Gates (1996), p. 271.

165 "BETWEEN NOVEMBER . . . 10": ibid., p. 272.

165 "THE GROUP . . . GERMANY": Paul Dibb, in Morton (2005).

166 "INFORMATION ABOUT . . . MISPLACED": Gates (1996), p. 273.

166 "LIFTING ITS . . . COUNTRIES": Mastny and Byrne (2005), Document No. 102, p. 490.

167 "NEVER, PERHAPS . . . EIGHTIES": Gorbachev, speech to the 27th Communist Party Congress, quoted in Newhouse (1989), I: 39.

167 "I FEEL . . . WANT?": Reagan (1990), p. 589.

167 "DO YOU . . . ABOUT": quoted in Oberdorfer (1992), p. 67.

TEN **THE WARHEADS WILL ALWAYS GET THROUGH**

168 "COLUMBUS DAY . . . WAR": quoted in Reagan (1990), p. 585.

169 NUCLEAR WINTER *SCIENCE* PAPER: R. P. Turco, O. B. Toon, T. P. Ackerman, J. B. Pollack, and C. Sagan (1983). Nuclear winter: global consequences of multiple nuclear explosions. *Science* 222, 1283–92.

169 "I KNEW . . . CELLULOID": quoted in Cannon (1991), p. 157.

169 "WHEN BILL . . . PRODUCE' ": Cannon (1991), pp. 156–57.

169 "THE FIRST . . . DEPRESSED' ": Morris (1999), p. 498.

170 SIOP TARGETS: Oberdorfer (1992), p. 65.

170 "WAS 'CHASTENED' . . . SCENARIO' ": Beth Fischer (1997), p. 121. Fischer believes that this late-October briefing was Reagan's first, but Thomas Reed reports attending a SIOP briefing with the president during the IVORY LEAF exercise of 1–4 March 1982. See Reed (2004), p. 243.

170 "A MOST . . . CRAZY": Reagan (1990), pp. 585–86.

170 "ANECDOTALLY, NOT ANALYTICALLY": Gelb (1985), p. 2.

170 "FIRSTHAND DISCOVERIES . . . EXPERIENCE": Cannon (1991), p. 287.

170 "MOST OF . . . LAZY": ibid., p. 55.

171 "THE SAD . . . RESPECT": ibid., p. 427.

171 "NOT ONE . . . BOOKS": Gelb (1985), pp. 1–2.

171 "REAGAN'S SEEMINGLY . . . IT' ": Cannon (1991), p. 308.

171 "HIS BIGGEST . . . COLLEGE": ibid., p. 130.

171 ("PLAYING IT . . . CAMPUS"): Wills (1987), p. 67.

172 "REAGAN COULD . . . ANALOGY": Pious (1991), p. 500.

172 "WITH HIM . . . FORCE": Blumenthal (1986), pp. 241–42.

172 "EVERYTHING IS . . . CHRIST": Cannon (1991), pp. 288–89.

172 "TWICE TEN . . . WORMWOOD": Revelation 9:18; Revelation 8:10–11 (RSV).

173 "WAS SIEZED . . . TRIUMPH": Cannon (1991), p. 288.

173 "FROM THE . . . EARTH": quoted in Cannon (1991), p. 290.

173 "HE WOULD . . . ARMAGEDDON": Cannon (1991), p. 291.

173 "HAIL AND . . . GRASS": Revelation 8:7 (RSV).

174 "GOD HAS . . . EVERYONE": quoted in Lettow (2005), p. 8.

174 "SEVEN SUMMERS . . . YOURSELF' ": Reagan (1965), pp. 19, 22.

174 "WE CAN . . . CREDIT": quoted in Clark's foreword to Reagan (2000), p. 9.

174 "THE SDI . . . PERSONAL": Wohlforth (1996), p. 35.

174 "I'VE BEEN . . . MORE": quoted in Lettow (2005), p. 117.

174 "IT KIND . . . DID": quoted in Lakoff and York (1989), pp. 6–7.

175 "ULTIMATE GOAL . . . OBSOLETE": Ronald Reagan, "Address to the Nation on Defense and National Security," 23 Mar. 1983.

175 "THAT MIGHT . . . RAIN": Ronald Reagan, "Remarks at the High School Commencement Exercises in Glassboro, New Jersey," 19 June 1986.

175 "LIFEGUARDS ARE . . . RESCUE": quoted in Lettow (2005), pp. 8–9.

175 "THE SUM . . . CAN DO IT": Freedman et al. (2005), p. 66.

175 "IN THE . . . TIME' ": Reed (2004), pp. 234–35.

176 "REAGAN THOUGHT . . . WEAPONS": Lettow (2005), pp. 30–31.

176 "ONE OF . . . WAR": Reagan (1990), p. 550, cited in Beth Fischer (1997), p. 104.

176 "HE WAS . . . WARFARE": Freedman et al. (2005), p. 67.

176 "REAGAN . . . WAR": Lettow (2005), p. 51.

176 "WHATEVER HAPPENS . . . CAN": quoted in Lettow (2005), p. 50.

177 "MADE ME . . . WAR": ibid.

177 "MATLOCK . . . UNACCEPTABLE' ": Lettow (2005), p. 133.

177 "I LISTENED . . . ANIMALS": Shultz (1993), p. 513.

177 "REAGAN ASKED . . . RESPOND": Newhouse (1989), I, p. 39.

178 REAGAN LAMENTED FAILURE OF BARUCH PLAN: See Lettow (2005), p. 75: "On several occasions, Reagan publicly expressed regret that the Soviets had not accepted the Baruch Plan of 1946, which would have abolished nuclear weapons and internationalized nuclear energy."

178 WEST POINT ADDRESS: Ronald Reagan, "Address at Commencement Exercises at the United States Military Academy," 27 May 1981.

178 "THE BEST . . . DEFENSE": quoted in Beth Fischer (1997), p. 106.

179 "THIRD GENERATION . . . WEAPONS": Teller, House Armed Services Committee testimony, Apr. 1983, quoted in Broad (1992), p. 143.

179 "NO DOCUMENTARY . . . 1967": Lettow (2005), p. 254, n. 92.

179 "HE TOOK . . . MIND": Strober and Strober (1998), p. 232.

180 "I WOULD . . . ENTIRELY": quoted in Oberdorfer (1992), p. 129.

180 "THE TRUTH . . . OF": Hunter (1992), p. 94.

180 "PRESIDENT REAGAN . . . CRISIS' ": Beth Fischer (1997), p. 134.

181 JAPANESE DIET SPEECH: Ronald Reagan, "Address Before the Japanese Diet in Tokyo," 11 Nov. 1983.

181 A CONVICTION EXPRESSED BEFORE: Ronald Reagan, "Radio Address to the Nation on Nuclear Weapons," 17 Apr. 1982; "Address Before the 38th Session of the United Nations General Assembly in New York, New York," 26 Sept. 1983.

181 "WHEN I . . . HANDS": Shultz (1993), p. 376.

181 16 JANUARY 1984 SPEECH: Ronald Reagan, "Address to the Nation and Other Countries on United States–Soviet Relations," 16 Jan. 1984.

181 FIFTY-FIVE HUNDRED NEW WARHEADS: Newhouse (1989), I, p. 42.

182 REAGAN ALLUDING TO WAR SCARE: "McFarlane, who helped draft the speech, notes that the president's references to 'dangerous misunderstandings and miscalculations' referred to the Soviet response to the war game. In a thinly veiled statement, Reagan declared that he sought to find 'meaningful ways to reduce the uncertainty and potential for misinterpretation surrounding military activities and to diminish the risk of surprise attack.' Likewise, the president's assurances that the United States 'poses no threat to the security of the Soviet Union' were meant to clarify U.S. intentions for the Kremlin." Beth Fischer (1997), p. 135–36.

182 "HACKNEYED PLOY": quoted in Newhouse (1989) I, p. 50.

182 FIVE LETTERS; TASS COMPARISON; "A SHAMELESS . . . END": Shultz (1993), p. 476.

182 "WHAT IS . . . SYSTEMS": quoted in Shultz (1993), p. 474.

182 NANCY REAGAN WORRIED: Newhouse (1989), I, p. 51. See also Prados in Cowley (2005), p. 451.

182   "HINTS CAME . . . PRESIDENT": Shultz (1993), p. 480.

183   "THE PRESIDENT . . . WEAPONS' ": ibid., p. 484.

183   "WHATEVER IS . . . OPERATIONS": Gorbachev (1995), p. 161.

183   "THE SOVIET . . . WEAPONS": quoted in Shultz (1993), p. 507.

183   "GORBACHEV HAD . . . SDI": Memorandum of Conversation, Meeting with British Prime Minister Margaret Thatcher, 22 Dec. 1984, p. 6 (online version), Margaret Thatcher Foundation Archive.

183   "THE TOUGHEST . . . TABLE": Shultz (1993), p. 504.

183   "RONALD REAGAN'S . . . GROUND": ibid., p. 505.

184   "TO SEE . . . GROMYKO": ibid., p. 515.

184   "THE SIDES . . . EVERYWHERE": quoted in Shultz (1993), p. 519.

184   "THE USSR . . . NOW": ibid., p. 530.

184   "THE RESULT . . . AIR": Shultz (1993), p. 532.

184   "A PERSONAL . . . UNDERSTANDING": quoted in Shultz (1993), p. 534.

184   "WE WERE . . . WAR": Shultz (1993), p. 501.

ELEVEN   **GOING AROUND IN CIRCLES**

187   "THE NEXT . . . OFF?": quoted in Kuhn (2004), p. 168.

187   GENEVA SUMMIT SESSIONS: this and all further session discussions paraphrased from the corresponding U.S. Memoranda of Discussions, available online in the Margaret Thatcher Foundation Archives.

189   "SECURITY CAN . . . SECURE": quoted in Sigal (2000), p. 317, n. 4.

189   ("WE MET . . . MEMOS"): quoted in English (2000), p. 324, n. 44.

189   GORBACHEV MEETING PALME: "Throughout that period, Arbatov was working with Gorbachev, and when the Commission met in Moscow in June 1981, Palme and a few members went to see Gorbachev and spoke with him and talked about their ideas and the Commission." Barry Blechman interview, Washington, D.C., Nov. 2005.

189   SOVIET MILITARY STRATEGY: see Odom (1998), passim.

189   "SHARED THE . . . CREDIBILITY": Brandt (1989), p. 396.

190   "I NEVER . . . DEFENSES": Knott Selverstone et al. (2002), p. 13.

190   "THERE WERE . . . THAT": Knott and Riley (2002), p. 10.

190   "NONE OF . . . END": Tannenwald (1999), p. 88.

190   "REAGAN'S SECOND . . . PEOPLE": Dobrynin (1995), p. 610.

190   "THROUGHOUT THE . . . DEVELOPED?": ibid., p. 611.

191   "ALTHOUGH THE . . . SPENDING": Gorbachev (1995), p. 405.

191   "WHAT ARE . . . NOT": quoted in Chernyaev (2000), p. 83.

191   "SINCE THERE . . . START": Wohlforth (1996), p. 37.

191   "MANY HUNDREDS . . . DISARMAMENT": Assembly of presidents of scientific academies and other scientists convened by the Pontifical Academy of Scientists, "Declaration on Prevention of Nuclear War," 24 Sept. 1982.

192   "MADE A . . . CONCLUSIONS": Cohen and vanden Heuvel (1989), p. 160.

192   "THE TASK . . . MEANS": quoted in Sigal (2000), p. 19.

192   "IN OUR . . . DESTRUCTION": ibid., p. 20.

192   "I CRITICIZED . . . UNION' ": Brandt (1989), pp. 65–66. Emphasis added.

192   "RENUNCIATION OF . . . EUROPE": Bahr (2003), p. 138.

193   "RAISE OUR . . . ACT": ibid., p. 140.

193   "THE PRINCIPLE . . . THEM": Palme (1982), p. 176.

193   "MAKE REFERENCE . . . PROBLEMS": Bahr (2003), p. 141.

194   "THE BLANK . . . PAPER"): Chernyaev diary, 24 Nov. 1985. National Security Archive

Electronic Briefing Book No. 192. (N.B.: Translation used here from an earlier posting, "Excerpt from Anatoly Chernyaev's Diary," same site.)

194 "HE WOULD . . . PRESIDENT' ": Alexander Yakovlev, Memorandum prepared on request from M.S. Gorbachev and handed to him on 12 Mar. 1985, National Security Archive Electronic Briefing Book No. 168.

195 "BUD AND . . . MEETING": Kuhn (2004), p. 169.

195 "ARE YOU . . . IS": Knott, Selverstone, et al. (2002), p. 26.

195 "RIPPED MY . . . SHEVARDNADZE": Kuhn (2004), p. 170.

195 "WREATHED IN SMILES": ibid.

197 "ASTONISHED": Tannenwald (1999), p. 68.

198 "SUCCEEDED IN . . . PROBLEMS"): Krepon (1989), p. 258.

198 "THEY ASKED . . . DINOSAUR!' ": Gorbachev interviewed on *CNN Perspectives, Episode 22: Star Wars.*

199 "THE FIRST . . . EASE": Chidester et al. (2003), p. 56; Adelman (1989), pp. 122–23. I have merged these two variant versions of Adelman's story.

200 "BLEEDING WOUND": Gorbachev first used this phrase publicly in his speech to the 27th Party Congress in Feb. 1986. Archie Brown (1996), p. 221.

201 "I CAN'T . . . DID": quoted in Lakoff and York (1989), p. 362, n. 68.

201 SDI AND REDUCTIONS IN OFFENSIVE MISSILES: according to Matlock (2004), p. 158.

201 "WE WILL . . . THUNDERED": quoted in Matlock (2004), p. 157.

202 "I OBSERVED . . . CHIN": Matlock (2004), p. 156.

202 "VELIKHOV AND . . . THING' ": Roald Sagdeev interview, Washington, D.C., Dec. 2003.

202 "GORBACHEV'S GENUINE . . . ECONOMY": Sagdeev (1994), p. 273.

203 "VACCINATIONS . . . 1972": Velikhov (1991), p. 368.

203 "A SPACE-BASED . . . DOWN": ibid., p. 369.

203 "THE 'BALANCE . . . EXPANDED": Velikhov et al. (1986), p. 112.

204 "OUR RESPONSE . . . SDI": Chernyaev (2000), p. 57.

204 TOPOL: Uhler (2003); Podvig (2001), pp. 230–34; www.globalsecurity.org, Weapons of Mass Destruction (WMD): RT-2UTTH - Topol-M (SS-27).

204 312 DEPLOYED BY 2006: See Podvig at http://russianforces.org/missiles/ (accessed 4 Aug. 2006). The Topol entered active service in Dec. 2006.

204 "HOW COULD . . . SILLY?": quoted in Robert Cottrell, "An Icelandic Saga," *NYRB* 51 (17), 4 Nov. 2004, n. 6 (online edition).

204 COMPOSITION OF VPK: Odom (1998), p. 51.

204 "EXPERTS AT . . . STATES' ": Oberdorfer (1992), pp. 29–30.

205 "A SURPRISINGLY . . . POSITIONS": Odom (1998), p. 115.

205 "CUTTING MILITARY . . . LEADERSHIP": ibid., p. 119.

206 "WITH RIGHTEOUS . . . DESTRUCTION": Gorbachev (1995), p. 406.

206 "WE HAD . . . WACKO": Chidester et al. (2003), p. 52.

206 "SHARPLY DISAGREE[D] . . . UNION": Second Reagan-Mondale debate, 21 Oct. 1984, Kansas City, Mo.

207 ("IF THE . . . 1985"): Mastny and Byrne (2005), Document No. 106, p. 509.

207 "RONALD REAGAN'S . . . REPLIED": Gorbachev (1995), p. 407.

208 "AND BESIDES . . . MOVIES": Arbatov (1992), p. 320.

208 "THE WALK . . . ME": Gorbachev (1995), p. 407.

209 "WITH SOME . . . SPHERE?": Memorandum of Conversation, Reagan-Gorbachev Afternoon Tête-à-Tête, 19 Nov. 1985, pp. 3–4. Margaret Thatcher Archives.

210 "WE WERE . . . MOSCOW": Gorbachev (1995), p. 408.

210   "THE DAY . . . POLITICS": Tannenwald (1999), p. 115.

210   "WE HAD . . . IT' ": Knott (2002), p. 21.

210   TWO A.M.: Gorbacheva (1991), p. 169.

211   "TRULY HISTORIC DOCUMENT": Gorbachev (1995), p. 411.

211   "THE SIDES . . . STABILITY": quoted in Oberdorfer (1992), p. 153.

TWELVE **NAYSAYERS HARD AT WORK**

212   "NOT ONCE . . . STATE": Reagan (1990), p. 641.

212   "GORBACHEV . . . WAS . . . IMPRESSION' ": Zubok (2000), p. 5.

212   "NUCLEAR WAR . . . WEAPONS": Gorbachev (1995), p. 411.

212   "DECIDED THAT . . . OFF": quoted in Newhouse (1989), II, p. 58.

212   "OBVIOUSLY THERE . . . ALL": Reagan (1990), p. 643.

213   "GORBACHEV TOLD . . . UNRESOLVED": Tannenwald (1999), pp. 112–13.

213   "IMPRESSION THAT . . . ECONOMY": Chernyaev (2000), pp. 45–46.

213   "I FEEL . . . ON": Tannenwald (1999), p. 79.

213   " 'IT'S JUST . . . SHOCK": ibid., p. 121.

214   "AS A . . . UNION": ibid.

214   "SUDDENLY, AT . . . EVERYTHING' ": Tannenwald (1999), p. 122. Emphasis added.

215   "WE IMMEDIATELY . . . PHONY": ibid., p. 122.

215   "WE PUSHED . . . PROGRAM": ibid., p. 123.

215   "AGREED ON . . . OFFENSIVE' ": Gorbachev (1995), p. 411.

215   TARASENKO PROPOSAL: For details see Tannenwald (1999), p. 124ff.

215   "IT TOOK . . . PROPOSAL": Tannenwald (1999), pp. 124–25.

216   "THIS WAS . . . FUTURE' ": Odom (1998), p. 127.

216   "GORBACHEV WAS . . . PROGRAMS": ibid.

216   "IT WAS . . . AGAIN": Tannenwald (1999), pp. 136–38.

217   "HE PROMPTLY . . . ENDORSED": Odom (1998), p. 127.

217   "NOT TO . . . DECEPTION": quoted in Evangelista (2001), p. 20.

217   "IN AND . . . DOCUMENT": Tannenwald (1999), p. 113.

218   "THE CHIEF . . . HICCUP": Archie Brown (1996), pp. 93–94.

218   GORBACHEV 15 JANUARY 1986 TEXT: *FBIS Daily Report*, 16 Jan. 1986, Vol. 3, No. 11, pp. AA1–AA9 (hereafter "FBIS 16 Jan. 86").

218   "[THE SOVIET . . . EARTH": FBIS 16 Jan. 86, pp. AA1–AA2.

218   "THE FIRST . . . POSSIBLE": ibid., p. AA2.

219   SECOND STAGE OF GORBACHEV'S PLAN: ibid.

219   "BY THE . . . ELABORATED": FBIS 16 Jan. 86, p. AA3.

219   ON-SITE INSPECTION: ibid.

219   "ACTUAL TROOP . . . BALANCED": Allin (1994), p. 82.

220   "IT WASN'T . . . TOLD": Ellman and Kontorovich (1998), p. 43.

220   "THUS, WE . . . COURSE": FBIS 16 Jan. 86, p. AA3.

220   "IS A . . . BE": ibid.

220   "OUR NEW . . . RACE": FBIS 16 Jan. 86, pp. AA7–AA8.

221   "PROGRAM OF . . . ARMS": Palme (1982), p. 177.

221   "THE VERY . . . LEADERSHIP": Chernyaev (2000), p. 59.

221   "GORBACHEV SURPRISINGLY . . . DOWN": Reagan (1990), pp. 650–51.

221   PERLE, HEARING FROM NITZE: Shultz (1993), p. 669.

221   "SECRETARY WEINBERGER . . . PROPOSING": Nitze (1989), p. 422.

222   "WHY WAIT . . . WEAPONS?": ibid.

222   WHITE HOUSE STATEMENTS: Statement on the Soviet–United States Nuclear and
      Space Arms Negotiations, 15 Jan. 1986; Statement on the Soviet Proposal on Nuclear
      and Space Arms Reductions, 15 Jan. 1986; Statement by Principal Deputy Press Secre-
      tary Speakes on the Soviet Proposal on Nuclear and Space Arms Reductions, 16 Jan.
      1986, Public Papers of Ronald Reagan.

222   "NSPG TIME . . . US": Reagan (1990), p. 651.

222   "THE NAYSAYERS . . . POLICY": Shultz (1993), p. 701.

223   "HE THINKS . . . WEAPONS": ibid.

223   COLD WAR TACIT COOPERATION: See, e.g., Kanet and Kolodziej (1991).

223   "ROZ RIDGWAY . . . THEM' ": Shultz (1993), pp. 704–5.

224   "OUR PROPOSAL . . . EUROPE": Reagan (1990), p. 658. For excerpts from Reagan's
      22 Feb. 1986 letter see pp. 656–58.

224   "THE MORATORIUM . . . GUARANTEES": Chernyaev (2000), pp. 56–57; Gorbachev
      Foundation Archive (combining variant translations).

224   "DESPITE ALL . . . ROLE": 3 Apr. 1986 Politburo meeting (Chernyaev's notes), Gor-
      bachev Foundation Archive.

224   "MORE THAN . . . BETTER?": Reagan (1990), p. 662.

224   "TO PORTRAY . . . POLICY": ibid., pp. 662–63.

225   "GORBACHEV . . . CONTROL!": Shultz (1993), p. 709.

225   "THE WESTERN . . . INITIATIVE": Gorbachev (1995), p. 412.

225   "WAS DISAPPOINTED . . . STEPS": Tannenwald (1999), pp. 154–55.

225   GORBACHEV AND . . . DIFFICULT": ibid., pp. 153–54.

226   SHEVARDNADZE ON DEALING WITH HUMAN RIGHTS: according to Jack Matlock
      in Tannenwald (1999), p. 178.

226   "WE LOOKED . . . OURSELVES": Tannenwald (1999), p. 196.

226   FORTY-EIGHT THOUSAND FEET: Many accounts give forty-six thousand, but cf.
      Joseph P. Kerwin, M.D., to Rear Admiral Richard H. Truly, 28 July 1986, at http://
      history.nasa.gov/kerwin.html, an official report on the deaths of the *Challenger*
      astronauts, which says forty-eight thousand. Details of the accident from this source
      and from James Oberg, "7 Myths about the Challenger Shuttle Disaster," Space News,
      MSNBC.com.

227   "THE FUTURE . . . GOD": Ronald Reagan, "Address to the Nation on the Explosion
      of the Space Shuttle Challenger," 28 Jan. 1986.

227   "CHERNOBYL WAS . . . FALLOUT": Petrosyants (1988), p. 54.

227   "TORE THE . . . EYES": Shevardnadze (1991), p. 175.

228   "COMRADE GORBACHEV . . . THIS": Mastny and Byrne (2005), Document No. 115,
      pp. 531–32.

228   "ONE PERSONAL . . . HANDS?": Wohlforth (1996), p. 33.

228   "THAT PHRASE . . . CONVICTION": ibid., p. 37.

228   "ALL THE . . . ELITE' ": Gorbachev (1995), p. 402.

228   LOCATION OF MEETING: Oberdorfer (1992), p. 162.

228   "THAT IN . . . DIMENSION": Gorbachev (1995), pp. 402–3.

229   THESE WERE NOT . . . KGB: e.g., ibid.

229   "FROM 1986 . . . 1994": Graham (2002), p. 51.

229   RICHARD PERLE ARGUMENT: "He persuaded Mr. Reagan to repudiate the SALT II
      treaty": "The Light and Darkness of Richard Perle," *New York Times* editorial, 16 Mar.
      1987.

229   "SINCE THE . . . GROUND": Ronald Reagan, "Statement on Soviet and United States
      Compliance with Arms Control Agreements," 27 May 1986.

229 "WAS SURPRISED . . . INITIATIVES": Chernyaev (2000), p. 58.

229 CASPAR WEINBERGER . . . ADVANTAGES": Talbott (1985), p. 17.

230 ABM TREATY'S "BROAD" INTERPRETATION: For a full treatment of this controversy see T. Graham (2002), pp. 143–84.

230 "THE PRODUCT . . . MACHINES": quoted in David (2000), p. 3 (online version).

230 "THERE WERE . . . PROCESS": Wohlforth (1996), p. 41.

230 IKLÉ, KAMPELMAN: Oberdorfer (1992), p. 171.

230 "RICHARD PERLE . . . THAT": Tannenwald (1999), p. 143.

231 "ON FEBRUARY . . . NOTHING": Shultz (1993), p. 708.

231 "WHO ASSURED . . . AMICABLY": ibid., p. 719.

231 "ONE OF . . . MATTERS": ibid.

231 "ABOUT THIS . . . PLOY": Tannenwald (1999), p. 148.

231 "IT MADE . . . DEFENSES": quoted in Lettow (2005), pp. 209–10.

231 "RIDICULOUS": quoted in Oberdorfer (1992), p. 173.

232 "HOPES FOR . . . WANING": Gorbachev (1995), p. 429.

232 "I ADMIT . . . PROPHECIES": Transcript of Conversation Between Mikhail Gorbachev and François Mitterrand, 7 July 1986, Gorbachev Foundation Archives, in document collection for Brown University Conference "Understanding the End of the Cold War," archival document no. 25.

232 " 'IT SEEMS . . . THINKING' ": Chernyaev (2000), p. 76.

232 "HE TOLD . . . RATIONAL": Gorbachev (1995), p. 430.

232 "I HAVE . . . INTEREST": Transcript of Mikhail Gorbachev–Richard Nixon conversation, Gorbachev Foundation Archives, 18 July 1986, p. 14 (translation from the Russian), in Mazo (2004), p. 20, and Zubok (2000), p. 10.

233 "AN ATTEMPT . . . AMERICANS": Gorbachev (1995), p. 414.

233 "I TOOK . . . CRAP!' ": Chernyaev (2000), p. 78.

233 "IT WAS . . . PROCESS": Gorbachev (1995), p. 414.

234 "HE STARTED . . . OFFENDED!' ": Chernyaev (2000), p. 78.

234 "IN HIS . . . PROGRAM": quoted in Chernyaev (2000), p. 79.

234 "WE SHOULD . . . CAPABILITIES": Transcript of Chernyaev notes from Politburo session of 4 Oct. 1986, Gorbachev Foundation Archives, in document collection for Brown University Conference "Understanding the End of the Cold War," archival document no. 32.

235 "IN ALMOST . . . PERSONALLY": Reagan (1990), p. 672.

THIRTEEN **LOOKING OVER THE HORIZON**

236 "ESSENTIALLY A . . . SUMMIT": Ronald Reagan, "Remarks on Departure for Reykjavik, Iceland," 9 Oct. 1986.

237 "THE OTHERS . . . COST": Academy of Achievement (1990), p. 2.

237 "WE COULD . . . POCKET": Nitze (1989), p. 429.

237 "TO INTERACT . . . UNION": Chernyaev (2000), p. 84.

237 "BY THE . . . BACK": Gorbachev (1995), p. 349.

237 "WE ARE . . . TETHER": quoted in Chernyaev (2000), pp. 83–84.

238 "OTHERWISE . . . DEAD END": Chernyaev (2000), p. 82.

238 "NOBODY EXCEPT . . . WARS": quoted in Pryce-Jones (1995), p. 114. See also Don Oberdorfer, quoting Chernyaev, in Wohlforth (1996), p. 5.

238 "STAR WARS . . . WAR": Lebow and Stein (1994), p. 37.

238 KIEV LEAVES: Mould (1988), p. xiv.

238   SARCOPHAGUS FINISHED: Z. Medvedev (1990), p. 80.

238   HOFDI HOUSE DETAILS: "Hofdi: The City of Reykjavik's House for Official Recep-
      tions," Reykjavikurborg official pamphlet, 1996, courtesy Terri and Randy Reece.

239   A LOT OF PAPER: All direct and indirect quotations from principals at Reykjavik are
      drawn from U.S. or translated Soviet memoranda of conversations unless otherwise
      indicated. U.S. memoranda online at Margaret Thatcher Archives. Soviet memo-
      randa from the Gorbachev Foundation Archives. First and final session Soviet mem-
      oranda translated by Glen Worthy. I have sometimes compressed "direct" quotations,
      which are not verbatim in the original.

240   "THE NEED . . . JOY' ": Mazo (2004), pp. 30–31.

241   "WHOOPS . . . HIS JUDGMENT": Matlock (2004), p. 220.

242   "GORBACHEV AND . . . DAYS": Reagan (1990), p. 675.

242   "OUTLINED THE . . . CONVERSATION": Gorbachev (1995), p. 416.

243   "HELL, THIS . . . NYET": Adelman (1989), p. 44.

244   "HE PROPOSED . . . DISADVANTAGE": Shultz (1993), p. 759.

245   "GORBACHEV WAS . . . WAYS": ibid., p. 758.

246   "SDI COOPERATION TREATY": Thomas Graham, Jr., personal communication,
      Sept. 2006.

246   "OBVIOUSLY DISAPPOINTED . . . PROPOSALS": Matlock (2004), p. 221.

246   "SOMEWHAT TAKEN . . . REACTION": Shultz (1993), p. 760.

247   "WAS RELIEVED . . . NEGOTIATIONS": ibid.

248   "THE SMALLEST . . . TANK": Adelman (1989), p. 46.

248   "WHY DID . . . YEARS": Shultz (1993), p. 760.

248   "TELL HIM . . . YESTERDAY": Adelman (1989), p. 47.

248   GORBACHEV AND ADVISERS ON THE MAIN DECK: Chernyaev (2000), p. 84.

250   KASHA FOREVER: quoted in Oberdorfer (1992), p. 196.

251   "I'M OLDER . . . THEN?": quoted in Winik (1996), p. 506.

252   "IT WAS . . . POSITIONS": Rozanne Ridgway interview, CNN Perspectives, Episode
      22: Star Wars.

252   "GORBACHEV FINALLY . . . PRAGMATIC' ": Matlock (2004), p. 222.

253   LAST OF THE MOHICANS: Shultz (1993), p. 763.

253   "MR. SECRETARY . . . SHOT": quoted in Chidester et al. (2003), p. 37.

253   "I'M NO . . . WANTS": quoted in Winik (1996), p. 507, and (a variant) Adelman
      (1989), p. 49.

254   ROWNY DISAGREEMENT AND CAUCUS: Adelman (1989), p. 50.

254   AKHROMEYEV AND KARPOV: Shultz (1993), p. 763.

254   "AT TWO . . . NEXT": Academy of Achievement (1990), p. 3.

254   "HOPED INTO . . . HOUR": Nitze (1989), p. 430.

254   "WHO DO . . . UP?": Shultz (1993), p. 764. Shultz misremembers Perle and others
      accompanying Nitze and Linhard; both Nitze and Rowny recalled otherwise.

254   "MARSHAL AKHROMEYEV . . . ACCEPT": Academy of Achievement (1990), pp. 3–4.

254   "IT WAS . . . LIMITED": Nitze (1989), p. 431.

254   "IT BECAME . . . LEVEL": ibid.

255   "WE MADE . . . A.M.": Academy of Achievement (1990), p. 4.

255   "DEFINING STRATEGIC . . . YEARS": Adelman (1989), p. 53.

255   SOVIET CARBON PAPER: ibid.

255   "DAMN GOOD . . . YEARS": Shultz (1993), pp. 764–65.

255   "FOR THE . . . REMAINED": ibid., p. 765.

257   "NO, LET'S . . . NOTHING": Oberdorfer (1992), p. 196.

258 "IT'S BEEN . . . ROUND": quoted in Winik (1996), p. 512.

258 "ALMOST TAUNTING . . . LINE": Shultz (1993), p. 768.

258 "AN EFFORT . . . IMPASSE": ibid.

258 "A LITTLE . . . WEAPONS": Tannenwald (1999), pp. 188–89.

259 LINHARD-PERLE PROPOSAL: quoted in full in Shultz (1993), p. 769.

259 "HE GETS . . . BALL GAME": quoted in Oberdorfer (1992), p. 199.

259 GORBACHEV PROPOSAL: quoted in full in Shultz (1993), p. 769.

260 "RON, IS THAT YOU?": Besides the official memorandum of conversation, this reconstruction draws on Mazo (2004), p. 52; Schell (2004), p. 7; and Shultz (1993), p. 771.

260 "POLICY OF . . . ANYBODY": Skinner et al. (2001), pp. 439–40. Emphasis added.

260 "WE CAN . . . US": ibid., p. 442.

260 "AN UNVARNISHED . . . PRESIDENT": ibid., p. 438.

262 "SOME OF . . . DECISION": quoted in Bosch (1998), p. 284.

262 "THE PRESIDENT . . . LIMITATIONS": Richard Perle conversation, Hoover Institution, Oct. 2006.

263 "THE USSR . . . OTHERWISE": quoted in Shultz (1993), pp. 770–71.

266 "I REMEMBER . . . HOPING": Chernyaev (2000), p. 86.

267 "ANGRIER AND ANGRIER": Reagan (1990), p. 679.

267 "MORE THAN . . . DRAINED": Shultz (1993), p. 773.

267 "IT WAS . . . UNHAPPY": Tannenwald (1999), p. 199.

268 "LEFT IN HIS CAR": Gorbachev (1995), pp. 418–19.

268 "GORBACHEV . . . US' ": Dobrynin (1995), p. 621.

268 "I REALIZED . . . ANGRY: Reagan (1990), p. 679.

269 "PERLE REGARDED . . . ACHIEVEMENTS": Thomas Graham, Jr., personal communication, Sept. 2006.

269 "I WALKED . . . FACE' ": Gorbachev (1995), p. 419. Emphasis added.

269 "THE POSITION . . . THRESHOLD": Thoughts about Reykjavik, Chernyaev notes, 12 Oct. 1986, Gorbachev Foundation Archives.

270 "IT SEEMS . . . MIND": Gorbachev (1987b), p. 29.

270 "WE FELT . . . ENDORSED": ibid., p. 25.

270 "REYKJAVIK GENERATED . . . WORLD": ibid., p. 66.

270 "AFTER ALL . . . START": ibid., p. 19.

FOURTEEN **THE SOVEREIGN RIGHT TO CHOOSE**

271 "WE SAT . . . SUBJECTS' ": Knott, Selverstone, et al. (2002), p. 8.

271 "COMPARABLE TO CHERNOBYL": quoted in Zubok (2000), p. 8.

271 "THE MEETING . . . CONTRADICTORY": Gorbachev (1987a), pp. 240–41.

271 "IRRESPONSIBILITY" . . . DROWN": Chernyaev notes, 16 Oct. 1986, Gorbachev Foundation Archives, in document collection for Brown University Conference "Understanding the End of the Cold War," archival document no. 24. Emphasis added.

272 "SDI IS . . . DISARMAMENT": Chernyaev notes, 12 Oct. 1986, Brown University Conference, archival document no. 23.

272 "A FEW . . . TIME": Roald Sagdeev interview, Washington, D.C., Dec. 2003. *Washington Post* story: Walter Pincus, " 'Modest' SDI Testing Called Compatible with BM Pact," 30 Oct. 1986.

273 "MAGINOT LINE . . . USSR": Sakharov (1991), pp. 22–23.

273 WARNED GORBACHEV TO SLOW DOWN: Oberdorfer (1992), p. 230. Oberdorfer gives many of the details of Rust's excursion that follow.

273 "VERY POLITICAL . . . WEST": Carl Wilkinson, "What Happened Next?" *Guardian Observer*, 27 Oct. 2002.

274 "MY PLAN . . . IT": ibid.

274 RUST MASSACRE, ORDER OF LENIN: Oberdorfer (1992), p. 230.

274 "GORBACHEV ALSO . . . CONFLICTS": English (2002), p. 84.

275 "THE TRUE . . . CONTROL": T. Graham (2002), p. 124.

275 "IN 1987 . . . SOLUTION": ibid., p. 125.

275 ASTROLOGER PICKED SIGNING TIME: Oberdorfer (1992), p. 259.

276 "AN UNFORGIVABLE . . . HEAD": Gorbachev (1995), pp. 443–44.

276 "FIRST NUCLEAR . . . TIMES": ibid., pp. 442–43.

276 SANDIA AND VERIFICATION REGIME: Dori Ellis, personal communication, Nov. 2005.

276 "A RECIPROCAL . . . WAS": T. Graham (2002), p. 111.

276 "A GREAT . . . EUROPE": Tannenwald (1999), pp. 206–7.

276 "WHERE WILL THEY FIGHT?": Emilio Segré, personal communication, 1982.

277 "I ALWAYS . . . WAY": Bush and Scowcroft (1998), p. 60.

278 "BRIEFLY TOUCHED . . . ON' ": Gorbachev (1995), p. 451.

278 "WAS FACILITATED . . . NEGOTIATIONS": ibid., p. 455.

278 "THE REMARKABLE . . . THINKING": Reagan (1990), p. 710.

278 "MERCILESS" . . . BLUNDERED": Yakovlev (1993), p. 3.

278 "OUR COUNTRY . . . DECEIVED": ibid., pp. 73–75.

279 "THE EXACT . . . DISARMAMENT": Gorbachev (1995), p. 459.

279 GORBACHEV ORDERING DEFENSE MINISTRY TO PLAN TROOP WITHDRAWALS: Evangelista (2001), p. 27.

279 AKHROMEYEV WORKED WITH HIM: Gorbachev (1995), p. 459.

280 "AS A . . . POSITION": quoted in Ellman and Kontorovich (1997), p. 267.

280 "FINALLY TO . . . INTIMIDATION": Chernyaev (2000), pp. 193–95.

281 "HOPED THAT . . . UNION": Gorbachev (1995), p. 460.

281 "I STARTED . . . ELOQUENCE": ibid., p. 461.

281 "TODAY, I . . . AIRCRAFT": Gorbachev (1990), pp. 36–37.

282 "AFTER AN . . . OVATION": Chernyaev (2000), p. 201.

282 "A SPEECH . . . NATIONS": quoted in Gorbachev (1995), p. 462.

283 "I KNOW . . . NONETHELESS": quoted in Oberdorfer (1992), p. 321.

283 "WEEKS . . . PASSED": Gorbachev (1995), p. 496.

283 MOSCOW SHOULD BE LEFT TO STRUGGLE: See Beschloss and Talbott (1993), p. 106.

283 "CHENEY BELIEVED . . . ALACRITY": Foer and Ackerman (2003), pp. 3–4. Emphasis added.

284 HEU PRODUCTION: ISIS, Military and Excess Stocks of Highly Enriched Uranium (HEU) in the Acknowledged Nuclear Weapon States, 11 June 2004, Revised 25 June 2004, Table 1, n. 1.

284 "CHANGED THE . . . INSPECTIONS": Harahan and Kuhn (1996).

284 GROMOV CROSSING, WAR DEATHS: Oberdorfer (1992), p. 243.

284 CSCE: For a detailed account of this and the following discussion, see Harahan and Kuhn (1996).

285 "KNOWN AS . . . ACCORD": Harahan and Kuhn (1996), Chapter 1a., p. 2.

285 "FOR US . . . IT!": Gorbachev (1995), p. 502.

285 "WANTED TO . . . BEGAN": T. Graham (2002), pp. 190–91.

286 "THE PRINCIPLE . . . ESTABLISH": Gorbachev (1995), p. 437.

286 "BARE-BONES . . . WANTED": T. Graham (2002), p. 192.

286 "ALL AROUND . . . PROPOSED": Chernyaev (2000), p. 226.

287 "RESPECT FOR . . . CHOICE": quoted in Kramer (2001), p. 126.

287 "IF WE . . . BACK": quoted in Beschloss and Talbott (1993), p. 96.

287 GRAHAM HIMSELF . . . IT . . . REPRESENTATIVE: T. Graham (2002), p. 193.

288 "ALWAYS BRIGHT . . . PEPPERED": Alex de Jonge, *The Weimar Chronicle,* London: Paddington Press, 1978, p. 130.

288 "ON A . . . REALIZED' ": Beschloss and Talbott (1993), p. 132.

288 "BEFORE THE . . . IT": ibid., p. 166.

288 "YOU KNOW . . . FAST": Lee Hamilton, conversation, Washington, D.C., 2004.

288 "LASTED ABOUT . . . 1990)": T. Graham (2002), p. 185.

289 "IT WAS . . . SCENES": ibid., p. 203.

289 "IN 1988 . . . POWER": Graham and LaVera (2003), p. 594.

289 "THE CFE . . . SECURITY": T. Graham (2002), p. 209.

289 "THEY DECLARED . . . FRIENDSHIP' ": Evangelista (2001), p. 23.

FIFTEEN **THE LITTLE SUITCASE**

290 "WE FINALLY . . . WAR": Gorbachev (1995), pp. 538–39.

290 "PUT THE . . . SIGNED": Graham and LaVera (2003), p. 885.

290 "START I . . . SIDE": Jentleson (2000), p. 111.

291 TACTICAL NUKE YIELDS: Millar (2002), p. 1.

291 "THE STRATEGIC . . . PROCEDURES": Gorbachev (1995), p. 514.

291 TWENTY-TWO THOUSAND SOVIET TACTICAL NUKES: Millar (2002) p. 4, n. 6.

291 TWENTY-THREE THOUSAND U.S.: Powell (1995), p. 541.

291 "PUT ON . . . TRUE": quoted in Beschloss and Talbot (1993), p. 316.

291 RICE INTERAGENCY GROUP: ibid.

291 "A RIGHT-WING JUNTA": quoted in Bush and Scowcroft (1998), p. 527.

291 "DURING THE . . . PRESIDENT]": Baker (1995), p. 526.

292 "A RUSSIAN . . . LEGISLATION": Sam Nunn, conversation, Washington, D.C., Sept. 2005.

292 "WHILE THERE . . . US": Bush and Scowcroft (1998), p. 544.

292 "I DON'T . . . SUNG": quoted in Nichols (2004), p. 108.

293 "I WANT . . . PROPOSALS": quoted in Powell (1995), p. 541.

293 "CHENEY'S DISTASTE . . . TIME": Bush and Scowcroft (1998), pp. 544–45.

293 "THE SUM . . . ONES)": ibid., p. 545.

293 CHENEY SIGNED ON: ibid.

293 "FAR EXCEEDED . . . WORLD": Powell (1995), p. 541.

294 "HE WANTED . . . AGREEMENT": Bush and Scowcroft (1998), p. 547.

294 "WE PROPOSE . . . ELEMENTS": "Text of President Gorbachev's Televised Statement on Nuclear Weapons," 5 Oct. 1991, Tass, Moscow.

295 "DISMISSING THE . . . DEMOCRACY": Archie Brown (1996), pp. 101–2.

295 "GORBACHEV, WHILE . . . ME' ": Chernyaev (2000), p. 280.

295 "IN THE . . . PROGRESS": Gorbachev (1991), pp. 104–5.

296 "IN THE . . . POLICY": quoted in Gorbachev (1995), p. 614.

296 "MR. PRESIDENT . . . OPINION": quoted in Chernyaev (2000), p. 274.

297 "BOTH THE . . . AMERICA": Gorbachev (1995), p. 539.

297 "FOOLISHNESS" . . . MANEUVER": quoted in John H. Cushman, Jr., "Defense Aide Rejects Concept of a World Free of Atomic Arms," *New York Times,* 1 Feb. 1987.

297 "A NUCLEAR . . . BOTH": Dobrynin (1995), pp. 468–69.

298 "CAME OUT . . . LIFE": Barnet (1985), pp. 484–90.

298 "IT IS . . . AFRAID": ibid., p. 490.

299 "DETERRENCE . . . FAILED": Kugler (1984), pp. 474–76.

299 "NUCLEAR NATIONS . . . OUTCOMES": ibid., pp. 478–79.

299 "THE MAIN . . . ARSENALS": ibid., p. 501.

300 "CHALLENGING THE . . . MAGIC": ibid.

300 SENATE HEARINGS: *Nuclear Testing Issues:* Hearing before the Committee on Armed Services, United States Senate, 99th Congress, 2nd Session, 29–30 April 1986.

300 "AT TIMES . . . DUDS": Rosengren (1983), p. 13.

300 "IN LATE . . . FORCE": ibid., p. 21.

300 MINUTEMAN AND W45S: ibid., pp. 21–22.

301 "THE COUP . . . COME": Gorbachev (1995), p. 646.

301 "IN GORBACHEV'S . . . CORNER": Yeltsin (1994), pp. 109–10.

302 "HAD TO . . . WAY": ibid., p. 111.

302 "WE WERE . . . UNION": ibid.

302 "A WONDERFUL . . . DIVISION": Yeltsin (1994), pp. 111–12.

303 "FIRST A . . . UNION)": Stanislav Shushkevich, personal communication, Aug. 2005.

304 "THE IDEA . . . PARTIES": Yeltsin (1994), p. 112.

304 FAX MACHINES: ibid.

304 "ON DECEMBER . . . UNION": Reed (2004), pp. 1–2.

304 "YUGOSLAVIA WITH . . . WEAPONS": Jentleson (2000), p. 111.

305 "THERE WAS . . . PRETENSE": Shushkevich interview, April 2003.

305 "PROTRACTED AND DIFFICULT": Yeltsin (1994), p. 121.

305 "IT WAS . . . SURVIVED": quoted in Archie Brown (1996), p. 342, n. 104, quoting Gorbachev interview with Jonathan Steele, *Guardian,* 24 Dec. 1992.

305 "MY DEAR . . . FAMILY!": quoted in Beschloss and Talbot (1993), p. 461.

305 "TO SUM . . . RUSSIA": Reed (2004), p. 2.

305 "I ATTACH . . . TONIGHT": quoted in Beschloss and Talbot (1993), p. 461.

306 $5.5 TRILLION: Schwartz (1998), p. 3.

306 "ENOUGH TO . . . LAND": C. Sagan (1992), p. 24.

306 "RESPONSIBLE FOR . . . REQUIREMENTS": quoted in Barnet (1971), pp. 171–72.

306 "THE EXTENT . . . MILITARY": Melman (1974), p. 122.

306 "THE PURVEYORS . . . SOCIETY": ibid., p. 123.

307 "SINCE FUTURE . . . YEAR": quoted in Melman (1974), pp. 122–23.

307 "THE DOLLARS . . . BUDGETS": Melman (1974), p. 117.

307 ASCE REPORT CARD: "2005 Report Card for America's Infrastructure," www.asce.org (accessed 6 Dec. 2006).

308 "ALL LEVELS . . . SECTOR": ASCE press release, 9 Mar. 2005, available at http://www.asce.org/reportcard/2005/page.cfm?id=108 (accessed 6 Dec. 2006).

308 "IF YOU . . . THING": Tannenwald (1999), pp. 52–53.

308 "THE VERY . . . LIFE": Oppenheimer (1953), pp. 527–29.

BIBLIOGRAPHY

Academy of Achievement (1990). Paul H. Nitze Interview, 20 October 1990. Academy of Achievement, Washington, D.C.

Adelman, Kenneth L. (1989). *The Great Universal Embrace: Arms Summitry, A Skeptic's Account.* New York: Simon & Schuster.

Alexievich, Svetlana (2005). *Voices from Chernobyl.* K. Gessen, Trans. Normal, IL: Dalkey Archive Press.

Allin, Dana H. (1998). *Cold War Illusions: America, Europe and Soviet Power, 1969–1989.* New York: St. Martin's Press.

Anders, Roger M. (1987). *Forging the Atomic Shield.* Chapel Hill: University of North Carolina Press.

Anderson, Martin (1990). *Revolution: The Reagan Legacy.* Stanford, CA: Hoover Institution Press.

Andrew, Christopher, and Oleg Gordievsky (1990). *KGB: The Inside Story of Its Foreign Operations from Lenin to Gorbachev.* New York: HarperCollins.

Andrew, Christopher, and Oleg Gordievsky, Eds. (1991). *Instructions from the Centre: Top Secret Files on KGB Foreign Operations 1975–1985.* London: Hodder & Stoughton.

Andrew, Christopher, and Vasili Mitrokhin (1999). *The Sword and the Shield: The Mitrokhin Archive and the Secret History of the KGB.* New York: Basic Books.

Anspaugh, Lynn R., Robert J. Catlin, and Marvin Goldman (1988). The global impact of the Chernobyl reactor accident. *Science* 242 (4885), 16 Dec., 1513–19.

Arbatov, Georgi (1992). *The System: An Insider's Life in Soviet Politics.* New York: Times Books.

Armstrong, David (2002). Dick Cheney's song of America. *Harper's* 305 (1829).

Arnold, Lorna (2001). *Britain and the H-Bomb.* Basingstoke, Hampshire: Palgrave.

Bahr, Egon (2003). Statements and discussion: Egon Bahr. *German Historical Institute Bulletin, Supplement 1: American Detente and German Ostpolitik, 1969–1972,* 2003, 137–43.

Baker, James A., III (1995). *The Politics of Diplomacy: Revolution, War and Peace, 1989–1992.* New York: G. P. Putnam's Sons.

Ball, Desmond, and Jeffrey Richelson, Eds. (1986). *Strategic Nuclear Targeting.* Ithaca, NY: Cornell University Press.

Barnet, Richard J. (1971). *The Economy of Death.* New York: Atheneum.

———(1985). The ideology of the national security state. *Massachusetts Review* 26 (Winter), 483–500.

Baucom, Donald R. (1990). Hail to the chiefs: The untold history of Reagan's SDI decision. *Policy Review* 53 (Summer), 66.

Bearden, Milt, and James Risen (2003). *The Main Enemy: The Inside Story of the CIA's Final Showdown with the KGB.* New York: Random House.

Berman, Harold J. (1963). The dilemma of Soviet law reform. *Harvard Law Review* 76 (5), 929–51.

Beschloss, Michael R., and Strobe Talbott (1993). *At the Highest Levels: The Inside Story of the End of the Cold War.* Boston: Little, Brown.

Betts, Richard K. (2003). Striking first: A history of thankfully lost opportunities. *Ethics and International Affairs* 17 (1) (Spring).

Blacker, Coit D. (1993). *Hostage to Revolution: Gorbachev and Soviet Security Policy, 1985–1991.* New York: Council on Foreign Relations Press.

Blake, George (1990). *No Other Choice: An Autobiography.* New York: Simon & Schuster.

Bleek, Philipp C. (2001). U.S. and Russian/Soviet strategic nuclear forces. *Arms Control Today,* May.

Blinken, Antony J. (2003). From preemption to engagement. *Survival* 45 (4) (Winter), 33–60.

Blumenthal, Sidney (1986). *The Rise of the Counter-Establishment.* New York: Times Books.

———(1987a). Richard Perle, disarmed but undeterred. *Washington Post,* 23 Nov.

———(1987b). Richard Perle's nuclear legacy. *Washington Post,* 24 Nov.

———(1987c). Perle and the diminished dream. *Washington Post,* 25 Nov.

———(2005). The long march of Dick Cheney. *Salon,* http://www.salon.com/opinion/blumenthal/2005/11/24/cheney/ (accessed 24 November 2005).

Bosch, Adriana (2000). *Reagan: An American Story.* New York: TV Books.

Brandt, Willy (1989). *My Life in Politics.* New York: Viking.

Broad, William J. (1992). *Teller's War: The Top-Secret Story Behind the Star Wars Deception.* New York: Simon & Schuster.

Brook-Shepherd, Gordon (1989). *The Storm Birds: Soviet Postwar Defectors.* New York: Weidenfeld & Nicolson.

Brown, Archie (1996). *The Gorbachev Factor.* New York: Oxford University Press.

Brown, Michael (1996). Phased Nuclear Disarmament and US Defense Policy (Occasional Paper No. 30). The Henry L. Stimson Center, Oct.

Bundy, McGeorge (1969). To cap the volcano. *Foreign Affairs* 48 (1) (Oct.).

———(1988). *Danger and Survival: Choices About the Bomb in the First Fifty Years.* New York: Random House.

Bunn, George (2003). The Nuclear Nonproliferation Treaty: History and current problems. *Arms Control Today,* Dec.

Burnham, James (1945). Lenin's heir. *Partisan Review* 12 (Winter), 61–72.

Burr, William, Ed. (2004). *The Creation of SIOP-62: More Evidence on the Origins of Overkill.* Washington, D.C.: National Security Archive Electronic Briefing Book No. 130.

———. (2005). *"To Have the Only Option That of Killing 80 Million People Is the Height of Immorality": The Nixon Administration, the SIOP, and the Search for Limited Nuclear Options, 1969–1974.* Washington, D.C.: National Security Archive Electronic Briefing Book No. 173.

Burr, William, and Robert Wampler, Eds. (2004). *"The Master of the Game": Paul H. Nitze and U.S. Cold War Strategy from Truman to Reagan.* Washington, D.C.: National Security Archive Electronic Briefing Book No. 139.

Bush, George H. W., and Brent Scowcroft (1998). *A World Transformed.* New York: Vintage.

Butler, Richard, Lee Butler, et al. (1996). *Report of the Canberra Commission on the Elimination of Nuclear Weapons.* Department of Foreign Affairs and Trade, Commonwealth of Australia.

Cahn, Anne Hessing (1998). *Killing Detente: The Right Attacks the CIA.* University Park: Pennsylvania State University Press.

Calabrese, Edward J., and Linda A. Baldwin (2003). Toxicology rethinks its central belief. *Nature* 421, 13 Feb., 691.

Callahan, David (1990). *Dangerous Capabilities: Paul Nitze and the Cold War.* New York: HarperCollins.

Cannon, Lou (1991). *President Reagan: The Role of a Lifetime.* New York: Simon & Schuster.

Carynnyk, Marco, Lubomyr Y. Luciuk, and Bohdan S. Kordan, Eds. (1988). *The Foreign Office and the Famine: British Documents on Ukraine and the Great Famine of 1932–1933.* Kingston, ON: Limestone Press.

Chernyaev, Anatoly (2000). *My Six Years with Gorbachev.* University Park: Pennsylvania State University Press.

Chidester, Jeff, Stephen F. Knott, and Robert Strong (2003). Interview with Kenneth Adelman, University of Virginia, 30 Sep. Charlottesville, VA: Ronald Reagan Oral History Project, Presidential Oral History Program, Miller Center of Public Affairs.

Cimbala, Stephen J., Ed. (1999). *Mysteries of the Cold War.* Aldershot, England: Ashgate.

Clem, Ralph S. (1986). The Soviet Union: Crisis, stability or renewal? *Air University Review* (Nov.–Dec.), http://www.airpower.au.af.mil/airchronicles/aureview/1986/nov-dec/clem .html (accessed 24 June 2005).

Cochran, Thomas B., et al. (1991). Report on the Third International Workshop on Verified Storage and Destruction of Nuclear Warheads held in Moscow and Kiev, Natural Resources Defense Council. Dec. 16–20.

Cohen, Avner (1998). *Israel and the Bomb.* New York: Columbia University Press.

Cohen, Avner, and Thomas Graham, Jr. (2004). An NPT for non-members. *Bulletin of the Atomic Scientists* 60 (3) (May/June), 40–44.

Cohen, Avner, and Steven Lee, Eds. (1986). *Nuclear Weapons and the Future of Humanity.* Totowa, NJ: Rowman & Allanheld.

Cohen, Stephen F. (2000). *Failed Crusade: America and the Tragedy of Post-Communist Russia.* New York: W. W. Norton.

Cohen, Stephen F., and Katrina vanden Heuvel (1989). *Voices of Glasnost: Interviews with Gorbachev's Reformers.* New York: W. W. Norton.

Conquest, Robert (1986). *The Harvest of Sorrow: Soviet Collectivization and the Terror-Famine.* New York: Oxford University Press.

———(1990). *The Great Terror: A Reassessment.* New York: Oxford University Press.

Cottrell, Robert (2004). An Icelandic Saga: Review of *Reagan and Gorbachev: How the Cold War Ended,* by Jack F. Matlock, Jr. *New York Review of Books* 51 (17), 4 Nov.

Cowley, Robert, Ed. (2005). *The Cold War: A Military History.* New York: Random House.

Cox, Arthur Macy (1975). *The Myths of National Security: The Peril of Secret Government.* Boston: Beacon Press.

———(1980). The CIA's tragic error. *New York Review of Books* 27 (17), 6 Nov., 1–8 (online version).

CRS (Congressional Research Service) (2006). U.S. Conventional Forces and Nuclear Deterrence: A China Case Study. Bolkom, Christopher, et al. 11 Aug.

Curtis, Adam (2005). *The Power of Nightmare* (BBC three-part series), DVD edition.

Dahl, Robert (1985). *Controlling Nuclear Weapons: Democracy Versus Guardianship.* Syracuse, NY: Syracuse University Press.

Dallin, Alexander (1985). *Black Box: KAL 007 and the Superpowers.* Berkeley: University of California Press.

Dam, Kenneth W. (1983). Challenges of U.S.-Soviet relations at the 50-year mark: Address before the International House, Chicago, 31 Oct. *Department of State Bulletin* (Dec.), 26–30.

David, Mark W. (2000). Reagan's real reason for SDI. *Policy Review* (103) (Oct.–Nov.), online version.

Department of State (1950). *NSC 68: United States Objectives and Programs for National Security.* 7 Apr.

Dobrynin, Anatoly (1995). *In Confidence: Moscow's Ambassador to Six Cold War Presidents.* Seattle: University of Washington Press.

Doder, Dusko (1988). *Shadows and Whispers: Power Politics Inside the Kremlin from Brezhnev to Gorbachev.* New York: Penguin.

Doder, Dusko, and Louise Branson (1990). *Gorbachev: Heretic in the Kremlin.* New York: Viking.

Dolot, Miron (1985). *Execution by Hunger: The Hidden Holocaust.* New York: W. W. Norton.

Ebel, Robert E. (1994). *Chernobyl and Its Aftermath: A Chronology of Events.* Washington: Center for Strategic and International Studies.

Eden, Lynn (2004). *Whole World on Fire: Organizations, Knowledge and Nuclear Weapons Devastation.* Ithaca, NY: Cornell University Press.

Ehrman, John (1995). *The Rise of Neoconservatism: Intellectuals and Foreign Affairs 1945–1994.* New Haven, CT: Yale University Press.

Eisenhower, Susan (1995). *Breaking Free: A Memoir of Love and Revolution.* New York: Farrar, Straus & Giroux.

Ellman, Michael, and Vladimir Kontorovich (1997). The collapse of the Soviet system and the memoir literature. *Europe-Asia Studies,* 49 (2) (March), 259–79.

Ellman, Michael, and Vladimir Kontorovich, Eds. (1998). *The Destruction of the Soviet Economic System: An Insiders' History.* Armonk, NY: M. E. Sharpe.

English, Robert D. (2000). *Russia and the Idea of the West: Gorbachev, Intellectuals and the End of the Cold War.* New York: Columbia University Press.

———(2002). Power, ideas, and new evidence on the Cold War's end: A reply to Brooks and Wohlforth. *International Security* 26 (4) (Spring), 70–92.

Ermarth, Fritz W. (2003). Observations on the "war scare" of 1983 from an intelligence perch. Parallel History Project on Cooperative Security, http://www.php.isn.ethz.ch/collections (accessed 11 Mar. 2007).

Evangelista, Matthew (1999). *Unarmed Forces: The Transnational Movement to End the Cold War.* Ithaca, NY: Cornell University Press.

———(2001). Norms, heresthetics and the end of the Cold War. *Journal of Cold War Studies* 3 (1) (Winter), 5–35.

Fainsod, Merle (1956). The Communist Party since Stalin. *Annals of the American Academy of Political and Social Science* 303 (Jan.), 23–36.

Feiveson, Harold A., Ed. (1999). *The Nuclear Turning Point: A Blueprint for Deep Cuts and De-Alerting of Nuclear Weapons.* Washington, D.C.: Brookings Institution Press.

Fischer, Benjamin B. (1997). A Cold War Conundrum. Center for the Study of Intelligence, Central Intelligence Agency.

———, Ed. (1999). *At Cold War's End: US Intelligence on the Soviet Union and Eastern Europe, 1989–1991.* Washington, D.C.: GPO.

Fischer, Beth A. (1997). *The Reagan Reversal: Foreign Policy and the End of the Cold War.* Columbia: University of Missouri Press.

Fischer, David (1997). *History of the International Atomic Energy Agency: The First Forty Years.* Vienna: IAEA.

FitzGerald, Frances (1976). The warrior intellectuals. *Harper's,* May, 45–64.

———(2000). *Way Out There in the Blue: Reagan, Star Wars and the End of the Cold War.* New York: Simon & Schuster.

Foer, Franklin, and Spencer Ackerman (2003). The radical. *New Republic* (1 Dec.), 3–4.

Fosdick, Dorothy, Ed. (1990). *Henry M. Jackson and World Affairs: Selected Speeches, 1953–1983.* Seattle: University of Washington Press.

Foster, Kenneth R., David E. Bernstein, and Peter W. Huber, Eds. (1993). *Phantom Risk: Scientific Inference and the Law.* Cambridge, MA: MIT Press.

Freedman, Lawrence (2000). Does deterrence have a future? *Arms Control Today,* Oct.

Freedman, Paul B., Stephen F. Knott, et al. (2001). Interview with Stuart Spencer, University of Virginia, 15–16 Nov. Charlottesville, VA: Ronald Reagan Oral History Project, Presidential Oral History Program, Miller Center of Public Affairs.

Gaddis, John Lewis (1997). *We Now Know: Rethinking Cold War History.* Oxford: Clarendon Press.

Garthoff, Raymond L. (1983). The NATO decision on Theater Nuclear Forces. *Political Science Quarterly* 98 (2) (Summer), 197–214.

———(1985). *Detente and Confrontation: American-Soviet Relations from Nixon to Reagan.* Washington, D.C.: The Brookings Institution.

Garton Ash, Timothy (1993). *In Europe's Name: Germany and the Divided Continent.* New York: Vintage.

Gates, Robert M. (1996). *From the Shadows: The Ultimate Insider's Story of Five Presidents and How They Won the Cold War.* New York: Simon & Schuster.

Gelb, Leslie H. (1984). Is the nuclear threat manageable? *New York Times Magazine,* 4 Mar. (online version).

———(1985). The mind of the President. *New York Times Magazine,* 6 Oct. (online version).

Genin, Vlad E., Ed. (2001). *The Anatomy of Russian Defense Conversion.* Walnut Creek, CA: Vega Press.

Gilpatrick, Roswell, et al. (1965). A report to the President by the Committee on Nuclear Proliferation. The White House, 21 Jan. National Security Archives.

Glaser, Charles L. (1990). *Analyzing Strategic Nuclear Policy.* Princeton, NJ: Princeton University Press.

Goldman, Marshall I. (1986). Keeping the Cold War out of Chernobyl: Just as the Soviets must be more open, so we in the West must not gloat. *Technology Review* 89 (2) (July), 18–19.

Gorbachev, Mikhail (1984). The people's vital creativity. *Current Digest of the Soviet Press* 35 (24), 9 Jan. 1985 (*Pravda,* 11 Dec. 1984), 1–10, 24, and No. 25, pp. 1–8.

———(1987a). *Perestroika: New Thinking for Our Country and the World.* New York: Harper & Row.

———(1987b). *Reykjavik: Results and Lessons.* Madison, CT: Sphinx Press.

———(1987c). *Selected Speeches and Articles.* Second Updated Ed. Moscow: Progress Publishers.

———(1990). *A Road to the Future: Complete Text of the December 7, 1988 United Nations Address.* Santa Fe, NM: Ocean Tree Books.

———(1991). *The August Coup: The Truth and the Lessons.* New York: HarperCollins.

———(1995). *Memoirs.* London: Doubleday.

———(2000). *On My Country and the World.* G. Shriver, Trans. New York: Columbia University Press.

Gorbachev, Mikhail, and Zdenek Mlynar (2002). *Conversations with Gorbachev on Perestroika, the Prague Spring, and the Crossroads of Socialism.* New York: Columbia University Press.

Gorbachev, Mikhail, et al. (1996). What did we end the Cold War for? *New Perspectives Quarterly* (Winter).

Gorbacheva, Raisa (1991). *I Hope.* D. Floyd, Trans. New York: HarperCollins.

Graham, Bradley (2001). *Hit to Kill: The New Battle Over Shielding America from Missile Attack.* New York: Public Affairs.

Graham, Thomas, Jr. (2002). *Disarmament Sketches: Three Decades of Arms Control and International Law.* Seattle: University of Washington Press.

Graham, Thomas, Jr., and Damien J. LaVera (2003). *Cornerstones of Security: Arms Control Treaties in the Nuclear Era.* Seattle: University of Washington Press.

Graham, Thomas, Jr., and Douglas B. Shaw (1998). Viewpoint: Nearing a fork in the road; Proliferation or nuclear reversal? *Nonproliferation Review* (Fall), 70–76.

Gray, Colin S., and Keith Payne (1980). Victory is possible. *Foreign Policy* 39 (Summer), 14–27.

Gusterson, Hugh (1996). *Nuclear Rites: A Weapons Laboratory at the End of the Cold War.* Berkeley: University of California Press.

Hadley, Stephen, Robert G. Joseph, et al. (2001). Rationale and Requirements for U.S. Nuclear Forces and Arms Control. National Institute for Public Policy (NIPP). Jan.

Hafemeister, David (1997). Reflections on the GAO Report on the nuclear triad: How much was enough to win the Cold War; was it Freud or Newton? (Occasional Report). *Science & Global Security* 6, 383–93.

———(2005). A secrecy primer. *Bulletin of the Atomic Scientists* (May/June), 23–25.

Harahan, Joseph P., and John C. Kuhn III (1996). *On-Site Inspections Under the CFE Treaty: A History of the On-Site Inspection Agency and CFE Treaty Implementation, 1990–1996.* Washington, D.C.: On-Site Inspection Agency, U.S. Dept. of Defense (online at www .fas.org).

Hartmann, Robert T. (1980). *Palace Politics: An Inside Account of the Ford Years.* New York: McGraw-Hill.

Hayes Holgate, Laura S. (1991). Fallout in the Fifties: The beginnings of environmentalism as arms control. *Breakthroughs* (Spring), 14–19.

Heilbrunn, Jacob (1996). Who won the Cold War? *The American Prospect* 7 (28) (Sept.).

Hendrickson, David C. (2002). Toward universal empire: The dangerous quest for absolute security. *World Policy Journal* (Fall), 1–10.

Herken, Gregg (1980). *The Winning Weapon.* New York: Alfred A. Knopf.

———(1985). *Counsels of War.* New York: Alfred A. Knopf.

Hersh, Seymour M. (1986). *"The Target Is Destroyed": What Really Happened to Flight 007 and What America Knew About It.* New York: Random House.

Hobbes, Thomas (1651). *Leviathan.* Reprinted by Oxford: Clarendon Press, 1909.

Hollander, Paul (1999). *Political Will and Personal Belief.* New Haven, CT: Yale University Press.

Holloway, David A. (1994). *Stalin and the Bomb.* New Haven, CT: Yale University Press.

Hopkins, Arthur T. (1993). *Unchained Reactions: Chernobyl, Glasnost and Nuclear Deterrence.* Washington, D.C.: National Defense University.

Hudson, George E., Ed. (1990). *Soviet National Security Policy Under Perestroika.* Mershon Center Series on International Security and Foreign Policy, Vol. IV, C. F. Hermann, Ed. Boston: Unwin Hyman.

Hunter, Kerry L. (1992). *The Reign of Fantasy: The Political Roots of Reagan's Star Wars Policy.* New York: Peter Lang.

Hunter, Thomas O., and C. Paul Robinson, Eds. (2005). *U.S. Strategic Nuclear Policy: An Oral History, 1942–2004* (4 DVDs). Albuquerque, NM: Sandia National Laboratories.

IAEA, Ed. (1997). *International Atomic Energy Agency: Personal Reflections.* Vienna: IAEA.

Iklé, Fred Charles (1973). Can nuclear deterrence last out the century? *Foreign Affairs* (Jan.), 267–85.

Jaworowski, Zbigniew (1999). Radiation risk and ethics. *Physics Today,* Sept. 1999, 24–29.

Jentleson, Bruce W. (2000). *Opportunities Missed, Opportunities Seized: Preventive Diplomacy in the Post-Cold War World.* Latham, MD: Rowman & Littlefield.

Jervis, Robert (1989). *The Meaning of the Nuclear Revolution: Statecraft and the Prospect of Armageddon.* Ithaca, NY: Cornell University Press.

Johnson, Chalmers (2004). *The Sorrows of Empire*. New York: Henry Holt.

Joseph, Paul (1983). Nuclear strategy and American foreign policy. In *The Socialist Register 1983*, R. Miliband and John Saville, Eds., pp. 202–18. London: Merlin Press.

Josephson, Paul R. (2000). *Red Atom: Russia's Nuclear Power Program from Stalin to Today*. New York: W. H. Freeman.

Jürgens, Urda (1990). *Raisa: The 1st First Lady of the Soviet Union*. S. Clayton, Trans. New York: Summit.

Kaiser, Robert G. (1992). *Why Gorbachev Happened*. New York: Simon & Schuster.

Kanet, Roger E., and Edward A. Kolodziej, Eds. (1991). *The Cold War as Cooperation*. Baltimore, MD: Johns Hopkins University Press.

Kaplan, Fred (1979). Warring over new missiles for NATO. *New York Times Magazine* (9 Dec.).

———(1983). *The Wizards of Armageddon*. New York: Simon & Schuster.

Keeney, L. Douglas (2002). *The Doomsday Scenario*. St. Paul, MN: MBI Publishing.

Kegley, Charles W., Jr. (1994). How did the Cold War die? Principles for an autopsy. *Mershon International Studies Review* 38 (1) (Apr.), 11–41.

Khrushchev, Nikita (1974). *Khrushchev Remembers: The Last Testament*. S. Talbott, Trans. Boston: Little, Brown.

Kistiakowsky, George (1976). *A Scientist at the White House: The Private Diary of President Eisenhower's Special Assistant for Science and Technology*. Cambridge, MA: Harvard University Press.

———(1979). False alarm: The story behind SALT II. *New York Review of Books* 26 (4), 22 Mar. (online version.)

Klotz, Frank Graham (1980). The U.S. President and the Control of Strategic Nuclear Weapons. D. Phil. Oxford University.

Knight, Amy (2003). The KGB, perestroika, and the collapse of the Soviet Union. *Journal of Cold War Studies* 5 (1) (Winter), 67–93.

Knott, Stephen, and Russell L. Riley (2002). Interview with Caspar Weinberger, University of Virginia, 19 Nov. Charlottesville: Ronald Reagan Oral History Project, Presidential Oral History Program, Miller Center of Public Affairs.

Knott, Stephen, Marc Selverstone, and James Sterling Young (2002). Interview with George Shultz, University of Virginia, 18 Dec. Charlottesville: Ronald Reagan Oral History Project, Presidential Oral History Program, Miller Center of Public Affairs.

Knott, Stephen, James Sterling Young, and Allison Asher (2001). Interview with Martin Anderson, University of Virginia, 11–12 Dec. Charlottesville: Ronald Reagan Oral History Project, Presidential Oral History Program, Miller Center of Public Affairs.

Kotkin, Stephen (2001). *Armageddon Averted: The Soviet Collapse, 1970–2000*. New York: Oxford University Press.

Kramer, Mark (1992). New sources on the 1968 Soviet invasion of Czechoslovakia. *Cold War International History Project Bulletin* 2 (1) (Fall), 4–13.

———(2001). Realism, ideology and the end of the Cold War: A reply to William Wohlforth. *Review of International Studies* 27 (1) (January), 119–30.

Kramish, Arnold (1993). Proliferation 101: The Presidential faculty. *Global Affairs*, Spring, 110.

Krepon, Michael (1989). *Arms Control in the Reagan Administration*. Lanham, MD: University Press of America.

Kristensen, Hans M., Matthew G. McKinzie, and Robert S. Norris (2004). The protection paradox. *Bulletin of the Atomic Scientists* 60 (2) (Mar./Apr.), 68–77.

Kugler, Jacek (1984). Terror without deterrence: Reassessing the role of nuclear weapons. *Journal of Conflict Resolution* 28 (3) (Sept.), 470–506.

Kuhn, Jim (2004). *Ronald Reagan in Private*. New York: Sentinel.

Kull, Steven (1988). *Minds at War: Nuclear Reality and the Inner Conflicts of Defense Policymakers*. New York: Basic Books.

Kunsman, David M., and Douglas B. Lawson (2001). A Primer on U.S. Strategic Nuclear Policy. Sandia National Laboratories. January.

Kurtz, Lester R. (1988). *The Nuclear Cage: A Sociology of the Arms Race*. Englewood Cliffs, NJ: Prentice Hall.

Lakoff, Sanford, and Herbert F. York (1989). *A Shield in Space? Technology, Politics, and the Strategic Defense Initiative*. Berkeley: University of California Press.

Lambright, W. Henry (2002). Changing course: Admiral James Watkins and the DOE nuclear weapons complex. In *Security in a Changing World: Case Studies in U.S. National Security Management*, V. C. Franke, Ed., 55–80. Westport, CT: Praeger.

Lebow, Richard Ned, and Janice Gross Stein (1994). Reagan and the Russians. *Atlantic* 273 (2) (Feb.), 35–37.

Leebaert, Derek (2002). *The Fifty-Year Wound: The True Price of America's Cold War Victory*. Boston: Little, Brown.

Leffler, Melvin P. (1991). Was the Cold War necessary? *Diplomatic History* 15 (2), Spring, 265–75.

Legasov, Valery (2000). Testament. In *Chernobyl Record*, R. F. Mould, Ed., 289–303. Bristol, England: Institute of Physics Publishing.

Lettow, Paul (2005). *Ronald Reagan and His Quest to Abolish Nuclear Weapons*. New York: Random House.

Levoy, Peter R. (2004). Predicting nuclear proliferation: A declassified documentary record. *Strategic Insights* 3 (1) (Jan.) (online).

Lodal, Jan M. (1976). Assuring strategic stability: An alternate view. *Foreign Affairs* 54 (3) (Apr.) (online version).

Luttrell, Clifton B. (1973). The Russian wheat deal: Hindsight vs. foresight. *Federal Reserve Bank of St. Louis Review* (Oct.), 2–9.

MacArthur, Brian, Ed. (1999). *The Penguin Book of Twentieth-Century Speeches*. London: Penguin Books.

MacLean, Douglas, Ed. (1984). *The Security Gamble: Deterrence Dilemmas in the Nuclear Age*. Totowa, NJ: Rowman & Allanheld.

Madariaga, Salvador de (1929). *Disarmament*. New York: Coward-McCann.

Malia, Martin ("Z," pseudonym) (1990). To the Stalin mausoleum. *Daedalus* 119 (1) (Winter), 295–344.

Malish, Anton F. (1984). Soviet agricultural policy in the 1980s. *Policy Studies Review* 4 (2) (Nov.), 301–10.

Maloney, Sean (2004). Fire brigade or tocsin? NATO's ACE mobile force, flexible response and the Cold War. *Journal of Strategic Studies* 27 (4) (Dec.), 585–613.

Mann, James (2004). *Rise of the Vulcans: The History of Bush's War Cabinet*. New York: Viking.

Marples, David R. (1986). *Chernobyl and Nuclear Power in the USSR*. New York: St. Martin's Press.

———(1993). Chernobyl's lengthening shadow. *Bulletin of the Atomic Scientists* 49 (7) (Sept.), 38–43.

———(1996a). *Belarus: From Soviet Rule to Nuclear Catastrophe*. New York: St. Martin's Press.

———(1996b). The Chernobyl disaster: Its effect on Belarus and Ukraine. In *The Long Road to Recovery: Community Responses to Industrial Disaster*, J. K. Mitchell, Ed. New York: United Nations University Press. Full text online (accessed 6 Oct. 2005).

Masters, Roger D. (1964). World politics as a primitive political system. *World Politics* 16 (4) (July), 595–619.

Mastny, Vojtech (2003). Did East German spies prevent a nuclear war? Parallel History Project on Cooperative Security, online at http://www.php.isn.ethz.ch/collections/coll_stasi/mastny.cfm (accessed 12 Mar. 2007.)

Mastny, Vojtech, and Malcolm Byrne, Eds. (2005). *A Cardboard Castle? An Inside History of the Warsaw Pact, 1955–1991.* Budapest: Central European University Press.

Matlock, Jack F., Jr. (1995). *Autopsy on an Empire: The American Ambassador's Account of the Collapse of the Soviet Union.* New York: Random House.

———(2004). *Reagan and Gorbachev: How the Cold War Ended.* New York: Random House.

Maynes, Charles William (1982). Old errors in the new Cold War. *Foreign Policy* 46 (2) (Spring), 86–104.

Mazo, Michael (2004). The Peak: Nuclear Arms Control and the End of the Cold War at the Reykjavik Summit. B.A. thesis, Yale University.

McLean, Scilla, Ed. (1986). *How Nuclear Weapons Decisions Are Made.* Basingstoke, England: Macmillan.

McNamara, Robert S. (1986). *Blundering into Disaster: Surviving the First Century of the Nuclear Age.* New York: Pantheon.

———(1995). *In Retrospect: The Tragedy and Lessons of Vietnam.* New York: Vintage.

Medvedev, Grigori (1991). *The Truth About Chernobyl.* New York: Basic Books.

———(1993). *No Breathing Room: The Aftermath of Chernobyl.* New York: Basic Books.

Medvedev, Zhores (1990). *The Legacy of Chernobyl.* New York: W. W. Norton.

Melman, Seymour (1970). *Pentagon Capitalism: The Political Economy of War.* New York: Basic Books.

———(1974). *The Permanent War Economy: American Capitalism in Decline.* New York: Touchstone.

Millar, Alistair (2002). The pressing need for tactical nuclear weapons control. *Arms Control Today,* May 2002, 1–5, online at http://www.armscontrol.org/act/2002_05/millarmay02.asp (accessed 12 Mar. 2007).

Millis, Walter, Ed. (1951). *The Forrestal Diaries.* New York: Viking.

Mlynar, Zdenek (1980). *Nightfrost in Prague: The End of Humane Socialism.* P. Wilson, Trans. New York: Karz.

Morris, Edmund (1999). *Dutch: A Memoir of Ronald Reagan.* New York: Random House.

Morton, Tom (2005). Episode 1: The Nuclear War We Nearly Had in 1983. In *Torn Curtain: The Secret History of the Cold War.* ABC Radio National. Australia.

Mould, Richard F. (1988). *Chernobyl: The Real Story.* Oxford: Pergamon Press.

———(2000). *Chernobyl Record: The Definitive History of the Chernobyl Catastrophe.* Bristol, England: Institute of Physics Publishing.

Moynihan, Daniel Patrick (1990). How America blew it. *Newsweek* (10 Dec.), 14.

Mueller, John (1988). The essential irrelevance of nuclear weapons. *International Security* 13 (2) (Fall), 55–79.

Nacht, Michael L. (1975). The delicate balance of error. *Foreign Policy* 19, (Summer), 163–77.

Newhouse, John (1989). Annals of diplomacy: "The Abolitionist" I & II. *New Yorker;* I: 2 Jan., 37–52; II: 9 Jan., 51–72.

Nichols, John (2004). *The Rise and Rise of Richard B. Cheney: Unlocking the Mysteries of the Most Powerful Vice President in American History.* New York: New Press.

Nielsen, J. Rud (1963). Memories of Niels Bohr. *Physics Today,* Oct.

Ninsic, Miroslav (1988). The United States, the Soviet Union and the politics of opposites. *World Politics* 40 (4) (July), 452–75.

Nitze, Paul (1976). Assuring strategic stability in an era of detente. *Foreign Affairs* 54 (2) (Jan.), 1–16 (online version).

———(1989). *From Hiroshima to Glasnost: At the Center of Decision.* New York: Grove Weidenfeld.

Nolan, Janne E. (1989). *Guardians of the Arsenal: The Politics of Nuclear Strategy.* New York: Basic Books.

Norris, Robert S., and William M. Arkin (1994). Estimated U.S. and Soviet/Russian nuclear stockpiles, 1945–1994. *Bulletin of the Atomic Scientists* 50 (6) (Nov.–Dec.), 58–59.

Nuenlist, Christian (2001). Cold War generals: The Warsaw Pact Committee of Defense Ministers, 1969–1990. Parallel History Project on Cooperative Security, online at http://www.php.isn.ethz.ch/ (accessed 12 March 2007).

Nye, Joseph S., Jr. (1987). Nuclear learning and U.S.-Soviet security regimes. *International Organization* 41 (3) (Summer).

Oberdorfer, Don (1992). *The Turn: From the Cold War to a New Era; The United States and the Soviet Union 1983–1990.* New York: Simon & Schuster.

Odom, William E. (1998). *The Collapse of the Soviet Military.* New Haven, CT: Yale University Press.

Oppenheimer, Robert (1953). Atomic weapons and American policy. *Foreign Affairs* 31 (4) (July), 525–35.

Palme, Olof (Independent Commission on Disarmament and Security Issues) (1982). *Common Security: A Blueprint for Survival.* New York: Simon & Schuster.

Park, Robert (2000). *Voodoo Science: The Road From Foolishness to Fraud.* New York: Oxford University Press.

Patman, Robert G. (1999). Reagan, Gorbachev and the emergence of "New Political Thinking." *Review of International Studies* 25 (Oct.), 577–601.

Paton, Boris E., Victor G. Baryakhtar, et al. (2003). The Chernobyl catastrophe in Ukraine: Causes of the accident and lessons learned. *Environmental Science & Pollution Research,* Special Issue 1, 3–12.

Perle, Richard (1987). Reykjavik as a watershed in U.S.-Soviet arms control. *International Security* 12 (1) (Summer), 175–78.

———(1992). *Hard Line.* New York: Random House.

Petrosyants, Andranik (1988). *Nuclear Engineering Before and After Chernobyl: Problems and Prospects.* Moscow: Progress Publishers.

Pious, Richard M. (1991). Prerogative power and the Reagan presidency: A review essay. *Political Science Quarterly* 106 (3) (Fall), 499–510.

Pipes, Richard (1977). Why the Soviet Union thinks it could fight and win a nuclear war. *Commentary* (July), 21–34.

———(1986). Team B: The reality behind the myth. *Commentary* (Oct.), 25–40.

———(2003). *VIXI: Memoirs of a Non-Belonger.* New Haven, CT: Yale University Press.

Podvig, Pavel, Ed. (2001). *Russian Strategic Nuclear Forces.* Cambridge, MA: MIT Press.

Potter, William C.(1985a). Nuclear proliferation: U.S.-Soviet cooperation. *Washington Quarterly* (Winter), 141–54.

———. (1985b). The Soviet Union and nuclear proliferation. *Slavic Review* 44 (5), Fall, 468–87.

———(1989). Soviet decision-making for Chernobyl: An analysis of system performance and policy change. National Council for Soviet and East European Research, Dec.

———(1991). The effects of Chernobyl on Soviet decision-making for nuclear safety. *Impact of Science on Society* 163, 257–67.

Potter, William C., and Lucy Kerner (1991). The Soviet military's performance at Chernobyl. *Soviet Studies* 43 (6), 1027–47.

Powaski, Ronald E. (2000). *Return to Armageddon: The United States and the Nuclear Arms Race, 1981–1999.* New York: Oxford University Press.

Powell, Colin L., with Joseph E. Persico (1995). *My American Journey.* New York: Random House.

Powers, Thomas (1996). Who won the Cold War? (Review of Robert M. Gates, *From the Shadows,* Simon & Schuster, 1996). *New York Review of Books* 43 (11), 20 June (online version).

Preble, Christopher (2005). The Uses of Threat Assessment in Historical Perspective: Perception, Misperception and Political Will. Threat Assessment Working Group of the Princeton Project on National Security. June.

Pry, Peter Vincent (1999). *War Scare: Russia and America on the Nuclear Brink.* Westport, CT: Praeger.

Pryce-Jones, David (1995). *The War that Never Was: The Fall of the Soviet Empire 1985–1991.* London: Phoenix Press.

Ramzaev, P. V., Ed. (1996). *Medical Consequences of the Chernobyl Nuclear Accident.* Commack, NY: Nova Science.

Read, Piers Paul (1993). *Ablaze: The Story of the Heroes and Victims of Chernobyl.* New York: Random House.

Reagan, Ronald (1990). *An American Life.* New York: Simon & Schuster.

———(2000). *Abortion and the Conscience of the Nation.* Sacramento, CA: New Regency Publishing.

Reagan, Ronald, with Richard G. Hubler (1965). *Where's the Rest of Me?* New York: Best Books.

Reed, Thomas C. (2004). *At the Abyss: An Insider's History of the Cold War.* New York: Ballantine.

Remnick, David (1991). Dead souls. *New York Review of Books* 38 (21), 19 Dec.

———(1994). *Lenin's Tomb.* New York: Vintage.

Rhodes, Richard (1995). *Dark Sun: The Making of the Hydrogen Bomb.* New York: Simon & Schuster.

———(1986). *The Making of the Atomic Bomb.* New York: Simon & Schuster.

Rippon, Simon (1986). The Chernobyl accident. *Nuclear News* (June) (LexisNexis Academic, accessed 3 May 2005), 87.

Robin, Corey (2004). *Fear: The History of a Political Idea.* New York: Oxford University Press.

Rodberg, Leonard S., and Derek Shearer, Eds. (1970). *The Pentagon Watchers: Students Report on the National Security State.* Garden City, NY: Doubleday & Co.

Rogers, Paul. (1988). *Guide to Nuclear Weapons.* Bradford Peace Studies Papers: New Series No. 2. Oxford: Berg.

Rosenberg, David Alan (1983). The origins of overkill: Nuclear weapons and American strategy, 1945–1960. *International Security* 7 (4) (Spring), 3–71.

Rosenberg, David Alan, and W. B. Moore (1981–1982). "A smoking radiating ruin at the end of two hours": documents on American plans for nuclear war with the Soviet Union, 1954–1955. *International Security* 6 (3) (Winter), 3–38.

Rosengren, J. W. (1983). Some Little-Publicized Difficulties With a Nuclear Freeze. Office of Internal Security Affairs, U.S. Department of Energy, Oct.

Rostow, Walt W. (1975). Robert S. McNamara Oral History Interview I, 8 Jan., Internet Copy, LBJ Library.

Roxburgh, Angus (1991). *The Second Russian Revolution: The Struggle for Power in the Kremlin.* London: BBC Books.

Rummel, Rudolph J. (1998). *Statistics of Democide.* Munich: Lit.

Sagan, Carl (1992). Between enemies. *The Bulletin of the Atomic Scientists* 48 (May), 24–26.

Sagan, Scott D. (1987). SIOP-62: The nuclear war plan briefing to President Kennedy. *International Security* 12 (1) (Summer), 22–51.

Sagan, Scott D., and Kenneth N. Waltz (2003). *The Spread of Nuclear Weapons: A Debate Renewed.* New York: W. W. Norton.

Sagdeev, Roald Z. (1994). *The Making of a Soviet Scientist.* New York: John Wiley & Sons.

Sakharov, Andrei (1990). *Memoirs.* R. Lourie, Trans. New York: Alfred A. Knopf.

———(1991). *Moscow and Beyond: 1986 to 1990.* A. Bouis, Trans. New York: Alfred A. Knopf.

Sanders, Jerry W. (1983). *Peddlers of Crisis: The Committee on the Present Danger and the Politics of Containment.* Boston: South End Press.

Satter, David (1996). *Age of Delirium: The Decline and Fall of the Soviet Union.* New Haven, CT: Yale University Press.

Sayle, Murray (1993). A reporter at large: Closing the file on Flight 007. *New Yorker* (13 Dec.), 90–101.

Scarry, Elaine (1991). War and the social contract: Nuclear policy, distribution and the right to bear arms. *University of Pennsylvania Law Review,* 139 U. Pa. L. Rev. 1257.

Scheer, Robert (1988). *Thinking Tuna Fish, Talking Death: Essays on the Pornography of Power.* New York: Noonday Press (Farrar, Straus & Giroux).

Schell, Jonathan (2004). Cold war to Star Wars. *Nation* (28 June), 7.

Schmid, Sonja (2005). Envisioning a Technological State: Reactor Design Choices and Political Legitimacy in the Soviet Union and Russia. Doctoral dissertation, Cornell University.

Schmidt, Helmut (1981). A policy of reliable partnership. *Foreign Affairs* 59(4) (Spring), 1–8 (online version).

Schneider, Barry R., and William L. Dowdy, Eds. (1998). *Pulling Back from the Nuclear Brink: Reducing and Countering Nuclear Threats.* London: Frank Cass.

Schwartz, Stephen I., Ed. (1998). *Atomic Audit: The Costs and Consequences of U.S. Nuclear Weapons Since 1940.* Washington, D.C.: Brookings Institution Press.

Schweizer, Peter (1994). *Victory: The Reagan Administration's Secret Strategy That Hastened the Collapse of the Soviet Union.* New York: Atlantic Monthly Press.

Shcherbak, Iurii (1989). *Chernobyl: A Documentary Story.* I. Press, Trans. New York: St. Martin's Press.

Sheehy, Gail (1990). *The Man Who Changed the World: The Lives of Mikhail S. Gorbachev.* New York: HarperCollins.

Sheldon, Robert (2004). Military Operations Research Society (MORS) Oral History Project interview of Alfred Lieberman, FS. *Military Operations Research* 9 (1), 57–73.

Shevardnadze, Eduard (1991). *The Future Belongs to Freedom.* C. A. Fitzpatrick, Trans. London: Sinclair-Stevenson Ltd.

Shultz, George P. (1993). *Turmoil and Triumph: My Years as Secretary of State.* New York: Charles Scribner's Sons.

Shvets, Yuri B. (1994). *Washington Station: My Life as a KGB Spy in America.* New York: Simon & Schuster.

Sigal, Leon V. (2000). *Hang Separately: Cooperative Security Between the United States and Russia, 1985–1994.* New York: Century Foundation Press.

Skinner, Kiron K., et al. (2001). *Reagan, In His Own Hand.* New York: Simon & Schuster.

Solomon, Fredric, and Robert Q. Marston, Eds. (1986). *The Medical Implications of Nuclear War.* Washington, D.C.: National Academy Press.

Steinbruner, John D. (1981). Nuclear decapitation. *Foreign Policy* 45 (Winter), 16–28.

Stelzer, Irwin, Ed. (2004). *The Neocon Reader.* New York: Grove Press.

Steury, Donald P., Ed. (1994). *Estimates on Soviet Military Power, 1954 to 1984: A Selection.* Washington, D.C.: Central Intelligence Agency.

Stockman, David A. (1986). *The Triumph of Politics: How the Reagan Revolution Failed.* New York: Harper & Row.

Stone, I. F. (1973). The Sakharov campaign. *The New York Review of Books* 20 (16), 18 Oct., 1–7 (online version).

Strober, Deborah Hart, and Gerald S. Strober (1998). *Reagan: The Man and His Presidency.* Boston: Houghton Mifflin.

Szporluk, Roman (2000). *Russia, Ukraine, and the Breakup of the Soviet Union.* Stanford, CA: Hoover Institution Press.

Talbott, Strobe (1984). *The Russians & Reagan.* New York: Vintage.

———(1985). *Deadly Gambits: The Reagan Administration and the Stalemate in Nuclear Arms Control.* New York: Vintage.

———(1988). *The Master of the Game: Paul Nitze and the Nuclear Peace.* New York: Alfred A. Knopf.

Tannenwald, Nina, Ed. (1999). *Understanding the End of the Cold War, 1980–87: An Oral History Conference, Brown University, May 7–10, 1998 (Transcript).* Providence RI: Watson Institute for International Studies.

Thomson, James A. (1984). The LRTNF decision: Evolution of US theatre nuclear policy, 1975–9. *International Affairs (Royal Institute of International Affairs 1944–)* 60 (4) (Autumn), 601–14.

Tilly, Charles (2003). *The Politics of Collective Violence.* Cambridge: Cambridge University Press.

Todd, Emmanuel (1979). *The Final Fall: An Essay on the Decomposition of the Soviet Sphere.* J. Waggoner, Trans. New York: Karz.

Tonelson, Alan (1979). Nitze's world. *Foreign Policy* (35) (Summer), 74–90.

Tuchman, Barbara (1984). *The March of Folly: From Troy to Vietnam.* New York: Ballantine Books.

Tucker, Robert C. (1981–82). Swollen state, spent society: Stalin's legacy to Brezhnev's Russia. *Foreign Affairs* 60 (2) (Winter).

Turner, Paul R., David Pitt, et al., Eds. (1989). *The Anthropology of War & Peace: Perspectives on the Nuclear Age.* Granby, MA: Bergin & Garvey.

Turpin, Jennifer, and Lester R. Kurtz, Eds. (1997). *The Web of Violence: From Interpersonal to Global.* Urbana: University of Illinois Press.

Uhler, Walter C. (2003). There he goes again. *The Nation,* 3 Feb.

Ukrainian Weekly (1983). *The Great Famine in Ukraine: The Unknown Holocaust.* Jersey City, NJ: Ukrainian National Association.

Underhill-Cady, Joseph B. (2001). *Death and the Statesman: The Culture and Psychology of U.S. Leaders During War.* New York: Palgrave.

van Oudenaren, John (1990). The tradition of change in Soviet foreign policy. *McNair Papers (Institute for National Strategic Studies, National Defense University, Fort Leslie J. McNair, Washington, D.C.)* 7 (Apr.).

Vargo, George J., Ed. (2000). *The Chornobyl Accident: A Comprehensive Risk Assessment.* Columbus, OH: Battelle Press.

Velikhov, Yevgeni (1991). Science and scientists for a nuclear-weapon-free world. In *Physics and Nuclear Arms Today: Readings from Physics Today,* D. Hafemeister, Ed., 368–72. New York: American Institute of Physics.

Velikhov, Yevgeni, Roald Sagdeev, and Andrei Kokoshin, Eds. (1986). *Weaponry in Space: The Dilemma of Security.* Moscow: Mir.

Viola, Lynne (2001). The other archipelago: Kulak deportations to the North in 1930. *Slavic Review* 60 (4) (Winter), 730–55.

Volkogonov, Dimitry (1988). *Stalin: Triumph and Tragedy.* H. Shukman, Trans. New York: Grove Weidenfeld.

———(1998). *Autopsy for an Empire: The Seven Leaders Who Built the Soviet Regime.* H. Shukman, Trans. New York: Free Press.

Warnke, Paul (1975). Apes on a treadmill. *Foreign Policy* 18 (Spring), 12–29.

Waskow, Arthur I. (1964). Disarmament as a special case in military strategy (review of three books). *World Politics* 16 (2) (Jan.), 322–27.

Wasserstrom, Richard A., Ed. (1970). *War and Morality.* Belmont, CA: Wadsworth.

Weinberger, Caspar W. (1990). *Fighting for Peace: Seven Critical Years in the Pentagon.* New York: Warner.

Westad, Odd Arne (2001). Concerning the situation in "A": New Russian evidence on the Soviet intervention in Afghanistan. *Cold War International History Project Bulletin* 8/9 (in Documents on the Soviet Invasion of Afghanistan, e-Dossier No. 4, Cold War International History Project, Woodrow Wilson International Center, Washington, D.C., Nov.), 128–32.

Whelan, Joseph G. (1988). *Soviet Diplomacy and Negotiating Behavior—1979–88: New Tests for U.S. Diplomacy.* Special Studies Series on Foreign Affairs Issues, U.S. House of Representatives (Committee on Foreign Affairs), II. 3 vols. Washington, D.C.: U.S. GPO.

Wieseltier, Leon (1985). When deterrence fails. *Foreign Affairs* 63(4) (Spring), 827–47.

Wiesner, Jerome (1984). We Need More Piefs. SSI Conference Proceedings, SLAC, Stanford University.

Wills, Garry (1987). *Reagan's America.* New York: Penguin Books.

Wilson, Richard (1987). A visit to Chernobyl. *Science* 236 (4809), 26 June, 1636–40.

Winik, Jay (1996). *On the Brink: The Dramatic, Behind-the-Scenes Saga of the Reagan Era and the Men and Women Who Won the Cold War.* New York: Simon & Schuster.

Wirls, Daniel (1992). *Buildup: The Politics of Defense in the Reagan Era.* Ithaca, NY: Cornell University Press.

Wittner, Lawrence S. (2004). Did Reagan's military build-up really lead to victory in the Cold War? *History News Network,* http://hnn.us/articles/2732.html. (Accessed 12 Oct. 2006.)

Wohlforth, William C., Ed. (1996). *Witnesses to the End of the Cold War.* Baltimore: Johns Hopkins University Press.

Wohlstetter, Albert (1974). Is there a strategic arms race? *Foreign Policy* 15 (Summer), 3–20.

Wohlstetter, Albert, Paul H. Nitze, et al. (1974). Is there a strategic arms race? (II): Rivals but no "race." *Foreign Policy* 16 (Autumn), 48–92.

Wolf, Markus, with Anne McElvoy (1997). *Man Without a Face: The Autobiography of Communism's Greatest Spymaster.* New York: Times Books.

World Health Organization (1987). Nuclear Accidents and Epidemiology: Reports on Two Meetings. WHO 25.

———(2005). Health Effects of the Chernobyl Accident and Special Health Care Programs (Report of the Chernobyl Forum Expert Group "Health"). EGH. 5 Apr.

Yakovlev, Alexander (1993). *The Fate of Marxism in Russia.* C. A. Fitzpatrick, Trans. New Haven, CT: Yale University Press.

Yaroshinskaya, Alla (1995). *Chernobyl: The Forbidden Truth.* M. Kahn and Julia Sallabank, Trans. Lincoln: University of Nebraska Press.

Yeltsin, Boris (1994). *The View From the Kremlin.* C. A. Fitzpatrick, Trans. New York: Harper-Collins.

Zanzonico, P. B., and D. V. Becker (2000). Effects of time of administration and dietary iodine levels on potassium iodide (KI) blockade of thyroid irradiation by ^{131}I from radioactive fallout. *Health Physics* 78 (6) (June), 660–67.

Zaslavskaya, Tatyana (1984). The Novosibirsk Report. *Survey* 28 (1) (Spring), 88–108.

Zubok, Vladislav M. (2000). Gorbachev's nuclear learning: How the Soviet leader became a nuclear abolitionist. *Boston Review* (Apr.–May), http://bostonreview.net/BR25.2/issue.pdf. (Accessed 10 June 2005.)

ACKNOWLEDGMENTS

Anne Sibbald and Mort Janklow ably represented this third volume in what has evolved into a multivolume history of the nuclear age, with one more volume to go. Jon Segal and Sonny Mehta at Knopf saw its value and supported it enthusiastically across five years.

At length or briefly, I interviewed many people for this book. Thanks first and foremost to Stanislav and Irina Shushkevich, whom I met originally in Belarus while researching *Masters of Death* and who subsequently visited California as my houseguests. Their contributions were invaluable.

An evening with Elena Bonner in Moscow in 1992 helped me understand her ordeal and Andrei Sakharov's. I corresponded by e-mail with Yuli Khariton at that time as well.

Hans Blix gave me a day out of his life for a long, rich interview, conducted improbably in Las Vegas. Tom Graham sat for many hours of interviews that supplemented his books. So did Sig Hecker, an old friend. More will be heard from all three the next time around. Susan Eisenhower and Roald Sagdeev welcomed me into their home and offered valuable eyewitness accounts; I wish I had been able to include the story of their courtship—another marker of when the Cold War ended—but both have told it in books. Berry Blechman clarified the work of the Palme Commission, wise Jim Goodby his understanding of summits and leaders. Robert McNamara, Sam Nunn, Lee Hamilton, Jack Matlock, Jr., General Eugene Habiger, Rozanne Ridgway, and Richard Perle responded helpfully to questions. So did Georgi Arbatov through the kind agency of his son Alexei, whose work contributed in its own right. I benefited from several pleasurable luncheon conversations with Sid Drell and a long dinner conversation with Jonathan Schell.

My colleagues at Stanford's Center for International Security and Cooperation deserve special thanks for their warm support and encouragement, particularly CISAC's director, Scott Sagan, and associate director, Lynn Eden. Seminars and lectures there, and conversations with Herb Adams, George Bunn, Gail Lapidus, Mike May, Pavel Podvig, and Dave Hafemeister deepened my understanding of U.S.-Soviet relations and U.S. diplomatic politics. Sonja Schmid expertly vetted my Chernobyl chapter.

Nina Tannenwald generously made available the invaluable transcripts and documents from the Brown University oral history conference. James Prados offered guidance on ABLE ARCHER 83, Finn Aaserud on Niels Bohr and common security, Stan Norris on Soviet and American nuclear weapons, Dori Ellis on Sandia. Mike Keller allowed me to wander the Stanford Library. Glen Worthy supplied fluent translations from Russian. Randy and Terri Reese explored Iceland on my behalf. Cornelia and Michael Bessie, cherished friends, recalled their work with Mikhail Gorbachev and Alexander Yakovlev. Julia Penrose transcribed, alphabetized, extracted, and sorted, indefatigably.

My wife is Ginger Rhodes, Ph.D., now, a clinical psychologist and skilled psychotherapist. She was there for me, as she is always.

PERMISSIONS ACKNOWLEDGMENTS

INDEX

PHOTOGRAPHIC CREDITS

Peacekeeper warheads: © 1993 by Paul Shambroom.
Reagan as lifeguard: Ronald Reagan Presidential Library.
Reagan shooting scene: Ronald Reagan Presidential Library.
SDI illustration: U.S. Air Force.
SS-20 missile: ITAR-TASS.
Pershing 2s: Defense Visual Information Center (DVIC).
"The Day After" scene: ABC/Photofest.
Greenham Common arrest: Sahm Doherty/Time Life Pictures/Getty Images.
NATO exercise: NATO.
Gromyko/Gorbachev: AP/Wide World Photos.
Gorbachev on Lenin Mausoleum: ITAR-TASS.
Eduard Shevardnadze: Eastlight/Getty Images.
Anatoly Chernyaev: Dr. Svetlana Savranskaya.

PHOTOGRAPHS APPEARING IN INSERT II

Reagan/Gorbachev: Ronald Reagan Presidential Library.
Challenger disaster: NASA.
Olof Palme: AP/Wide World Photos.
Schmidt/Bahr: Robert Lackenbach/Time Life Pictures/Getty Images.
Yevgeny Velikov: Private collection.
Arbatov–Eisenhower: Private collection.
Garwin–Sagan: Richard Garwin.
Sidney Drell: Sidney Drell.
Andrei Sakharov: AP/Wide World Photos.
Paul Nitze: AP/Wide World Photos.
Sergei Akhromeyev: © Peter Tunley/CORBIS.
Gorbachev/Reagan at Reykjavik: Ronald Reagan Presidential Library.
Reagan/Perle: Ronald Reagan Presidential Library.
Reagan/Gorbachev leaving Hofdi House: Ronald Reagan Presidential Library.
Matthias Rust's plane over Red Square: unknown.
Lithuanian succession: © Pascal le Segretain/CORBIS SYGMA.
Gorbachev at the UN: John Chiasson/Liaison/Getty Images.
Celebrants on Berlin Wall: AP/Wide World Photos.
Wolfowitz-Sununu: George Bush Presidential Library.
Baker/Shevardnadze: AP/Wide World Photos.
Scrapped Soviet tanks: © TASS/Sovfoto.
Boris Yeltsin on tank: AP/Wide World Photos.
Kravchuk/Shushkevich/Yeltsin: ITAR-TASS.

ALSO BY RICHARD RHODES

*"Through his fine and accessible account, Rhodes deepens our sense
of the Holocaust's utter evil."*
—The New York Times Book Review

MASTERS OF DEATH
The SS-Einsatzgruppen and the Invention of The Holocaust

In *Masters of Death*, Rhodes gives full weight, for the first time, to
the Einsatzgruppen's role in the Holocaust. These "special task
forces," organized by Heinrich Himmler to follow the German army
as it advanced into eastern Poland and Russia, were the agents of the
first phase of the Final Solution. They murdered more than 1.5 million men, women, and children between 1941 and 1943, often by
shooting them into killing pits, as at Babi Yar. These massive crimes
have been generally overlooked or underestimated by Holocaust historians, who have focused on the gas chambers. In this painstaking
account, Pulitzer Prize–winning author Richard Rhodes profiles the
eastern campaign's architects as well as its "ordinary" soldiers and
policemen, and helps us understand how such men were conditioned
to carry out mass murder. Marshaling a vast array of documents and
the testimony of perpetrators and survivors, this book is an essential
contribution to our understanding of the Holocaust and World War II.

History/Holocaust Studies/978-0-375-70822-0

JOHN JAMES AUDOBON
The Making of an American

John James Audobon came to America as a dapper eighteen-year-old
eager to make his fortune. He had a talent for drawing and an interest in birds, and he would spend the next thirty-five years traveling
to the remotest regions of his new country—often alone and on
foot—to render his avian subjects on paper. The works of art he created gave the world its idea of America. They gave America its idea
of itself. Here Richard Rhodes vividly depicts Audobon's life and
career: his epic wanderings; his quest to portray birds in a lifelike
way; his long, anguished separations from his adored wife; his
ambivalent witness to the vanishing of the wilderness.

Biography/978-0-375-71393-4

WHY THEY KILL
The Discoveries of a Maverick Criminologist

Lonnie Athens was raised in a violent world. His father was a hot-tempered man who shot at strangers and beat his wife and literally bashed his sons' heads together. So when Athens began studying for his doctorate in criminology at Berkeley, it was only natural that he was fascinated with the question of what makes people violent. He decided to conduct in-depth interviews with several hundred violent prison inmates, an endeavor which spanned a decade and reaped the discovery of "violentization," the four-stage process by which almost any person, regardless of race, gender, genetic heritage, or socio-economic status, can become someone who will assault, batter, rape, mutilate, or murder another human being. Richard Rhodes traces Athens's journey into the fiercest corners of our world's most brutal souls and has produced an indispensable book for anyone who has wondered why people become violent and what we can do about it.

Current Affairs/Criminology/978-0-375-70248-8

VINTAGE BOOKS
Available at your local bookstore, or visit
www.randomhouse.com